Phonological Development

Applied Language Studies
Edited by David Crystal and Keith Johnson

This new series aims to deal with key topics within the main branches of applied language studies – initially in the fields of foreign language teaching and learning, child language acquisition and clinical or remedial language studies. The series will provide students with a research perspective in a particular topic, at the same time containing an original slant which will make each volume a genuine contribution to the development of ideas in the subject.

Phonological Development

The Origins of Language in the Child

Marilyn May Vihman

BLACKWELL
Publishers

First published 1996
2 4 6 8 10 9 7 5 3 1

Blackwell Publishers Inc.
238 Main Street
Cambridge, Massachusetts 02142, USA

Blackwell Publishers Ltd
108 Cowley Road
Oxford OX4 1JF
UK

Library of Congress Cataloging-in-Publication Data
Vihman, Marilyn May.
    Phonological development: the origins of language in the child / Marilyn May Vihman.
      p.   cm. – (Applied language studies)
    Includes bibliographical references and index.
    ISBN 0–631–16353–0 (hbk.: alk. paper). – ISBN 0–631–16354–9 (pbk.: alk. paper)
    1. Language acquisition.   2. Grammar, Comparative and general –
Phonology. I. Title. II. Series.
P118.V54 1996
401'.93 – dc20   95-15094
                                                                        CIP

British Library Cataloguing in Publication Data

A CIP catalogue record for this book is available from the British Library.

Typeset in 10 on 11.5pt Ehrhardt
by Best-set Typesetter Ltd., Hong Kong

Printed in Great Britain by T. J. Press Ltd, Padstow, Cornwall
This book is printed on acid-free paper

To the memory of
Viviane May Scott
and
Eerika Ungerson Vihman,
who nurtured me.

Contents

Figures

Tables

Acknowledgments

This book has been some years in the making; it has been perhaps the most satisfying learning experience of my life. For this I have to thank, first and foremost, the much-tried patience of my editor at Blackwell, Philip Carpenter. The long gestation period has, however, given me ample opportunity to reflect on and savor the very special apprenticeship which I enjoyed with Charles Ferguson, or Fergie. His natural inclination to let the data speak for themselves certainly struck a harmonious chord in me; I believe that his broad tolerance for and interest in opposing points of view have also had a positive effect, though that involved a more effortful adaptation on my part. I should also mention my long collaboration with Lorraine McCune. Our ten years of intense discussion (sometimes argument!) have played an important role in my understanding of every aspect of children's development; I am deeply grateful to her for that, as well as for her consistent friendship and support.

Next, I would like to warmly thank the friends and colleagues who read drafts of one chapter or another and took the trouble to respond to them. Shelley Velleman is first among them: She read and commented on virtually every chapter. Fergie was particularly helpful with chapter 2. Both Bruno Repp and Michael Studdert-Kennedy provided extensive and invaluable comments on chapters 3 and 4. Bénédicte de Boysson-Bardies and Kim Oller responded to chapter 5. Lorraine commented on chapter 5 and also on chapter 6, much of which reflects our collaborative work. Sarah Christman, Rory DePaolis, Barbara Davis and Susan Nittrouer also provided helpful comments on some sections of the book. Finally, David Crystal, who has read it all, repeatedly managed to supply words of encouragement from Wales with unexpectedly good timing.

I am immeasurably grateful to the National Science Foundation, which supported much of the research from which I draw my own data here. In particular, the Stanford Child Phonology Project, which Fergie founded in 1968, was funded by NSF throughout the period that I was there (1980–8). The "Stanford data" on

1-year-olds acquiring English were collected as part of that project in 1980–1, with the help of Marcy Macken, Ruth Miller, and Hazel Simmons; the 3-year-old data were collected from the same children in 1982–3, with Hazel and Kathie Carpenter. The "Rutgers data" were collected in the same time period by Lorraine, prior to our meeting; those data were phonetically transcribed and analyzed in the course of a joint Stanford/Rutgers project involving Fergie, Lorraine, Ruth and myself, again with NSF funding.

Finally, the cross-linguistic data from French, Japanese and Swedish were collected as part of my last project at Stanford. The Japanese data were collected in the Stanford area in the essentially monolingual homes of young Japanese business-men in training; Fumiko Arao visited every family (including several who returned to Japan before the planned data collection could be completed), coordinated all of the data collection, transcribed the data phonetically, and identified words. Bénédicte and Catherine Durand collected the French data, transcribed them, identified words, and performed unending quantitative analyses; I have benefited in many ways from the pleasure of working with them, both here and in Paris. Similarly, Liselotte Roug-Hellichius, with the help of Ingrid Landberg, collected, transcribed and analyzed most of the Swedish data, and received me most hospit-ably on my short working visits to Stockholm. The other members of both the French and Swedish teams (Pierre Hallé; Björn Lindblom, who made Swedish participation possible, and later Olle Engstrand and Francisco Lacerda) provided lively and productive discussion of every aspect of our joint studies.

It remains only to mention my family. The book was planned and written in periods of major upheaval for us; my children and stepchildren cheerfully bore with me through all of this, helping in whatever way they could. Thank you, Virve, Raivo, Jenny, and Stephen.

Hammond, Louisiana

Conventions

As is customary in the child language literature, child age is given here throughout as years; months. days, e.g. 1;4.10 for "one year, four months and ten days." Adult glosses are given in single quotes; adult form is given either orthographically, in italics, or phonemically, in slant brackets. Child forms are given in square brackets. In chapter 6, in reference to the gestural expression of child meanings, the presumed meaning is given in capitals (e.g. BYE–BYE), followed by the observed gesture in square brackets (e.g. [wave hand]).

Emphasis in quoted passages is from the original unless noted otherwise.

1 Introduction

In recent years the question of the origin of language – once virtually a taboo subject, in some linguistic circles at least (Hewes, 1992) – has begun to be widely discussed by linguists, psychologists, ethologists, neurologists, and others (Bickerton, 1981, 1990; Lindblom, MacNeilage, and Studdert-Kennedy, 1984; Edelman, 1989; Lieberman, 1984, 1991; Pinker and Bloom, 1990; Studdert-Kennedy, 1991b; MacNeilage, in press). Since the notion of an analogy, if only a partial one, between phylogeny and ontogeny naturally arises in this connection, interest in language origins has led to discussion and active investigation of the nature of language acquisition, particularly the earliest stages, when "something" (a linguistic system) seems to arise out of "nothing" (prelinguistic resources which may or may not bear some relation to the system which appears later). At least one speculative account of the origins of consciousness (Edelman, 1989) suggests that the anatomical changes in the vocal tract which are among the features which distinguish man from the other primates – changes recapitulated in the infant's development over the first year – are themselves at the root of higher neurological development and thus of human thought as well as language. These vocal tract changes, which create the basis for the highly differentiated articulatory structure underlying language, similarly potentiate the child's expanding vocal capacities and consequently, according to the view we adopt here, lead to critical refinements in the child's receptivity to the patterning of sounds in the ambient language as well.

The central goals of this book are to survey what has been learned about phonological development and to raise questions for further study. We will interpret these goals broadly, however, going well beyond the phonological rules or processes which were the primary concern of linguists interested in child phonology in the 1970s. Placing our topic within the wider domain of inquiry into the possibility of a system arising out of no system – that is, the question of whether language could in principle "be learned by an organism initially uninformed as to its general character" (Chomsky, 1965, p. 58), we will adopt a functionalist approach along the lines suggested by Lindblom (1992): We will be concerned with tracing the beginnings of phonology (and of language) in the infant's perceptual capacities, now understood to be quite remarkable already at birth or soon thereafter, in the growing repertoire of vocal resources of the first year, and in the emergence of a link between perception and production. We will then consider the transition to language, endeavoring to identify critical communicative and cognitive developments which permit the construction of a system of interconnected sound patterns along with a dawning understanding of the nature of naming and reference.

Before embarking on a roughly chronological account of development in the first 18 months of life (first of perception, chs 3 and 4, then of production, chs 5 and 6), however, we will review the history of attempts to develop a theoretical formulation which does justice to the forms and processes seen to characterize phonological development (ch. 2). As is the case with theorizing about language acquisition in general, none of these attempts has so far met with general approval. The pair of contrasting perspectives – formalist and functionalist – which dominates most linguistic discourse pervades current discussion of child phonology as well. Few substantive current formalist accounts are available, however (see Macken, 1995), while the functionalist position continues to generate research programs, descriptive and instrumental studies, and efforts to integrate biological and cognitive perspectives. Little attention will be given to the formulation of rules in the present account, nor will we attempt to specify a detailed model of the development of phonological organization. Instead, avoiding narrowly technical terminology, we will bring together relevant materials from the many fields of study pertinent to that development and hope thus to appropriately constrain as well as inspire future work along both formal and functional lines.

Once we have described the process by which first word production is followed by the development of production templates and the gradual construction of a phonological system, we will be in a position to consider later aspects of phonological development. We will discuss the development of linguistic perception and the response of the older child to the more complex task of understanding running speech, and we will consider the role of vocabulary growth in the development of phonological processing. We will review recent work demonstrating the importance for reading an alphabetic script of sensitivity to phonological "connections" – rhyme, alliteration, assonance – and the substructure of the syllable (ch. 7). We will trace what has been established or proposed regarding prosodic development, from its origins in biologically given rhythms to accommodation to the individually patterned stress- or pitch-accent systems of different adult languages (ch. 8). We will then turn to later stages of production (ch. 9). We will examine the first rule-based phonology and the data which point to the word or syllable as the first unit of phonological organization. We will consider evidence from instrumental studies of coarticulation which suggest that the segment emerges as an independently controlled element only in later childhood, well after the preschool years. And we will examine the relationship of phonology to the emergence of morphosyntax, a relationship long disregarded by students of language acquisition.

Design features of language

In the early years of this century, based on experience with the many divergent Native American languages in addition to the classical and living languages of Europe and others, linguists observed that no "primitive languages" have been identified; that is, all human languages appear to exhibit a comparable level of complexity in lexicon and grammatical structure (Sapir, 1921; contrast, however, Givón, 1979 and Kalmár, 1985). More recently, the sign languages of the deaf have come to be understood as belonging to the set of all natural languages, the properties of which can be taken to define, in part, what it is to be human. It is perhaps appropriate, then, to open an inquiry into the origins of language in the child by reviewing properties of language in relation to other communication systems, adapting for that purpose the design features of language identified by Hockett in 1960 (see Appendix 1.1, at the end of this chapter).[1]

The first six properties listed in Appendix 1.1 characterize a number of communicative systems, including human language but in each case excluding certain other systems. Some of these properties are particularly interesting from a developmental point of view. The choice of modality (1), for example, appears to remain open until well into the second year. Children generally develop a small repertoire of communicative gestures before they begin to make intentional use of vocal signals; some hearing children, exposed only to oral language, develop more lexical gestures than (vocal) words in the early period of transition into symbolic communication (Acredolo and Goodwyn, 1988). The properties of interchangeability (2) and complete feedback (3) are important as well. The first ensures that empathic identification with the caregiver will provide motivation and model enough for the normally developing child to muster the attention and effort needed to make the transition to language (Locke, 1993); the second may provide the critical means for that shift, as the child discovers within his or her own vocal resources the equivalent of some elements of adult speech. Finally, in relation to discreteness (6), Fernald (1992) has suggested that the powerful affective meaning inherent in the prosody of infant-directed speech is a phylogenetically prior mode of communication, graded rather than discrete, which may serve as a bridge, guiding the child toward the units of language.

The remaining five properties are to an increasing extent uniquely characteristic of language. For example, linguistic symbols are typically arbitrary (7) – although the relatively small number of onomatopoeic word forms which constitute exceptions to this rule play a disproportionately large role in the early vocabularies of children, suggesting that a partially iconic or natural (non-arbitrary) sound–meaning link is an advantage for the novice language user.[2] Productivity (9) – the hallmark of syntax, as has been well understood since Chomsky (1957) – is similarly central to language form and content; unlike the property of arbitrariness, productivity does not appear to constitute a difficulty for the child but is, rather, evident from the first consistent and conventional formal expressions of intentional meaning, that is, from the first communicative uses of gesture, word or "protoword" (a word form of the child's own creation).

Displacement (10) is not typical of a child's early uses of language – although this may be due in part to the instability of form and possible unconventionality of reference which may make a child's early words difficult or impossible for adult observers to identify out of context.[3] Similarly, duality of patterning (11) is not characteristic of the first words of precocious language users, whose early forms are situationally embedded or "context-limited" (Bates et al. 1979; Vihman and McCune, 1994). Beyond that, these early word forms usually contrast as whole units (Ferguson and Farwell, 1975); only gradually do the syllables and segments that make them up come to achieve contrastive status in a fully viable phonological system. Evidently, then, the one clearly human yet demonstrably primitive language – lacking in at least two of the critical properties of the adult system – is the first language of the child.

The phonetics/phonology interface, or the emergence of complexity

An issue which appears to divide formalist and functionalist approaches was raised by Macken (1992): "Where's phonology?" Macken suggests that the study of phonological development in the eighties was largely concerned with the "phonetics of acquisition," which seemed to imply that no abstract phonology is learned. Arguing for an autonomous phonological component, she presents data illustrating nonlinear advances, which – as will be seen below (ch. 6, ch. 9) – are to be found in any closely observed longitudinal study which goes beyond the earliest period of word production. In phonological development, as in language acquisition in general, learning can be seen to take the shape of a "U-shaped curve": Following a presystematic period of correct production of a small number of input forms, the child begins to develop a system of his or her own, assimilating new adult forms appropriate to that system and frequently showing errors of over-generalization as adult forms reflecting a different pattern are included in an as yet overly restricted or idiosyncratic structure – and then reorganizing the system to encompass more data, resulting in more complex structure or more complete or accurate representation.

As our review of theories of phonological acquisition will suggest, both continuity and discontinuity can fairly be illustrated from children's development. The resources developed through vocal production in the prelinguistic period (babbling) serve as a basis for the first word forms and thus for the development of a first phonological system. This essential continuity of development was presumably the basis for early behaviorist accounts of phonetic learning; it provides clear evidence of the biological rootedness of phonology. Once the first words are in place, however, reorganization and restructuring can be seen to operate repeatedly as the child implicitly compares lexical representations, develops production templates which reconcile targeted forms with output constraints, enlarges the internalized lexicon while at the same time outgrowing certain constraints, and reenters the cycle. Such restructuring is not unique to language development but may instead be seen as analogous to the "phase shifts" characteristic of self-organizing systems in many domains (Thelen, 1989):

Phonologically, the first words show minimal accommodation to the adult language. They reflect instead perceived matches between pre-existing vocal schemata and adult word patterns, and constitute the disparate pieces of a system yet to cohere. An increase in variability accompanies the beginnings of systematicity, signalling the onset of a phase shift from context-bound babble-as-words to more consistent and interrelated word forms alongside more flexible and established word use. As the shift . . . proceeds, one or more stable production patterns or "canonical forms" emerge, reflecting the phonological interaction of prevalent adult patterns and the child's developing vocal motor schemes. At the same time, the child attempts a wider range of adult word shapes and assimilates them more radically to fit the emergent production patterns, leading to more relatedness (systematicity) among child words but less accuracy in reproduction of adult models. Non-linearity or "regression" in production accuracy marks emergent organization. (Vihman, 1993a, p. 418)

Macken follows Chomsky in seeing the overgeneralized forms typical of phases of restructuring as evidence of "the operation of an innate, highly specific phonological grammar," permitting learners to "arrive at, not just any grammar, but essentially a single grammar . . . relatively quickly" (Macken, 1992, pp. 260f.). In contrast, we will take the position that language belongs to the class of "open systems in nature that have the property of increasing the complexity of organization . . . " (Mohanan, 1992, p. 650); it will in part be the burden of this book to illustrate Mohanan's conclusion, that "phonological development . . . is pattern formation and adaptation, not knowledge discovery and deduction" (p. 659).

A test of this perspective will come with additional study of children acquiring complex adult morphophonological systems. The "rules" (N. V. Smith, 1973; Ingram, 1974) or "processes" (Stampe, 1969) of younger children learning English resemble adult phonological rules only superficially, since they do not relate variant surface forms of a single underlying lexical representation but instead translate an adult form, which may or may not be represented as such (i.e., be correctly perceived and retained) by the child, into a child output form. Once the child's immaturities of perception, production and organization have been overcome, none of these rules is expected to play a role in the mature grammar. On the other hand, a representation of the production templates which positively characterize the child's own system in early stages may be retained at some level even in the mature production system; there is, to my knowledge, no evidence that adult speakers of a language share an identical grammar, despite nativist assumptions (see again Mohanan, 1992). On the contrary, individual differences are exhibited by adults as well as children in performance on experimental phonological tasks and in second language learning, retention of spelling patterns and a host of other skills indirectly drawing on phonological knowledge (see, e.g., Fillmore, Kempler and Wang, 1979, as well as the extensive sociolinguistic literature initiated by Labov's (1963) classic study of Martha's Vineyard).

In English there are few phonological variants of the high frequency morphemes learned in early childhood – and thus little abstract adult phonology to which the child is exposed early in the acquisition period. In the few cases of phonetically variable inflectional morphemes (e.g., plural, possessive, past tense), children make appropriate use of the regular variants from early on but fail to show productive knowledge of the relevant rules (Berko, 1958). Most of the abstract apparatus of English phonology is required for irregular inflectional variants and for derivational morphology; the learning of these rules or relationships is far from complete even for linguistically advanced first-grade children (Jones, 1991[4]). Jones speculates that

> children may become aware of a meaning relationship between a word and its deriva-tive form before they have learned the adult phonological form for one of the items. A child may say *eight* correctly but pronounce the cardinal number as [eyθ]. Given the opportunity to convert *eight* to *eighth*, and the reverse, in meaningful situations, the child may develop an abstract morphophonemic representation capable of alternative surface representation, as appropriate . . . Another possibility is that a child might learn an inflected form and its base form as separate items. For example, *wolf* might be learned as [wʊf] at time 1, and *wolves* learned as [wʊlz] at time 2, in different contexts. Either of these words might move toward the adult form independently prior to the time that a common underlying representation is formed. Conversion of one form to the other with a meaning association is presumably the learning experi-ence that would generate the abstract representation. (pp. 234f.)

In short, the more abstract rules of adult English phonology are based on lexical and grammatical relationships which are not typically internalized until well into the primary school years. There is thus little reason to hypothesize that an adult-like phonological grammar is completed early or "quickly," based on data from the acquisition of English. Studies of languages with more complex morphophonology affecting high frequency or early learned items can provide more pertinent infor-mation about the rate and process of acquisition of abstract phonology. Although few such studies are available as yet, Demuth's (1993) case study of the acquisition of Sesotho tone sandhi provides one example. Demuth suggests that while some straightforward rule applications are learned relatively early, in other cases correct underlying representations can only be recovered once certain complex sandhi effects have been disentangled; in such cases, as one might expect, phonological acquisition remains incomplete as late as age 3.

Themes in phonological development

In the chapters which follow we will be concerned at least as much with the origins of phonology in the first 18 months of life as with later development – in accordance with the existing bias in the literature to be reviewed. Four aspects of phonological development which will be central to our account are briefly identified below.

The interaction of perception and production

The effort to trace links between perception and production in order to arrive at a more complete understanding of phonological development received little em-pirical or theoretical attention until the nineties; studies adopting this perspective have been few and relatively isolated. In the remarkably dynamic field of infant speech perception concern with production has been minimal. As regards adults, proponents of the motor theory of speech perception presuppose a critical link between the two domains but generally lack interest in its development, taking a biologically based connection between perception and production to be axiomatic: The perceptuomotor link underlying speech is "not a learned association . . . but innately specified, requiring only epigenetic experience to bring it into play" (Liberman and Mattingly, 1985, p. 3). This point of view is not universal, however. Studdert-Kennedy (1993), for example, emphasizes that "a central function of perception in the infant is surely to guide production: by learning to listen the child learns to speak" (p. 150); he goes on to endorse the view that "with the discovery of correspondences between the sounds it hears and the sounds it makes, the infant begins to focus attention on the phonetic (articulatory) properties of native sounds" (p. 152; cf. Vihman, 1991). Walley (1993a) takes this further, stressing the need for studies of perceptual development beyond infancy and for taking account of the relationship between changes in perception, such as postulated changes in the weighting of auditory information (an integral part of Jusczyk's (1992, 1993) perceptual model), and other areas of development, including cognitive or representational, lexical and (expressive) phonological advances: "Traditionally, perceptual abilities have been assumed to undergo little, if any development . . . We still know very little about how individual variation in perceptual abilities or proclivities contributes to developmental advances" (Walley, 1993a, p. 175).

It is our view that the interaction of perception and production is key to an understanding of the early stages of phonological development. Accordingly, we begin by surveying the separate literatures on infant speech perception and infant vocal development; in our review of the transition to language we will bring the two areas together as we sketch a model of their mutual influences and growing linkage over the course of the first year.

Prosodic and segmental approaches

The central role of the word in early phonological development was an implicit tenet of Waterson (1971), in which the kind of holistic (non-segmental or "prosodic") analysis developed by J. R. Firth was sensitively applied to a single acquisitional case study. This theoretical position, more explicitly articulated, amplified and illustrated by Ferguson and his colleagues in the succeeding decade (e.g., Ferguson and Farwell, 1975; Ferguson, 1978; Macken, 1979; Ferguson, 1986), was anomalous in the American context dominated by generative phonology (Chomsky and Halle, 1968). Since then, however, whole-word-based phonological organization has come to be generally accepted for the early stages, although the nature (and extent) of the shift toward a phonological system in which the segment plays a critical role alongside the word and syllable remains little understood (see chs 7 and 9).

Despite concurrent efforts to encourage the study of prosodic development in its primary sense – that is, the acquisition of intonation and accentual systems (Crystal, 1970, 1973, 1979; Allen and Hawkins, 1978, 1980), this important area of research has remained underdeveloped. The shift in theoretical attention since the 1970s toward tonal systems and, in consequence, nonlinear approaches to phonology (see Goldsmith, 1990) has led to a new focus on the syllable alongside the segment in current studies (e.g., Kent, Mitchell, and Sancier, 1991), on rhythmic and accentual development (e.g., D. Snow, 1994), and on the specific relationship of prosodic factors to morphosyntactic development (e.g., Gerken and McIntosh, 1993; Peters and Menn, 1993).

Our review of studies of prosodic development to date (ch. 8) is meant to draw attention to the many intriguing questions which arise in this connection, to the relative paucity of available data on which to base conclusions, and also to some of the methodological difficulties which may explain the lack of information in this area. As descriptive studies are undertaken of larger numbers of children acquiring languages which pose differing challenges as regards accentual system, characteristic relationship between word and morpheme, and degree of morphophonemic complexity, we will be in a better position to consider the funda-mental issue of the long-term process of integration of prosodic and segmental aspects of language.

Cross-linguistic perspectives

Although studies of phonological development in a variety of languages have long been available, much of the literature continues to make reference to specific characteristics of the acquisition of English as if they were universal properties of child development. To take just one example, the prevalence of monosyllables among the early word productions of English-learning children is often cited as characteristic of early stages of phonological development. A consideration of the structure of the vocabulary used in addressing children in English suggests that there is a language-specific bias in the input (see Hart, 1991), however, and com-parison with the phonetic structure of the input in other languages confirms this impression (Vihman et al., 1994). In fact, even within the period of production of the first 50 words, over half the words produced by children acquiring French, Japanese and Swedish are disyllabic or longer, in accordance with the adult models which they are attempting, while monosyllables dominate the production of chil-dren acquiring English (Boysson-Bardies et al., 1992; Vihman, 1993c).

Studies of the earliest period of development have revealed influence from the ambient language on both perception and production – alongside strong evidence of universal perceptual biases and production constraints. Our review will thus include explicit consideration of such early ambient language effects. In the later period, however, cross-linguistic research has been sporadic. The study of linguis-tic perception in the older child as well as in the adult, for example, includes little consideration of languages of differing prosodic or morphological structure; experi-mental research on such languages might lead to important changes in the way the processing of running speech is understood. We have already alluded to the signifi-cance of cross-linguistic data for the study of prosodic development. With regard to the "discovery of the segment" and changes in coarticulation, cross-linguistic research has so far been minimal. Case studies of phonological development *per se* are available for a number of languages, though the numbers of children on which our information is based remain small. Finally, Peters and Strömqvist (in press) have emphasized the clear need for cross-linguistic data in the emergent study of the interaction of prosody and morphosyntax.

The significance of individual differences

Each child must individually forge a path to language. Despite the popularity of Chomsky's view that "in language learning 'a rich and complex system of rules and principles is attained in a uniform way, rapidly, effortlessly, on the basis of limited and rather degenerate evidence'" (1981a, cited in Elbers and Wijnen, 1992, p. 339), every careful study of more than one child – in so far as individual patterns of development rather than group results are at issue – has revealed a range of differences and individual strategies (for overviews, see Nelson, 1981; Bates, Bretherton, and Snyder, 1988).[5] Macken (1992) goes so far as to propose that

> the central acquisition mechanism is a constrained hypothesis formation mechanism . . . where the linguistic constraints are not so restricted as to result in invariance but, rather, so closely replicate the formal constraints on languages in general as to render any set of ten or twenty learners (of even the same language) a virtual typological study of language parameters. (p. 250)

We would argue that both biological predispositions and salient aspects of the ambient language constrain the child's initial progress in language acquisition; nevertheless, multiple individual factors enter into the child's approach to language, as regards both timing and manner of acquisition. Attempts to reduce this individual variation to a single pair of contrasting styles (such as referential vs. expressive, analytic vs. holistic) have not, on the whole, yielded definitive or generally satisfying results. Instead, it seems that, within the given constraints, the child has a great deal of scope for variation – including such matters as rate of maturation along several parameters, both broadly social (interest in communicative interaction) and more specifically language-related (sensitivity to vocal patterns, motoric skill). Even more important perhaps is apparent variation in the child's deployment of the cognitive elements of acquisition, attention and effort (see note 5) and the work of integration through which the internalized representations of adult forms and of the child's own vocal capacities are interrelated and molded into a viable set of production patterns which can then gradually be brought into line – over a period of two to three years at the very least – with the target adult system. The chapters which follow should provide ample documentation of the remarkable range of creativity and initiative exhibited by the individual child, who is after all the central character in this account.

NOTES

1   The comments on chimpanzees in Appendix 1.1 are drawn from Boehm's (1992) discussion of Hockett's design features with specific reference to chimpanzees.
2   The iconic elements in sign language do not appear to hasten the acquisition process, however (Newport and Meier, 1985).

3   An example taken from the diary account of the language development (in Estonian) of
Virve Vihman: At age 1;5, in response to her mother's joking suggestion that she go and
tell daddy (outside, mowing the lawn) that dinner is ready (*söök on valmis*), she says to her
father, [masi, masi] (for *valmis* 'ready'). When her father fails to understand, she adds,
[mi:ma, eiba] *piima, leiba* 'milk, bread' – to which her father, still unable to interpret her
attempt at a decontextualized message, responds (in Estonian), "If you want milk and
bread, go and ask your mother!"

4   See also Templeton and Scarborough-Franks (1985), who suggest that knowledge of
orthographic relationships precedes phonological knowledge for English-speaking children (grades 6 and 10), and Carlisle (1988), who found strong evidence of continuing
progress in knowledge of derivational morphology across grades 4, 6 and 8.

5   Noting that "the only constituents of Chomsky's contention that do not seem to have
invited much criticism are the claim that language knowledge consists of 'a rich and
complex system of rules' and the claim that language acquisition is effortless" (Elbers
and Wijnen, 1992, p. 339), these authors comment that

> the rich-and-complex claim is a professional judgment . . . [while] the no effort
> claim . . . is a layman's contention, based on casual and superficial impression rather
> than on careful observation and research . . . It seems just as mistaken to hold that
> development is effortless because it *seems* effortless, as it would be to hold
> that language itself is simple because it *seems* rather simple to the ordinary speaker.
> (p. 340)

APPENDIX 1.1   PROPERTIES OF LANGUAGE IN COMPARISON WITH OTHER COMMUNICATION SYSTEMS

Properties especially characteristic of human language are starred.

1   *Modality (or mode of expression)*   The full complexity of human language can be expressed in one of two modalities, vocal/auditory or gestural/visual. The sign languages of
the deaf (e.g., American Sign Language) are fully equivalent to vocal language.

Tactile, kinetic, and chemical modalities form the basis for some animal communication
systems: for example, bee dancing is kinetic in part; crickets use the auditory modality
but not the vocal; other primates ues both vocal and gestural modalities.

2   *Interchangeability*   Members of the speech community serve as both transmitters and
receivers of linguistic signals; sender and receiver may exchange roles at will.

In contrast, among some species of crickets, for example, only the males chirp, though
both males and females respond to chirping.

3   *Complete feedback*   The transmitter of a linguistic signal normally also receives the
signal (at the same time as the intended recipient). This allows monitoring of message
transmission and error correction.

Chimpanzees show evidence of deliberate suppression of vocalization while on patrol, or
in listening to a distant call, suggesting a similar capacity to that of humans for feedback
and monitoring.

4 *Specialization* Speech production serves no direct biological function in itself, so that language is not a byproduct of some other behavioral goal but is specifically intended for communication; it is the flexible behavioral consequences of language as a signalling device that are of benefit to the species.

In contrast, crying (in the newborn infant, for example) serves a direct physiological and affective function; additionally, it may be interpreted and receive a response, thus inadvertently functioning as a communicative signal as well.

5 *Semanticity* Linguistic signals are conventionally associated with specific meanings or denotations.

Vervet monkeys have been found to communicate a small number of specific messages distinguishing between different potential predators; chimpanzee vocalizations have not yet been clearly shown to have such specific meanings.

6 *Discreteness* Languages use a repertoire of discrete sound and meaning units; there is no continuous grading possible between these to express, for example, shades of meaning.

It is unclear whether some chimpanzee calls are discrete, in this sense; to the human observer, at least, they appear often to be graded and blended.

*7 *Arbitrariness* There is generally no necessary connection between linguistic symbols and the meanings they express. That is, language is generally not iconic – although there are exceptions in vocal language, as in onomatopoeic expressions (*woof, clang*). There is a greater iconic element in sign languages (e.g., point to self for "I"; point to head for "think/ thought"), though a conversation in sign is wholly opaque to the uninitiated (Klima and Bellugi, 1979).

Bee dancing is in large part iconic, expressing direction by movement in the relevant direction.

*8 *Cultural transmission* Although language has a biological base (predisposition to babble, to perceive contrasts in speech sounds, to draw analogies and combine patterns, for example), it must be learned in a social setting, generally in the context of "intersubjectivity," or mutual empathic interaction, with one or more caretakers.

There is an element of learning in the songs of some birds, but extensive interaction with a particular community member does not appear to be required.

*9 *Productivity, or openness* Flexible rules of combination of linguistic elements (words, sounds, meanings) allow the creation of an infinite number of messages. The rules of syntax allow new sentences to be created virtually every time we speak; new combinations of sounds also occur (neologisms, adaptation of foreign terms), though less often; and new applications of existing words occur daily as well, extending meaning to novel situations or to express novel perspectives on the familiar.

Only very limited productivity is possible in any other known animal communication system.

*10   *Displacement*   The meanings expressed in language are independent of the actual situation of use, so that communication is not limited to the "here and now."

This is true of bee dancing as well, but is not typically applicable to communication by other primates.

*11   *Duality of patterning*   A limited set of meaningless symbols (sounds or gestures) are combined to create meaning-bearing units (words or signs); these in turn may be combined to generate an unlimited number of messages.

No other animal communication system is known to share this feature.

2 Theoretical Perspectives

Up until the seventies, in the absence of any reliable data pool other than sporadic diary accounts by scholar parents, competing models of phonological development were drawn up largely on theoretical grounds, some rooted in behaviorist psychology, others in structural linguistics. Then methodological advances made possible the explosion of experimental research on infant speech perception (Kaplan, 1969; Eimas, et al. 1971; Moffitt, 1971), while a database of meticulous observations of children's phonological development, facilitated by the general availability of first audio, then video recording equipment, began to accumulate at about the same time, though at a more moderate pace (Menn, 1971; Waterson, 1971; Ferguson, Peizer, and Weeks, 1973; N. V. Smith, 1973). Leopold (1939, 1947, 1949a, 1949b) served as precursor and standard-setter to this trend. Though some features of the earliest models continue to be of current interest (e.g. the role of input frequency, central to Olmsted's behaviorist account, or the role of contrast, central to Jakobson's structuralist view), these models are largely ignored today. Instead, on the basis of growing evidence from both purely observational and experimentally controlled data, two types of models have emerged, sometimes termed "biological" and "cognitive." It may be taken as a sign of genuine progress in the understanding of phonological development over the past two decades that these current models, unlike the earlier ones, do not so much compete as complement one another.

This historical survey of the theoretical perspectives which have informed the study of phonological development will be organized according to a loosely chronological plan. Each of the major theoretical models we identify will be ordered by the date of its first influential publications; subsequent elaborations of the model or related theoretical formulations will then be treated in sequence under the same general heading. In the closing section we will review themes which arise in several of the models and also consider some of the issues which remain central to the developmental study of phonology.

Behaviorist models

A behaviorist or "learning theory" perspective on phonological development was first elaborated by O.H. Mowrer in the late 1940s, based on the study not of human infants but of parrots and other "talking birds" (Mowrer, 1952, 1960). Four steps were postulated: (1) attention to and identification with the caretaker; (2) the development (in the learner, bird or child) of an association between caretaker vocalizations and such "primary reinforcement" as food or expressions of affection (speech sounds are "positively conditioned"); (3) the extension of reinforcement value to the bird's (or child's) own vocalizations by virtue of their similarity to those of the caretaker; (4) additional selective reinforcement of sound patterns closest to those of the caretaker, both "extrinsic," through caretaker responses, and "intrinsic" or "autistic," through the child's own experience of the similarity (cf. also Winitz, 1969).

Chomsky (1959) definitively demonstrated the limitations of (animal) learning theory as a source of understanding of the acquisition of human language, which is typified above all by its open-ended creativity or generative capacity. Nevertheless, the extensions of Mowrer's theoretical formulation by both Murai (1963) and Olmsted (1966, 1971) raise issues which remain relevant today.

Murai (1963) reports observations and insights drawn from a longitudinal study of normal and disordered language development, with only occasional reference to the behaviorist notion of reinforcement. He begins by noting that it is the emergence of language use, with its implication of a specific social and cultural context, which promotes the child to human status, and suggests that the study of ontogeny may eventually shed light on phylogeny or the origins of speech – a goal of scholars at the end of the last century (Romanes, 1888; Franke, 1899) which has only recently reappeared as a central concern of contemporary linguists, psychologists and cognitive scientists (see, for example, Pinker and Bloom, 1990 and the commentaries that follow).

Murai goes on to detail his reasons for viewing babbling rather than crying as the precursor of speech. Crying develops function as a (non-arbitrary) communicative signal early in the child's life but it cannot be flexibly used to represent a range of different meanings. Babbling, on the other hand, occurs in a wide range of situational contexts; it is copious and variable in form; it is not "extinguished" when needs are satisfied but rather tends to increase in comfort situations; and it has no inherent (biological) value or meaning as a signal, which leaves it free to be shaped by experience or learning. Furthermore, the abundance of babbling in normally developing infants stands in contrast with the comparative poverty of vocalization in the chimpanzee as well as in deaf, mentally handicapped, or institutionalized infants, all of whom develop language late or not at all. He concludes that babbling should be seen as a stage in speech development proper, providing the phonetic material – repeatedly and pleasurably reproduced – out of which language is formed. Furthermore, Murai remarks that the child plays an active role in this process, by choosing "objects to accommodate itself to" (1963, p. 25). That is, selection from adult models plays a role in early speech development.

Murai emphasizes the separate developmental trajectories of comprehension and production. Because comprehension involves (conditioned) responses to contextual cues, Murai sees it as closely related to animal use of *signals*, whereas the representation of objects or events through the production of an (arbitrary or "free") sound pattern is the beginning of *symbolic* behavior. The role of maternal "rewards" for word-like vocal productions is mentioned but minimized: "The symbolizing sounds do not always agree with the sounds reinforced by the mother . . . because an infant has its own peculiar concepts or schema concerning sounds and things" (1963, p. 32). Furthermore, Murai insists on the centrality of play, not the satisfaction of needs, as the factor leading to optimal symbolic and linguistic development (cf. Ferguson and Macken, 1983).

Olmsted (1966) takes Mowrer's learning theory as the starting point for a series of deductive "postulates" which predict the course of phonological acquisition, defined by the accurate pronunciation of phones, as a function of (1) frequency of occurrence in input speech and (2) ease of perception. He elaborates and tests this predictive account with an empirical study closely focused on the same postulates (1971).

Olmsted argues that once the child has learned to distinguish between "cries of distress" and other vocalizations, the sound of the human voice acquires "secondary reinforcing properties" which provide the child with motivation for engaging in further vocal activity. In support of these ideas he reviews contemporaneous research on the infant's behavioral repertoire (e.g. Wolff, 1966), interpreted as showing that the components of articulation present from birth (to serve the primary functions of respiration and ingestion) are available for relearning as part of the secondary function of communication. He notes that infant attention is most effectively captured a few minutes after the child has begun to suck.

> The infant feeding in his mother's arms is getting primary reinforcement for feeding behavior and for certain orienting behavior important to his perceptual development; in addition, he is attaching secondary reinforcing power to other constant stimuli in the situation. One of the most pervasive of these other stimuli is the sound of his mother's voice. (Olmsted, 1971, p. 31)

As the child spends more time awake and begins to vocalize or "coo," the sounds of his or her own vocalizations resemble adult speech sounds. "The more similar the child's voice is to the mother's, the more secondary reinforcement he can supply for himself" (p. 33). As cooing is replaced by babbling, "this [vocal] exercise represents only a gradual increase from the "accidental" sounds of the cooing period and apparently has little to do with communication . . . with *others* . . . However, it is likely that the delivering of secondary reinforcement to oneself is a kind of communication" (p. 34). Olmsted goes on to suggest that when, toward the end of the first year, the infant begins to produce adult words, some of his productions elicit direct parental reinforcement ('maternal smiles, cries of delight, and increased attention generally"). This should lead the child to pay closer attention to the adult's word forms, with the goal of producing better matches as a path to the associated parental response.

Olmsted deduces that "the most difficult task facing the infant beginning to speak . . . is *perceptual and imitative*, rather than articulatory" (1971, p. 35). The sounds produced in the vocal exercise of babbling are free from intentional sequencing constraints; during this period the impression of adult speech is consolidated in a few often repeated expressions which lend themselves to "latent learning" (which "can be demonstrated even in the rat", p. 37, n. 1). When the child now produces approximations to some of these expressions, the more successful matches will be noticed and reinforced by adults and older children, leading to especially rapid progress in the case of vocal infants with one or more consistent and attentive caretakers.

Olmsted assumes that "stretches of speech . . . gain secondary reinforcing properties in proportion to their frequency" (1966, p. 361), and that the distribution of speech sounds in child-directed speech is about the same as in adult-directed speech. The basic thesis of the empirical study then follows: Since auditory cues must be discriminated under variable conditions of competing ambient noise, the phones consisting of components found to be more discriminable to adults (based on Miller and Nicely, 1955) should be accurately produced by more children at an earlier age than those consisting of less discriminable components.

Olmsted's predictions are based on perceptual factors, explicitly disregarding *ease of articulation* (or production factors), which he views as difficult to test, as well as phonological context (or possible syntagmatic effects), which he does not address. He interprets his results (combining vowels and consonants, based on a sample of 100 children aged 15 to 54 months) broadly, finding support for the predicted difficulty in the following order: place of articulation < frication < nasality. However, voicing, predicted to be roughly equivalent to nasality, proves unexpectedly difficult, especially in the acquisition of later-learned sounds such as fricatives. Detailed analysis of each sound by age groups strongly supports the idea that error-free production is a gradual attainment, with coexistence of success and error the most common pattern for all phones and all children. As Olmsted admits in conclusion, "the notion of secondary reinforcement is not directly tested in this study," though "none of the results . . . are inconsistent" with it, "and alternative explanations of those results (e.g., dependence on the concept of biological maturation) appear to be less satisfactory" (1971, p. 243).

Structuralist models

Roman Jakobson first published his deductive account of the systematic unfolding of phonological oppositions in child language in German in 1941; the work was translated into English only in 1968, although Jakobson's model of adult phonology as essentially based on *opposition* or *contrast* (extending the work of Trubetzkoy and the Prague School of Linguistics) was available earlier (Jakobson and Halle, 1956).[1]

Jakobson drew on contemporary diary accounts of early phonological development (particularly Grégoire, 1937) for the facts to be explained; he drew on "structural analysis" and the "general laws of irreversible solidarity which govern the languages of the world synchronically" for his ordering of those facts into a theoretical explanation (Jakobson, 1949, p. 370). Citing Grammont (1902) to the effect that the language of the child is most impressive in the consistency of its errors, Jakobson sees the beginnings of phonology in the selection of sounds which accompanies the transition into word use, or the first meaningful use of remembered sound patterns. For communicative purposes the child requires "simple, clear, stable phonic oppositions, suitable to be engraved in memory and realized at will" (p. 369); Jakobson contrasts this phonologically constrained system (which must characterize the intentional production of early word forms) with the phonetic abundance of vocalizations not directed toward a communicative goal (*gazouillis*: 'burbling' or 'warbling').

Jakobson emphasizes the universal character of the "rigid regularity in the order of [phonological] acquisitions," based on anecdotal reports from a wide range of languages over more than a century of observation by his time. He envisages the unfolding of a phonological system as the progressive differentiation of a sequence of oppositions affecting successively smaller sound classes, based on the principle of maximum contrast and corresponding to the *implicational universals* of adult phonological systems (e.g. the presence of velar consonants implies the presence of labials and dentals (or alveolars); fricatives imply stops, nasal vowels imply nasal consonants). The first oppositions are the most general and the most strongly predicated: The earliest syllable to be produced will include a vowel, normally the low vowel [a], and a front consonant, usually a labial stop; thus the first syllable should be [ba], or sometimes [da]. The first consonantal opposition is expected to be oral vs. nasal ([ba] : [ma] or [da] : [na]), then labial vs. dental ([ba] : [da]); the first vocalic opposition, high vs. low ([i] : [a]), then high : mid : low ([i] : [e] : [a]) or high front : high back : low ([i] : [u] : [a]). The less common vowels (front rounded, back unrounded) imply the more common ones in the successive stages of a child's phonological system as they do in adult languages; similarly, the least common consonants, such as the Czech fricative /ř/ or the ejective consonants of several Native American and Caucasian languages or Ethiopian, for example, imply the corresponding plain consonants and are among the last to be acquired by children learning those languages. Jakobson concludes that "the choice of different elements within a language is far from arbitrary and random; rather, it is governed by universal and constant laws (or tendencies)" (1949, p. 378).

It is important to point out that Jakobson is treating the child's developing system as a succession of self-contained and lawful phonological structures in their own right. In addition, he allows for marginal phenomena, "vocal gestures" reflecting adult onomatopoeia and exclamations, which coexist with the phonological system proper. The consistency or "constancy" to which Grammont referred may be found not only in the growing set of phonological oppositions which make up the child's inventory but also in the regular relationship of substitutions (or errors), in which a particular sound from the child's repertoire is consistently used to replace an adult sound not yet mastered (cf. Ingram, 1974, 1986; Oller, 1975).

Jakobson has been praised for bringing order "into the bewildering array of facts accumulated by observation, which seemed to lack a common denominator until his broad principles were applied to them" (Leopold, editorial comment, in Bar-Adon and Leopold, 1971, p. 75). On the other hand, Olmsted (1966) explicitly rejects

Jakobson's structuralist formulation of the acquisition of phonology with its emphasis on oppositions as the essential core of a phonological system, since "some of the interesting parts of the learning process have already taken place before opposition learning is possible" (p. 533). He also objects to Jakobson's rejection of babbling as a stage in speech development. He argues cogently that exclusive attention to the learning of oppositions would lead to insurmountable sampling problems, given the small number of word productions at the onset of language use, and could create an inevitable illusion of abrupt acquisition of phonemic contrasts if early sporadic and variable usage of phones were to be disregarded in principle (see also Kiparsky and Menn, 1977). Similarly, Ferguson and Garnica (1975) observe that Jakobson "gives only the barest outline of his universal order of acquisition" (p. 167) and fails to address the effect of position in a word on the acquisition of sounds (e.g., fricatives may be acquired earlier word-finally, stops word-initially: Ferguson, 1975).

The most often cited criticism of Jakobson's views concerns the postulated discontinuity between babbling and speech and the characterization of babbling as random, involving the production of a wide range of human sounds including "clicks, palatalized and labialized consonants, affricates, sibilants, uvulars, etc." (1949, p. 368), most of which are said to disappear from the child's repertoire with the advent of the first meaningful (or intentional) word production. With the benefit of tape-recorded observations it has been possible in the decades since Jakobson first formulated his broad principles of sound acquisition to make direct comparisons, not limited to inventories but considering also token frequencies, of the sounds used in vocalizations serving different functions (word, protoword, or babble), in different social settings (solitary play, mother–child dialogue), and in different ambient language contexts (Nakazima, 1962, 1970, 1980; Cruttenden, 1970; Oller et al., 1976; Labov and Labov, 1978; Stark, 1980; Boysson-Bardies, Sagart, and Bacri, 1981; Elbers, 1982; Boysson-Bardies et al., 1992). These studies suggest that the "random" impression of babbling gained from diary reports was inaccurate, and furthermore they provide evidence that babbling should be viewed as a critical "phonetic substrate," facilitating subsequent phonological development (Ferguson and Macken, 1983).

Ferguson and Macken (1983) suggest that "there are systematic relationships between the phonetic characteristics of a child's babbling and those of his/her early speech," including

> the development of "speechiness" in babbling [or increasing clarity of contrast in consonant–vowel sequences] parallel to development in permitted phonetic complexity in speech, similarities in the order of acquisition and relative frequency of particular sound types, the progression in vowel qualities which seems to cut across babbling and speech, and the appearance (or increased frequency) of sound types in a child's babbling which are about to appear or have just appeared in his/her speech. (p. 143)

Vihman et al. (1985) found that the "wild sounds" of babbling – such as syllabic consonants, bilabial trills, or labio-lingual consonants (Oller et al., 1976) – may also be found in the early words, especially if onomatopoeia are not excluded from the comparison a *priori*. With regard to the more basic issue, the significance of prelinguistic vocal exploration for the subsequent development of phonological organization, Vihman et al. (1985) concluded that "an individual child's babble repertoire will be reflected . . . in choice of adult words to say and in the phonetic rendition of those words . . . Words emerg[e] naturally from the sound system which the child has been developing in his babble . . ." (p. 438; cf. the earlier speculative remark of MacNeilage, 1979: "The child's first words can be seen as . . . a matter of choosing from the babbling repertoire a set of approximations to adult word forms" (p. 30)).

What then are we to make of Jakobson's laws of irreversible solidarity? If early words largely resemble babbled vocalizations instead of reflecting a sharp diminution in phonetic diversity, and if oppositions are not easily identified in a child's small repertoire of lexical types, how should we understand Jakobson's statement of great regularity in the order of emergence of contrasting sounds? The predicted sequence of oppositions, meant to apply only to intentional word production, can plausibly be reinterpreted as a schematic expression of the sound types which typically emerge with the earliest syllable-based or "canonical" babbling (Oller, 1980) and which make up the highest frequency patterns to be found cross-linguistically in babbling as well as early words (Vihman, 1992).[2] Though Jakobson's sources, together with his theoretical bias, appear to have misled him into overemphasizing the formal distinction between babbling and early words, his analysis of the limited core of sound types which underlies both babbling and first word production, its universality across infants regardless of the ambient language and its similarity to the subset of sounds to be found in virtually all adult languages, remains valid half a century later (see Locke, 1983; Lindblom, 1992).

Though subsequent studies of phonological development were influenced by Jakobson's theoretical position, with diarists weighing his predicted acquisition order against the early word forms which they observed (e.g. Velten, 1943; Pačesova, 1968; Jeng, 1979), the only serious effort to extend Jakobson's schematic account of the regularity of phonological development in the same spirit was made by Moskowitz (1971, 1973). Whereas Jakobson restricted his remarks to the child's overall inventory of contrasting sounds, Moskowitz focuses on the gradual increase in phonotactic complexity.

Dismissing the distinction between a "pre-linguistic" and a "linguistic" stage as arbitrarily based on adult recognition of the first words,[3] Moskowitz traces development from short babbling utterances to longer vocalizations which bear adult-like intonation patterns. She sees the first production unit as the (babbled) sentence, followed by the minimum intonation bearer, the CV syllable. The syllable itself is at first unanalyzed, and comes to be equated with the word. Reduplicated words (CV CV) are succeeded by partial reduplication (with consonant or vowel harmony). Progress in comparing parts of these production units will eventually lead the child to "discover" the segment and the distinctive feature.

Moskowitz suggests that at first the child's phonetic ability goes beyond what "can be displayed through the structural sieve of phonology" (1973, p. 69). As a result, early words may be most accurate when first produced, while later productions are adapted to the child's phonological system. She also emphasizes the presence of extra-systemic elements in the child's phonology, both progressive idioms (words produced more accurately than the child's current production system would warrant) and regressive idioms, words reflecting an earlier stage in the child's phonology.

Generative linguistic models

In 1965, as part of the elaboration of his theory of syntax, Chomsky linked linguistic theory and language learning. One way to conceptualize the goal of linguistic theory at the deepest, "explanatory" level is to consider the problem of the child-learner, who is faced with acquiring the grammar of a language merely from exposure to "primary linguistic data." Only on the assumption that the child is innately provided with "tacit knowledge" of universal principles of language structure does the task become feasible:

> As a precondition for language learning, [a child] must possess, first, a linguistic theory that specifies the form of the grammar of a possible human language, and, second, a strategy for selecting a grammar of the appropriate form that is compatible with the primary linguistic data. As a long-range task for general linguistics, we might set the problem of developing an account of this innate linguistic theory that provides the basis for language learning. (1965, p. 25)

> It seems plain that language acquisition is based on the child's discovery of what from a formal point of view is a deep and abstract theory – a generative grammar of his language – many of the concepts and principles of which are only remotely related to experience by long and intricate chains of unconscious quasi-inferential steps. A consideration of the character of the grammar that is acquired, the degenerate quality and narrowly limited extent of the available data, the striking uniformity of the resulting grammars, and their independence of intelligence, motivation, and emotional state, over wide ranges of variation, leave little hope that much of the structure of the language can be learned by an organism initially uninformed as to its general character . . . The real problem is that of developing a hypothesis about initial structure that is sufficiently rich to account for acquisition of language, yet not so rich as to be inconsistent with the known diversity of language. (p. 58)

The same general points were made in brief summary form in the introduction to *The Sound Pattern of English* (Chomsky and Halle, 1968):

> General linguistics attempts to develop a theory of natural language as such, a system of hypotheses concerning the essential properties of any human language . . . those that must be assumed to be available to the child learning a language as an *a priori*, innate endowment. That there must be a rich system of *a priori* properties . . . is fairly obvious from the following empirical observations. Every normal child acquires an extremely intricate and abstract grammar, the properties of which are much underdetermined by the available data. This takes place with great speed, under conditions that are far from ideal, and there is little significant variation among children who may differ greatly in intelligence and experience. The search for essen-

tial linguistic universals is, in effect, the study of the *a priori faculté de langage* that makes language acquisition possible under the given conditions of time and access to data. (p. 4)

These provocative inferences regarding the nature of first language learning, and this linkage of language acquisition as a logical problem with the most fundamental goals of linguistic theory, stimulated a flow of activity in language acquisition research which continues unabated, though the issues and controversies have shifted considerably since that time.

The publication of *The Sound Pattern of English* in 1968 established the dominant features of generative phonological theory, most of which have remained stable over the intervening years. According to Dinnsen's succinct summary (1984), the basic tenets of that theory which are still widely accepted include the following:

1 Phonological descriptions can be formulated in terms of precise and explicit statements and notations;
2 segments are analyzable as a complex of features;
3 there are two levels of representation, one corresponding to the underlying (abstract) level and the other to the (surface) phonetic level;
4 phonological rules mediate between the two levels;
5 phonological rules interact.

In the area of phonological acquisition two linguists soon responded to the challenge of explaining how generative rules might come to be acquired, and what the nature of the pertinent "innate knowledge" might be, with somewhat different models: David Stampe's Natural Phonology (1969, 1979[4]) and Neil Smith's model, here referred to as the "Generative Phonology" model (1973).

Natural phonology

Stampe's model of phonological development focuses on automatic phonological rules, which he terms *phonological processes* (as opposed to "phonetically unmotivated" alternations, involving morphological or other exceptional conditions). These processes, which relate the alternating forms of morphemes as they are reshaped or adjusted in different phonological contexts, reflect "natural responses to phonetic forces" (Donegan and Stampe, 1979, p. 130), based on the limitations on human speech perception and production. It follows from the natural phonetic basis for phonological processes that they should not have to be "learned" by children. Instead, Natural Phonology assumes that the processes are universal and innately available; what the child needs to learn from exposure to the phonology of a particular language is to suppress, limit, and order these processes as required by the language.

The child enters upon language production with the full set of natural phonological processes. The initial phonological system represents a "language-innocent state" (i.e., an absence of specific adult language influence); in this state *all* the natural processes apply, "unlimited and unordered" (Stampe, 1979, p. ix). As a result of the expression of "the most extreme processes" – deletion of unstressed syllables, simplification of clusters and coarticulations, stopping of fricatives, merging of all vowels as low central [a] – the first attempts at speech or speech-like production, both "post-babbling" and the first words, yield simple CV sequences like those described by Jakobson ([dadada], [mamama]: Stampe, 1979, p. x).[5]

In order to begin to produce the wider range of phonological oppositions found in the adult inventory the child must learn to "suppress" those processes which do not make up a part of the phonology of the input language, or to limit or order processes so that they apply only in certain contexts. For example, the natural phonological process of "stopping" (replacing fricatives and affricates by stops) must be gradually suppressed, or limited to just those stop: fricative oppositions which do not occur in the ambient language (e.g., in the velar position in English). "Each new phonetic opposition the child learns to pronounce involves some revision of the innate phonological system . . . The mature system retains all those aspects of the innate system which the mastery of pronunciation has left intact" (1979, p. x).

Stampe explicitly rejects the idea that the child has a "phonemic system of his own" (1979, p. xiii). Instead, he insists that the child's representations of words are close to (the surface forms of) adult speech. He argues that this is shown by the fact that phonological oppositions appear suddenly and wherever needed in the child's speech: "He pronounces the new segment in precisely the appropriate morphemes, without rehearing them, and the old substitute does not reappear again" (1979, p. xiii). Finally, Stampe cites with approval the attribution of (historical) phonetic change to children's "imperfect imitation" of adult speech (from Passy, 1890; cf. also Kiparsky, 1965, 1968, but contrast Vihman, 1980, Kiparsky, 1989).

Stampe's account is meant to "explain" the implicational laws which Jakobson had proposed; in general, the effort to relate synchronic phonological rules or relationships between alternating forms, diachronic processes, and the systematic substitutions reflected in child attempts at adult words is very much in the synthesizing spirit of Jakobson; what is new is the formulation of phonology in generative terms, as a set of rules (or processes) rather than a system of oppositions. As Donegan and Stampe (1979) emphasize, moreover, the basic premise of their model, the rootedness of phonological processes in natural phonetic forces, has a long history, dating back to the last century, though it is at odds with the mainstream positions of both structuralist and generative phonology.

Generative phonology

The single most important characteristic of phonological development, from a linguistic perspective, is its regularity: Errors or segment substitutions in child forms as compared with the adult target forms are predictable or "rule-based." Regularity may also be said to characterize the changes to the system as the child approaches the adult pronunciation. Accordingly, N. V. Smith (1973) devises a set of *realization rules*, using distinctive features and other notational devices drawn from generative phonology, to express the regularities in his son Amahl's phonological development from age 2 to 4. He actually provides two sets of analyses: (1) a mapping from the adult surface forms, which are hypothesized to serve as the child's underlying representations, to the observed child productions; and (2) a self-contained "independent system," based solely on the phoneme inventory and phonotactic constraints observed in the child's forms. Smith also presents in full the longitudinal data on which his rule formulations are based.

In addition to the use of a generative rule format and distinctive features, Smith shares with Stampe the conviction that "there is no useful sense in which the child can be said to have his own system" (1973, p. 132); that is, he rejects the validity of the second analysis. Smith concludes that the child's phonology consists of a set of psychologically valid rules (or processes) which operate on underlying lexical representations derived from adult surface forms, which are assumed to be accurately perceived and stored; he notes in passing that the realization rules of his model, which are in effect "a kind of filtering device of the child's competence, and have gradually to be unlearned as the child approximates more and more closely to the adult language," have much in common with Stampe's "general constraints" or processes (Smith, 1973, p. 133).

Smith points out that it is always possible (and thus a trivial exercise) to write rules relating any forms the child might produce to the intended adult target form. For the rules to be of real interest, there must be independent evidence that they actually reflect the child's linguistic competence. Two issues are critical: (1) Is there good reason to believe that the child accurately perceives adult forms? This is necessary to justify use of the adult surface form as the input to a set of rules. If the child's forms sometimes reflect misperception of the adult word, the underlying lexical representation cannot always correspond to the form of the adult word. (2) Are the rules themselves psychologically real? Smith dismisses the view that the child's deviations from the adult form are solely due to articulatory difficulties or "motor problems" (a position he ascribes to Kornfeld, 1971), arguing that structural pressure from the realization rules must be invoked to account for some of the complexities in the child's phonological development. If the rules can be shown to have a "life of their own," this will validate their status as psychologically real for the child. Figure 2.1 (from N. V. Smith, 1978) illustrates the production model implied by Smith's account.

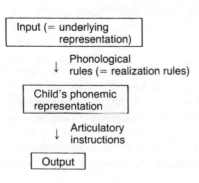

Figure 2.1 Smith's (1973) model.
Source: N. V. Smith, 1978, p. 260, used by permission

Smith notes that, like adults, children have a greater passive knowledge of language than their active repertoire reveals (they understand more than they can say), citing specific examples to show that the child's merger of different adult forms into homophones in production need not reflect a failure in discrimination of the adult forms. His main argument, however, concerns the "across-the-board" nature of the acquisition process (mentioned also by Stampe): "The fact that changes occur in precisely the correct set of words is further evidence that it must be the adult forms that the child has internalised" (p. 139).

Finally, Smith outlines four functions served by the realization rules: vowel or consonant harmony, consonant cluster reduction, systemic simplification (or merger of contrasting adult phonemes), and "grammatical simplification" (e.g., his son's use of a fixed "dummy" prefix for unstressed initial syllables of adult words). He argues that these are universal constraints or "part of a universal template which the child has to escape from in order to learn his language" (1973, p. 206); Smith is inclined to view these constraints as innately available to the child, limiting the range of possible child solutions to phonological problems posed by the ambient language (1978).

It is a great virtue of Smith's book that the data from his extensive longitudinal case study are presented in sufficient detail to allow reanalysis by other investigators; such reanalysis has allowed Macken (1980a) and Grunwell (1982) independently to show, on the basis of Smith's own data, that new sounds are not always acquired "across-the-board" in all and only the relevant forms. For example, Amahl first produced both the affricate /ʧ/ and the cluster /tr/ as [t]; when he developed the ability to produce the cluster, he treated some affricate-initial words as if they were /tr/-initial: *chalk* [tɑk ~ tɹɑk], *chocolate* [tɑklit ~ tɹɑklit] (Grunwell, 1982, p. 141). This suggests misperception of the adult form in the period when the child was not yet producing either affricates or clusters, followed by a period of variability between competing forms, and requires eventual restructuring of the underlying representation for the affricate-initial forms (for similar examples of protracted /f : θ/ confusion from another child, see Vihman, 1982).

In a penetrating review, Braine (1976) suggests that Smith has oversimplified the arguments in favor of the child's "own system" and has consequently overstated the case for a child phonology consisting solely of adult-like lexical representations plus the realization rules. In particular, Braine maintains that the child must have "an output system . . . [that has] some sort of psychomotor reality" (p. 491). The "phonemes" of the child's system reflect the "small set of features for which he has articulatory control . . . and through which the realization of his words has to be funneled" (p. 491). Although Smith succeeds in showing that the child has more knowledge about adult surface forms of words than the child's productions can exhibit directly, his analyses also unwittingly reflect the fact that there is also systematicity in the child's own productions and their interrelations.

With regard to the child's lexical representations, Braine proposes the following contrasting positions, the first of which is close to that which Smith espouses:

1   The "articulation hypothesis": Adult forms are generally perceived accurately and are represented in terms of adult articulatory features. "The relations

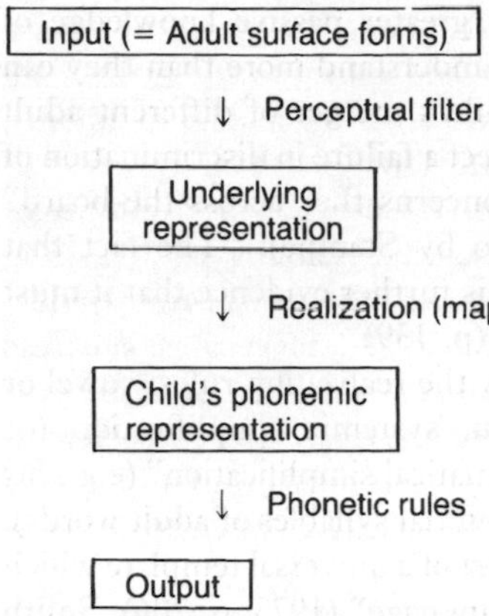

Input (= Adult surface forms)

↓ Perceptual filter

Underlying representation

↓ Realization (mapping) rules

Child's phonemic representation

↓ Phonetic rules

Output

Figure 2.2 Smith's (1978) model.
Source: N. V. Smith, 1978, used by permission

between perception and articulation are given innately, so that a child never has to work out the articulatory representation of a form heard" (1976, p. 491).

2 The "perception hypothesis": Perception is represented in terms of auditory features. The interpretation in terms of vocal production has to be discovered by the child; a representation in terms of articulatory features is gradually added to the lexicon in the course of development (cf. also Braine, 1974). Perception may be assumed either to be accurate from the first or to contain systematic biases, leading to partially inaccurate initial auditory representation in the lexicon.

Macken's extensive reanalysis (1980a) of the effects of some of Smith's core rules strongly supports Braine's arguments in favor of partially inaccurate representation of adult forms in some cases, with apparently accurate representation of others. Following Braine, she argues for a two–level rule system, with (a) perceptual–encoding rules, which serve as a perceptual filter on adult forms, converting them into the child's lexical representation, and (b) output rules, which function as an articulatory filter, relating the lexical representation to the child's actual production forms (see figure 2.2, which expresses N. V. Smith's 1978 revision of his model to include a perceptual filter). With regard to Smith's anecdotal evidence that Amahl perceived adult phonological contrasts that he could not differentiate in production, Macken comments that "it is dangerous to generalize from the evidence of [perceptual] discrimination in a few cases to the conclusion that the child can discriminate all instances of a contrast . . ." (p. 13).

In order to show that articulatory difficulties alone are insufficient to explain the child's substitutions for adult sounds Smith presents evidence that Amahl appeared "unable to produce a particular sound or sound sequence in the correct place, but [was] perfectly capable of producing it as his interpretation of something else" (p. 4); for example, he substituted [g] for /d/ before syllabic (dark or velar) /ḷ/ (*puddle* → [pʌgḷ]), but [d] for /z/ in the same context (*puzzle* → [pʌdḷ]). In addition, Smith adduces instances of "recidivism," or "loss of a contrast which has already been established" (p. 4) and of "absolute exceptions," or words which are produced more accurately than the child's system would appear to allow; these are what others have labeled "regressive" and "progressive" phonological idioms, (Moskowitz, 1973, and Ferguson, 1978 respectively). While Smith interprets all of these complexities and exceptions as deriving from "the psychological validity of the realisation rules, and the structural pressure these exert" (Smith, 1973, p. 152), Braine and Macken argue that inaccurate perception (leading to inaccurate underlying representations) offers a more satisfactory explanation in most cases. Whereas Braine doubts that formal properties of the realization rules or their ordering ever afford a cogent way of explaining a child's production errors, Macken prefers to leave open the question of whether errors reflecting regression, for example, may not sometimes reflect "other factors related to the child's active systematization or organization of phonology" (1980a, p. 17).

Prosodic phonology

Like the other linguistic models described so far, Waterson's "prosodic phonology" represents the application to child data of a specific linguistic theory, namely that developed by J. R. Firth. Anticipating the current nonlinear models by several decades, Firth's prosodic analysis (1948) went beyond the segment-oriented analysis of structural linguistics to allow for the phonetic consequences of the continuous and partially overlapping flow of articulatory gestures which characterizes speech. Phoneme-like or "phonematic" (C and V) units are supplemented in this model by *prosodies*, phonological structures of any length. Like nonlinear analysis within the generative framework, prosodies have been effectively used to deal with relations of length, stress, and tone, as well as with harmonic constraints and with "spreading" phonetic features such as palatalization, retroflexion, nasalization, and glottalization.[6]

Waterson attributes to Firth many of the elements of her own work which are most original and which have proven most influential. Above all, her focus on whole words rather than segments as the relevant unit for early phonologies derives directly from the theory:

> It is the whole-unit or holistic approach of prosodic phonology which brought to light the patterned relationships between a child's hardly recognizable words and the adult models and thus made it possible to explain the somewhat bizarre forms of early words, as well as why sounds that children are capable of producing are not used in all the contexts in which they occur in adult forms. (Waterson, 1987, p. 2)

In *Prosodic Phonology*, chapter 1: "An introduction to the theory" (1987, pp. 4–14) Waterson lays out several key concepts and illustrates them from her own data and analyses. For example, the notion of "restricted language" is intended to allow for the clear delimitation of the domain of application of a linguistic description, combined with "renewal of connection," which specifies the relationship of that domain to different situational contexts of language use. Waterson uses the concept to describe the child's succession of stages, each with its own "total system." Another important concept is "polysystematicity," which Waterson interprets as allowing for different subsystems of phonological elements in different phonotactic positions – content vs. function words, or stems vs. suffixes – and imitations – onomatopoeia or recitations vs. everyday language use.

Waterson (1971), the most widely cited of Waterson's studies of her son's phonological development, has three explicit goals: (1) to illustrate and defend the value of discovering the child's system on its own terms; (2) to demonstrate that the patterning of the child's forms is best understood to be holistic rather than based on segment-by-segment substitutions for adult sounds; (3) to support the contention that the child's perception is different from the adult's, and is at first schematic and incomplete. Each of these issues remains of central concern today.

Waterson's detailed and discerning analyses of her son's early word patterns provide a rich illustration of the notion of "the child's own system"; these patterns, or "word-level acoustic schemata, by means of which the child is claimed to perceive words and to represent and organize them in the lexicon" (Queller, 1988, p. 464), are taken to reflect the child's perceptual filtering of the input. For each pattern, the child forms reproduce only the most salient acoustic features shared by a set of adult words (e.g., the "nasal structure," *finger, window, another,* and *Randall,* produced at 1;6 as reduplicated CVCV forms in which C is a palatal nasal). Waterson insists on the differential perceptual salience of adult words as the basis for the child's choice of a production pattern; what is salient for the child is related both to what is already in his repertoire and to "the most strongly articulated features" (1971, p. 41). Unfortunately, no independent evidence is provided for the characterization of certain features (such as nasality, in the above examples) as "most strongly articulated," so that the explanation has an inescapably circular ring.

Queller's sympathetic appreciation (1988) describes Waterson's model as

> essentially embryological. While acknowledging the child's active role in constructing and systematizing a lexicon, W. wants to explain phonological development in terms of a gradual loosening of constraints on the complexity of internal lexical representations. Permitted complexity constraints are in turn assumed to reflect limitations on what the child is capable of perceiving linguistically, at any given time. W's cognitivism thus tends inexorably to be eclipsed by her perceptual determinism. (p. 465)

Nevertheless, perhaps due to the emphasis of the Firthian approach on the analysis of "specific language material" (rather than on the more abstract search for universals) as well as to her repeated insightful applications of the theory to different aspects of her son's phonological development, Waterson supplied many of the elements later highlighted in the more eclectic cognitive model to which we now turn.

Cognitive models

The models we have discussed up until now have been deductive at least in part, based on a preexisting theoretical stance and illustrated with anecdotal examples or, in the case of Smith and of Waterson, a single extended diary study. With the cognitive model we come to the first attempt to develop a theory of phonological acquisition inductively, based on first-hand experience with a range of different children. The model was developed interactively over a period of about ten years by several investigators, but primarily by Menn and by Ferguson and his colleagues at the Stanford Child Phonology Project (1968–1988).

Menn (1983) contrasts two versions of the "implicit defining question" of research on phonological acquisition:

> We used to ask: What linguistic theory will explain the order in which the various language behaviours develop? This question assumed that there is such an order, and that it should be explainable by linguistic theory. The new question is roughly: What behavioural predispositions and abilities does the child bring to the task of learning to communicate with language, and how does the individual go about solving the articulatory and phonological problems posed by the language to be learned? (p. 45)

The replacement of the order of acquisition issue – central to Olmsted's work on perception as well as to Jakobson's predictions regarding the production of phonological oppositions – by issues of early capacities and the child's active role in problem-solving is clearly expressed here, and constitutes the fundamental difference between the cognitive model and its predecessors. In addition, linguistic theory is no longer expected to provide ready-made "solutions" or explanations for developmental questions; instead, Menn envisages a dialogue between theory and acquisition data:

> As for the old assumption that linguistic theory can explain what we find in acquisition . . . the more likely scenario is that linguistic theory and acquisition data will have to come to terms with one another. A theory based only on the performance of the mature skilled user cannot anticipate the temporary learning devices and detours of the unskilled learner. (p. 45)

In perhaps the earliest published attempt to articulate a cognitive position[7] Ferguson and Farwell (1975) explicitly reject the deductive approach, choosing instead "to try to understand children's phonological development in itself so as to improve our phonological theory, even if this requires new theoretical constructs . . ." (p. 437; cf. also Ferguson, 1986). Starting from this pretheoretical perspective, they encounter "surprises" in the analysis of their longitudinal data from three one-year-old children: (1) an unexpectedly high level of variability in the production of word forms; (2) relative accuracy in the earliest renditions of a word, sometimes followed by less accurate production (termed "regression" in Ferguson, 1978); (3) evidence of sound-based selectivity in the particular words a child will attempt. The unifying lesson which they draw from these surprises is "the primacy of lexical items in phonological development" (p. 437).

Ferguson and Farwell find that children "construct their own phonologies" (p. 437): "Individual paths of development" may be traced for each child, reflecting different strategies and resulting in an idiosyncratic early lexicon. In addition to emphasizing the word as a central unit in phonological development (alongside other elements and relations, such as syllables, prosodies, features, and rules), their model, in explicit contrast with Jakobson, "would de-emphasize the separation of phonetic and phonemic development, but would maintain in some way the notion of 'contrast' . . . It would emphasize individual variation . . . but incorporate the notion of 'universal phonetic tendencies' which result from the physiology of the human vocal tract and central nervous system" (Ferguson and Farwell, 1975, p. 437). This early formulation of the cognitive model thus already looks forward to the complementary biological models which began to be developed somewhat later.

Active discovery of structure by the child, hypothesis testing and problem solving, with experimentation (and variability) followed by overgeneralization and regression are all hallmarks of the cognitive model (Menn, 1976a; Kiparsky and Menn, 1977; Macken, 1978, 1979; Macken and Ferguson, 1981, 1983; cf. also Menn, 1971). As in other aspects of language acquisition (such as the past tense: Berko, 1958; Cazden, 1968; or lexical and semantic domains: Carey, 1978; Bowerman, 1982), the child's progress typically involves an early presystematic period of piecemeal learning (the mastering of special cases, including "phonological idioms"), followed by the discovery (and overgeneralization) of patterns (compare the shift from individual item learning to whole word patterns posited in Waterson, 1978). Phonological selectivity is seen as a complement to the child's construction of a small number of canonical output forms (Ferguson, 1978); Kiparsky and Menn (1977) argue that the use of relatively complex rules, such as metathesis, to achieve an "acceptable" output form (e.g., *snow* → [nos]) are good evidence that the child's phonological processes are not the automatic consequence of innate articulatory constraints, but serve instead an information processing function, reducing the number of different forms to be stored and accessed for production (see also Menn, 1978).

In theoretical formulations spanning a decade Menn (1974, 1976, 1978, 1979, 1983; Kiparsky and Menn, 1977) wrestled with models of the relation between perception and production in phonological development. An information processing approach was already evident in 1974: "The recognition processes must impose a sufficiently regular structure on the incoming stream of sound so that it can be coded for memory storage; the production-phase processes essentially concern recoding the stored phonetic features as articulatory instructions" (p. 2). Kiparsky and Menn (1977) propose a three-level model which allows for the abstract underlying representations (A) which will eventually be learned as part of the adult system, as well as for storage of the child's pronunciation (C), which will eventually cease to be distinct from the adult surface forms; intermediate between these are the "phonetic representations perceived by the child" (B), which may or may not differ at first from the adult surface or phonetic forms (see figure 2.3).[8]

In 1978 Menn developed this model further, renaming (B) the "input lexicon" (or "recognition store") and restructuring (C) into two levels, the "output lexicon" ("production store") and the "articulatory instructions" (see figure 2.4, adapted from Menn, 1983). In this model, the child first "stores for recognition some of the information available from the adult target words . . ." (p. 164). In order to produce a word, however, the child must "invent" reduction rules which simplify the forms to be produced, yielding a small set of canonical forms, or output patterns. The

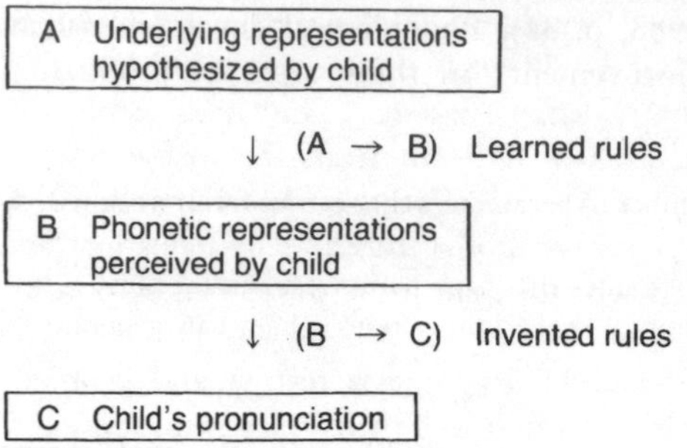

```
┌─────────────────────────────────┐
│ A  Underlying representations   │
│    hypothesized by child        │
└─────────────────────────────────┘

    ↓  (A  →  B)   Learned rules

┌─────────────────────────────────┐
│ B  Phonetic representations     │
│    perceived by child           │
└─────────────────────────────────┘

    ↓  (B  →  C)   Invented rules

┌─────────────────────────────────┐
│ C  Child's pronunciation        │
└─────────────────────────────────┘
```

Figure 2.3 Kiparsky and Menn's (1977) model.
Source: Kiparsky and Menn, 1977

output lexicon then stores only canonical forms ("articulatory subroutines") and the distinctive aspects of each of the child's pronounceable words; production rules supply the predictable articulatory specifications which derive from the established output patterns.

Menn (1983) elaborates the notion of an "output constraint" which (like the "conspiracies" sometimes invoked for adult phonological rules, e.g., Kisseberth, 1970) may motivate several of a child's rules or production strategies, including the avoidance or exploitation of particular sounds or sound patterns (referred to above as "selection"), the use of assimilatory rules such as consonant harmony, and "template matching," in which adult patterns may be radically distorted to fit a child's production pattern (e.g., Waterson, 1971; Priestly, 1977; Macken, 1979).[9] Menn relates the output constraints to "the state of a child's knowledge" of articulatory possibilities, as arrived at through vocal exploration, although the physiological factors usually understood under the term "ease of articulation" also play a role in shaping these constraints.

The child's construction of one or more canonical forms simplifies speech production by acting "like a [computer] program in which some parameters are fixed, but others are settable . . . Once [such a program] has been learned, it can be

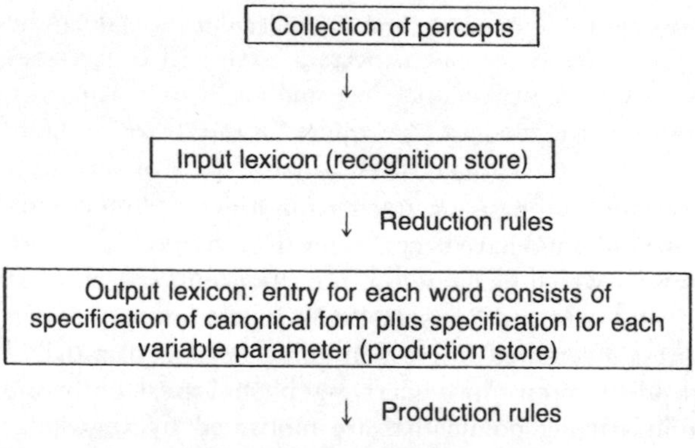

```
            ┌─────────────────────────┐
            │ Collection of percepts  │
            └─────────────────────────┘
                        ↓
         ┌───────────────────────────────┐
         │ Input lexicon (recognition store) │
         └───────────────────────────────┘
                ↓  Reduction rules
┌─────────────────────────────────────────────────┐
│      Output lexicon: entry for each word consists of │
│ specification of canonical form plus specification for each │
│      variable parameter (production store)       │
└─────────────────────────────────────────────────┘
                ↓  Production rules
            ┌─────────────────────────┐
            │ Articulatory instructions │
            └─────────────────────────┘
```

Figure 2.4 Menn's (1983) model.
Source: Adapted from Menn, 1983

highly automatic to 'run'" (Menn, 1983, p. 31). Phonological development can then be understood as involving improvement "in three areas of production control":

1 [the child] learns to increase the number of parameters that can be freely assigned values in a given word . . .
2 she learns to increase the number of values that each parameter can take on . . .
3 she learns to link up short programs to make longer ones which can generate polysyllabic words. (p. 31)

The various expressions of a cognitive model of phonological development typically share the expectation that the child comes to the acquisition problem equipped with general, "natural" capacities for perception and sound production, but not with specialized or "innate" knowledge of linguistic categories (recall the reference to "universal phonetic tendencies" in Ferguson and Farwell, 1975, quoted on p. 29). The babbling period is seen to allow for "practice" in the motor activities which subserve speech production (Zlatin, 1975; Oller, 1981; Ferguson and Macken, 1983); early words are understood as drawing on that vocal preparation (Vihman et al., 1985). The precise *mechanism* of early vocal activity in paving the way to language is not specified, although some work within a cognitive perspective sought to order the "emergence of the sounds of speech in infancy" (Oller, 1980; cf. also Stark, 1978, 1980). For example, Menn (1983) posits

a two-stage discovery process [for] a child's establishment of a new articulatory gesture as her way-of-saying a particular target sound. The first stage is a matter of trial-and-error attempts to match the sound sequence; the second stage is one of deliberate or accidental overgeneralization of the success of that articulatory gesture – that is, the use of it to render similar adult targets. (p. 21)

The development through babbling of a repertoire of voluntarily producible sound patterns (somewhat different for each child), which may play a significant role in the *first* of these stages, is assumed, but is not a central concern of the model.

Biological models

The biological models place their emphasis on tracing the origins of phonology back to perceptuomotor constraints, and have begun to make more specific suggestions regarding the mechanisms which facilitate the transition into speech (e.g., Kent, 1992; Locke, 1986, 1990; Locke and Pearson, 1992). Furthermore, theorists within this framework express a renewed interest in going beyond data-driven models to arrive at independent motivations, deriving phonological units and processes deductively, "from starting points that are motivated by knowledge independent of the facts to be explained" (Lindblom, 1992, p. 135). "'Arguing from data' is a common, and initially an often necessary, procedure in model making and theory construction. But it is not an end in itself and, in the long run, it is non-explanatory" (p. 134).

Continuity model

Locke (1983) was one of the first to articulate an explicitly biological approach to phonological acquisition. He is interested in defining the beginning of phonology:

> If to have phonology a child must reveal a rigidly patterned system of segments, syllable shapes and stresses, phonotactic rules, and pitch contours – a system whose properties resemble those of the adult system, and are available to convey lexical meaning – then . . . most children have phonology long before their first "true word" is evident. If to have acquired phonology the child's prelexical sound system must perceptibly change in the direction of the ambient system – in a way that could only be due to exposure – then I feel just as certain that a child's (expressive) phonological system may not be acquired until well after the appearance of his early words. (p. 2)

He goes on to reject both Jakobson's contention that babbling is an entirely random activity, unrelated to the later systematic unfolding of speech sound oppositions, and R. Brown's (1958) suggestion, consistent with the behaviorist model current at the time, that babbling "drifts in the direction of . . . [ambient] speech" (p. 199). Locke presents sound inventories and frequencies from a wide range of different studies to show that a small core of "repertoire" sounds account for babbling vocalizations in children learning a number of different languages. He sees the babbling repertoire as a universal pool of possibilities out of which early word productions will be shaped: "The infant – as he begins to speak – brings forth a set of sounds which are somewhat like those he is attempting to replicate . . . [He] does not substitute some sounds for other sounds. Rather, he projects what he has into contexts where it seems to fit . . ." (pp. 60f.).

Locke's continuity model includes physiological, perceptual, and cognitive components. The physiological component is predicated on the preexisting match between the universal repertoire of infant phonetic capacities and the universal core of adult language inventories, while the perceptual and cognitive components are based on the child's approximate ability to identify matches between the sounds in his repertoire and the target patterns of the adult language. What is *not* available in the beginnings of phonology is knowledge of linguistic structure, including oppositions and their communicative function: This is the child's "systemic innocence."

Locke posits three stages for early phonological development:

1 In the pragmatic stage the child begins to recognize the auditory consequences of his own phonetic gestures; this is the "beginning of the *function* of phonology for the child" (p. 94; cf. also Fry, 1966), reflecting "the demonstrated desire to vocally communicate" (p. 96).
2 The cognitive stage begins with the first attempts at adult words "through the operation of cognitive processes such as attention, storage, retrieval, and pattern matching" (p. 97), although the early word shapes show little change from "premeaningful" vocalizations. First words show little accommodation to the adult system, but use sound-based selection to produce adult-like forms while relying primarily on the mechanism of maintenance of those preexisting pho-

netic patterns of babbling which are present in the ambient adult language. (Recall the surprising accuracy of early forms noted by Ferguson and Farwell, 1975.)

3   The systemic stage "is marked by changes, not of intentionality or in the nature of the lexicon, but rather in the phonetic characteristics of the child's . . . system" (pp. 97ff.), which now moves in the direction of the particular ambient language through loss of sounds outside the adult structure (cf. the loss of [h] in children acquiring French: Vihman and Boysson-Bardies, 1994) as well as learning of sounds outside the babbling repertoire. "Where phonology is concerned, it appears that the first genuine stage may well await the first 50 words, and may not be discerned until 18 months or more" (p. 98).

The relationship between this model and cognitive approaches was clarified in several subsequent papers. Vihman, Ferguson, and Elbert (1986) saw the strong evidence of variability and individual differences in early phonology as supporting a cognitive over a biological approach, as did Goad and Ingram (1987) – who dispute the extent of early variability, however. Elaborating on Studdert-Kennedy's (1983, 1986) contention that pervasive (phonetic) variability is the "stuff" of development, Locke (1988) replied to Goad and Ingram (1987) that

> according to the principles of evolutionary biology, every species is composed of genetically diverse individuals . . . The primary mechanism of adaptation, natural selection, requires that there be genetically transmitted variation across the individual members of a species . . . Many of the so-called "individual differences" in children's behaviour are undoubtedly an expression of their biological differences. (p. 664)

Similarly, Kent and Bauer (1985) maintain that

> individual differences . . . [are] recognized as critical in phonological acquisition because they would be expected to have both developmental and evolutionary significance . . . The selection of individual resources of cognitive and sensorimotor experience to become expressive skills in pragmatically and semantically significant contexts is the heart of the developmental side of the selectionist paradigm. (p. 493)

Vihman (1993c) concluded that "high individual variation across children early in the period of transition to speech, whatever its origins (in brain or vocal tract structure or other), can be accommodated within a biological model" (p. 62).

In what can be seen as a continuation of the cognition/biology debate, MacNeilage and Davis (1990b) seek to derive the acquisition of motor representation and control for speech from a single universal motor base: the rhythmic alternation between open and closed jaw, or mandibular oscillation, which characterizes canonical babbling – the first adult-like syllable production. MacNeilage and Davis see these "pure frames" as constituting "dynamic prototypes" for the syllable frames of adult language. The "content" for these syllables, provided by a limited number of fixed consonant–vowel sequences, is at first the mechanical consequence of lip and tongue placement in relation to the moving mandible. Mid or high front vowels tend to occur after dentals or alveolars, for example, as a consequence of the raising of the tongue tip for the consonantal closure. In varie-gated babbling, "local modulations in this reduplicated oscillatory envelope" con-stitute the chief advance (p. 462), and it is these local modifications of frame structures that give rise to the first word forms. Longitudinal data from one child's acquisition of English are presented in support of this hypothesis (cf. also Davis and MacNeilage, 1990).

In response, Vihman (1992) endeavored to test "the relative contributions to early vocal production of biological constraints, the phonetic characteristics of particular languages, and the child's individual creativity or initiative in the con-struction of patterns" (p. 394). She analyzed the C–V associations found in the most common syllables used by each of twenty-three children in the earliest stages of acquiring one of four languages (English, French, Japanese, or Swedish) in order to determine whether the postulated "mechanical" associations between alveolars and non-low front vowels, velars and non-low back vowels, and labials and central vowels would be found in these cross-linguistic data. Though the predicted associations did appear in part, individual differences across children learning the same language proved to be more salient than the hypothesized biological con-straint (for further discussion, see MacNeilage and Davis, 1993; cf. also Boysson-Bardies, 1993, who provides data from English, French, Swedish and Yoruba to tease out the role of motor and ambient language factors; and also Oller and Steffens, 1994).

An additional test of the force of perceptuomotor constraints in early phonologi-cal development involves the close analysis of the construction of individual first phonological systems by different children learning the same or different lan-guages, as undertaken in several studies mentioned earlier (by Ferguson, Macken, Menn, Vihman, Waterson; cf. also Branigan, 1976; Berman, 1977; Stoel-Gammon and Cooper, 1984; and Appendix C, below). In these studies a variety of different organizational strategies are reported. In some cases, which Vihman and Roug-Hellichius (1991) characterize as "controlled expansion," strict constraints on pos-sible syllable types appear to obtain at first, but are gradually relaxed over time (cf. the phonological development of Jonathan (Braine, 1974), who exhibits in his early word forms the C–V associations predicted by Davis and MacNeilage, as does Virve (Vihman, 1976); see also Timmy (Appendix C)); such developmental profiles readily lend themselves to a biologically oriented description such as MacNeilage and Davis envisage, in which the child slowly emerges from the constraints of his or her particular early sound-patterns. On the other hand, other children seem to begin with a far wider range of possible sound sequences and to "crystallize" a canonical word pattern only as the apparent result of active exploration of possible "matches" between their own repertoire and the affordances of the adult language (cf. Si in Macken, 1979; Molly and Alice (Appendix C)).

The timing of adult language influence has also been investigated in several studies since Locke's model was first developed, leading to persuasive evidence that already in the prelinguistic period the ambient language has a global effect on vowel shape (Boysson-Bardies et al., 1989), intonation (Whalen, Levitt, and Wang, 1991) and place of articulation (Boysson-Bardies and Vihman, 1991). It is thus now possible to document Brown's notion of phonetic drift toward the ambient language; this does not, however, invalidate the relevance of biological constraints in the period of transition into speech. Rather, it is probably necessary to think in terms of a somewhat more complex model of the interaction of physiological and environmental influences and cognitive or individual system-building activity.

In 1993 Locke elaborated a socio-biological account and proposed an interpretation in developmental neurological terms of the shift from prelinguistic to linguistic behavior (see also Locke, 1994). According to this model, there are not one but *two* specialized systems in humans which are relevant to language. The first is present at birth: This is the "specialization in social cognition," which biases the infant toward faces and voices and toward the prosody of infant-directed speech. This specialization (not a "module," since it is not necessarily altogether unique to humans) not only directs the child's attention toward input speech (or "data sources" for constructing knowledge of language) but also *motivates* the child by enlisting affect and communicative interaction in the service of language acquisition. This prelinguistic specialization is thus responsible for vocal accommodation, which leads to the development of contextualized word use and the learning of whole (unanalyzed) formulaic utterances (and their appropriate situations of use), resulting in the data base needed to activate the more specifically linguistic analyses imputed to the second specialized system, usually known as "the language module." This module handles the "language internal" systems shared with no other species, specifically, phonology and morphosyntax.

Self-organizing models

A complementary biological approach to phonological development, with emphasis on the precursors to motor speech control in infancy, draws on the notion of "autoorganization" (Kent, 1984), or self-organizing systems (Edelman, 1987; Thelen, 1985, 1989). The idea is suggested in Kent (1981):

> The acquisition of speech motor control is a continuous but nonlinear process. "Sensitive" periods of nonlinearity occur when certain neural, musculoskeletal, environmental, and cognitive changes combine (or "get together") in the individual organism. The points in time at which a particular number of these factors combine can result in "jumps in performance" [periods of "discovery" and reorganization (Kent, 1984)]. (p. 136)

Kent (1984, 1992) proposes several basic principles for a theory of speech development, or factors to be reckoned with in such a theory. These start from the premise that language is rooted in auditory perception and speech production as well as in cognitive (and social or communicative) experience and in exposure to an ambient language.[10] Kent's principles include the following:

1   The anatomy of the vocal tract changes dramatically over the first year of life; this has a direct effect on the range of possible infant sounds. More speculatively, maturation appears to involve a "progressively ascending level of central nervous system control over vocalization" (1984, p. R889); cortical control is

achieved only in the second half of the first year. The timing of the emergence of reduplicated babbling, which has been related to the first signs of handedness (Ramsay, 1982), may be tied to this development.

2   Rhythmicity is a natural basis for the organization of movement systems; it contributes to skill acquisition by facilitating emergent coordination within and among motor systems. The importance of rhythmicity in speech motor control is suggested by the fact that trains of adult-like syllables first emerge at a time of widespread rhythmicity in infant motor development in general (Thelen, 1981). Thus reduplicated babbling may constitute a "vocal manifestation of a general tendency toward repetitive or rhythmic movement patterns" (Kent, 1992, p. 70; see also Kent et al., 1991).

3   Production and perception have separate origins and must come to be integrated in the course of the first few months, in interaction with exposure to the ambient language. "The process involves the infant's sensitivity to, and use of, the multiple sensory consequences of movement" (1992, p. 78). In Edelman's (1987) terms, a gradual global process of neural mapping between a motor gesture and its sensory consequences leads, with sufficient repetition, to stable action categories. These could provide the "canonical forms" (or word production patterns) around which the child's earliest phonological organization is constructed.

4   The child's first unit of contrast in speech production may be the word (based on the work of Ferguson, Macken and others). In that case, the child "must relate an intended word to a motor plan or [phonetic] gestural score" (Kent, 1992, p. 80); this "gestural score" or "stable prearticulatory representation" might arise through the development of well-mastered babbling patterns, or "vocal motor schemes" (McCune and Vihman, 1987). The vocal motor scheme, in turn, may represent the "stable action categories" which, when linked with phonetically similar adult word targets, develop into canonical forms, providing the basis for lexical development.

Kent (1992) outlines a biological model of perceptual and motor factors in phonological development. Genetic factors are represented by universal perceptual categories (Jusczyk, 1992) and by cross-linguistic constraints on early production ("early movement synergies"). In addition, the model includes attentional and orienting subsystems which interact to mediate ambient language effects through a "stable self-organizing neural recognition code" (Kent, 1992, p. 83, based on Carpenter and Grossberg, 1987). The attention system "processes familiar events to maintain stable representations for these events and to effect learned expectations (top-down processing). The orienting system detects unfamiliar events so as to reset the attentional system" (p. 84). Sensorimotor trajectories for production are developed through exercise of the available speech motor functions and through neural representation of emergent patterns of motor control.

Another self-organizing model, compatible with that of Kent, focuses on the next logical step in phonological development (Lindblom, 1992). Lindblom draws on structural linguistic principles as well as considerations of perception and production in order to explain the ontogenetic origins of (segment-based) phonological systems (cf. also Lindblom, MacNeilage, and Studdert-Kennedy, 1984). Lindblom's work on acquisition is part of a long-range research strategy based on the assumption that

> languages tend to evolve sound patterns . . . as adaptions to biological constraints on speech production . . . Speech perception and speech development . . . introduce their own boundary conditions on linguistic form. The constraints of speaking, listening, and learning thus interact in complex ways to delimit humanly possible sound patterns. (1983, p. 217)

Lindblom (1992) begins with the observation that the complexities of linguistic systems cannot be understood as the product of either a genetic program or environmental processes alone; rather, it is the interaction of the two which allows for novelty and complexity, generating "qualitatively new phenomena, *emergents*, whose complexity is not explicitly preformed, but arises as an automatic consequence of the interaction, that is, by *self-organization*, and goes beyond that found either in the initial conditions or in the input" (p. 133). Lindblom's functional model views phonetic forms as adaptations to universal constraints on perception and production ("performance factors") as well as to language-specific and child-specific factors; phonological units are the "spontaneously assembled emergent consequences of lexical development" (p. 135).

Given that the child begins with a small number of word-forms or "articulatory scores" (or "motor" or "gestural" scores), it is assumed that these scores are made up of anatomically distinct components, corresponding to the separable loci of motor control (e.g., lips, tongue tip, tongue body, jaw, etc.).[11] It is assumed further that these separable activity patterns for different control units are stored in distinct neuronal spaces ("somatotopically"); once stored, such an activity pattern need not be stored again but merely marked for appropriate lexical access, that is, for synchronization with the other elements of a given motor score. The "segments" of linguistic analysis are an automatic byproduct – or "emergent" – of the economy of this neurophysiological storage system. As the number of different "known" (producible, mastered, stored or "represented") vocal motor schemes or canonical word forms increases, self-segmentation will result, an automatic consequence of vocabulary growth and the repeated use of a small number of motor control units (cf. also Studdert-Kennedy, 1987).

Lindblom describes this process as "a spontaneous and unsupervised mechanism for supplementing the input speech" (p. 159), in which perceptual invariance is notoriously unavailable for listener or learner (cf., for example, Klatt, 1979; Blumstein and Stevens, 1981). As he points out, a methodological advantage of self-organization as a theoretical construct is that we need not attribute foreknowledge of goals to the child:

> Clearly children do not develop phonemes "in order to" solve the problem of acquiring a large lexicon at a rapid rate. In the parlance of ecological psychologists (Bellugi and Studdert-Kennedy, 1980), the mechanism of emergence makes it unnecessary to "take loans on" cognition – a risk facing proponents of cognitive models. (p. 159)

Current formal models

In discussions of phonological development today two approaches dominate discussion of formal modeling: Nonlinear models, which derive from the generative models of the sixties but are substantially different in kind, and connectionist models, which were developed by psychologists and cognitive scientists who did not have *phonological* acquisition specifically in mind. Neither of these types of model has as yet been extensively tested on child data; the potential benefits thus remain unclear. It is striking, however, that these two quite different developments should share one important formal characteristic: the emphasis on representations and constraints at the expense of rules and processes.

Nonlinear phonology

In the decades since the publication of Chomsky and Halle's *The Sound Pattern of English* (1968) linguistic theory has seen a proliferation of proposed alternative phonological models and theoretical approaches; by 1977 at least nine alternatives were in contention (Dinnsen, 1979). Paradoxically, Chomsky and Halle's relative success in meeting their goal of reducing phonological phenomena to a purely formal calculus through expression in rules and representations has been seen to constitute one of the main problems with the theory (Anderson, 1985). In particular, as Chomsky and Halle themselves recognized in their last chapter, the lack of a connection between formal expression and phonetic content leads to a virtually unconstrained – and thus non-explanatory – model. However, one of the chief advantages of a formal theory is that its defects can be readily detected as it is extended to new material:

> Our growing awareness of the range of problems that cannot be reduced to notational decisions has only been achieved by attempting to carry out the logicist program comprehensively. This has had the effect of refining our understanding of the significance of the results that can be obtained by a study of phonological formalisms, just as the latter contribute to a proper appreciation of the phonological role of phonetic content. (Anderson, 1985, p. 335)

Applications of the generative model to prosodic phenomena – tone and stress – led to the development of the "autosegmental" (Goldsmith, 1976) and "metrical" models (Liberman and Prince, 1977, who radically reformulated the unwieldy apparatus designed by Chomsky and Halle, which had nevertheless served the purpose of bringing to light the wide range of phenomena encompassed by English stress alternations). Such nonlinear models are able to more directly express the phonetic bases of rules of assimilation and to encompass word- and syllable-based phonological effects such as harmony, or assimilation at a distance, as well as incorporating such previously extra-theoretical phenomena as the internal structure of syllables.[12]

An important difference between nonlinear models and the generative model from which they derive is the shift of emphasis from rules to representations; in the new models, representations are regarded less as a sequence of segmental "beads on a string" than as analogous to an orchestral score in which the synchronization of each instrument with the other instruments is as much a part of the score as the actual notes each is to play. In phonological terms, the "instruments" are the various separable components of the speech apparatus ... (Anderson, 1985, p. 348; the relevance of these comments to Browman and Goldstein's model as well should be clear.)

A promising recent outgrowth of this perspective is optimality theory, in which rules are dispensed with entirely (Paradis, 1988; Prince and Smolensky, in press; McCarthy and Prince, in press).

Nonlinear models offer important advantages in accounting for developmental data. Menn (1978) was the first to attempt to describe some of the facts of child phonology using such a model. She identifies two properties of autosegmental formalism which are particularly apt for the description of children's phonological systems: (1) the possibility of specifying domains of application for phonetic features which extend beyond the segment, such as the syllable or the word; (2) the freedom from sequential ordering of features which results from placing them on

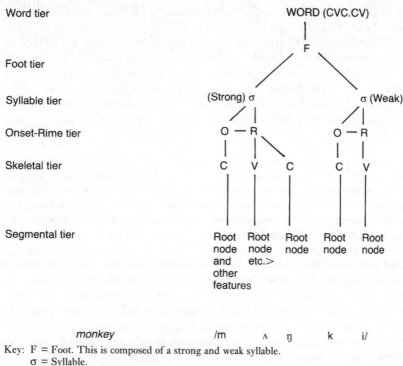

Key: F = Foot. This is composed of a strong and weak syllable.
σ = Syllable.
O = Onset. This includes all prevocalic consonants (C) in a syllable.
R = Rhyme/Rime. This includes the vowel (V) and postvocalic consonants in a syllable.

Figure 2.5 Nonlinear representation of the word *monkey*.

Source: Bernhardt and Stoel-Gammon (1994), reprinted by permission of the American Speech-Language-Hearing Association

separate tiers, or levels of organization (see figure 2.5). The separate specification of features which affect only consonants (glottalization, retroflexion) or only vowels (vowel harmony, advanced/retracted tongue root) in adult language provides a natural formal treatment for consonant harmony, notoriously prominent in child phonology while correspondingly rare in adult languages. The reordering of adult segments, or apparent metathesis, is also often reflected in child forms. The notion of specifying different features on different tiers provides a useful account for the reordering of heterogenous segments; Menn (1978) proposed to enrich the theory to permit the lexically unspecified ordering of segments on the same tier as well (e.g. two stops, as in a child form such as [dæge] for *alligator*).

In another early reflection on developmental consequences of the new theoretical orientation Goldsmith (1979) suggested that the first stage in phonological acquisition may involve "autosegmental" representation of certain features – that is, placement of the feature on a separate tier (e.g., a tier for nasals or velars only), which would lead to "rampant harmony processes in early speech" (p. 215). In a vein reminiscent of Stampe's account of innate processes in need of suppression in the course of phonological learning, Goldsmith goes on to predict that the course of language acquisition will involve "de-autosegmentalization," or the incorporation at the segment level of features initially specified at a higher level, except in the case where particular aspects of the language – for example, tonal melodies in some African languages, nasalization in Guarani or Desano, vowel harmony in Hungarian, Turkish, Nez Perce, and so on – provide reasons to maintain the feature at a higher level in prosodic structure. An extensive developmental account of the acquisition of an adult phonology characterized by one of the classic autosegmental properties – e.g., a tonal language, such as Sesotho, or a vowel harmony language, such as Finnish – would provide an interesting test of Goldsmith's (1979) notion of "de-autosegmentalization." In particular, would longitudinal observation of a number of children provide evidence for the early word-level presence of one of the tones or vowel qualities which play a role in the adult system?

Later applications of nonlinear models to child data have made bolder departures from the Chomsky and Halle model, supported by ongoing advances in nonlinear theory (Fee, in press; Fikkert, 1994). For example, Velleman (1992) suggested that whole levels of representation may be lacking in the initial stages of phonological representation, notably skeletal (CV) or segmental levels (see figure 2.6 and compare figure 6.2 below; cf. also Menn and Matthei, 1992). Similarly, the child's representation may lack branching, either at the word level (if only monosyllabic words are produced: see fig. 2.6, 14 and 15 months) or at the syllable level (no clusters, diphthongs, or syllable-final consonants are produced: contrast the first and second syllables of *monkey* in fig. 2.5).

The notion of "planar segregation," introduced into adult phonological theory to account for Semitic languages with morphological templates requiring only consonants (McCarthy, 1989), now permits an especially elegant formal account of both harmony and metathesis (cf. McDonough and Myers, 1991; Macken, 1992). Underspecification of features and the inclusion in lexical representation of "default" features also play a role in these models, though the interpretation of particular data as motivating one or another of these accounts remains controversial

14 months

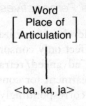

Word
$\begin{bmatrix} \text{Place of} \\ \text{Articulation} \end{bmatrix}$

|
<ba, ka, ja>

15 months

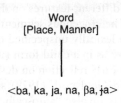

Word
[Place, Manner]

|
<ba, ka, ja, na, βa, ɟa>

16 months (a)

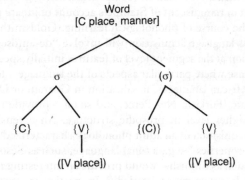

Word
[C place, manner]

σ   (σ)

{C}   {V}   {(C)}   {V}

([V place])   ([V place])

16 months (b)

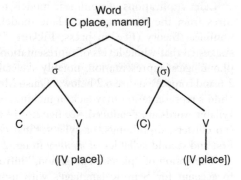

Word
[C place, manner]

σ   (σ)

C   V   (C)   V

([V place])   ([V place])

Key
( )   Optional elements
{ }   Emerging elements
σ   Syllable

Figure 2.6 Development of a lexical representation.
Source: Vihman et al., 1994. In Yavas (ed.), *First and Second Language Phonology*.
Reprinted with the permission of Singular Publishing Group.

(Spencer, 1986; Iverson and Wheeler, 1987; Stemberger and Stoel-Gammon, 1991; Goad, 1991). In short, planar segregation, underspecification of features and default features are all ways of expressing a relative lack of complexity in the child's initial representations.

Nonlinear models are, in principle, equally compatible with nativist and functionalist developmental approaches to the acquisition of phonology. Following Chomsky's (1981b) parameter-setting model of language acquisition, Bernhardt (1994) has proposed a nativist interpretation:

> If a child comes to the language-learning situation with a representational framework and a set of universal principles, "templates" are then available to utilize for decoding and encoding . . . Exposure to the input language(s) will both confirm the universally-determined representation (e.g., that, as expected, the language has CV units and stop consonants) and also result in "setting" of parameters where options are available (e.g., that the language has final consonants and that stress is syllable-initial in a given language) . . . (p. 161; see also the excellent tutorial in nonlinear phonology and its application to phonological disorders: Bernhardt and Stoel-Gammon, 1994)

In this book, we will adopt an alternative functionalist interpretation of the establishment of the "expectation" of CV syllables and stop consonants, which follows quite naturally from the character of vocal development in the first year (see ch. 5). However,

> whether these options are available to all children, specified by innate parameters, determined by some characteristics of the language to which the child is exposed, "chosen" by the child based on idiosyncratic perceptual, physiological, or cognitive biases, or some combination of the above is an open and widely debated question. In any case, the course of phonological development includes the addition of complexity to any or all of these aspects of the representation. (Vihman et al., 1994, p. 20).

Connectionist models

With the publication in 1986 of the two-volume work, *Parallel Distributed Processing* (or *PDP*), by Rumelhart and McClelland a radical new computer-based model of cognitive processing became available, one which has appeared to many to offer an intuitively attractive alternative to the linear computer model underlying "classical" cognitive science.

The role of both (input) frequency and (output) variability, minimized in the structuralist and universalist models which dominated theorizing through the early 1970s, has been revived in applications of the connectionist model to language acquisition. In this model, a network of units interconnect a set of input and output nodes. The connections are "weighted" to express the degree of relatedness or potential influence (positive or negative) between each pair of units; in addition, each unit filters the input it receives through its "threshold" or "activation level," which may increase or decrease as a function of its recent activity. Units may be arranged in multiple layers; within each layer, units compete to participate in a pattern of activity. Multiple influences may be expressed in parallel, as in the case of effects on word recognition ("top-down" lexical effects, from the syntactic or semantic context, and "bottom-up" phonetic effects from the auditory signal: McClelland and Elman, 1986).

In connectionist learning models, the distribution or frequency of different patterns in the input plays a central role in modulating the weighting and also the threshold level for activation of network connections to output forms (e.g., Rumelhart and McClelland, 1986). The regularities and symbolic relations usually expressed by ("explicit but inaccessible") rules are replaced in these models by the associative pairing of input and output patterns. "Associations are simply stored in the network, but because we have a superpositional memory, similar patterns blend into one another and reinforce each other. If there were no similar patterns . . . there would be no generalization . . . It is statistical relationships among the base forms themselves that determine the pattern of responding" (p. 267). In addition to highlighting frequency factors such learning models tolerate the coexistence in the output of competing forms in response to a single input type, thereby exhibiting stages in a process of gradual change with "transitional" or variable behavior not normally allowed for in rule-based accounts.

Connectionist models have been severely criticized as a "new associationism," reviving approaches discredited over thirty years ago (Pinker and Mehler, 1988). In a lengthy, closely argued comparison of "classical" and connectionist cognitive models, Fodor and Pylyshyn (1988) refer the essential difference to the nature of mental representations (expressed as nodes interpreted as units or aggregates of units in the networks of a connectionist model). In the classical account, mental representation is a *symbol system*, in which symbols have combinatorial (and hierarchical) syntactic and semantic structure and the processes operating on these symbolic expressions are sensitive to that structure. Connectionist models, on the other hand, can be seen as "analog machines for computing [statistical] inferences" (p. 68), while learning is "basically a sort of statistical modeling" (p. 31). In the contrasting classical cognitive view, learning involves "theory construction, effected by framing hypotheses and evaluating them against evidence" (p. 69).

Explicit attempts to model the child's acquisition of phonology within a connectionist framework have just begun to be made (Menn et al., 1993; Stemberger, 1992). Menn and Matthei (1992) provide a lucid account of difficulties posed by children's phonological data for the "two-lexicon" model developed primarily by Menn herself some 15 years ago. These include competing child output forms (Menn, 1971, 1979; cf. also Ferguson and Farwell, 1975); ill-defined variant forms (Priestly, 1977); frequency effects, as illustrated by both regressive and progressive phonological idioms; "fuzzy boundaries" or "cross-talk" interactions between words (Waterson, 1971; Menn, 1976a; Vihman, 1981); and the operation of word-level phonological constraints *between* words (Donahue, 1986; Stemberger, 1988; Matthei, 1989). Connectionist models offer several potential advantages in dealing with such unruly aspects of developmental data, since in such models

we expect fuzzy boundaries, we expect forms to interact with each other, we expect frequency effects – and, crucially, we also expect both input and output forms to be stored in some linked way. We also have instance-based learning . . . If we have storage of both input and output forms, we at least have the potential for modeling all of the good things that the two-lexicon model buys us, and we may be able to get rid of the aspects of the model that were getting oppressive. (Menn and Matthei, 1992, p. 228)

Stemberger's (1992) connectionist model agrees with Olmsted's earlier behaviorist model in highlighting frequency as one of two factors contributing to "accessibility" (or the relative strength of a unit). Stemberger supplements frequency with the time-honored factor, ease of articulation (cf. Schultze's "principle of least effort" (1880)); Olmsted's second factor, ease of perception, is dismissed out of hand ("I assume that the child's representations are identical to that of adults" (Stemberger, 1992, p. 172)). Errors are traced to erroneous weighting of connections, failure to inhibit non-target units, and other errors in the setting of processing parameters. The model is capable of "explaining" – or restating with connectionist terminology – a wide range of error types, including "chain-shifts," fusions, and a variety of interference effects. The discussion of frequency is weakened by Stemberger's failure to distinguish between external input (from the child's caretakers) and internal input (feedback from the child's own vocalizations). Furthermore, a critical feature of the model is the implicit internal comparison of child productions and adult target forms; the mechanism for locating errors is not discussed, however. Nor is the model developmental: There is little discussion of changes in error types as the child's lexicon increases. The long-debated question of phonological units is decided by fiat ("I will assume features; segments; syllable units . . . ; and a coarse phonological representation . . . that codes only the number of segments involved" (p. 171)).

Stemberger does not speculate as to the possible system-external sources of error. Biological explanations do not appear to be intended, since connection weights are said to be "initially random" (p. 173). Babbling, which is said to allow "tuning" of the system, is also characterized as "random." However, in accord with reported findings of continuity between babbling and first words, Stemberger posits an adjustment of perceptuomotor control functions for "a small number of learned mappings between perception and production, which can then be used to realize [adult] words" (pp. 173f.). This tuning results in a few strong output states which tend to be overused, substituting for less common target patterns.

It is important to note that the effort to model child errors in phonological production without imputing phonological processes or rules differs in principle from the attempt to model the child's progress in acquiring past tense forms in connectionist terms, since the "rules" for past tense formation are understood to be part of adult competence, while phonological processes merely express the systematicity in a child's substitutions or error patterns.[13] The child's phonological "rules" are destined to be eliminated as the adult system is acquired (these are the "invented rules" of figure 2.3). Pinker and Prince (1988) point out that the connectionist model for past-tense learning tends to overapply the "subregularities" which characterize small sets of verbs (*slept* not **sleeped*), successfully exhibiting instance-based learning but failing to appropriately model the critical shift in which children move from correct use of irregular past tense forms to the generalizations underlying the rule-generated regular system. They argue that a "one box" model, in which memorized forms and generalizations are handled by a single mechanism, is incapable in principle of modeling acquisition of more abstract linguistic structure, such as distinctions between morphology and phonology, the role of roots in morphology, preservation of stem and affix identity, and so on (p. 126; cf. also Macken, 1987). A comparable phonological model would be concerned with later-learned rules deriving the abstract underlying representations of adult phonology (box A in figure 2.3); no such connectionist model has yet been proposed, to my knowledge. Stemberger's program is thus not vulnerable to the kinds of objections raised in response to the past tense acquisition model. On the other hand, it also lacks the impressive specificity of that model: It has not so far been simulated on a computer; its actual learning capacity remains to be demonstrated.

Summary: Themes and issues

We have critically reviewed a range of theoretical models, extending from an early period when the idea of child phonology as a distinct area of interest was scarcely imagined, to the present time, when an annual meeting is devoted to the topic (the Midwestern Child Phonology meetings, held on different university campuses in the United States since 1979) and two international conferences have been convened (Bethesda, Maryland, in 1978 – resulting in the two-volume publication edited by Yeni-komshian, Kavanagh and Ferguson, *Child Phonology*, 1980 – and Stanford, California in 1989, resulting in a single substantial volume, edited by Ferguson, Menn, and Stoel-Gammon, *Phonological Development: Models, Research, Implications*, 1992). We have tracked shifting approaches and perspectives over this period; we will now summarize some of the dominant themes and issues which emerge from this review before going on to consider the empirical findings to date.

We noted that early theoretical models were arrived at deductively, based on theoretical constructs within the fields of origin, typically linguistics or psychology. These models were generally narrow in scope and focused on a few specific issues, which allowed the theorist to use child data to illustrate some broader principles of interest within the larger discipline. Today, developmental phonological models are truly cross-disciplinary: They draw on psychological theories to arrive at an understanding of the nature of learning and development, including models of attention and memory and action or systems theories as well as models of cognitive processing in general, and they draw on linguistic theories to understand the nature and complexity of the language structures to be learned, including the appropriate units for both perception and production.

The theoretical approaches at first were based largely on individual case studies, although large-scale studies of phonetic and lexical development have been available from the early part of this century (McCarthy, 1930, 1954; Wellman et al., 1931; Poole, 1934; Irwin, 1957; Templin, 1957; Winitz and Irwin, 1958; K. Snow, 1963). Only in the 1970s did intensive studies of small samples of children begin to accumulate, many of them longitudinal and some of them cross-linguistic. As Macken and Ferguson pointed out, "These data document the existence of significant, wide-spread individual differences between children acquiring the same language and show that the acquisition process, in certain key aspects, is not a linear progression of unfolding abilities – as assumed by the universalist model" (1981, p. 114). Thus, the central concern of many studies today – to reconcile universalist accounts with the pervasive evidence of variability – grew out of the confrontation of theory with data, once a serious research effort had begun.

Finally, the chronological focus of observational studies has shifted downward since the early seventies, from the "2-year-old stage" (Moskowitz, 1970; N. V. Smith, 1973) to the 1-year-old and the transition into speech. In part, this shift no doubt reflects currents in the larger fields of language acquisition and communicative development, where attention also shifted to the transition period (Lock, 1978; Bates et al., 1979; Bullowa, 1979; Golinkoff, 1983). In addition, however, the motivating factor for the change in research may have been the theoretical formulations themselves: A good many issues were raised, in comparing behaviorist and structural approaches, for example (as in Ferguson and Garnica, 1975), which only the study of younger children could begin to resolve (as in Ferguson and Farwell, 1975). Let us turn now to some of those issues, and others which arose later in the course of two decades of intensive research activity.

In this brief review we will touch on five topics mentioned earlier in connection with one or more theoretical models: (1) continuity vs. discontinuity in the relation between babbling and early words; (2) the relation of perception to production; (3) relational (adult-model-based) vs. independent system accounts of the child's phonology; (4) the relative weight of factors invoked as influences on early simplified word forms; (5) universals of phonology and the nature of development.

1   Continuity vs. discontinuity: This issue was central to the difference between behaviorist and structuralist models. Schematically, behaviorists assumed that babbling provided the basis for selective reinforcement, which, together with imitation of the adult, could lead the child to the sounds of speech. Structuralists denied any connection between preverbal "wild sounds" and the regular patterning of the later emerging phonological systems. Generative models have not, on the whole, been concerned with the preverbal period; interest has centered instead on modeling the regularities of later child phonology, using a variety of popular formalisms; Stemberger's connectionist model follows in that tradition. Cognitive models, on the other hand, have reflected the shift in research attention from two- to one-year-olds and from early words to precursors in babbling (e.g., Macken and Ferguson, 1983; Ferguson and Macken, 1983); Menn and Matthei (1992) look forward to connectionist modeling of the transition.

2   The relation of perception to production: Many of the models we have discussed have preferentially focused on one of these two sides of the coin of language use. Olmsted, for example, was primarily interested in testing the role of perceptual discriminability on the accuracy and timing of phone production in his large-scale study of phonological development; Waterson places the emphasis on the role of perceptual salience in guiding the child's early steps into phonological structure in all of her studies. Jakobson, on the other hand, and with him Moskowitz, is concerned only with the unfolding of the phonological oppositions as

observed in production; similarly, Stampe, Smith, and later Stemberger dismiss perception as irrelevant, given their assumption that the child has overcome any perceptual difficulties or constraints before embarking on phonological acquisition. Cognitive models have given due attention to perception, but have drawn their data primarily from production, which is amenable to simple observational study. Biological accounts, on the other hand, have tended to be sensitive to the problems posed by perceptual as well as motor aspects of production. What is lacking, despite the ever increasing sophistication of perception studies, is an adequate paradigm for the investigation of perception in individual subjects, which would allow us to look for relationships between individual differences in perceptual response and differences in early production patterns.

3 Relational vs. independent system accounts: Here again, earlier models tended to be doctrinaire, while current modeling assumes the need for multiple perspectives. N. V. Smith (1973) specifically addresses this issue and comes to the conclusion that the child's "own system" has no psychological validity. Waterson operates with the opposite assumption, exploring the child's forms in a richly detailed way as an object of interest in their own right; the adult forms are taken to provide differentially salient structures which are the source of the child's system, but do not make up an essential element in that system. Menn's two-lexicon models, on the other hand, mediate between these positions, allowing for creativity in the construction and interrelationship of canonical forms but relating these back to the adult models.

4 The relative weight of different factors: Both ease of discrimination (Olmsted) and ease of articulation (Stampe) have sometimes been invoked as primary factors in shaping early phonology; this relates to the role of perception and production discussed under (3). More linguistically oriented models have usually invoked "systemic pressures" as well, arguing that emergent structures will develop a "life of their own" and can accordingly be expected to exert structural pressure analogous to the effects of sound systems or inflectional paradigms, for example, on language change (Martinet, 1955; Malkiel, 1968; Weinreich, Labov, and Herzog, 1968). Attention to systemic factors shaping emergent phonologies can be identified particularly in the work of Smith, Waterson, Macken, and Vihman. Finally, information processing considerations have been central to Menn's approach from the beginning; her eclectic pursuit of the best model for child phonology reflects advances in related fields of cognitive science.

5 Universals of phonology and the nature of development: Beginning with Jakobson, and continuing with Ferguson and his colleagues as well as recent attention to child phonology by Lindblom, linguists have been intrigued and puzzled by the problem of universals and near-universals of language and their relationship to individual differences and variation in production (Macken, 1980b, 1986; Ferguson, 1986). The nativist tradition, which currently holds that innate (universal) language structures are adjusted to the particulars of the ambient language through the appropriate "parameter setting," triggered by exposure to the input language, has so far yielded few studies specifically devoted to phonological acquisition (Lleó (1991) is one such study). It may be that such studies are not encouraged by nativist framing of the issue: Dore (1983) quotes George Miller

as comparing "the failure of behaviorist explanations to the mystery in nativist ones," concluding that we are caught between "the impossible and the miraculous" (p. 167). Dore advocates a functionalist approach rooted in mother–child interactions: "The origin of words occurs in the immediate context of affective conflict, arising as solutions to maintain and negotiate relationship through dialogue" (p. 168). Such a functionalist and dyadic perspective has begun to inform efforts to conceptualize phonological development as one strand in a net of developing (perhaps self-organizing) abilities, which also includes symbolic or cognitive and communicative advances (Bloom, 1983; Vihman et al., 1985; C. E. Snow, 1988; McCune, 1992; Vihman et al., 1994).

NOTES

1   See also the shorter French version of the "sound laws of child language and their place in general phonology," presented orally in 1939 but first published as an appendix to the French translation of Trubetzkoy, *Principes de phonologie* (1949) and included in English translation in Jakobson (1971). References to Jakobson (1949) below reflect my own translation.

2   Leopold (1953) illustrates this point when he speaks of the orderly "oppositions" of vowels, stops and nasals which he finds in his daughter's canonical babbling, "a sort of experimental prepatterning . . . [found also in] the early structural syllable pattern, consonant-vowel, both of which were carried over without break or relearning into imitative speaking with meaning" (p. 5).

3   Moskowitz later returned to a position closer to that of Jakobson, however: "The syllables and segments that appear when the period of word learning begins are in no way related to the vast repertory of babbling sounds. Only the intonation contours are carried over from the babbling stage into the later period" (1978, p. 106A).

4   Stampe's 1969 paper and 1973 dissertation are reprinted, together with additional notes, in Stampe, 1979; that is the version to which I shall refer here.

5   Stampe's comments on the issue of babbling and its relation to speech are worth noting here: "Since the structure of post-babbling utterances can be accounted for by the innate phonological system, one might further speculate that they are underlain by phonological representations, in some sense, perhaps as crude imitations of adult speech, prior to the recognition of its distinctions and semanticity" (1979, p. xxi). This remark could be taken to foreshadow later studies suggesting global (unsegmented) representations of the adult language as the source of phonetic influence from the specific adult language on babbling and the earliest words: Boysson-Bardies et al., 1989; Boysson-Bardies and Vihman, 1991.

6   For illustration and references to prosodic analyses of a range of different languages and phenomena, see Palmer (1970) and Robins (1989), in addition to the first chapters of Waterson (1987), a partially revised collection of earlier papers.

7   Elements of this position are already implicit in Ferguson, Peizer, and Weeks (1973), but they are not identified as such.

8   I will from here on disregard the "learned rules" (fig. 2.3) or "abstraction processes" which yield adult-like underlying representations relating morphological variants of words only some years later; as noted in chapter 1, few studies have addressed this more abstract aspect of phonological acquisition, which occurs relatively late in English.

9   Chapters 6 and 9, below, provide illustration of these concepts.

10 See also McCune (1992), who discusses the interconnected contributions of representational, or cognitive level, communicative understanding, and articulatory prepared-
ness in the emergence of flexible word use within a dynamic systems framework.

11 The notion of an articulatory or gestural score has been elaborated by Browman and
Goldstein in the framework of their model, "articulatory phonology" (1989, 1991,
1992), which may be considered an exponent of the nonlinear phonological models to be
discussed next. At least one application of this model to child data is available
(Studdert-Kennedy and Goodell, 1992).

12 Kim (1982) sets forth a lucid brief account of the development and interconnected
justification for several nonlinear models; van der Hulst and Smith (1982) offer a more
extended discussion of these models and of areas of continuing controversy. Kaye
(1989) provides an introductory exposition of the workings of such models, while
Goldsmith (1990) constitutes a far more complete but also more advanced text (see
Rice, 1992, for a useful review). Levelt's (1989) chapter 8, on "phonetic plans for words
and connected speech," also offers a useful exposition of the main points of the model,
set within a psycholinguistic framework for speech production.

13 Adult speech errors are sporadic and have never been viewed as remnants of the child's
phonological processes (though the types of substitutions are often similar, as
Stemberger points out).

3 Initial Perceptual Capacities

In a now famous phrase, William James (1890) characterized the world of sensory impressions into which the infant is born as one of "blooming, buzzing confusion."[1] Such a characterization reflects the empiricist outlook long prevalent in American psychology. The empiricists saw infant perception as beginning with immediate, unstructured sensory experience: "The starting point of perceptual development was generally believed to be modality specific, two dimensional, and meaningless sensations . . ." (Von Hofsten, 1983, p. 241). Two theoretical frameworks have largely replaced empiricist views about the nature of speech perception (primarily rooted in auditory capacities or hearing) as well as about the perception of objects (rooted in visual and haptic capacities, or sight and touch: Spelke, 1988).

According to modularity theory, perception is based on a hierarchy of computations performed by modality-specific, largely autonomous mechanisms or "modules" (Marr, 1982; Fodor, 1983). For speech perception, the theory postulates a specialized mechanism (the "speech module") designed to identify and decode the acoustic signals which represent speech (e.g., Liberman and Mattingly, 1985; Mattingly and Liberman, 1988). As a corollary of the relative insulation of speech from other aspects of perceptual and cognitive processing, units specific to language are posited as innately available to the newborn, such as phonetic feature detectors (Eimas, 1982).

Ecological theory (J. J. Gibson, 1966, 1979; E. J. Gibson, 1969, 1984), on the other hand, postulates "direct perception" of rich environmental stimuli afforded by a functionally relevant context in relation to action by the perceiving organism (see also Fowler, 1986, Fowler and Rosenblum, 1991, who apply these views to speech). In this view, the infant is biologically preadapted to the "ecological niche" into which it is born; in particular, it should have the means to extract from the social as well as the physical world around it the information it needs to begin to arrive at a functional conceptual model of that world.

In a review of perceptual development which includes a brief account of speech perception alongside a more detailed consideration of visual perception, Aslin and Smith (1988) distinguish three structural levels in the perceptual processing of adults: (1) sensory primitives (e.g., for vision: color hue or saturation; line orientation; for audition: intensity, frequency), (2) perceptual representations ("based on the bundling of one or more sensory primitives," p. 441, e.g., color, object shape; consonantal segment or syllabic onset, pitch contour), and (3) higher order representations (e.g., faces; word shapes). One striking difference between auditory and visual perception which emerges from their review concerns the status of sensory primitives in the two modalities in infancy.

Most of the basic auditory capacities needed to discriminate speech sounds have been found to be present from the earliest ages tested (typically, 1 to 2 months) – whereas visual capacities are known to be limited in a number of ways in early infancy. The evidence suggesting this rather startling infant sophistication was at first taken to support nativist views of speech perception (Eimas et al., 1971), but subsequent research and theorizing have resulted in other interpretations. Indeed, in accordance with the ecological view of perception as the product of action by the organism, recent studies of newborn auditory "preferences" in relation to specific fetal experiences (e.g., DeCasper and Fifer, 1980) suggest an explanation of the difference in status of auditory as compared with visual perceptual capacities at birth: Auditory activities occur in the womb in the last trimester of pregnancy, when middle ear structures are normally complete (although the liquid medium of the fetus will limit available sound frequencies: Querleu and Renard, 1981; Querleu et al., 1988; Lecanuet, 1993); visual activities, in contrast, cannot begin to structure perception until *after* birth.

Let us follow Aslin and Smith, then, in considering that in infancy the sensory primitives, or "elements of sensation," combine into "bundles" to make up perceptual representations – representations which, in the case of the auditory modality, are capable early on of discriminating relatively well between simple speech patterns. In ecological terms, the "proximal stimuli" of direct auditory perception are acoustic signals detectable by the ear; for the infant, the "distal stimuli" or natural objects of perception are not, as for the adult, meanings or messages expressed in word forms and phrases but auditory signals whose parsing into units and interpretation into meanings will require considerable additional processing.[2]

We will begin by reviewing briefly some of the classic issues in the study of speech perception by adults; it was the effort to advance our understanding of those issues which led to the study of infant discrimination of speech contrasts. We will then take up the early findings which suggested remarkable perceptual capacities in very young infants, followed by efforts to interpret these findings in relation to competing models of perceptual processing in adults. Finally we will consider more recent efforts to extend our understanding of infant responses to speech.

Problems posed by speech perception

Three basic characteristics of speech complicate the decoding task of a listener despite the appearance of effortlessness in ordinary adult conversation.

1   Speech flows. Although pauses occur at the ends of some sentences, clauses or phrases, stretches of spontaneous speech of five to ten words are often produced without interruption (Goldman Eisler, 1968). Where brief moments of silence *can* be identified in spectrographic recordings of speech, they may correspond to the production of stop consonants rather than to word boundaries (Martin, 1970). This lack of any reliable overt marking of boundaries is one aspect of the segmentation problem: How does the listener segment the flow of speech in order to recognize words and retrieve the speaker's meaning?

2   Speech sounds vary. Every aspect of speech production is subject to multiple sources of variation. Across different speakers the size of the vocal tract has an important effect on the acoustic output, for example. There is no direct proportional relation between the vocal tracts of men, women, and children (Fant, 1973). The formant frequencies which define the vowel space therefore differ from speaker to speaker in complex ways (Peterson and Barney, 1952). Furthermore, even for a single speaker, rate of speech and loudness of delivery each exert significant effects on the signal (Lindblom, 1991). This presents a problem of perceptual constancy: How are two vocal productions (tokens of a single utterance type) recognized as "the same?"

3   Articulatory gestures interact. As a result of the dynamic nature of speech production, the same identifiable phonetic segments will be expressed by different acoustic patterns even within a single utterance, depending on their position in the word (initial, medial, final) or syllable and on the phonetic context. Coarticulation (or coproduction) refers to the overlapping of articulatory movements associated with two or more phonetic segments; it is in part a function of the relative independence of the various articulators: the lips, tongue, velum, etc. If the two or three segments preceding a rounded vowel such as /u/ do not involve lip movement, for example, the lips may begin to round well in advance of production of the /u/, yielding sub-phonemic (non-significant) variation in the preceding segments. Similarly, in a language like English with no contrast between oral and nasal vowels, the velum may be lowered well in advance of the moment when oral closure marks the onset of a nasal stop such as /n/, creating a non-contrastively nasalized stretch of speech preceding the nasal consonant proper.[3]

From the point of view of production, coarticulation can be seen as facilitating the smooth flow of speech, thus increasing the speed of transmission (Liberman et al., 1967); from the point of view of perception, it ensures the redundant coding of phonemes, which may boost intelligibility, but it also has been taken to complicate the decoding process for the listener, creating the problem of lack of invariance in the signal (Perkell and Klatt, 1986): No single acoustic cue suffices to identify a phonetic unit in all contexts. Furthermore, there is no direct relationship between the order of acoustic events and the listener's perception of a sequence of individual segments making up a string of phonemes (the "linearity" problem: Chomsky and Miller, 1963).

These "problems" were originally identified in the course of attempts to design machines capable of automatic speech recognition; they do not normally impede communication among adults. Several factors account for the ease of speech perception for the mature listener who is also a native speaker of the language. Above all, "top-down processing," or knowledge of the discourse context and the semantic and syntactic constraints on an utterance, once some portion of it has been decoded, may render detailed decoding of the actual phonetic sequence unnecessary (Frauenfelder and Tyler, 1987); this would explain why we frequently fail to detect speech errors, slips of the tongue, spoonerisms, and so forth (Boomer and Laver, 1968). Another factor is the redundancy in the phonetic signal itself, to which we have already alluded. The overlapping of gestures for different segments means that portions of a word can be "heard" ("restored" or guessed at) even when competing noise or listener inattention leads to "loss" of some portion of the signal (Warren, 1970; Samuel, 1981a and b; Ohala, 1986).

If the signal itself is not sufficient to allow decoding of the message in all cases, and in particular if prior familiarity with the words, grammar, and probable meanings of an utterance are prerequisite to a listener's interpretation, then how does the child succeed in entering the speech code? How does the child begin to parse the speech stream into words before acquiring a lexicon? How does the child adjust to differences in speaker or tempo in order to begin to recognize words across a variety of different discourse events? In other words, how does the child overcome the ever present "noise" of variable production to "hear through" to the intended phonemes and recognize repeated tokens of the same word, if knowledge of the phonemic system of the ambient language has yet to be acquired? And how can a child identify individual segments within words if there is no one-to-one relationship between intended segments and identifiable slices of the acoustic signal? The past two decades of intensive research on infant speech perception have begun to provide at least partially satisfactory answers to these questions; a review of research on infant vocal production (ch. 5, below) and the transition to speech (ch. 6) will be needed to address others.

Categorical perception

The initial impetus to investigate infant discriminatory capacities did not derive from developmental concerns at all but arose out of attempts to understand and model adult speech perception.[4] In the 1950s and 1960s experimental tests of adult discrimination of contrasting syllables using synthetic speech, based on spectrographic representation of the acoustic signal, led to an appreciation of the extremely complex relationship between phonetic perception and the underlying acoustic events. Among other things, such tests revealed the striking phenomenon of categorical perception.

In order to test the efficacy of an acoustic cue for perception, a continuum of syllables can be synthesized in such a way that the acoustic dimension of interest is altered in small equal steps. The first acoustic dimension to be tested in this way was the cue to place of articulation differences between the stop phonemes /b, d, g/. Identification of the place categories was found to depend on the relationship between the frequency of the stop release burst and that of the second formant in the following vowel (Cooper et al., 1952). In a later study, Liberman et al. (1957) discovered that listeners shifted abruptly in their labeling of the utterance-initial consonant (e.g., from /b/ to /d/ or /d/ to /g/), despite the fact that the stimuli with which they were presented (representing the onset frequency of the second formant transition into a fixed following vowel) were evenly graded along a continuum. Most strikingly, listeners showed very poor discrimination of sounds *within* each category, but discriminated easily *between* categories.

Categorical perception was also found to characterize adult discrimination of voiced and voiceless stops (e.g., /b : p/, which depends on voice onset time (VOT), or differences in the timing of release of the stop closure and the onset of voicing for the following vowel (Lisker and Abramson, 1964). Since we will have numerous occasions to refer to this important articulatory phenomenon in relation to phonological development, let us stop to give it some consideration, both from a cross-linguistic and a psychophysical perspective.

Languages which maintain a two-way "voiced : voiceless" contrast do so in one of two ways. Some, like English (or Cantonese), contrast (in word-initial position) (1) "voiceless" stops (/p/, /t/, /k/), characterized articulatorily by a delay or "long lag" (in voicing) before the onset of the vowel – creating the perceptual effect traditionally referred to as "aspiration" of the consonant – and (2) "voiced" stops (/b/, /d/, /g/), whose release is timed to coincide very closely with the onset of voicing; such "short lag" consonants are more accurately characterized as "voiceless unaspirated," since voicing does not actually occur during the consonant closure (see figure 3.1). Other languages with a two-way contrast, like Dutch, Hungarian or Tamil (or French), allow voicing to begin before the release of the voiced member of a pair of stop phonemes (/b/, /d/, /g/: these stops thus show "voicing lead"; they are "pre-voiced"), but do not "aspirate" the voiceless members (/p/, /t/, /k/), which are thus phonetically voiceless unaspirated, or physically closely similar to English /b/, /d/, /g/. Finally, some languages, like Thai, include stops of all three kinds: (1) pre-voiced, (2) voiceless unaspirated, and (3) voiceless aspirated (see figure 3.2).

As regards the auditory signal itself, the shifts in relative timing of the stop release and the onset of laryngeal pulsing, or voice, are reflected in striking psychoacoustic differences: "voicing lead" is characterized by a low-amplitude, low-frequency buzz during the "silent" interval represented by stop closure; "short lag," in contrast, involves "the sudden full unfolding of the formant pattern for the syllable," while "long lag" is accompanied by the noise excitation of "aspiration," followed by the "sudden shift to a train of voicing pulses" (Abramson, 1977).

For the perception of consonants, then, absolute identification of specific phonemes proved to be generally almost as accurate as discrimination of differences. This finding is quite remarkable, as becomes clear by comparison with the perception of pitch in music, for example, or the perception of color: We normally experience considerable difficulty in identifying the absolute pitch of two neighboring tones or in specifying two shades of color, though we are easily capable of determining that they are not the same ("discrimination"; Liberman et al., 1961; Berlin and Kay, 1969).

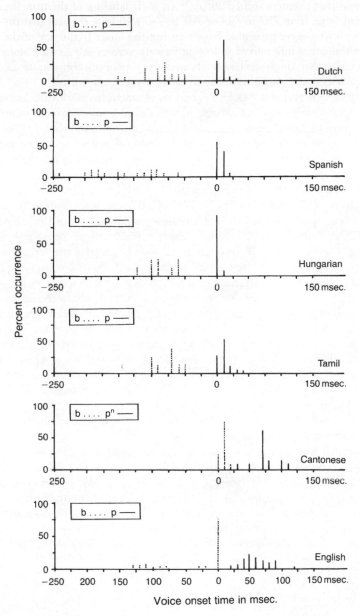

Figure 3.1 Voice onset time distributions: Labial stops of two-category languages.
Source: Lisker and Abramson, 1964

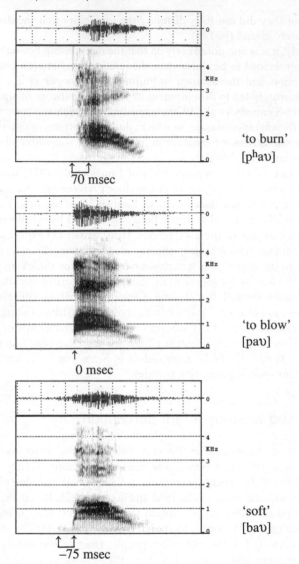

'to burn'
[pʰaʊ]

70 msec

'to blow'
[paʊ]

0 msec

'soft'
[baʊ]

−75 msec

Figure 3.2 Three conditions of voice onset time: Wide-band spectrograms and amplitude waveforms showing (from bottom to top) voicing lead, short voicing lag and long voicing lag. (Examples from Thai, with thanks to Thom Huebner, who provided a selection of minimal triplets, to Manit Janesathit, who spoke the words for us, and to Rory DePaolis, who created the spectrograms.)

Liberman et al. (1961) initially argued that categorical perception most likely reflected the effects of long-term learning or experience in producing and perceiving the categories of the native language ("acquired distinctiveness"), especially in light of the probable differences between languages in the location of phonemic boundaries, but they did not fully dismiss "the possibility that the discrimination peaks are innately given" (p. 178).

Alternatively, it was also noted early on that the relationship between perception and articulation seemed to be closer than the relationship between either articulation or perception and the acoustic stimulus itself (Cooper et al., 1952). This observation ultimately led to development of the "motor theory of speech perception" (Studdert-Kennedy et al., 1970), according to which the speech signal is a (particularly efficient) special code, in which, due to the effects of coarticulation, "a single acoustic cue carries information in parallel about successive phonemic segments" (Liberman et al., 1967).

The pioneering infant perception study of Eimas et al. (1971) was directed at this issue: If infants gave evidence of responding preferentially to the categorical voice onset time contrasts characteristic of English (/ba/ vs. /pa/) as compared with the acoustically comparable distinctions represented by synthesized syllables selected from *within* one of these categories, then neither (1) experience with the sounds of language (the learning theory account) nor (2) reference to the articulatory patterns underlying speech sounds (the motor theory account) could reasonably be invoked as the source of the categorical nature of the adult response. Indeed, the results showed that 1- and 4-month-old babies "discriminate" the stimuli – or react to a change – only when the synthetic syllables (which differed by 20 msec in all cases) *cross* the VOT category boundary characteristic of English and not when they are drawn from *within* either the short-lag (/b/) or the long-lag (/p/) category. It was this finding, published in *Science* in 1971, which launched the field of infant speech perception research.

Methods used to study infant perception

The method most often used to test very young infants' perception of speech sound contrasts is the High-Amplitude Sucking technique (HAS; the various methods used in infant speech perception are illustrated and described in considerable detail in both Aslin et al., 1983 and Kuhl, 1987). It was first developed for use in testing infant visual perception (Siqueland and De Lucia, 1969), and was adapted for testing responses to speech by Eimas et al. (1971). It is based on a simple observation: Infants, like older people, react to changes they perceive in their environment and become bored by ("habituate to") repetitions of the same event.

In this technique, the infant controls the presentation of a speech stimulus by sucking on a pacifier attached to a pressure transducer which records the sucking responses. Once the infant's baseline sucking rate has been established, a repeating speech stimulus such as [ba ba ba] is presented. The frequency of repetition of the sound is controlled by the infant's sucking rate; the rate increases as the child learns the contingency between his or her activity and the sound stimulus. Increased sucking is thus taken to reflect the child's attention to or interest in the speech-like sound, which serves as a "reinforcing stimulus." After several minutes, the infant's sucking rate typically levels off and then decreases. The decreased rate is taken to indicate that the infant is no longer interested in the stimulus (has habituated). For an experimental group of infants the stimulus is then changed to a minimally different repeated syllable (e.g. [pa pa pa]) for two to four minutes, while a control group continues to hear the sound stimulus first presented.

The sucking responses of the experimental group during the period *after* the change in stimulus ("post–shift period") are compared with the post–shift responses of the control group, which receives only a single stimulus throughout the experiment. A "difference score" is obtained for each infant by subtracting the mean response rate for the two minutes immediately preceding the shift from the mean response rate for the minutes following the shift. A significant difference between the mean difference score derived from the experimental group and that derived from the control group is taken to mean that the experimental group discriminated the speech sound contrast to which they were exposed. In figure 3.3, from Eimas et al. (1971), there are two experimental groups: The group labeled "20

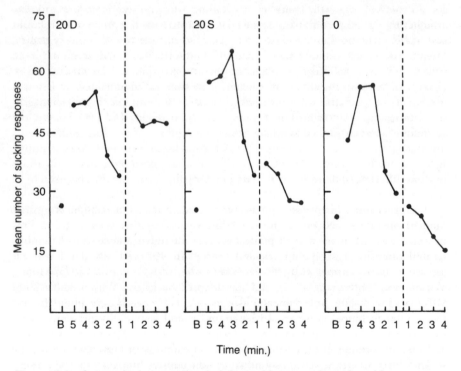

Figure 3.3 Categorical perception in infants. Mean number of sucking responses are shown for the 4-month-old infants, as a function of time and experimental condition. The dashed line indicates the occurrence of the stimulus shift or, in the case of the control group, the time at which the shift would have occurred. The letter B stands for the base-line rate. Time is measured with reference to the moment of stimulus shift and indicates the 5 minutes prior to and the 4 minutes after shift.
Source: Reprinted with permission from Eimas et al., 1971, copyright 1971 American Association for the Advancement of Science

D" (for "different categories") was exposed to the contrasting pair, /ba/ : /pa/, while group "20 S" ("same category") was exposed to within-category changes of the same magnitude. The third group, "O", was the control, which heard no change in stimuli.

Although this technique has been widely used and has led to major advances in our understanding of infant discriminatory capacities, it has several inherent limitations. First, negative results are difficult to interpret, since they may reflect a lack of infant interest in the stimulus (or "lack of motivation") rather than failure to detect a change. Second, only group data may be obtained, since comparison with a control group is the only way to differentiate a stimulus-related change in sucking rate (which can only occur in an experimental group, not in a control) from natural fluctuations in sucking rate, which should be observed to an equivalent extent in both experimental and control groups. Third, the testing lasts up to 15 minutes, demanding a long period of cooperation and attention from young infants. Not surprisingly, a very large percentage of infants fail to complete the procedure, for a variety of reasons (fussing, crying, falling asleep); there is no way to know whether the 25–50 percent of infants who *do* complete the test are in some relevant way different from those who do not. That is, differences in auditory acuity, attentional capacity, and other individual child variables could account for an infant's failure to habituate or to tolerate the test situation, at least in some cases. (Information regarding differential behavior in such an auditory test situation is potentially of predictive value for late speech onset, for example, but no longitudinal data testing relationships of this sort have been reported so far.) Finally, the technique is largely limited to infants under four months of age, since older infants are more active and less content merely to suck and listen. Within those constraints, however, the basic findings to be reviewed below have been replicated many times over, in different laboratories by different investigators, and can thus be taken to be quite reliable.

The other procedure most often used to test infant speech perception is another kind of operant conditioning, namely, the visually reinforced head turn. This procedure, which is most appropriate for older infants, capitalizes on the child's natural orienting response to a sound source. It was originally developed for assessing auditory thresholds (Moore, Thompson, and Thompson, 1975; Moore, Wilson, and Thompson, 1977), and was adapted by Eilers, Wilson, and Moore (1977) to investigate developmental aspects of infant speech perception. In this localization technique a repeated background sound is typically presented for a time, followed by presentation of a minimally different stimulus for a few seconds and then by a repeat of the original background stimulus. A head turn toward the sound source when the second sound is introduced is reinforced with the presentation of a lighted, animated toy which "rewards" the infant for discriminating the new sound from the old. If the infant turns his or her head during change trials (in which a new sound is introduced) but not during control trials (in which the same sound continues to be presented), the infant is taken to be discriminating the two contrasting sounds.

Although the head-turn technique, unlike HAS and other techniques sometimes used to test infant perception, can provide reliable information about individual subjects, it too is limited by age (it works best in the range 6–10 months: Kuhl, 1980). In addition, provision of a sufficient number of trials for statistical assessment of individual results can be a problem. In particular, attrition rates in tests of difficult discriminations, in which the infant's experience of rewards may be relatively infrequent, tend to be even higher than usual (Aslin et al., 1983).

Discrimination: Infant capacities

The simplest answer to the question "Are very young infants capable of discriminating between speech sounds?" is clearly, though somewhat surprisingly, "Yes." The majority of contrasts tested (with 2-month-olds, typically) in the decade following the first published study (Eimas et al., 1971) proved discriminable, and in the case of consonantal distinctions, something resembling categorical perception was often shown as well (see especially the studies by Eimas and his colleagues). So, for example, infant discrimination was shown for voicing distinctions, or VOT ([ta] : [da] in addition to [pa] : [ba]), using both synthetic syllables (Eimas et al., 1971; Eimas, 1975b) and natural speech tokens (Trehub and Rabinovitch, 1972). Contrasts in place of articulation of stop consonants were discriminated in both syllable-initial (Eimas, 1974; Miller and Morse, 1976) and syllable-final position (Jusczyk, 1977). Discrimination of manner of articulation contrasts was shown for stops vs. nasals (Eimas and Miller, 1980), stops vs. glides (Hillenbrand, Minifie, and Edwards, 1979), and [ra] vs. [la] (Eimas, 1975a). In addition, vowels were discriminated in tests using natural speech tokens of [a] vs. [i] and [a] vs. [u], as well as whole syllables containing these vowels ([pa] : [pi], [ta] : [ti]: Trehub, 1973). As is the case with adults, infant vowel discrimination appears to be continuous rather than categorical. That is, discrimination of vowel tokens within a phoneme category generally proved no more difficult than discrimination across category boundaries (Swoboda, Morse, and Leavitt, 1976).

Contrasts between fricatives are among the few which have been reported to resist discrimination in the early months and thus to require learning by the child (e.g., using naturally produced syllables, [sa] vs. [za], [fa] vs. [θa], [fi] vs. [θi]: Eilers and Minifie, 1975; Eilers, 1977). However, when computer-synthesized tokens are used, 2- to 3-month-olds appear to be able to discriminate [fa] vs. [θa] (Jusczyk, Murray and Bayly, 1979). A later study showed discrimination by 2-month-olds of both voiced and voiceless labiodental vs. interdental pairs of naturally produced fricatives (Levitt et al., 1988).

Another instance of infant failure to discriminate was reported by Trehub (1976b). She embedded a stop voicing contrast in a multisyllabic context, using relatively short syllables (less than 300 milliseconds: [ataba] vs. [atapa]).[5] Her subjects also failed to discriminate two-syllable sequences in which only the ordering of the syllables was changed ([mapa] vs. [pama]), but did discriminate the voicing contrast in a minimal two-syllable sequence ([apa] : [aba]). In other studies medial consonantal place contrasts were successfully discriminated in simple disyllabic sequences in both stops (Jusczyk and Thompson, 1978) and glides (Jusczyk, Copan, and Thompson, 1978). The nature of the difficulty posed by a "long word" context was further explored in a later study. Goodsitt et al. (1984) found that it was significantly more difficult for (6-month-old) infants to detect a new syllable embedded in a trisyllabic pattern when the "background" phonetic pattern itself was varied (e.g., [kotiba] : [kotidu], target syllables [ba] vs. [du]), as compared with a repeating background ([kokoba]), though the infants did "succeed" (perform above chance) in making the discrimination in both cases. Placement of the target syllable (initial, medial or final position) did not affect the infants' performance; on the other hand, the syllable [ba] proved unexpectedly easier to detect than the syllable [du].[6]

Notice that, even in the case where natural speech sounds were used as stimuli, the goal of most of these studies was not to simulate natural listening conditions but to isolate for testing, as far as possible, the individual acoustic cues known to signal contrasts between speech sounds – such as the direction and extent of second and third formant transitions or, alternatively, the nature of the release burst (Miller, Morse, and Dorman, 1977), both of which signal contrast of place in stops; the duration of the first formant, which distinguishes [ba] from [wa]; or nasal resonance ([ba] vs. [ma]). In general infants appear to be sensitive to most such basic cues, at least when tested with isolated syllables, with minimal attentional distraction and no irrelevant phonetic variation. However, as MacKain (1982) has pointed out, "evidence of infants' sensitivity to spectral changes in speech stimuli during a discrimination task in the laboratory says little about whether or not the infant is affected by the same parameters in the natural speech situation" (p. 534). Similarly, Jusczyk (1992) comments that, in a HAS procedure, "repeated exposure to [a given] sound may enable the infant to build up a much more detailed representation . . . than would be possible in most natural settings . . . " (p. 26).

The effect of variability in the speech signal

Just as the successful visual recognition of objects depends on maintaining "perceptual constancy" despite the different transformations (in rotation and distance from the observer) which result from movement in space of either object or perceiver (E. J. Gibson, 1969), so the recognition of the phonetic categories of speech must depend on the listener's capacity to ignore irrelevant within-category variation due to context or change in speaker. In order to learn more about what infants might actually be able to extract from the speech around them, investigators have attempted to test perceptual constancy in infants by gradually introducing complications into the test situation – such as variability in the phonetic context and in the voices used as stimuli.

Perceptual constancy

Using the HAS procedure, Kuhl and Miller (1975b) tested 1- to 4-month-old infants on tokens of the vowels [a] and [i], each produced both on a monotone and with a rise-fall in pitch as a distractor. The infants were able to discriminate the vowels, despite the differences in pitch. When the situation was reversed, however, such that the two pitch contours were the target changes to be identified, with random shifting between [a] and [i] as a distractor, the infants failed to discriminate the pitch contrast. Thus, young infants showed perceptual constancy only with respect to the vowel-color dimension (i.e., [a] vs. [i]), which apparently was more salient to them than the pitch contour dimension (monotone vs. rise-fall). Kuhl (1980, 1983; Kuhl and Hillenbrand, 1979; Kuhl and Miller, 1982) further pursued the question of the effect on infant perception of variability in vowel production, using the head-turn technique to test slightly older infants (5.5–6.5 months) on vowel contrasts produced by adult male, female, and child talkers. The results showed that, regardless of changes in speaker, infants discriminate even the acoustically very similar vowels /a/ and /ɔ/, which sometimes actually overlap (Peterson and Barney, 1952), although this task was more difficult.[7] Furthermore, in a new test of vowels pitted against pitch contour, the older infants could be trained to disregard vowel changes when pitch change was the target stimulus; the relative similarity of the vowels used (/a/ : /i/ vs. /a/ : /ɔ/) did not affect the results (see Kuhl, 1987).

Perceptual constancy for consonantal contrasts has also been tested with the head-turn method (Kuhl, 1980). The fricatives /s/ vs. /ʃ/ and /f/ vs. /θ/ were tested with the vowels /i/, /u/, and /a/ as distractors. Here again it was possible to train infants to attend to the target consonantal contrast in spite of changes in vowel and talker. Discrimination of the relatively low intensity fricatives /f/ and /θ/, often confused by adults under noisy conditions (Miller and Nicely, 1955), proved the most difficult.

As Kuhl (1987) points out, the evidence that infants can be trained to generalize responses to speech sounds produced by speakers with vocal tracts as different as those of adult males, adult females, and children is particularly important in view of the critical role that imitation, or matching own vocal production to input speech, must play in the process of learning to talk, since matching would be impossible unless children could perceive the underlying similarity in sound patterns produced by quite different vocal tracts.

Prosodic effects

One of the earliest studies of infant perception focused on stress (present or absent on the last word) and pitch contour (rising, as for a question, or falling, as for a statement) in a short sentence, *See the cat* (Kaplan, 1969; a measure of change in heart rate was the response indicator). The 4- and 8-month-old subjects showed a change in heart rate only when the pitch change was accompanied by stress on the last word. In later studies, Morse (1972) showed that 6- to 8-week-old infants could discriminate changes in pitch contour; Spring and Dale (1977) showed that 4- to 17-week-old infants could discriminate syllables differing only in duration – one of the cues to stress used by adults. In addition, as noted above, Kuhl and Miller (1975b) showed that infants responded to a pitch change only when vowel variation was not added as a distractor.

Against this background of earlier research, Karzon (1985) designed a systematic series of experiments to ascertain the influence of prosodic enhancement on infant capacity to detect a change in onset consonant in the syllables [ra] vs. [la] (clearly discriminated in isolation) when they are embedded in a trisyllabic pattern ([marana] vs. [malana]). One- to 4-month-old infants were tested with synthesized stimuli, using a female voice. The syllables were *not* discriminated when presented without perceptible stress differences (as judged by adult listeners), nor when presented with a rise in pitch contour centered on the target syllable, similar to the "bell-shaped" pitch contour typical of mother's talk to children (Fernald and Simon, 1984). However, when this exaggerated pitch contour was further enhanced with an increase in both intensity and duration on the target syllable (the remaining components of naturally occurring stress, together with pitch change), the infants did respond to the change in syllables. Displacement of the "stress" to the initial (non-target) syllable of the word resulted in loss of discriminability for the target syllable. Finally, a test of adult-like stress on the target syllable, without the exaggeration of pitch, intensity, and duration typical of infant-directed speech, also resulted in loss of discriminability.

This is an especially informative study, defining ever more precisely the factors needed to make a difficult or subtle change in phonetic pattern stand out for the infant. Additional study of intensity and duration alone in a similar test situation would be needed to establish as fully as possible the limiting factors on perception of speech for infants under ideal conditions – that is, when they give it their full attention. We will consider in the next chapter the kinds of situation in which such attention might actually occur in the every-day experience of a developing child.

Mechanisms underlying infant perception

A major research goal of infant studies has been to explore the mechanism underlying apparent categorical perception: Does evidence of such perception indeed ratify the interpretation of phonetic categories as innately specified in the human brain, and of attention to speech as mediated by a specialized set of language processors or phonetic feature detectors?

Discrimination of speech vs. non-speech signals

Recall that the first investigation of infant speech perception using the HAS method revealed the categorical effect found in adults: between-category differences (/ba/ vs. /pa/) were discriminated, while within-category differences (syllables which are *acoustically* distinct but phonemically the same, labeled "/ba/$_1$" vs. "/ba/$_2$") were not (Eimas et al., 1971). This result was confirmed in several later studies, for a range of different consonantal contrasts (Eimas, 1974; 1975a, 1975b; Eimas and Miller, 1980). The initial investigation of infant speech perception was intended to shed light on the theoretical issue raised by studies on adults: Are the phonetic categories which affect responses to speech sound contrasts the result of long-term "overlearning" of the contrasts underlying the phonological system of the native language (at least for consonants)? Or, given apparent differences in adult responses to contrasting speech vs. nonspeech signals, are there specific mechanisms to support speech perception, such as specially designed phonetic feature detectors (Eimas and Corbit, 1973), perhaps located in a self-contained speech module? The finding of categorical perception in infants seemed to validate the latter line of interpretation. This led investigators skeptical of those conclusions to return to experiments designed to test both adult and infant responses to speech-like discriminations in non-speech signals.

At least two experiments successfully demonstrated a categorical effect in the perception of nonspeech signals. Miller et al. (1976) mimicked the acoustic characteristics of VOT by varying the onset of a noise relative to a succeeding buzz; Pisoni (1977) varied the relative onset time of two pure tones (creating a "TOT" continuum). Whereas earlier tests of nonspeech perception (using very simple acoustic stimuli) had failed to evoke a categorical response, these later studies employed relatively complex stimuli (which were thus more comparable to speech), varying only one component relative to a stable background; in both cases areas of enhanced discriminability were found, corresponding to the category boundaries of experiments on speech perception.

The finding of a categorical effect in these studies allowed investigators to conclude that there must be a more general psychophysical basis for the categorical perception of speech (recall fig. 3.2 and the comments of Abramson, 1977, on the psychophysical discontinuities corresponding to the articulatory VOT contrasts). According to one interpretation, there are acoustic "quantal regions" in which the human perceptual mechanism is particularly sensitive to change, separated by regions in which sensitivity is relatively low. The former regions would correspond to the discrimination peaks marking phoneme boundaries for consonants (Stevens, 1972, 1989; for critiques of this view, see Studdert-Kennedy, 1980, 1989). Such a psychophysical analysis is not incompatible with the view that "speech is special." As Kuhl points out, "mechanisms may have evolved especially for the perception of speech, but not be designed so as to exclude nonspeech signals mimicking the critical features in speech . . . It is possible that [such] nonspeech stimuli . . . work because they "fool" the relevant feature-detecting mechanisms" (1987, p. 327). That is, the mechanisms underlying speech perception may indeed be "tuned" for speech, but not so narrowly as to exclude nonspeech signals. On the other hand, it may be that the general auditory processing mechanisms which respond differentially to certain acoustic regions were in place even prior to the evolution of speech, and themselves contributed to the shaping of the phonological categories of human language (Kuhl, 1986b).

What of infant responses to nonspeech signals? There are no conclusive experimental results on this issue so far. A study of 2-month-olds' discrimination of tone onset time, designed to test Pisoni's (1977) conclusion that the human auditory system is structured to respond in a certain way to temporally ordered events, whether speech or nonspeech, produced categorical discrimination, but with the regions of highest discriminability shifted toward larger stimulus values than are observed in adults (Jusczyk et al., 1980). It may be that a longer interval is needed to permit infants to perceive a separation between two tones when temporal information alone is provided (20-msec VOT differences are discriminated in the presence of additional cues to voicing, but not alone: Eilers et al., 1981).

Speech perception by humans vs. other animals

At the same time that some experimenters were beginning to explore the speech-specificity of categorical perception by devising analogues in nonspeech sounds,[8] others addressed the same issue by presenting speech sound contrasts to non-human mammals whose auditory mechanisms are close to that of humans. Kuhl and Miller (1975a) were able to show "categorical perception" in chinchillas. The animals were trained by an avoidance conditioning procedure to respond differentially to extreme values of VOT for computer-synthesized versions of /da/ : /ta/ and then tested on intermediate stimuli. They typically switched responses (showing evidence that they had "generalized" from the syllables on which they were trained, grouping the intermediate stimuli together with one or the other end of the continuum) at a change-over point closely corresponding to the phonetic (and psychoacoustic) short vs. long lag boundary used by English-speaking listeners. In a later study, Kuhl and Miller (1978) replicated and extended this experiment, testing labial, alveolar and velar pairs contrasting in VOT. For the chinchillas, as for humans, the boundary VOT values shifted with place of articulation, the cross-over point between voiced and voiceless being lowest for bilabial stimuli and highest for velars (see figures 7.1 to 7.3). It was thus possible to conclude from these studies that auditorily salient boundaries, based on the structure of the mammalian hearing system rather than on either learned or innate knowledge of specific speech values, could be held responsible for the categorical perception of VOT.

Kuhl and Padden (1982, 1983) used a different operant training method to test macaque monkeys on VOT and place contrasts in stop consonants; in both cases responses typical of categorical perception were obtained, revealing that the same regions of these acoustic continua afford enhanced discriminability for the macaques as for humans and chinchillas, regions coinciding with the boundaries between human phonetic categories. Kuhl (1987) concluded that, in the evolutionary origin of language, "the choice of the particular phonetic units used in communication was strongly influenced by the extent to which the units were ideally suited to the auditory system" (p. 336). Furthermore, the results with non-human animals constitute a strong challenge to claims regarding specialized human perceptual processing of speech.

More recently, Kluender, Diehl, and Killeen (1987) demonstrated that even a non-mammal species, the Japanese quail, can be trained to form the phonetic category [d], generalizing the varying acoustic cues to alveolar as opposed to labial and velar voiced stops across a range of different vowel contexts. Since these categories may be seen as "examples of polymorphous concepts . . . not definable in terms of any single stimulus dimension" (p. 1196), Kluender et al. argue that their study provides strong evidence that "phonetic" categorization is possible even in the absence of "a knowledge of articulatory commonalities," as is postulated in the motor theory account, or any other "uniquely human perceptual processes," such as the use of phonetic property detectors.

Categorization, units, and prototypes

The flow of studies documenting infant capacities for the discrimination of a wide variety of speech sounds, sometimes in the face of potentially distracting variation in the signal, has provided us with a knowledge base with which to begin to respond to the questions raised earlier. We have seen that infants are sensitive to many of the basic acoustic cues which signal phonetic contrasts, especially as regards those which make up the core of the world's phonological systems (Lindblom, 1992). We have also seen that the boundaries for phonetic categories tend to correspond to regions of enhanced auditory discriminability for the structure of the mammalian hearing system (although, for adult listeners, the psychoacoustic advantage of these naturally occurring regions is, in turn, most likely modified by experience with language-specific phonetic categories: Repp, 1984). The human infant, like the chinchilla or macaque, is responsive to those natural boundaries and shows categorical discrimination when tested on stimuli which cross them. What remains unclear, however, is the extent to which infants in the first year of life are actually able (like the quail trained by Kluender et al.) to form phonetic categories, or to group certain stimuli together despite differences between them in values irrelevant to the grouping. Research designed to shed light on issues of categorization and representation has proven difficult and results remain tentative and, to some extent, inconclusive; nevertheless, these issues constitute a critical element in our effort to understand development from initial capacities to language comprehension and use.

Categorization, or equivalence classification

Experimental results showing apparent categorical perception tell us that infants are able to discriminate between (consonantal) phonetic categories while remaining relatively insensitive to contrasting sounds within categories. Since this may reflect psychoacoustic factors, or strictly auditory rather than phonetic processing, the studies do not tell us whether infants can treat *discriminable* variation within a category as irrelevant. That is, we would like to know whether they are able to hear differences between speech sounds and disregard them. Kuhl was one of the first to attempt to investigate such "equivalence classification" by infants, as described above in conjunction with perceptual constancy. Kuhl maintains that "the use of an active response to code the perceived similarity between percepts [in the face of change along two dimensions, such as vowel quality and pitch or talker] provides strong evidence of the ability to categorize" (1987, p. 340).

Using Kuhl's head-turn transfer of training paradigm, Katz and Jusczyk (1980) conducted an experiment focused on the phonetic categories [b] and [d] across four different vowel contexts. Testing included two groups of infants, one presented with stimuli so organized as to lead to generalization of the target phonetic contrast, the other presented with a randomized ordering of the same stimuli. This made it possible to test for the role of memorization in test responses, as opposed to generalization of a linguistically relevant category. As expected, only infants in the "phonetic group," for whom reward, or reinforcement, was contingent on generalization according to initial consonant, performed above chance. However, even infants receiving the phonetically organized training proved unable to reach criterion on testing involving more than two vowel contexts. A similar test of younger infants on the same stimuli using the less demanding HAS procedure also failed to produce evidence of categorization based on perception of similarity across four consonants in different vowel contexts (Jusczyk and Derrah, 1987).

Hillenbrand (1983, 1984) included "phonetic" and "random" groups of subjects in transfer-of-training categorization experiments focusing on generalization of the phonemic contrast /m/ vs. /n/ (in open syllables with three different vowels) and of the feature contrast stop vs. nasal (in open syllables with the vowel /a/ and three different places of articulation for the consonants). In both cases, infants in the random group responded correctly only to the first stimulus which produced a reward, while infants in the phonetic group showed a relatively high level of correct responses. As Aslin et al. (1983) point out, however, the linguistic category "nasal" is represented acoustically by the rather salient feature of nasal resonance, which could in itself guide infant responses. Thus, a strong interpretation of relative success in such tasks in terms of a learned generalization involving a relatively abstract linguistic category, such as a phonetic segment or feature, may be unjustified. Some more limited kind of experience of relative similarity between stimuli may be involved.

Segments and features, or syllables?

Categorization studies such as those reviewed above raise the question of the unit of infant representation of speech. Early studies often assumed that phonetic segments or features were being discriminated; this was the initial interpretation favored by those who saw the infant as innately equipped for language learning through specialized mechanisms for the processing of speech (e.g., Eimas et al., 1971; Eimas and Corbit, 1973). More recently, the syllable has come to be regarded as a more plausible basic unit for the infant (Eimas, 1985; Jusczyk, 1985, 1986b). Persuasive evidence favoring one over the other has proven elusive, however.

Miller and Eimas (1979) made a rare attempt to focus directly on the nature of infants' organization or structuring of perceived CV syllables. In a first experiment, infants aged 2 to 4 months were tested on syllable pairs involving either a single consonant or vowel contrast (e.g., [ba-bæ] vs. [da-dæ]) or a "recombined" contrast ([ba]-[dæ] vs. [bæ]-[da]). In a second experiment, the features of voicing and place (in stops) and manner and place (stops and nasals) were recombined (e.g., [ba]-[ta] vs. [da]-[pa]; [ba]-[na] vs. [da]-[ma], on the grounds that "only if infants are sensitive to the relation between feature values will they discriminate these pairs" (p. 361). The results essentially showed successful discrimination in all experimental conditions. However, as Miller and Eimas acknowledged at the outset, these experiments demonstrate only that infants are able to discriminate complex stimuli, that is, to recognize that the test pair of syllables (post-shift) is somehow different from the pair used for habituation (pre-shift). It is not possible to distinguish here between holistic perception, based on unanalyzed syllables, and analytic perception, based on recognition of the individual segments and features which make up the syllable organization, though Miller and Eimas preferred the latter interpretation.

Experiments showing perceptual constancy for consonants in varying vocalic contexts (e.g., syllable-initial and syllable-final /s/ vs. /ʃ/ or nasals /m/ vs. /n/) also appear to provide evidence of infant representation of phonetic units below the level of the syllable. However, alternative interpretations are possible here as well (see Aslin et al., 1983; Kuhl, 1985, 1987). In general auditory terms, the results may be characterized as reflecting attention to the beginning portion of the stimulus, or to the end point. It is not clear how evidence for such specifically *linguistic* units as phonetic segments or features might be distinguished from this broader interpretation, although Kuhl (1985) suggested that

> the claim that the parts listed in the representation consist of phonetic units or phonetic features would require that the code contain much more specific information . . . [such as] a notational system that specifies that CV syllables have exactly two segments, not one or three, and that CVC syllables contain three segments. Moreover, a phonetic-unit representation should allow a unit's recognition regardless of its position in an utterance. (p. 257)

There are a number of reasons to favor the syllable as a basic unit of perception (Studdert-Kennedy, 1975, 1977, 1980; Klatt, 1979). Aside from the fact that most tests of discrimination have relied on syllable-sized phonetic patterns, the syllable affords a relatively stable perceptual object: It is less liable to contextual variation than are consonant and vowel segments. Identification of consonants often requires reference to information available only from a larger context (e.g., in addition to the place of articulation and VOT information for consonants which derives in part from the following vowel, syllable duration information is needed to calibrate relative transition duration in discriminating [b] from [w]: Eimas and Miller, 1980; Miller and Eimas, 1983). Coarticulation primarily operates within syllables in production; processing of syllables can thus be expected to provide the most effective access to the parallel information encoded for successive segments as well as for individual segments (Eimas, 1985).

On the other hand, attempts to provide positive evidence specifically supporting the syllable as a basic perceptual unit for the infant have been disappointingly inconclusive. For example, Bertoncini and Mehler (1981) used a sucking paradigm to compare infant responses to contrasting CVC syllables ([pat] vs. [tap]) as opposed to CCC sequences which do not constitute "canonical" (typically well-formed) syllables (in English or French, at least: [pst] vs. [tsp]). The same CCC sequences were also inserted in a vocalic frame (VCCCV: [upstu] vs. [utspu]). All three contrasts were discriminated, although response to the CVC sequence appeared to be somewhat superior to the other two sequences. The noisy sibilant [s] might have masked information about the neighboring consonants, thereby making discrimination of both of the contrasting sequences including CCC more difficult

(Aslin et al., 1983). Definitive conclusions regarding the syllable as a unit of perception for the infant cannot be drawn from this study.

In a later attempt to identify perceptual units for infants, Bertoncini et al. (1988) carried out categorization experiments with 2-month-olds and newborns. The first experiment was a replication of Jusczyk and Derrah (1987), with the addition of the younger group of infants. The habituation stimuli consisted of a set of different syllables which shared an initial consonant ([bi], [ba], [bo], [bə]), randomly presented. For post-shift testing a syllable token was added into the set of stimuli which differed in either vowel ([bu]) or consonant ([da]), or both ([du]). Results for the two groups of infants differed: The 2-month-olds responded with increased sucking rates to all post-shift stimulus sets (as did those in the earlier study), showing no evidence of having formed a [b]-category based on the habituation stimuli. The newborns, on the other hand, responded to sets including a token with a new vowel ([bu], [du]), but failed to respond to sets in which the novel token differed from the habituation stimuli in consonant only ([da]). Bertoncini et al. concluded that, for newborns, only vowels, which tend to be longer and louder than the accompanying stop consonant, are sufficiently salient to elicit a response.[9]

In a second experiment the investigators first presented habituation stimuli differing in manner or place of initial consonant but sharing a vowel ([bi], [si], [li], [mi]). The test stimuli involved a change in consonant, vowel, or both (with either a similar or a distant vowel: [dɪ] vs. [da]). Here again 2-month-olds discriminated all new sets of stimuli, giving no evidence of sub-syllabic structuring, while newborns again responded only to those sets which included tokens involving a change in vowel. A final follow-up experiment re-ordered the stimuli so that the novel token was [si], in order to better equate the salience of consonant and vowel portions of the new stimulus. As in the other trials, newborns failed to detect a change in consonant only.

While these results are consistent with the view that early representations of speech-like sound patterns are holistic syllables, undifferentiated with respect to phonetic segments, as Bertoncini et al. suggest, they provide no clear evidence that syllables, rather than smaller or larger units, provide a first basis for perceptual processing.

Prototypes

We noted earlier that vowels, unlike consonants, are typically perceived in a graded rather than a categorical fashion. That is, listeners usually find it as easy to distinguish vowels *within* a phonemic category as to distinguish between different vowels. Kuhl (1986a, 1991) and her colleagues (Grieser and Kuhl, 1989) undertook a series of studies to examine the internal structure and organization of vowel categories. The goal of these studies was to determine whether vowel categories, like basic object categories or color, for example, exhibit internal structure. In other areas, psychological categories have been shown to have a prototype structure, in which some members of the category are judged to be more typical, central, better exemplars; such prototypes are privileged in cognitive processing in many ways:

For example, they are more easily encoded and remembered (Rosch, 1975; Rosch and Mervis, 1975). For vowel categories, some areas of perceptual space may be expected to serve as "category centers," or prototypes, because they show greater perceptual stability (cf. Stevens, 1989, who relates vowel category structure to what he sees as the quantal nature of perception).

Kuhl and her colleagues based their studies on the idea that prototypes, or central exemplars of a category, ought to provide a better reference point for generalization to novel exemplars than poorer, more marginal exemplars ("nonprototypes"). They began by eliciting "category goodness" judgments from adults on synthetic vowels designed to represent a range of points in acoustic space corresponding to a single vowel category (/i/) (Grieser and Kuhl, 1989). In a test of adult perception of differences between these within-category exemplars, they found, as expected, that adults discriminate vowel variants of a single phoneme quite successfully (over 75 percent correct).

In addition to calculating percent-correct scores, however, Kuhl and her colleagues used the number of "miss responses" (failures to discriminate) to derive a "generalization score," reflecting the extent to which listeners implicitly perceived referent and comparison vowel stimuli as similar. Subjects proved significantly more successful at discriminating differences between the nonprototype and other stimuli than between the prototype and other stimuli – or, alternatively, they "generalized" more readily from prototype to comparison vowel than from nonprototype to comparison vowel. The investigators interpreted this finding to mean that "a prototype acts like a perceptual 'magnet'":

> Surrounding members of the category are perceptually assimilated to it to a greater degree than would be expected on the basis of real psychophysical distance. Relative to a nonprototype of the category, the distance between the prototype and surrounding members is effectively decreased; in other words, the perceptual space appears to be "warped," effectively shrunk around the prototype. The prototype of the category thus serves as a powerful anchor for the category, and the prototype's functional role as a perceptual magnet for the category serves to strengthen category cohesiveness. (Kuhl, 1991, p. 99)

In a follow-up study the same stimuli were used in a head-turn procedure to test 6-month-olds on their capacity to generalize from a prototype vs. a nonprototype to comparison stimuli. Although the overall discrimination scores were lower than those of adults, the pattern of generalization was the same. Most striking was the fact that for a subset of four identical stimuli included in tests of both prototype-as-referent and nonprototype-as-referent and ranging between "center" and "periphery" in acoustic space along the same vector, infants discriminated significantly less often between prototype and comparison stimulus than between peripheral exemplar and comparison stimulus, lending support to the idea that the central vowel acts as a kind of magnet, "assimilating" exemplars surrounding it. Thus, the internal structure of the vowel category demonstrated for adults appears to obtain for infants as well.

In contrast, a test of the same stimuli with Rhesus monkeys showed better than chance discrimination of the stimuli overall and a clear psychoacoustic effect of the relative distance between referent and comparison stimuli, but no evidence of a prototype effect (Kuhl, 1991). From this Kuhl drew the conclusion that category structure, unlike categorical perception, is demonstrable only in the human species and thus arguably reflects a phonetic level of representation rather than auditory salience alone.

Summary: The infant listener

We reviewed evidence that the basic sensory capacities needed to discriminate speech sounds are present in infants by 2 months of age, if not at birth – while bearing in mind that speech discrimination under laboratory conditions is not typical of the infant's task in a natural setting. The next structural level of perceptual processing, in the Aslin and Smith (1988) model with which we began, is the "bundling" of sensory primitives into the elements or "perceptual representations" out of which higher order representations will be constructed. In the case of speech perception, the relevant perceptual representations would be phonetic segments or syllable.

We opened our account of infant speech perception by reviewing the theoretical problems encountered by investigators attempting to understand speech perception by adults. Against that background, we asked how the child succeeds in entering the speech code. The issues which initially led to research on infant speech perception have remained at the center of debate ever since: What is the basis for adult speech sound discrimination, or the extraction of phonetic categories (whether features, segments or syllables) from the speech signal – learned patterns ("acquired distinctiveness"), reference to articulatory gestures (the motor theory of speech perception), innate phonetic feature or property detectors (e.g., quantal theory), "natural" psychoacoustic salience in relation to the sensitivities of the mammalian auditory system, or some unknown factor or factors? Our review of the modeling, argumentation and supporting evidence regarding the initial capacities of the child and the mechanisms underlying perception has led to one major conclusion: The partitioning of the speech stream is at first dictated by psychophysical salience as filtered by the human auditory system. At the same time, the continuing flow of findings regarding infants – as well as non-human animals – has opened new vistas on the nature of speech development.

We reviewed studies designed to demonstrate categorization of speech sounds. Infants from the earliest ages tested, like non-human mammals, showed perceptual constancy, or the capacity to disregard incidental variation while focusing on a vowel or consonant category (in studies by Kuhl and her colleagues). On the other hand, where more than two aspects of the "base" or input stimuli varied (a series of different syllables, as in studies by Jusczyk and his colleagues), infants seemed to find categorization more difficult. Attempts to determine whether infants perceive whole syllables or individual phonetic segments as units have so far proven inconclusive. We also considered evidence that human infants, but not Rhesus monkeys, are susceptible to a "magnet effect" in which prototype vowels prove more difficult to discriminate from other similar stimuli than do nonprototype vowels.

NOTES

1   "The baby, assailed by eyes, ears, nose, skin, and entrails at once, feels it all as one great blooming, buzzing confusion" (p. 488).
2   Fowler and Rosenblum (1991) argue that the distal object of speech perception is neither the acoustic signal nor auditory patterns but the "linguistically organized (phonetic) gestures" which are the source of those patterns (p. 36); for alternative views, see the response by MacNeilage (1991) and the chapter by Lindblom (1991) in the same volume.
3   For a vivid illustration (and quantification) of coarticulatory effects in the production of VCV sequences, see Öhman (1966).
4   Kuhl (1987) offers a lucid historical account of the issues and shifting theoretical stands which led to work on infant perception; Jusczyk (1986a) provides a comprehensive review of speech perception research on adults, while Aslin, Pisoni, and Jusczyk (1983) review research on general auditory as well as speech perception in infants, and relate the latter to the literature on acoustic phonetics and the problems it poses for an understanding of speech perception by adults.
5   Cowan, Suomi, and Morse (1982) provide a plausible explanation of these findings: "The useful lifetime of an echoic trace . . . may last longer in . . . infants than in adults . . . The added processing time might be achieved at the cost of a reduced ability of infants to analyze rapid sequences of stimuli that exceed a single echoic trace (e.g., a multisyllabic string)" (p. 990).
6   The authors do not report how many of their twenty-four 6.5-month-old infant subjects were already producing canonical babbling – though the question arises as to whether the added salience of [ba] might not be related to the emerging vocal capacities of these children, who could be expected to be at the threshold of babbling (see ch. 5). The syllable [du] is far less likely to be familiar to an early babbler than [ba].
7   Similar effects have been reported for both dogs and chinchillas exposed to the human speech contrast /a/ vs. /i/, with pitch and talker variation as distractors (Baru, 1975; Burdick and Miller, 1975).
8   For a recent such analogue, see Fowler and Rosenblum (1991), who compare "monosyllables and slamming doors."
9   See also Moon and Fifer (1990), who show that newborns are capable of learning to discriminate a contrasting pair of syllables – [pæt] vs. [pst] or [a] vs. [i] – in order to activate a recording of their mother's voice as opposed to quiet.

4 Developmental Change in Perception

In the last chapter we reviewed findings and theoretical discussion pertaining to infants' discrimination of syllable tokens incorporating phonological distinctions of the language to which they are exposed. Very little evidence of developmental change was reported in these studies. Exceptions include studies of fricative perception by Eilers and her colleagues, mentioned earlier (see also Eilers, 1980). Other investigators have questioned these results on methodological grounds, however, while later studies by Jusczyk and his colleagues showed discrimination of the most difficult pair, [fa] vs. [θ], by 2-month-olds. As a general rule both older and younger infants were found to discriminate whatever isolated syllables experimenters chose to present to them.

In this chapter we will broaden our purview to consider, first, the now extensive literature demonstrating ambient language influence on perception. We will also consider early evidence of cross-modal perception and the role it may play in providing a foundation for speech. We will then review the role of the prosodically enhanced speech patterns associated with "intuitive parenting" (Papoušek and Papoušek, 1987) and early affective bonding in guiding the child into speech recognition and comprehension. We will close our overview of infant speech perception with recent work which appears to be uncovering the origins of word recognition surprisingly early in the first year.

Influence from the ambient language

Among the early studies of infant speech perception were several which investigated responses to sounds which play no contrastive role in the native language. These studies also typically showed successful discrimination. For example, Trehub (1976a) reported that 1- to 4-month-old infants from English-speaking homes discriminated natural speech tokens of [pa] : [pã] (recorded by a French speaker), despite the fact that English lacks a contrast between oral and nasalized vowels (which does occur in a large fraction of the languages of the world, however: Maddieson, 1984). Similarly, Trehub used natural speech tokens of [ža] and [řa] (from Czech: the contrast occurs rarely in the world's languages) to test both infants and adults. Infants discriminated the fricatives, while English-speaking adults found the contrast considerably more difficult than a native pair [ri] vs. [li]. Such findings contributed to the impression of "universal" infant capacities for discrimination of speech sound contrasts.

One aspect of non-native contrasts which escaped attention in these early studies is the incidence of the sounds tested *per se* – at a phonetic, non-contrastive level – in the language of the child's environment, or "ambient language." There is a potentially important difference between the two non-native contrasts tested by Trehub, for example. Specifically, nasal vowels do occur, and with high frequency, in the *phonetics* of English running speech (see p. 52), even though they are contextually determined and thus do not play a contrastive role in the phonology of English. The Czech fricative [ř], on the other hand, is unlikely to be heard at all in an English-speaking home. We will take up the question of "exposure" to a speech sound and its relation to the notion of infant "experience" in the next section. First, we review the literature on non-native contrasts in voicing, which yielded mixed and often controversial results.

Recall that in the study of Eimas et al. (1971) infants displayed categorical discrimination for /ba/ (or short lag [pa]) vs. /pa/ (long lag [pʰa]), representing the VOT boundary characteristic of English; this result was then replicated in other laboratories.[1] In a follow-up study, Eimas (1975b) failed to find clear evidence of categorical perception (by infants exposed to English) of voicing lead [ba] vs. short lag [pa], representing the VOT boundary which plays no phonological role in English. Two studies undertaken with infants exposed to languages which make some use of voicing lead but not the long lag boundary (Spanish: Lasky, Syrdal-Lasky, and Klein, 1975, using Guatemalan infants as subjects, and Kikuyu: Streeter, 1976) reported discrimination of two VOT boundaries, one of which corresponds to the English long lag boundary which plays no phonological role in those languages.

Eilers, Wilson, and Moore (1979) used a head-turn procedure to test 6-month-olds exposed to English on VOT. This procedure also revealed categorical perception for the English VOT boundary. In the first study to use a single procedure to test infants from two linguistic communities on a contrast differentially functional in the two languages, Eilers, Gavin, and Wilson (1979) tested children from Spanish-speaking as well as English-speaking homes on the same VOT continuum. They too reported that the children exposed to English discriminated only the English long lag, not the voicing lead boundary, while infants exposed to Spanish discriminated both. They concluded that exposure to a language in which the voicing lead boundary is phonemic serves to enhance infant sensitivity to this distinction, as suggested by the earlier studies of Spanish and Kikuyu.

Aslin and Pisoni, who criticized aspects of the methodology used by Eilers and her colleagues (1980a; see also the reply by Eilers et al., 1980), conducted their own study of the VOT continuum with infants exposed only to English, using a variant of the headturn procedure (Aslin et al., 1981). They presented stimuli according to an adaptive staircase algorithm designed to identify the smallest discriminable VOT difference. This involved the use of repeated trials, beginning with extreme and thus easily discriminated values. With the focused attention engendered by the procedure, infants from English-speaking homes could discriminate both voicing lead and long lag boundaries, but the latter required smaller VOT differences (i.e., were easier to discriminate). This study, as well as the cross-language studies and studies mentioned earlier showing non-human animal discrimination, lends further support to the contention that the long lag category is particularly salient for purely psychophysical reasons: "The poorer discrimination of both TOT [tone onset time] and VOT differences in the lead (prevoiced) region of these continua is probably due, in part, to the poorer temporal resolving power of the auditory system for a high-frequency component preceded by a low-frequency component" (Aslin et al., 1983, p. 640). Thus, exposure to a language which makes frequent use of contrasts involving the less salient voicing lead boundary may be necessary to boost infant sensitivity to this VOT difference. On the other hand, it is not necessary to invoke innate feature detectors, as investigators had once thought, to account for infant response to the long lag category; analysis in purely sensory or psychophysical terms provides a sufficient explanation.

What is the role of experience?

In the early years of infant speech perception research there was a tendency to couch theoretical discussion of the role of experience in somewhat simplistic terms (Aslin and Pisoni, 1980b), invoking a dichotomy between nativist and empiricist interpretations which fails to do justice to the complexity of genetic–environment interactions (cf. also Oyama, 1989; Thelen, 1989). Research on development of the visual system, for example, has revealed that some neural mechanisms are not yet present at birth but develop over time, partially in response to early visual experience but also within genetically determined limits. Figure 4.1 (from Aslin and Pisoni, 1980b) illustrates a range of possible ways in which postnatal experience might interact with genetically given potential to shape the development of a sensory system such as that required for speech perception.

Four distinct modes of interaction between potential perceptual capacity and environmental influence are schematized in the figure. The perceptual ability to discriminate a particular pair of speech sounds is

1 present at birth, but will be partially or completely lost if no experience of that contrast is afforded by the speech to which the child is exposed;
2 only partially developed at birth and requires specific experience to be facilitated or attuned, in order that full development of the capacity should ensue;
3 absent at birth, but may be induced if specific experiences are afforded within the appropriate time frame;
4 either present or absent at birth, but in either case is not amenable to experiential shaping.

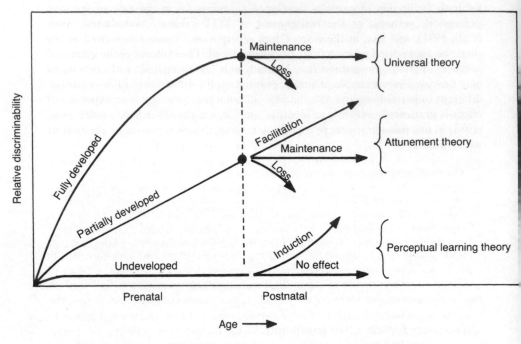

Figure 4.1   Effects of early experience on phonological development.
Source: Aslin and Pisoni, 1980b

Corresponding to these hypothetical modes of interaction, Aslin and Pisoni propose as plausible four types of theory of perceptual development:

1   "Universal theory" would reflect the view that infants are born with the sensory capacity to discriminate all the phonetic contrasts that might be found in any natural language. In the absence of early experience, these capacities are subject to loss – whether neural, attentional, or both.
2   "Attunement theory" assumes that at least some of the discriminative capacities required by the possible phonetic contrasts of natural languages will develop only in case of exposure to appropriate speech sounds, which will serve to "align and/or to sharpen" abilities which are "quite broadly tuned" (p. 79).
3   "Perceptual learning theory" assumes that only exposure to phonological contrasts in the ambient language will lead to discriminatory capacities in the infant.
4   "Maturational theory" assumes that discriminatory abilities unfold according to a genetically determined timetable, irrespective of early experience.

Aslin and Pisoni suggest that "some hybrid of the theories" is most likely to be needed to account for all of the data on the development of speech perception (1980b, p. 80; cf. also Aslin et al., 1983, p. 661). Attunement theory, which provides for both facilitation of partially developed capacities (as in the case of fricative perception, perhaps, or the realignment of VOT category boundaries: Aslin et al., 1981), and loss, in the case of lack of exposure, is sometimes cited as the single best supported position (e.g., Burnham, 1986). The evidence of the increased salience of stop consonants for 2-month-olds as compared with newborns may provide a rare example of simple maturation (of the capacity to discriminate different stops), although as Aslin and Pisoni point out, "absence of an experiential effect is particularly difficult to identify" (p. 78). On the other hand, Aslin et al. (1983) in one passage appear to espouse Universal theory as providing the best fit with the data:

> The most important factor controlling the young infant's responsiveness to speech appears to be a set of innate perceptual mechanisms [based on a sensory or psychophysical, not phonetic, mode of processing] rather than exposure to specific types of early linguistic experience . . . Whatever the nature of infants' early experiences with language, the discrimination results to date suggest that they do not . . . manifest themselves during the first few months of life. (Aslin et al., 1983, p. 642)

Given an interpretation of infant discriminatory capacities as initially based on psychophysical properties of speech sounds rather than on phonetic categories, the essential question regarding the role of experience is not how and when it comes to shape sensory capacities, but how it leads to the formation of phonetic categories incorporating these properties. Before going on to consider more recent studies of infants' changing capacities to discriminate non-native contrasts, then, we must examine the concept of "experience" with speech sound contrasts and its relation to "exposure" to the speech of a particular language community.

In a telling critique of the logic and underlying assumptions of the various studies seeking to determine the "role of experience" in infant discrimination, MacKain (1982) pointed out that it is inaccurate to describe infants from English-speaking homes as lacking "listening experience" with the voicing-lead boundary. At a phonetic (not phonologically contrastive) level, voicing lead is the rule, not the exception, for non-initial voiced stop production in English. Even in initial position (the only one tested in the perceptual studies under consideration), voicing lead is an option taken by some speakers, according to the classic study by Lisker and Abramson (1964; see figure 3.1). "Optional" production of "true voicing" was evident in as much as one-third of English speakers' word-initial productions of phonemic voiced stops in another study (based on twenty speakers: Zlatin, 1974). Thus, infants raised in an English-speaking home should have ample opportunity to *hear* prevoiced stops, even in word-initial position, despite the fact that such stops are not (linguistically speaking) contrastive in English, but instead vary freely with short lag "voiced" stops in initial position and regularly represent the voiced member of the voiced vs. voiceless stop opposition medially, in the context of other voiced sounds.

The critical question is the significance of the contrastive vs. incidental, optional, or co-varying status of a phonetic feature in its potential for resulting in infant "experience." MacKain takes issue with two unspoken assumptions regarding the nature of a child's effective experience of the sound system of a given language: (1) the negative assumption that a phonetic contrast can influence a child's discriminatory capacities – or count as "experience" – only in the case where the contrast is phonologically significant in the ambient language, and (2) the positive assumption that mere "exposure" to the speech stream will lead to "experience" of those contrasts which do have functional significance.

MacKain points out that in order to be specifically affected by phonologically contrastive features but not phonetic variants in attending to speech the infant must be presumed to be deploying such processes as

- segmentation of the speech stream into discrete units,
- recognition of contrasting units (i.e., phonemes) and disregard of redundant covarying changes in the signal (perceptual constancy),
- identification of recurrent instances of the contrast (categorization),
- registration of the relative frequency of those instances.

All of this presupposes, furthermore, a "phonetic" processing of speech long before there is evidence of infant awareness of sound–meaning correspondences, or of the function of speech as communication. Finally, MacKain calls for cross-linguistic investigation of infant vocal production, as an indirect but potentially more reliable indication of the effect of exposure to a particular ambient language (see chs 5 and 6, below, for review and discussion of the growing literature on this topic).

A number of well-controlled studies, including Trehub (1976a), support anecdotal evidence suggesting that adults speaking different languages differ strikingly in their capacities to make perceptual distinctions, and show in particular the strong influence exerted by the categories of the native language (e.g., Abramson and Lisker, 1970, 1973; Miyawaki et al., 1975; and Elman, Diehl, and Buchwald, 1977, who demonstrate differing effective VOT values for bilinguals, depending on their language set). It was thus to be expected that some change in discriminatory abilities would eventually be experimentally revealed for infants vs. older children in different communities, in relation to their acquisition of different adult languages.

As Jusczyk (1981) has pointed out, however, following MacKain, it is not sufficient to assume, by analogy with the course of development of the visual system, that "mere exposure to the sounds of a particular language serves to bias the responding of the underlying auditory mechanisms in a particular direction, resulting ultimately in a shift in the sensitivity of these mechanisms" (p. 210). Instead, it can be expected that infants from different language communities will begin to respond differently to speech sound contrasts which are difficult for adults only around the time when they become "actively engaged in trying to attach meaning to . . . utterances" (p. 210). Once particular sound patterns begin to be tied to particular meanings or situations of use, it is no longer implausible to assume that the child is engaging in at least some active processing of speech along the lines MacKain specified as needed for "experience" of phonological contrasts:

- identification of recognizable stretches of sound (familiar segments, syllables, or words), to yield incipient segmentation of the speech stream – with concomitant development of sensitivity to the distinction between meaning-bearing (contrastive) units (phonemes) and non-distinctive variation;
- recognition of repeated instances of the same sound – with concomitant emergent susceptibility to frequency effects based on the recurrence of contrastive units.

Attenuation of sensitivity to non-native contrasts

About the same time that this advance was being made in the formulation of the theoretical problem of the role of experience in shaping infant responses to speech sounds, a new line of research into the discrimination of non-native contrasts was opened as Werker and Tees and their colleagues began reporting a series of studies designed to determine the age of changeover from a "universal" pattern of speech perception to the language-specific mode characteristic of adults.

One of the initial goals of this research was to test infants and adults on a comparable discrimination procedure, so as to rule out unpredictable method or task effects on the findings. For this purpose Werker et al. (1981) adapted Kuhl"s head-turn procedure, using a "multiple natural tokens" approach to ensure that any discriminatory response would be based on linguistic category differences, not on minor acoustic variations. Adults indicated their response by pressing a button, while infants were conditioned to turn their heads in response to a change in stimuli to see a moving toy.

Werker et al. (1981) tested twenty English-speaking adults, five Hindi-speaking adults, and twelve infants aged 6–8 months who had been exposed to English only. The test stimuli involved three contrast pairs: English /ba/ vs. /da/ (as a baseline to test performance on the procedure itself) and /Ca/ syllable tokens recorded by Hindi speakers, contrasting in the C-slot (1) dental /t/ vs. retroflex /ʈ/ and (2) voiceless aspirated ("long lag") /tʰ/ vs. breathy voiced ("murmured": Ladefoged, 1971) /dʰ/. Half of the English-speaking adults received training on the Hindi contrasts comparable to that required to "shape" the infant responses to criterion. The results agreed with previous studies showing "universal" discriminatory abilities in infants but not adults: All of the Hindi-speaking adults and most of the infants met a pre-set discrimination criterion for the two Hindi contrasts, while only one of the English-speaking adults reached criterion on the retroflex pair without training. The Hindi voicing contrast was less difficult for English-speaking adults, though only four reached criterion without training.

This study provided several noteworthy clues to the nature of the interaction between perceptual development and experience. First, the basic finding of a significant difference in performance on two different non-native contrasts between infants exposed only to English and English-speaking adults, in conformity with previous findings (particularly Trehub, 1976a), provided a solid basis for further inquiry in this important area. Second, the inclusion of "naive" and "trained" subgroups of English-speaking adults allowed the authors to draw a tentative conclusion regarding the nature of the decline in performance between infancy and adulthood: Adults are not incapable of discriminating non-native contrasts, but they do not do so as readily as infants. This suggests that it is more appropriate to speak of *attenuation* of discriminatory capacity than of loss (cf. Tees and Werker, 1984; Werker and Logan, 1985, for validation and further exploration of this finding), or perhaps of attentional rather than neural change. Finally, because two different Hindi contrasts were included, neither of which corresponds directly to any naturally occurring phonetic variation in English, it was possible for the authors to uncover the interesting fact that one non-native contrast is considerably more difficult for English-speaking adults than the other.

As the next logical step in the investigation of the phenomenon of decline in discriminatory capacity Werker and Tees (1983) used the same two Hindi contrasts to test children of three different age levels: 4-, 8-, and 12-year-olds. Their initial expectation was that the change would date from puberty, following Lenneberg (1967), who maintained that an important loss of neurological flexibility is associated with puberty and underlies the well-known decline in ability to learn a second language with native-like accent. Contrary to expectation, all three groups of children performed similarly to the English-speaking adults in the previous study; even 4-year-olds resembled the adults rather than the infants in their relative inability to discriminate the Hindi contrasts – and in fact none of the 4-year-olds discriminated the relatively easier voicing pair, while half of the children in each of the older age groups did so. As Werker and Tees suggest, this difference may be connected with the tendency of children to display a relatively rigid adherence to newly acquired rules or language structures, often exceeding adult norms in the period when a grammatical form is in focus, for example (cf. Slobin, 1977).[2]

The culminating study in this series, after pilot testing of children between the ages of 8 months and four years (Werker, 1991), focused on the last months of the first year, looking for evidence of a *reorganization* rather than a loss of perceptual responses to speech. Werker and Tees (1984) began by testing twelve 6-month-old infants, ten English-speaking adults, and five adult native speakers according to the procedures described in Werker et al. (1981), using as stimuli another pair of "exotic" non-native speech sounds unlikely to occur at all in the phonetics of English speech: the contrasting glottalized velar and uvular stops found in Nthlakapmx, also known as Thompson, an Interior Salish (Native American) language spoken in British Columbia. Specifically, three natural tokens each of [k?i] and [q?i] (contrasting velar and uvular ejectives) were used as stimuli. The results replicated those of the Hindi study: All Thompson adults, three out of ten English-speaking adults, and eight out of ten infants discriminated the contrast.

In the critical second experiment, infants aged 8–10 months and 10–12 months were tested on three place of articulation contrasts, the "baseline" pair from English, /ba/ : /da/, and the difficult pairs from Hindi and Thompson. At 8–10 months over half the infants discriminated the non-native contrasts, while at 10–12 months most did not. In a follow-up experiment, six subjects who had been cooperative in the procedure at 6–8 months were tested again at 8–10 and 10–12 months on all three contrasts. By 8–10 months only three of the infants discriminated the Thompson contrast, and by 10–12 months neither the Hindi nor the Thompson contrast was discriminated, essentially replicating the cross-sectional results (cf. also Best, 1994, who reports replication of the results with infants on the Thompson contrast using a "visual fixation" paradigm developed by Miller, 1983). Werker and Tees concluded that a "selective tuning of initial sensitivities in accordance with a specific phonology . . . occurs at about the age that the child is beginning to understand and possibly produce sounds appropriate to his/her native language" (1984, p. 62).

Finally, Werker and Lalonde (1988) extended these findings by testing English-speaking adults and English-learning infants aged 6–8 months and 11–13 months on a synthesized place of articulation continuum designed to include the "common" labial vs. dental (or alveolar) contrast found in both English and Hindi, the "Hindi-only" contrast of dental vs. retroflex, and a contrast found in neither. They found that even the younger infants showed relatively poor discrimination of the contrasts characterizing neither adult language, while the older infants showed a decline in discrimination of the Hindi-only contrast, as in the earlier study. The authors concluded that their findings provide "further cross-language verification that infants are sensitive to the universal set of phonetic distinctions and evidence another instance [in addition to those based on the VOT continuum] . . . of a failure to discriminate an arbitrary contrast that is not phonetically relevant" (p. 681). However, they also note that their findings do not permit us to decide whether these "phonetically relevant sensitivities result from specifically linguistic or generalized auditory processing mechanisms" (pp. 681f.).

Two theoretical frameworks have been proposed to explain the finding that some non-native contrasts are more difficult than others. Burnham (1986) attempts to relate degree of difficulty for adults to age of "loss" in the infant or child, the prevalence of the contrast in the world's languages, and its psychoacoustic basis, positing a continuum from "robust" to "fragile" perceptual contrasts. The proposal is inherently plausible, although an independent definition of relative "robustness" in psychoacoustic terms remains to be provided. Unfortunately, there appears to be insufficient evidence at present regarding a range of different contrasts to permit serious evaluation of the developmental application of the hypothesis.

Best, McRoberts, and Sithole (1988) propose an alternative perceptual model (cf. also Best, 1994). They distinguish four ways in which a non-native speech contrast might be assimilated to the phonological categories of the listener's native language; the assumption is that adults will tend, whenever possible, to filter even unfamiliar speech sounds through their native phonemic system. According to this perceptual assimilation model, contrasting non-native phones may (1) resemble two different native phonemes (a "two-category" non-native contrast); (2) both resemble a single category of the native language, as if they were phonetic variants ("single-category"); (3) resemble a single category, but with a better phonetic fit with the category for one member of the contrasting pair ("category-goodness"); and (4) fail to resemble any native categories ("non-assimilable").

Examples of contrasts which have been tested experimentally include the following:

1 Ethiopian labial vs. dental ejectives, assimilated to different English categories (/p/ vs. /t/), pose little problem for adult discrimination.

2   Thompson velar and uvular ejectives, which assimilate to a single English category (/k/), are particularly difficult for adults to discriminate, even with training.
3   Zulu voiceless plain velar stop /k/ vs. velar ejective /kʔ/ both assimilate to English /k/, but with the plain stop constituting a more typical expression of the category; the contrast is less well discriminated than two-category contrasts, but is easier than a single-category contrast.
4   Zulu clicks, which adults discriminate readily, as do infants throughout the age range 6–14 months, exemplify a "non-assimilable" contrast and appear to be treated as non-speech sounds by both English-speaking adults and infants exposed to English: "We suggest that the high performance on the Zulu clicks occurred because no . . . phonemic influence . . . operated for them, thus permitting subjects more direct perceptual access to their auditory (nonspeech) or phonetic (articulatory) properties" (Best et al., 1988, p. 352).

The timing of the apparent perceptual reorganization is striking. It comes at the outset of the transition to speech, when the child is first beginning to make receptive sound–meaning connections, showing evidence of the first word recognition and of an intention to communicate as well as producing an idiosyncratic babbling repertoire, broadly similar across different languages but varying considerably from one child to the next within an ambient language group (see ch. 6). Best (1994) contrasts several hypotheses regarding the mechanism underlying the perceptual shift demonstrated by Werker and colleagues for the end of the first year, including a general cognitive shift, the development of a phonological representation involving segmental contrasts like those underlying adult linguistic behavior, and the development of a more global recognition of "patterns of [phonetic] gestural coordination" (cf. also Vihman, 1991, 1993c; Werker and Pegg, 1992).

Recent work in infant perception of musical patterns (sequences of tones) suggests that 6–8-month-old infants, unlike adults, are sensitive to subtle changes in "exotic" as well as Western melodies (Lynch et al., 1990) and to within-key as well as to key-violating changes in Western melodies (Trainor and Trehub, 1992; Trehub and Trainor, 1993); it has not yet been established whether 10–12-month-olds differ from younger infants with regard to "non-native" musical as well as speech patterns. If the timing of this shift from "universal" to culturally specific perception of a non-speech pattern should be found to occur at roughly the same time as the shift in speech sound discrimination, a rather different range of theories – with less emphasis on linguistic structure and function – may have to be considered.

Differences in infant processing of vowels vs. consonants

Some recent work on infant perception of non-native vowel contrasts may force yet another reevaluation of the developmental course of perceptual "entry" into the ambient language. It was established early on that vowels tend to be perceived more "continuously" (less "categorically") than consonants, by infants as well as adults.

This means that non-native contrasts between vowels should be less difficult than non-native contrasts between consonants, assuming that the difficulty in perceiving foreign language contrasts derives from the development of language-specific phonetic categories and on consequent categorical filtering in perception. There is evidence that this is the case for adults (e.g., Stevens et al., 1969). What is the developmental profile for infant perception of non-native vowels?

In a cross-linguistic study of prototype effects, Kuhl et al. (1992) demonstrated that 6-month-old American infants experienced a stronger "perceptual magnet" effect when tested on English /i/ than when tested on Swedish front-rounded /y/. Swedish infants showed the reverse – although English /i/ does in fact closely resemble Swedish /i/, a core vowel found in most languages.

Werker and Polka (1993) tested adults and infants on two German front-rounded vs. back-rounded vowel contrasts, tense /y:/ vs. /u:/ (the latter corresponding to English *gooed* /gud/) and lax /y/ vs. /u/ (corresponding to English *good* /gʊd/). They presented multiple natural tokens of the contrasting vowel pairs inserted in the carrier syllable frame /dVt/. Adults were found to discriminate the German vowel contrasts, but indicated that the back-rounded vowels were "better exemplars" of English vowels than the front-rounded vowels. Notice that although only the back-rounded vowels tested occur as phonemes in English, the front-rounded vowels do occur as contextual variants of these vowels, in the environment of palatal consonants (affricates /ʧ/ and /ʤ/, fricatives /ʃ/ and /ʒ/, glide /j/). This test is thus quite similar to Kuhl et al.'s prototype study, but is not comparable to the earlier Werker studies of the Thompson glottalized consonant contrasts, in which both speech sounds are entirely foreign to English.[3]

Werker and Polka's tests of infants (aged 6–8 and 10–12 months) suggested a different developmental profile from any of those reported previously. The older infants, unlike the adults, were generally unable to discriminate the two German contrasts, while the younger infants were able to discriminate them only if the non-English-like (front-rounded) vowel was presented first, as referent, and the English-like (back-rounded) vowel provided the test or comparison. Werker and Polka consider this result to constitute a validation of the cross-linguistic finding of Kuhl et al., best interpreted as revealing a perceptual magnet effect for 6-month-olds in which the English vowel is already sufficiently familiar to assimilate the non-native vowel (and thus block or interfere with discrimination) when it is heard first, as a background or referent speech sound (cf. Repp and Crowder, 1990, who found order effects in vowel discrimination by adults). Follow-up work with younger infants reported by Werker and Polka suggests that the prototype structure of vowel categories as defined by Kuhl may be an early effect of experience with the native language: It does not appear to be present at 4 months of age.

Werker and Polka note that it is reasonable that experiential effects should be found at earlier ages for vowels than for consonants, since vowels carry affective prosodic information as well as important cues to speaker identity and are thus ecologically (as well as acoustically) salient at an earlier point in infant development. Further speculation as to the meaning of the differences between findings regarding vowels vs. consonants is scarcely warranted at this point, since so few comparable studies are available. However, studies of cross-modal matching indicate that auditory-visual recognition of vowels occurs as early as 4 months of age, and at that age infants listening to vowels are inclined to produce vocal responses (Legerstee, 1990; cf. also Kuhl, 1987). This suggests that both motor and attentional factors may be involved in infant processing of vowel patterns within the first six months of life. Before turning to evidence relevant to developmental changes in attention over the first year, we will consider the data on cross-modal perception.

Cross-modal perception

It is evident that the perception of speech is facilitated by visual cues: The hearing-impaired can learn to "read lips" as a supplement to the residual auditory signal, and in noisy circumstances it is easier to follow a conversation face-to-face than on a telephone – especially when other conversations constitute the competing noise. The role of visual information in adult speech perception has been explored experimentally in several studies (see Massaro, 1988; Summerfield, 1991); the nature of the effects obtained when the percepts afforded by ear and by eye are made to conflict – as when the listener hears [VgV] but sees a (temporally synchronized) face forming the pattern [VbV], resulting in a reported percept of [VbgV] – has been taken to support the motor theory or ecological models of perception, according to both of which "proximal acoustical stimuli [are related] to their distal origins in articulation" (Summerfield, 1979, p. 329; see also ch. 3, n. 2 above).

Kuhl and Meltzoff (1982, 1984), echoing the goals of the original categorical perception study with infants of Eimas et al. (1971) – is the integration of auditory and visual cues the result of *learning* to associate the relevant cues with speech over "a protracted period during which [adults] both watch and listen to others speak?" (1984, p. 364) – undertook to explore the development of auditory-visual interaction in speech perception. They presented infants aged 4 to 5 months with two filmed images of a female talker producing each of two visually distinguishable vowels (/ɑ/ vs. /i/) in synchrony with each other and with a sound track of a woman saying each of the vowels. Following a familiarization phase in which the faces were shown without sound, each infant was briefly exposed to the taped sound of one of the vowels. The results were clear: Infants generally looked longer at the matched face.[4] In a follow-up experiment the investigators confirmed that temporal matching alone (given the possibility of subtle differences between the two visual gestures) was not the source of the effect: Removal from the signal of the spectral information specifying the vowel eliminated the finding.

How did these infants make the connection between the sight and sound of a vowel? As Kuhl and Meltzoff point out, infants aged 4 or 5 months are typically producing vowels resembling adult [ɑ] themselves, and perhaps also [i]. It is possible that they refer both auditory and visual percepts to their knowledge of their own production, since "during this period infants are mapping out the enormously complex relationship between articulatory maneuvers and their auditory results" (1984, p. 375). In fact, some of the children listening to vowels in the first experiment produced imitative responses, typically reproducing the pitch contour of the recorded vowel and also shaping their own vowel in the direction of the model (i.e., producing /a/-like vowels in response to /a/ and /i/-like vowels in response to /i/: Kuhl and Meltzoff, 1988). Infant recognition of the equivalence between the vowel articulation heard and seen and his or her own vocalizations would be based on the same somewhat mysterious responsive capacity which leads infants to imitate mouth opening/closing or tongue protrusion within the first weeks of life (Meltzoff and Moore, 1977, 1983). In essence, this constitutes yet another "perceptual constancy," or capacity for disregarding irrelevant variation (in the productions of men, women and children) in listening for a particular vowel. In this case, the infants reveal an intuitive empathic identification of the movements and sound productions of others with those in their own behavioral repertoire (Meltzoff and Moore, 1993).

The role of attention in mediating ambient language influence

Aslin et al. (1983) introduce their discussion of "auditory development and speech perception in infancy" with the following "cautionary note":

> Typically, developmentalists are interested in the change in auditory function across age and experiential history. Given an organism that is clearly undergoing rapid advances in motor, attentional, and motivational systems in parallel with presumed changes in sensory and perceptual sensitivity, it is crucial to be aware of the potential confounding of these various systems as one draws conclusions about the infant's perceptual development. When any improvement in performance on an auditory task is documented in the developing infant, it is absolutely essential to ask whether such an improvement could be due to non-perceptual factors, such as improvements in response systems, attentiveness, or familiarity with the testing situation. (p. 585)

We reviewed literature which appears to reveal a fairly sudden change in infant sensitivity to non-native consonant contrasts at the end of the first year. We have also reported a growing consensus to the effect that the change involves a "reorganization" which amounts to a shift from a "psychophysical" to a "phonetic" or "phonological" basis for responses to speech sounds. Thus, purely sensory changes cannot be invoked to explain the shift. What remains at issue is the mechanism for this shift, or its explanation in terms of the other changes affecting the infant; namely, changes in motor, attentional, and motivational systems. It is likely that the actual effect of experience with speech sounds in the child's environment is filtered through these other maturing systems. We will consider changes in motor capacity in connection with speech production in the next two chapters; changes in "motivation," which we will frame in terms of an emergent understanding of communication and the development of an "intention to mean," will be discussed in chapter 6. Here we consider briefly the idea that attention plays an important role in shaping the child's initial sensory capacities in the direction of the phonological repertoire of a specific ambient language.

Jusczyk (1981) suggests that it is only with the onset of active processing of speech signals as potential meaning bearers that the child first begins to be susceptible to differences in ambient language phonological structure: "It is hard to imagine that these phonological constraints could have much relevance for the infant outside of the important role that they serve in the communicative context" (p. 210). He goes on to relate dawning awareness of sound–meaning association to attention as a conduit for phonological effects on discriminatory capacities:

> The view here . . . is that the impetus to attach meaning to utterances promotes the assignment of different weightings to various acoustic cues according to their salience in marking a distinctive contrast in the language the infant is acquiring. The actual assignment of these weightings might translate into no more than a bias to focus more closely on one region of the acoustic spectrum rather than another. Changes in the relative weightings of the acoustic cues underlying a particular phonetic contrast could shift the region of highest discriminability along some selected stimulus continuum. Because phonological constraints do differ from language to language, the weightings assigned to the acoustic cues would also differ, thus resulting in cross-language differences in the perception of various speech continua. (p. 210)

One of the few studies to specifically manipulate attention as a variable affecting infant speech perception is Jusczyk et al. (1990) – a follow-up study to Bertoncini et al. (1988), reviewed in chapter 3 above – which suggested that newborn infants' failure to detect consonantal change was due to the greater salience of the vocalic portion of the syllabic stimuli. In the 1990 study newborns and 2-month-olds were again tested with the same paradigm, but the habituating stimuli were designed to be either relatively similar, thereby defining a "more limited perceptual space" and thus focusing infant attention on finer-grained distinctions (among the hard-to-discriminate consonants), or relatively distant, thereby defining a larger perceptual space and perhaps rendering fine-grained distinctions relatively more difficult (for vowels, inherently easier to discriminate). The responses of the newborns were of primary interest, since two-month-olds in the previous studies detected novel stimuli of every type presented.

In the first experiment, the similar stimuli were [pa], [ta], [ka], with [ma] as the test token, while [pa], [ka], [ma] made up a mixed set (similar and dissimilar consonants), with [ta] as the test token. Both sets of test stimuli resulted in comparable "release from satiation" for the newborns as well as the older infants. Jusczyk et al. concluded that detection of the novel stimulus was indeed facilitated by the relative similarity of the habituation stimuli, even in the "mixed" set.

In the second experiment, a dissimilar set of initial stimuli was presented to test the complementary possibility that focusing infant attention on "coarser-grained distinctions" might *impede* discrimination of test stimuli including a novel token relatively similar to one of the tokens in the habituation set. The dissimilar set was [bi], [ba], [bu], with [bʌ] as test token; for comparison, a mixed set was also presented, consisting of [bi], [ba], [bʌ], with dissimilar [bu] as the test token. The results supported the hypothesis that the setting of attentional focus will affect discrimination: Whereas 2-month-olds discriminated all novel sets, the newborns responded with a change in sucking rate only to the stimulus set including a dissimilar novel token ([bu]). They failed to discriminate the novel vowel of [bʌ] when "primed" with syllables consisting of a dissimilar set of vowels – although a direct test of the [ba] : [bʌ] distinction resulted in discrimination by another group of newborns.

The results of the two studies by Bertoncini, Jusczyk and colleagues provide intriguing evidence regarding the role of variable phonological input in guiding attention to distinctions in the input, with the ultimate result of differentially "weighting" different phonetic dimensions, depending on frequency of occurrence in the input (cf. also Jusczyk, 1992, 1993). Such weighting could contribute to the shift from "universal" discriminatory capacities such as appear to characterize the first half-year of life to the more selective attention to the phonological contrasts between consonants of the native language which emerges in the last months of the first year.

The role of prosody and infant-directed speech

Over fifty years ago, in his insightful "study of the beginnings of language," based on diary data as well as on a careful sifting of the theoretical and experimental literature then available, Lewis (1936) anticipated the most recent area of research in infant speech perception when he focused on the role of affect in the child's "early response to speech" (his chapter 4): "From the outset, heard adult speech comes to the child steeped in affective quality" (p. 42); "When . . . we consider the child's response to speech we must recognize that apart from its expressive functions and conventional meaning it will have an effect upon him merely because of its musical and affective qualities" (p. 44). Reviewing the debate already raging in his time between "intrinsic" (or innate) factors and the effects of training or conditioning (i.e., experience), he concludes that

> The child's attention is determined by his biological needs; at first his interest is aroused by the mere affective quality of the heard voice, then increasingly by the nature of the accompanying conditions. The "whole" which these interests fashion out of the continuum of experience embraces, as time goes on, a wider range within the situation in which the voice is heard. (p. 50)

Research on the development of "non-segmental phonology" or intonation and its role in caretaker talk was only sporadic until the last decade (Kaplan, 1969; Crystal, 1973, 1979; Garnica, 1977). Since then, the natural affective salience of prosody in speech to the infant early in life (Papoušek and Papoušek, 1981; Stern, Spieker, and MacKain, 1982; Fernald, 1984) and its possible significance as a bridge to specifically linguistic structure (Gleitman and Wanner, 1982; Peters, 1983; Morgan, 1986) has essentially been "rediscovered"; its importance is now far more widely acknowledged (cf., e.g., Morgan and Demuth, in press). What is new in current research, moreover, is the use of experimental methods to determine the actual salience to infants and the relative universality of such speech, to identify the properties which make it attractive to infants, and to define its functions.

Finally, recent work has placed what is now generally known as "infant-directed speech" (Werker and McLeod, 1989) in a broader biological and evolutionary context (Sachs, 1977; Papoušek and Papoušek, 1987; "innately guided learning," Jusczyk and Bertoncini, 1988). Fernald (1992) has proposed that "the characteristic vocal melodies of human mothers' speech to infants are biologically relevant signals that have been shaped by natural selection" (p. 393). In her view, the prosodic aspect of speech constitutes an adaptation of the continuously graded signal systems of non-human primates; this non-discrete system, well designed to convey subtle changes in the speaker's emotions and intentions, is also uniquely adapted to the perceptual capacities of infants "using phylogenetically older and simpler auditory processing mechanisms than those that will eventually develop to process the linguistic units in speech" (p. 420).

The salience and ubiquity of infant-directed speech

Several studies have demonstrated the special status of infant-directed speech, particularly its prosodic characteristics, for infants in the first half-year of life. Newborns prefer the sound of their own mother's voice over that of another female (DeCasper and Fifer, 1980), for example, while 1-month-olds have been found to recognize their mother's voice only when it is accompanied by the characteristic prosodic modulations of infant-directed speech (Mehler et al., 1978). Similarly, infants aged 3–4 months have been shown to imitate the pitch contour presented by their mothers, but only when it is marked by exaggerated prosody (Masataka, 1992). Newborns as well as 4-month-olds have been shown to prefer infant-directed over adult-directed speech (Cooper and Aslin, 1990; Fernald, 1985; cf. also Werker and McLeod, 1989, who found greater responsiveness in 4- as compared with 7-month-olds to videotapes of speech directed to younger infants). Finally, newborns are able to discriminate between different languages, but only when one of them is the native language – presumably as a result of prenatal experience with the mother's speech; the discrimination is unaffected by the filtering out of segmental structures, leaving only prosodic features of the signal (Mehler et al., 1988; cf. also Bahrick and Pickens, 1988).

As a complement to these findings, Fernald and Simon (1984) showed that even first-time German mothers make dramatic adjustments in their prosody when addressing their 3- to 5-day-old infants, using higher pitch, wider pitch excursions, shorter utterances, longer pauses, and more prosodic repetition. Similarly, Jacobson et al. (1983) showed that American fathers and mothers alike, whether experienced with infants or not, significantly increased their pitch height and variability in talk addressed to an infant (aged 4 to 8 months) as well as to a small child. A longitudinal study showed prosodic modulation to be at its most extreme in maternal speech to 4-month-olds as compared with newborns and 1- and 2-year-olds (Stern et al., 1983).

Whereas some form of "baby talk" has long been known to occur in a range of different languages, based on the observations of linguists and anthropologists (cf., e.g., Ferguson, 1964), only recently have studies been designed to examine the universality of prosodic features of speech addressed to infants in the first year of life. Grieser and Kuhl (1988) investigated the acoustic characteristics of prosody in Mandarin Chinese in the speech of mothers to their 2-month-old infants. They found effects very similar to those reported for speakers of English or German, including higher mean pitch, expanded range, shorter phrases, longer pauses, and slower tempo. As they point out, further research would be needed to determine how the prosodic modifications of speech to infants are reconciled with the linguistic functions of tone in Mandarin. Other studies of both Japanese (Masataka, 1992; cf. also Fernald et al., 1989) and Mandarin Chinese (Papoušek and Hwang, 1991) revealed significantly smaller prosodic adjustments to be typical of those languages as compared with English and German, while nevertheless confirming the general finding of prosodic modification in speech to infants.

What makes the prosody of infant-directed speech naturally salient?

Fernald and Kuhl (1987) devised a series of experiments to discover which acoustic properties of infant-directed speech are the basis for the previously established infant preference for that register (Fernald, 1985). Based on the natural speech samples of Fernald's early study and using the same preference paradigm, Fernald and Kuhl synthesized sine wave signals which maintained the temporal structure of the contrasting natural samples of adult- and infant-directed speech but differentially reproduced either the frequency or the amplitude modulation characteristics. In a third experiment, they held both frequency and amplitude constant and reproduced only the contrasting temporal structure of the natural speech samples. The results were clear-cut: The 4-month-old subjects showed a strong listening preference for samples preserving the pitch characteristics of infant-directed as compared with adult-directed speech, while they showed no such preference for samples preserving only the amplitude or durational characteristics of the original infant-directed speech samples.

In the absence of any evidence of absolute infant preference for female over male voices, Fernald and Kuhl assume that it is the expanded range rather than the increased height of pitch modulation in the infant-directed speech samples which was attractive to the infants in these studies.[5] They note further that visual as well as auditory stimuli characterized by contrast and change are generally found to arouse the most infant response: "Although looking and listening are different in fundamental ways, neural activation [optimized by the visual scanning of newborns: Haith, 1980] in the infant auditory system may be maximized by the exaggerated frequency sweeps typical of infant-directed speech" (p. 291).[6]

Additional perspective on early perception of prosodic patterns is afforded by research on infants' auditory processing of temporal and relational information in complex non-speech patterns such as music (Trehub and Trainor, 1993). Early results using a heart-rate procedure showed that 5-month-old infants process tone patterns as gestalts, discriminating scrambled patterns from a trained six-tone "standard," but not transposed patterns which maintain the same auditory configuration (Chang and Trehub, 1977). In a more elaborate study using somewhat older infants (8–11 months), Trehub, Bull, and Thorpe (1984) replicated the finding of holistic rather than absolute perception of melody, similar to that of adults but unlike that of non-human primates (Trehub and Trainor, 1993). Finally, in a study of infant capacity to discriminate changes in melodic contour in the context of irrelevant variation in key or interval size, Trehub, Thorpe, and Morrongiello (1987) found that 9- to 11-month-old infants detected changes in both contexts, again supporting the idea of holistic categorization of relational properties in complex sound sequences.

On the other hand, results of comparable tests of infant processing of temporal structure have had less striking results, revealing greater difficulty for infants in forming rhythmic categories, especially under conditions of irrelevant variation in both pitch and rate, or tempo (Thorpe and Trehub, 1989; Trehub and Thorpe, 1989). Trehub and Trainor (1993) conclude that "pitch contours . . . dominate perception at a time when the infant's world is uncluttered with referential meaning," revealing a bias toward "extracting the pitch contours of melodies and spoken utterances and ignoring many of the details within such contours," despite their well-established capacity for discrimination of single sounds in "impoverished auditory contexts, such as the typical laboratory experiments" (p. 313). These results, which appear to support Kuhl and Fernald's conclusions regarding the relatively greater power of pitch contour over temporal structure (rhythm) in organizing the infant's perceptual experience, cast some doubt on models which claim a basic "periodicity bias" for infants ("It may be the case that the characteristic rhythmic pattern of a language is sufficiently salient to assist the newborn child in segmenting the continuous speech stream into discrete units", Cutler and Mehler, 1993, p. 105).

Functions of prosody in infant-directed speech

Over the past decade a number of different investigators have sought to establish empirically the developing functions of prosody in speech to infants. Stern et al. (1982) identified distinct pitch contours used by mothers in specific interactional contexts, including rising contours to capture infant attention (that is, when the infant is looking away) and sinusoidal or bell-shaped contours to maintain infant positive affect and attention (when the infant is already gazing at the mother and smiling). Sullivan and Horowitz (1983) demonstrated the effectiveness of a rising contour for capturing the attention of 2-month-olds. Fernald (1989) tested the relative communicative value of spontaneous speech addressed to 12-month-old infants as compared with that addressed to adults when both are "content-filtered," leaving only the "melody" (prosodic contour); as predicted, adult listeners were more successful in identifying the "messages" (the speaker's intent, such as approval, comfort, prohibition) in the infant-directed than in the adult-directed speech. Finally, Werker and McLeod (1989) demonstrated that infants show both attentional and affective response to infant-directed speech, and that their affective responses make them more attractive to naive adult judges. They suggest that this latter effect may contribute to the success of early parent–infant interactions, lending support to the notion that one of the functions of infant-directed speech is to facilitate the establishment of an affective relationship between infant and caretaker.

The consensus achieved by these mutually supportive studies corresponds closely to Lewis's position, cited on p. 87: The modulated prosody of infant-directed speech is inherently salient for the child, serving biologically necessary functions in regulating infant attention and arousal.

Long before the mother can influence her child's behavior through the symbolic power of language, she can influence the infant more directly through her use of intonation . . . Although infants eventually learn to associate arbitrary speech sounds with arbitrary meanings in a linguistic system, the first meanings conveyed through the mother's voice are emotional in nature and non-arbitrary in form . . . (Fernald, 1991, p. 75)

Based on earlier evidence that adult listeners are sensitive to a number of markers of phrasal and clausal structure in the acoustic signal, such as lengthening of syllables, change in pitch contour, and placement of pauses (e.g., Crystal, 1969; Grosjean and Gee, 1987), it has been suggested that children may make use of prosody to identify the syntactically meaningful structures of their language (Crystal, 1970). This "prosodic bootstrapping hypothesis" (Gleitman and Wanner, 1982) has received support from a number of recent empirical studies.

In order to determine whether infants too are sensitive to the natural "perceptual grouping" effected by the congruent acoustic markers of syntactic clause structure, Hirsh-Pasek et al. (1987) presented to 7–10-month-old listeners child-directed speech which included one-second pauses inserted either between or within clauses (creating coincident vs. noncoincident samples, respectively). The observed preference for the "coincident" samples (evidenced by longer looking toward the loudspeaker which played those samples, in a modification of Fernald's 1985 procedure) provided evidence that infants hear the continuous speech stream as having coherent internal structure.

Later research in the same paradigm suggested further that this preference applies only to child-directed, not to adult-directed speech (Kemler Nelson et al., 1989), and that it is evident as early as 4 months, obtains even when segmental information is removed from the signal by low-pass filtering, and applies to non-native as well as native language material (Jusczyk and Kemler Nelson, in press). Jusczyk et al. (1992) also tested infant preference for child-directed speech containing interruptions between or within phrases. In this case, 9-month-old but not 6-month-old infants showed a preference for the coincident over the noncoincident speech samples, suggesting that greater familiarity with the structures of the native language may be necessary before infants can detect prosodic marking of phrasal units.

Evidence that infants are sensitive to syntactically relevant groupings in input speech when they are manifested in heightened prosody suggests that a secondary consequence of the inherent affective and attentional appeal of the prosody of infant-directed speech is its role in directing the child to attend to aspects of the linguistic signal, helping to parse the speech stream into lexical units (clauses and phrases, initially) which will gradually come to be associated with situations of use.

Fernald (1991) has provided a model of the "developmental functions of prosody in speech to infants" over the first year of life (p. 60).

1   From the early weeks on the intrinsic perceptual and affective salience of infant-directed speech can serve to alert, soothe, please or alarm the infant.

2   Later, as the child's experience of parental speech combines with the "accompanying conditions" of everyday life to which Lewis alluded, the modulation of attention, arousal and affect is effected increasingly successfully by prosodic contour.

3   As the infant continues to mature, parental "intention and emotion" are communicated through vocal and facial expression; the literature on social referencing provides supporting evidence (e.g., Klinnert et al., 1983). Following Lewis, Fernald hypothesizes that "stereotyped prosodic contours occurring in specific affective contexts come to function as the first regular sound-meaning correspondences for the infant" (see also Fernald, 1989, p. 1498).

4   As the culmination of this developmental sequence, individual words begin to emerge from the melody of speech. Here again, speech addressed to the language-learning child includes a variety of clarifying phonetic features (Bernstein-Ratner, 1987), including the placement of content words in positions highlighted by the prosodic contour (Fernald and Mazzie, 1991).

Origins of word recognition

Recently, some investigators have begun to explore the heretofore little studied period between 6 months, when non-native consonantal contrasts are generally still discriminated with ease, and 10 months, when the first evidence of both word comprehension and attenuation of sensitivity to non-native contrasts is reported. These studies provide some insight into children's initial construction of a set of familiar phonetic patterns, patterns likely to reflect those aspects of the ambient language rendered most salient to children by virtue of frequent use in infant-directed speech, prosodic highlighting and common association with events of high interest for the child, such as feeding situations, interaction with siblings or pets, dressing and bathing, outings, favorite toys.

Many of the results to date may be summed up as a series of contrasting effects from experiments with 6-month-old vs. 9-month-old infants, pointing up infants' accumulation of specific knowledge about their language across that short developmental span (see table 4.1). At 6 months of age a group of American infants showed a "preference" (based on length of listening time in a modified head-turn procedure) for a list of English words over a list of Norwegian words recorded by a fluent bilingual speaker (Jusczyk et al., 1993). The preference apparently was based on the relative unfamiliarity of the prosodic properties of the Norwegian list, since low-pass filtering to remove segmental detail did not decrease the effect. In contrast, comparison of a list of Dutch vs. English words elicited no such preference at 6 months but did show the effect at 9 months; low-pass filtering eliminated the effect even for the older children. The investigators concluded that greater experience was needed to distinguish a list of English from a list of Dutch words because these

Table 4.1 Recognition of familiar sound patterns in the first year

Stimulus	*Response: Prefer the familiar pattern? Age group in months*		
	6.0	*7.5*	*9.0*
English vs. Norwegian words	yes		
– prosody only	yes		
English vs. Dutch words	no		yes
– prosody only			no
English words: trochaic vs. iambic stress pattern	no		yes
– prosody only			yes
Dutch: words with permissible vs. impermissible clusters			yes
English: common vs. uncommon phonotactics	no		yes
Familiarize with words; test with story passage stocked with these words	no	yes	
Familiarize with story passage; test with words			yes
– change initial consonant			no

Source: Based on studies by Jusczyk and colleagues as described in text

languages do not greatly differ at the more global level of the prosodic envelope. The findings provide the first experimental evidence that the infant is able to retain a global impression of the prosodic patterns characteristic of the native language before the more detailed segmental patterns have attained a comparable level of familiarity.

In another study, Jusczyk, Cutler, and Redanz (1993) compared infant listening times for a list of English words with the more common trochaic accentual pattern (strong-weak) vs. the less common iambic pattern (weak-strong; e.g., *pliant*, *falter* vs. *comply*, *befall*). In this case, the older (9-month-old) infants preferred the trochaic words, even when they were low-pass filtered, but the younger infants did not. Thus, within this time period the characteristic English disyllabic stress pattern apparently passes some threshold of familiarity for a sufficient number of infants to yield a significant group effect at 9 months although not at 6 months.

Two studies considered phonotactic structure. Friederici and Wessels (1993) found a preference for monosyllabic words with permissible vs. impermissible consonant clusters in Dutch 9-month-old listeners; Jusczyk, Luce, and Charles-Luce (1994) revealed a preference for common English phonotactic structures over less common ones in 9-month-olds but not in 6-month-olds. They concluded that at this age children "seek out regularities (or "islands of reliability") in the input" (p. 636).

In a study designed to focus in more specifically on infants' capacity to learn word patterns in the native language in the period just before they show evidence of relating sound patterns to meanings, Jusczyk and Aslin (1995) first familiarized infants aged 7.5 months with one of two pairs of monosyllabic words (*cup*, *dog*; *feet*, *bike*) and then tested them immediately afterwards with short passages which included in each sentence either the words to which they had been selectively exposed or the pair not used in the familiarization phase. These infants showed longer listening times to the passages containing the familiar words; 6-month-olds failed to show the effect. In a complementary experiment, 9-month-old infants were familiarized with target words embedded in the sentences used for testing in the earlier experiment and then tested on the word blocks originally used for familiarization. These infants also showed a listening preference for the target words. Finally, a third group of 9-month-olds was familiarized with pairs of non-words differing from the original targets only in their initial consonant (/tʌp/, /bɔg/, /zit/ and /gaɪk/); they were then tested on the passages containing the original target words. In this case the preference effect was not elicited, leading the investigators to conclude that "the infants were matching rather detailed representations of the sound patterns of the target words in the familiarization phase to comparable patterns that appeared in the passages during the test phase" (p. 14).

In a related study of slightly older French children (11- and 12-month-olds) Hallé and Boysson-Bardies (1994b) used the same head-turn paradigm to contrast lists of words expected to be familiar to infants (based on the first words produced by five children in a longitudinal study: Boysson-Bardies and Vihman, 1991: e.g., *bonjour* 'hello,' *gâteau* 'cake,' *lapin* 'rabbit,' *chaussure* 'shoe') vs. extremely rare words of the same length (*beaudroie* 'a kind of fish,' *charpie* 'bits of rag,' *iguane* 'iguana,' *tangage* 'forward/backward rocking motion of a boat'). A significant preference for the familiar words was found in both age groups, but was more pronounced in the older children.[7] Although the phonetic constituents of the two word lists were comparable, the unfamiliar words included more clusters and CVC syllables and were thus somewhat more complex phonotactically than the familiar words. A second experiment was therefore conducted to control this difference, using 11-month-old subjects only. All words in both lists were disyllabic; the rare words now had simpler structures (*busard* 'hawk,' *cobaye* 'guinea pig,' *bigot*). The infants again showed significantly longer listening times for the familiar words.

In a later study (Hallé and Boysson-Bardies, 1994a) 11-month-old French infants were found to show the same preferential listening effect when the familiar words were distorted by changing the first consonant – a result in apparent contradiction with that of Juszcyk and Aslin (1995). The French infants were older than the American subjects who seemed not to recognize the familiar words once the initial consonant had been changed; it is thus unlikely that the French infants as a group had a "less detailed" representation of the familiar words. Two reasons for the contrasting results come to mind. First, the test itself was not the same, in that the French infants were asked to display only a general familiarity with (or "preference for") words that almost certainly occurred frequently in the language to which they were exposed at home, while the English-learning infants were expected to display familiarity with two specific words to which they had just been repeatedly exposed. The fact that the American infants showed a familiarity effect *both* to isolated words first heard in running speech and to passages of running speech including words learned through repeated isolated presentations makes it improbable that any highly specific word-form learning was involved. Instead, a second explanation seems more plausible: Rather than showing a "detailed representation" of the target words, the American infants may have failed to "prefer" the words distorted by initial consonant substitution because they had oriented particularly to the initial consonant of these words during the familiarization phase. This would agree with several studies of early word production in English, which consistently show special attention to the first consonant (e.g., Shibamoto and Olmsted, 1978; cf. also Shvachkin, 1973, who reported earlier discrimination of word-initial as compared with word-final sounds in Russian). In French, on the other hand, the initial consonant is apparently less salient, since it is more often omitted in early word production; the difference in salience may in turn be traced to the prosodic difference between the two languages, since the weak French accentual pattern is word- or phrase-final.

The earliest evidence of preference for specific phonetic patterns reported so far involves the child's own name. Early word production patterns sometimes seem to reflect special sensitivity to phonetic characteristics of the child's name (tentatively proposed in Vihman, 1993a and b: Both Laurent, whose real name is /l/-initial, and Alice, nicknamed *Ais* /eɪz/, seem to show such effects in their early phonology, for example, as shown in Appendix C and fig. 6.2). Mandel, Jusczyk, and Pisoni (1994) tested 4.5-month-olds for preference for their own name over three foils, one with matching stress pattern and two with opposite stress patterns. Interestingly, children oriented longer to their own names not only in comparison with names bearing unmatched prosodic patterns but even in comparison with names whose prosodic pattern was the same as their own (e.g., *Christopher* vs. *Agatha* as well as *Samantha*), so that their familiarity with the phonetic pattern embodied in the name goes beyond purely prosodic characteristics.

Since the child's name is a prime example of a pattern which may be expected to be salient in input to the child – uttered frequently, with prosodic emphasis, often in isolation (out of sentential context), we should not be surprised to find that it plays a role in the child's incipient phonetic organization, at least in some cases. To complete the picture, one might further explore the relationship between the phonetics of particular child names and the "favorite sounds" used in variegated babbling and first words. It is worth noting that despite the well-known privileged status of *mama* and *papa* among early words (Jakobson, 1960), the word *baby* – used by caretakers to refer to the child in lieu of or in addition to the child's own name in many families – is about as common an early word in production (see Appendix B).[8]

Summary: From universal to particular

The infant's initial auditory biases are only gradually shaped into phonetic categories derived from the particular affordances of the language to which he or she is exposed. The evidence of over twenty years of research on infant speech perception is sufficient to show that in general neither "learning" nor "maturation" need be invoked to account for sensitivity to speech sounds in the first six months of life; within that period, perhaps not surprisingly, infants are well prepared to accommodate to any language-particular selection from the universal store of possible phonetic categories. It is only in the latter half of the first year, when the child begins to orient toward the meaning potential of speech, that changes in the direction of the native language begin to be observed. A series of studies by Werker and colleagues have established the timing of the shift from broad discriminatory abilities to more adult-like language-particular biases as late in the first year for consonantal contrasts, while recent work by Kuhl and Werker and their colleagues suggests an earlier change in orientation for the more salient vowel categories.

The mechanism for the shift toward the phonological patterning of the native language remains controversial. Studies of cross-modal perception have demonstrated infant sensitivity to auditory-visual matches; unelicited imitative vocal behavior in the course of these experiments suggests that the child's response is mediated by reference to proprioception, or emergent knowledge of his or her own articulatory capacities. Attentional factors are undoubtedly also implicated in this shift from general auditory perception to perception mediated by a particular ambient language; the role of development in motoric and "motivational" systems (that is, the development of vocal production and intentional communication) will be considered further in the next two chapters, as we go on to ask how the child achieves higher order representations, or particular language forms (phonological shapes of words).

In reviewing the literature on prosody and infant-directed speech we suggested that the natural affective value, first of the mother's voice, then of the modulated intonation patterns instinctively used in addressing infants, may guide the infant toward specifically language-relevant syntactic units of the native language. Recent studies have explored children's growing familiarity with the prosody, phonotactic structure and frequently occurring word forms of the native language in the period immediately preceding the usual first evidence of word comprehension. This evidence, like the studies of an attenuation of sensitivity to non-native contrasts, points to a rapid increase in the store of language-specific phonetic knowledge in the latter half of the first year of life.

NOTES

1   See MacKain and Stern (1985) for a clear account of the perceptual cues involved in voicing contrasts and the experimental manipulation of these acoustic parameters typical of infant perception tests using synthetic syllables to simulate a VOT continuum.

2   More specifically, whereas "older children and adults have the flexibility to switch between phonologically based performance and alternative processing strategies . . . when required by task conditions," 4-year-olds may be constrained to "adhere strictly to a phonemic processing strategy" which would "preclude discrimination of even acoustically salient non-native contrasts" (Werker and Pegg, 1992, pp. 289f.); in other words, the virtually unlimited flexibility of the language-innocent infant is replaced, in the

young child, by an over-rigid adherence to a particular language-related strategy; only later is a relatively greater degree of flexibility again possible. We will encounter other instances of such "U-shaped curves" when we discuss prosodic development (ch. 8) and developmental changes in coarticulation (ch. 9).

3 A comparable contrast pair could be found among vowels. For example, in Estonian front rounded and back unrounded mid-vowels contrast (/ö/ vs. /ɤ/). These are close in acoustic space, and thus could be expected to provide a relatively difficult pair to discriminate, and neither constitutes a common allophonic variant of any English phoneme.

4 In a later study the vowels /i/ vs. /u/ were tested, with similar though somewhat weaker results (Kuhl and Meltzoff, 1988).

5 Werker and McLeod (1989) have since provided empirical evidence to support the assumption that infants will respond preferentially to prosodically modulated speech from male as well as female talkers. Although attentional response was unaffected by the gender of the talker, however, *affective* response was found to be greater for the female than for the male talker in this study.

6 In another experiment, a linear pure-tone sweep, designed to simulate the exaggerated contours of infant-directed speech, using values from Fernald and Simon (1984), proved insufficient to engage infant attention, however (Colombo and Horowitz, 1986).

7 Attempts to test 9–10-month-old French infants were unsuccessful; preliminary testing of slightly younger Japanese infants (mean age: 10.5 months) revealed only a non-significant trend toward a preference for familiar words (Hallé and Boysson-Bardies, 1994a).

8 *Baby* – or [baba] – is as well suited for early production on phonetic grounds as [papa] or [dada], and slightly more so than [mama], since nasal stops are less common than oral stops in the vocal repertoire of infants at the onset of word production, according to Locke (1985).

5 Infant Vocal Production

One approach to an understanding of the infant's progress in learning to produce speech sounds is to see the child as facing and surmounting a series of increasingly complex challenges, ranging from varied vocal production *per se* to communicative use, in appropriate settings, of adult-based sound patterns, or words (Menyuk, Menn, and Silber, 1986). A task analysis of this sort exemplifies the cognitive approach to phonological development and emergent speech. An alternative but not incompatible perspective is the functional, "dynamic" or "self-organizing" approach (Kent, 1984; Lindblom, MacNeilage, and Studdert-Kennedy, 1984; Thelen, 1991; McCune, 1992; Vihman, 1992; Vihman, Velleman, and McCune, 1994). In such a functional framework, three factors interact over time, in parallel, to shape the child's advances toward word production and phonological organization: (1) the physiological constraints and perceptual biases of infants, (2) the phonetic profile or "affordances" of the particular language of the child's environment ("the ambient language"), and (3) individual patterns of communicative and vocal effort, attention, and integration. Thelen (1991) elaborates several of the processes involved:

> First, there are natural categories of sounds that emerge when the oral, facial, respiratory, and ingestive apparatus at particular stages of anatomical and functional maturation are combined and activated. Second, perceptual biases make infants sensitive to certain features of the sound and visual environment and to the proprioception of their own vocal behavior. And third, infants select from the universe of possible natural categories of sounds by matching their own motor output to the sounds and sights of the natural language environment. The core assumption . . . is that speech coordination is in principle no different from other motor skills that arise as the actor continually matches the task requirements with the self-organizing capabilities of the perception-action system. (p. 340; cf. also Netsell, 1981)

In addition, in studying vocal production it is important to be mindful of the critical social context and, from very early on, the communicative value of the child's activity. It is only in this context that naturally emergent phonetic capacities are linked with the expression of meanings and thus lead into language.

In our account of prelinguistic vocalization we will consider both vocal production and, where relevant findings are available, related communicative advances in the first several months of life. We will begin with the early stages of vocal production, focusing on both the anatomical changes and the role of the social context in encouraging exploratory use of emerging vocal capacities. We will then devote special attention to the chief production milestone in the prelinguistic period, the emergence of syllable–like vocalizations, and will also trace the development of vowel production over the first year. Next, we will turn to a consideration of the evidence of ambient language influence in each of these domains within the prelinguistic period. In our concluding summary we will take up what we see as the critical role of proprioception in early vocal development.

Early vocal production

Rudimentary information regarding infant vocalization and the earliest forms of speech production has been available considerably longer than findings on infant speech perception, which had to await the development of suitable technology.[1] At the same time, perhaps as a consequence of the relatively greater ease of observation, contemporary studies of vocal production are more unified in general outlook than are the studies of perception. The various specialists in the area have each focused on somewhat different aspects of phonetic development in this period, but the studies tend to confirm and complement one another. There is nothing comparable to the proliferation of competing theoretical models that we see in infant speech perception research.

Diary studies began to provide documentation of the infant's vocal production as early as 1877, when accounts of their children's development by both Hippolyte Taine and Charles Darwin appeared in the British journal *Mind*.[2] When Lewis (1936) undertook to review and interpret what was then known about "early utterance" and babbling, however, he complained of "the meagreness of most available accounts," in which a sketchy list of the child's "speech sounds" was rarely accompanied by a statement of the circumstances in which they occurred (p. 23).

Lewis's analysis of vocal development in the first six months of life was seriously hampered by a paucity of objective information, due to the lack of tape recordings as well as acoustic analysis (Lynip, 1951; Oller, 1986). Nevertheless, his thoughtful consideration of the available data (including his own observations of the child K, transcribed with the symbols of the International Phonetic Alphabet (IPA) – "on line," presumably) led him to focus on the processes which enable a child to move from one stage of motor and communicative ability to another, thus anticipating much of what is most exciting in current description and theory.

One basic question, for example, concerns the vocal substrate of speech: Is it to be found in cry or in "non–cry," usually known as "comfort sounds"? And can emergent differences between the two be interpreted in purely anatomical or physiological terms, or should they be traced to differences in function? Similarly, in his discussion of babbling (later in the first year) Lewis is concerned with the transformation of discomfort as well as comfort sounds through "play," or the child's repetitive production of vocal patterns out of sheer pleasure in the activity itself, which Lewis likens to aesthetic activity (art for art's sake). Once play has thus emerged from "instinct," or the "natural categories of sounds" to which Thelen refers, it can provide a transition, launching the child onto vocal exploration through babbling, which will provide the vocal substrate for the next functional level, speech.

Contemporary models: Goals and methods

Oller (1980) and Stark (1980) provide compatible descriptions of vocal production over the first year of life (based on infants exposed to English) that have become a standard reference point in the field. Since then, Koopmans-van Beinum and Van der Stelt (1986) and Roug, Landberg, and Lundberg (1989) have provided similar descriptions of the early stages of vocal development in Dutch and Swedish infants, respectively. The research goals of some of these studies were quite different. Furthermore, the investigators were well aware of the inherent difficulty of arriving at an objective account of infant vocalizations; they developed different strategies to circumvent the difficulty. Yet despite differences in design as well as in ambient language, the results of the various studies are clearly comparable and yield a strong impression of commonality in development for infants in this period.

Oller (1980) focuses on the relationship between infant vocalizations and linguistic universals: "We must look below the surface to see the sense in which these vocalization types represent the fabric of a phonology" (p. 100). He therefore excludes "reflexive" vocalizations, or sounds that arise as automatic responses to internal or external stimulation, such as hunger or discomfort (including cries, burps, hiccoughs). His stages are meant to trace advances in "speechiness," or the emergence of language-like phonetic properties in infant vocalizations. Since what he terms "concrete phonology" (the phonetic features conventionally used to describe adult speech) is inappropriate for the description of many infant sounds, Oller supplements those descriptors with "metaphonological" features, such as pitch, voice quality, resonance pattern, timing and amplitude.

Oller (1986) elaborates what he now terms the "infraphonological" perspective as a way of bridging the gap between the two descriptive methods normally used in the empirical study of infant production, phonetic transcription and instrumental acoustic analysis (cf. also Oller and Lynch, 1992; Oller and Steffens, 1994). Phonetic transcription at its best uses the full symbology of the IPA, as Lewis did, to capture potential sound distinctions made in any adult language, and is based on tape-recordings, which can be reviewed over and over in the transcription process.[3] Nevertheless, its disadvantages, particularly for the younger infant, are clear: Such a transcriptional system interprets infant productions through the limiting filter of adult segmental categories, which may result in an "illusory" equation of "the elements of infant sounds with adult phonetic elements" (p. 22). Acoustic analysis, on the other hand, provides potentially unlimited detail regarding the pitch, duration, amplitude, and areas of concentration of periodic or aperiodic energy; it has the advantages of apparent objectivity and quantifiability. Yet its disadvantages are equally clear: Without a framework for interpretation, the detail afforded by such information is meaningless. Oller therefore proposes the meta- or infraphonological perspective, which is meant to "specify how acoustic parameters (frequency, resonance, intensity, timing) are manipulated to generate well-formed concrete phonetic units in any natural spoken language" (p. 24). This provides a basis for the comparison of any vocalization, "mature or immature, normal or abnormal, human or nonhuman" (p. 24), against the standard of normal adult speech.[4]

In response to the same methodological challenge, Stark and her colleagues (Stark, Rose, and McLagan, 1975; Stark, Rose, and Benson, 1978) developed a system for classifying early vocalizations as cry, discomfort, vegetative and comfort (cooing and laugh) sounds, based on the nonvocal behaviors which accompanied them, including facial expression, direction of gaze, and limb movements and posture, as well as the mother's responses. Samples from each of these classes were then subjected to both auditory and spectrographic analysis. Many of the features used distinctively in adult languages were found in these early productions (voicing, modulation of pitch, glottal stop and several supraglottal consonantal manner features) as well as features rarely so used (such as ingressive breath, breathy voice and vocal fry, or creaky voice). The method proved particularly effective for the earliest stages of vocal production (up to the age of about 4 months).

Koopmans-van Beinum and Van der Stelt (1986) sought to avoid using adult speech categories altogether, focusing instead "on the infants' phonatory and articulatory movements as part of the total development" (p. 38). They determined that, given a complete respiratory cycle, listeners could easily distinguish comfort from non-comfort sounds. Like Oller, they excluded crying and vegetative sounds in developing a descriptive system based on the elements of speech movements.

With the respiratory cycle as the basic unit, Koopmans-van Beinum and Van der Stelt distinguish continuous versus interrupted phonation and presence versus absence of supraglottal articulatory movements. Using the tape-recorded transcription of two male infants for a pilot study, they identified three syllable like (and thus in Oller's terms "speechy") milestones of development: the onset of interrupted phonation, involving the production of glottal stops in series; the first use of supraglottal articulatory movement; and the production of rhythmic series of repetitive articulatory movements within a single respiratory unit. This then led to the development of a screening test for infant speech development in the first year, designed for use with non-specialist parents; cross-sectional presentation of this test to the mothers of seventy infants resulted in sixty-nine satisfactory responses, with the distribution of infants by age largely confirming the expected developmental sequence.

The first six months

Figure 5.1 provides a chronology and a comparison across studies (and language groups). Both Oller and Stark divide the first six months into three sequential

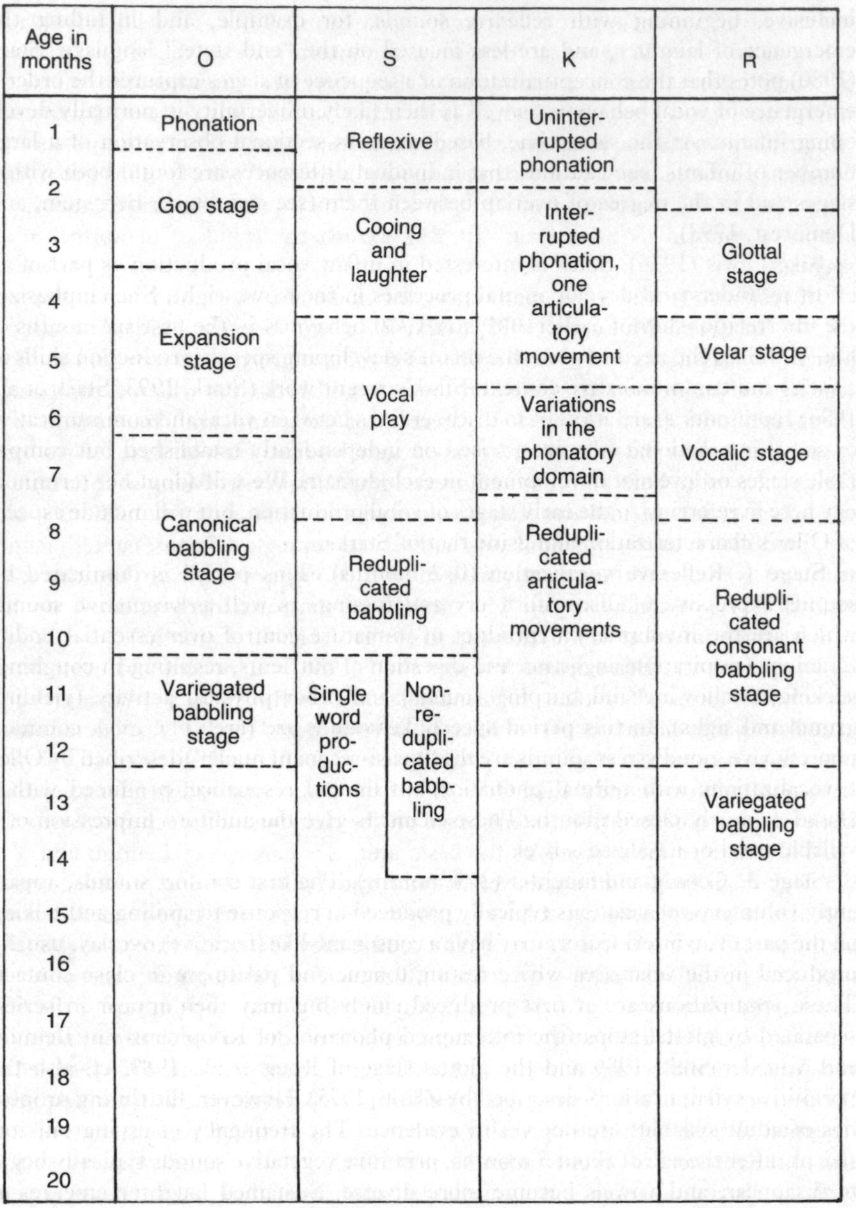

Age in months	O	S	K	R
1	Phonation	Reflexive	Uninterrupted phonation	
2	Goo stage			
3		Cooing and laughter	Interrupted phonation, one articulatory movement	Glottal stage
4				
5	Expansion stage	Vocal play		Velar stage
6			Variations in the phonatory domain	Vocalic stage
7				
8	Canonical babbling stage	Reduplicated babbling	Reduplicated articulatory movements	
9				Reduplicated consonant babbling stage
10				
11	Variegated babbling stage	Single word productions	Non-reduplicated babbling	
12				
13				Variegated babbling stage
14				
15				
16				
17				
18				
19				
20				

Figure 5.1 Stages in infant vocal production: O, Oller, 1980; S, Stark, 1980; K, Koopmans-van Beinum and van der Stelt, 1986; R, Roug, Landberg, and Lundberg, 1989.

Source: Adapted from Roug, Landberg, and Lundberg, 1989. Reprinted with the permission of Cambridge University Press.

stages. Stark's stages (1980, 1986), while closely similar to those of Oller, are more inclusive, beginning with reflexive sounds, for example, and including the emergence of laughter, and are less focused on the "end state," language. Stark (1980) notes that the conceptualization of a sequence of stages captures the orderly emergence of vocal behaviors as well as their likely universality in normally developing infants. At the same time, based on cross-sectional observation of a large number of infants, she cautions that individual differences are found both within stages and in the degree of overlap between them (see also Stark, Bernstein, and Demorest, 1993).

Like Lewis (1936), Stark is interested in infant vocal production as part of an effort to understand developmental processes in their own right. She emphasizes the interrelationship of earlier and later vocal behaviors in the first six months of life, as well as the need to place the infant's developing speech-production skills in a social and communicative context. Stark's recent work (Stark, 1993; Stark et al., 1993) represents a rare attempt to discover links between vocal and communicative or social interactional advances, based on independently established but comparable stages or levels of development in each domain. We will adopt her terminology here in referring to the early stages of vocal production, but will include aspects of Oller's characterization alongside that of Stark.

Stage 1. Reflexive vocalization (0–2 months). This period is dominated by sounds expressive of discomfort, cry and fussing, as well as vegetative sounds which are the involuntary byproduct of immature control over essential bodily functions (respiration, ingestion and digestion of nutrients, resulting in coughing, sucking, swallowing and burping sounds) and other physical activity (yielding grunts and sighs). In this period speechlike sounds are rare. The most common nonreflexive, nondistress sounds are the "quasi-resonant nuclei" described by Oller – vocalizations with normal phonation but limited resonance, produced with a closed or nearly closed mouth. These elements give the auditory impression of a syllabic nasal or nasalized vowel.

Stage 2. Cooing and laughter (2–4 months). The first comfort sounds, apparently voluntary vocalizations typically produced in response to smiling and talking on the part of an interlocutor, may have a consonant-like (fricative) overlay, usually produced in the velar area where resting tongue and palate are in close contact. These vocalizations are at first produced singly but may then appear in series, separated by glottal stops (the interrupted phonation of Koopmans-van Beinum and Van der Stelt, 1986 and the glottal stage of Roug et al., 1989; cf. also the "primitive syllabification" described by Zlatin, 1975). However, the timing properties of adult syllables are not yet in evidence. The frequency of crying falls off sharply after the age of about 3 months, primitive vegetative sounds typically begin to disappear, and vowels become more diverse. Sustained laughter emerges at around 4 months.

Stage 3. Vocal play (4–7 months). In this period the child appears to gain increasing control of both laryngeal and oral articulatory mechanisms. Both periodic and aperiodic sound sources of the vocal tract are explored (Roug et al., 1989): Prosodic features such as pitch level and pitch change (resulting in "squeals" and "growls") and loudness (resulting in "yells" and possibly whisper) are manipulated, as are consonantal features, yielding friction noises, nasal murmurs, and bilabial and (ingressive) uvular trills ("raspberries" and "snorts"). "Fully resonant nuclei" (adult-like vowels) begin to be produced in this period, as does "marginal babbling," in which consonant-like and vowel-like features occur but lack the mature regular-syllable timing characteristics of canonical babbling (Oller, 1980, 1986).

The infant vocal tract

The infant vocal tract is not simply a miniature or smaller version of the adult's. In fact, according to Lieberman, Crelin, and Klatt (1972), it resembles that of the nonhuman primate more closely than that of the human adult (cf. also Bosma, 1972): See Figure 5.2. Differences include (1) high placement of the larynx, resulting in a much shorter vocal tract; (2) a relatively shorter pharyngeal cavity, which leaves little room for the posterior portion of the tongue to maneuver; (3) a tongue that is large in relation to the size of the oral cavity, leaving little room for distinct vertical movements of tongue tip or blade; (4) a gradual rather than a right-angle bend in the oropharyngeal channel and a close approximation of the velopharynx and epiglottis, allowing little opportunity for oral exhalation without relatively wide mouth opening (Stark, 1980; Kent, 1981).

The differences in anatomical structure are in themselves sufficient to strongly mark infant vocal productions. For example, the range of potentially distinguishable vowel sounds is limited, due to the size and placement of the tongue in relation to the oral cavity. Similarly, the close relationship of laryngeal and velopharyngeal cavities leads to nasal breathing and early nasal vocalizations by the infant. Neuromuscular factors are also relevant, however. For example, the infant tongue, adapted at birth to sucking and swallowing, is capable of "thrusting and rocking" but is ill-equipped for more complex movements due to the immaturity of the intrinsic muscles (S. G. Fletcher, 1973).

The vocal substrate of speech

Stark (1978, 1980, 1986, 1989; Stark and Nathanson, 1974; Stark et al., 1975) has attempted to trace the "natural history" of various speech elements in early vocal production (cf. also Bosma, 1975; Wolff, 1969). She finds that some speech-like elements of early vocalizations derive from cry, which is essentially present from birth. In cry, produced with open mouth, we find the respiratory timing characteristic of speech, with brief intake of breath followed by prolonged expiration (Lieberman, 1967, 1985; Stark, 1989). Vocalic elements also derive primarily from cry, the only oral sound production in the early weeks of life. Finally, prosodic elements such as variation in intensity and pitch, rhythmic patterning, and phrasing are all present in cry long before they enter into vocal play. On the other hand, "consonantal noises" (stops, clicks, friction noises, and trills) and transitions to and from a closed vocal tract are not typically found in cry but are the hallmark of the vegetative sounds of the earliest period. They are voiceless, while cry is generally voiced throughout, and they occur on ingressive as well as egressive breath.

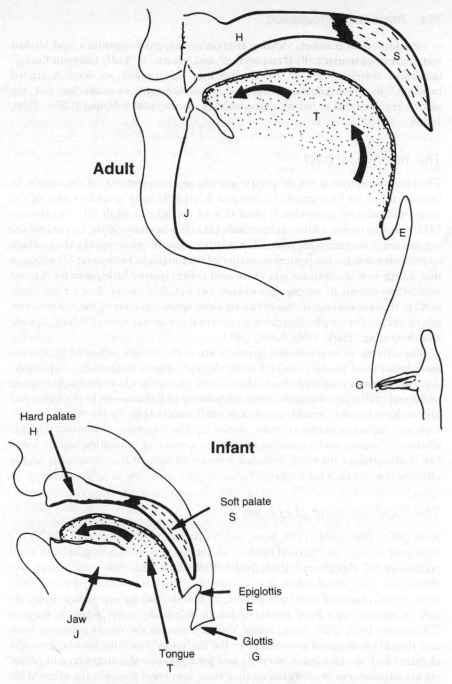

Figure 5.2 Adult and infant vocal tracts. The filled arrows within the outline of the tongue indicate differences in orientation of the tongue in the infant as compared with the adult.

Source: Adapted from Kent, 1992

The first comfort sounds, defined as sounds produced in pleasurable interaction with the mother (Stark, 1978) and typically observed in the context of mutual gaze accompanied by smiling, are brief low intensity grunts or breathy sounds (sighs), which represent a "regression in vocalization" relative to the more varied phrasing and rhythms that have already developed in cry (Stark, 1993). Interestingly, mutual gaze itself reflects an advance in postural control, depending on the infant's ability to hold up its head to some extent (Palthe and Hopkins, 1984). Vocalization in the form of primitive grunts appears to be the direct result of the physical effort involved in phonating in a new postural context.

According to Stark (1978, 1980), the emergence of cooing is dependent on increased control over voicing, which is first found only in cry. The new co-occurrence of voicing, egressive breath direction and consonant–like closures results from the overlap between the maturation in voluntary laryngeal control and continuing reflexive activity of the vocal tract, which produces the consonantal overlay.[5] Stark sees the acquisition of control over this new behavioral combination as deriving from the interaction of maturation and the experience of exercising the new behavior, initially in response to social stimulation.

Once the facial skeleton has grown downward and forward, increasing the size of the oral cavity relative to the tongue, the stage is set for an increase in the diversity of vowel types the child can produce. In addition to the anatomical changes, neural changes in the control centers for vocal production have been implicated in the timing of this landmark (Netsell, 1981). Changes have also taken place in the concentration of mucosal sensory receptors in the pharyngeal area, and the capacity for discrimination of touch, pressure and movement at the tongue tip and at the lips is thought to have increased (Bosma, 1975).

The vocal behaviors observed in the period following these changes, referred to above as "vocal play," have been seen as serving to "map the vocal tract" (Mattingly, 1973; Zlatin, 1975), allowing the infant to "update sensory information about oral and pharyngeal spaces by touch, pressure, and activity within these spaces" (Stark, 1986, p. 167).[6] Stark (1986) has referred to the infant's "improvisations and inventions" in the period of vocal play, and has noted that primate vocalization appears to offer no parallel for this developmental expansion.

Vocal production in its social context

Stark (1980) observed that "between 6 and 12 weeks of age, the infant forms the habit of playing with the tongue and lips when he is awake, alert, and not in distress. The tongue is protruded and retracted, the lips rounded, the mouth silently opened and closed" (p. 85; cf. also Trevarthan, 1977). These silent play movements, like the first brief voiced comfort sounds, are likely to occur in a social context, especially in mutual gaze with the mother, although both are *later* produced when the infant's attention is focused on interesting (especially moving) objects as well as on faces.[7] As the anatomical changes in the vocal tract free up the tongue, it becomes possible to combine consonantal closure with pleasure voicing. The stimulation of social interaction further promotes the production of voiced sounds with mouth postures previously exercised in that context, though not used in cry, eventually permitting longer lasting comfort sounds which combine irregularly with spontaneous oral gestures, similar to the seemingly irregular (but cyclic) flailing of limbs in this same age range (Stark, 1993).

In an interesting series of experimental studies, K. Bloom and her colleagues (Bloom, 1975, 1977, 1988; Bloom and Esposito, 1975; Bloom, Russell, and Wassenberg, 1987) have sought to establish the nature of the facilitative effect on vocal production of conversation-like "turn taking" between adults and 3-month-old infants. In the early studies Bloom showed that infants increase their rate of vocalization in the presence of an interlocutor, whether or not the adult's talk is timed to be contingent on the infant's vocalization. Interestingly, eye contact was an essential ingredient: "In essence, eye contact gave social relevance to the adult's response" (Bloom et al., 1987, p. 213). The patterning of infant vocal responses was differentially affected by the contingency of the adult's response, however: The infants tended to vocalize in bursts in the face of noncontingent adult talk, while in the contingent stimulation condition they paused, "became quite attentive, and sometimes smiled immediately after the adult's response . . . The infant then became active, produced another vocalization and the cycle was repeated" (Bloom, 1977, p. 368).

Based on informal observation that infant responses seemed more speech-like during contingent social interaction, the authors went on to test the hypothesis that turn taking affects the quality of infant vocal production (Bloom et al., 1987, Bloom, 1988). In order to operationalize the notion "more vs. less speech-like," they developed a simple categorization system based entirely on adult judgments of infant sounds. In a somewhat misleading choice of terms, they divided infant productions, all of which "fit the description of comfort, cooing or goo sounds" as defined by Oller and Stark (Bloom et al., 1987, p. 215), into "syllabic" vs. "vocalic". The terms were a shorthand way of referring to two basic adult reactions: "the baby was really talking" ("syllabic") and the converse. From pilot coding the "syllabic" sounds were further characterized as those with greater oral resonance, pitch variation, and possible consonantal constrictions, and often appeared to be produced toward the front of the mouth and to be more relaxed and better controlled (in terms of the descriptors used here, the "vocalic" sounds involve cooing or comfort sounds, while the "syllabic" sounds appear to approach vocal play).

As predicted, rate of vocalization increased in both contingent and non-contingent social interaction, but production of less adult-like ("vocalic") vocalizations decreased only in the contingent condition (cf. also Masataka, 1993, who replicated this finding using Japanese mother–infant dyads interacting in the home, and extended it longitudinally to 4-month-olds as well). Bloom (1988) tested the specific contribution of the adult vocal model by exposing infants to contingent vs. non-contingent interactions involving only a non-verbal vocal response (the click, "tsk-tsk"). Rate and patterning of infant responses replicated the previous studies, but less speech-like vocalizations dominated in both conditions. More precisely, in comparison with baseline rates, less speech-like vocalizations were significantly more frequent in both non-verbal conditions as compared with the two verbal conditions in the 1987 study.

Bloom et al. (1987) speculate that the proportionate boost in "speech-like" vocalizations in the course of turn taking with verbal responses might be due to "vocal contagion," stimulated by the state of positive arousal induced in the infant by the experience of turn taking. Bloom (1988) supports this interpretation by drawing on Vinter's (1986) proposal (set forth in an effort to account for the imitation of facial gestures by newborns, as in the studies by Meltzoff and Moore cited in ch. 4) that a subcortical mechanism involving kinesthetic stimulation is responsible for neonatal imitation.

Some earlier accounts of vocal imitation also fit in with this interpretation. Lewis (1936) distinguished three stages: In the first, "the child responds to human utterance by making sounds" (p. 71) – but only when attentive to the speaker (as evidenced by eye-gaze). In the second stage (lasting for several months in the middle of the first year) Lewis observed a regression in vocal imitation, which he ascribed to the child's new orientation to language as potentially meaningful, with attention to the affective value of speech replacing the former "simple arousal of speech by the hearing of speech" (p. 85). This newly meaningful character of the speech addressed to the child supports the linking of particular vocal patterns to their characteristic situational context, and thus prepares the groundwork for comprehension. Finally, in the third stage, vocal imitation reappears around the same time as the first evidence of comprehension, including the production of "delayed imitation," or appropriate but contextually limited word forms (to be discussed in ch. 6).

Užgiris (1973) describes 3-month-old infants as "responding to the model, though in a diffuse way" when presented with a vocalization from within their own repertoire (p. 601), while in a later study of older infants (11 months or more – corresponding to Lewis's third stage), she found that "infants imitated those acts that they saw as meaningful" (1984, p. 12). She observes that "imitation or matching during interpersonal interaction serves a social function, [conveying] mutuality or sharing of a feeling, understanding, or goal" (p. 25).

In recent studies, very early infant imitation of the mother's prosodic patterns has been reported in cases where the mother initiates the cycle by imitating the infant's pitch contour (e.g., in a 5-week-old child: Lieberman, 1984). Most reports concern children aged 3 months or more, however, typically matching "absolute pitch" (Kessen, Levine, and Wendrich, 1979; contrast Kuhl and Meltzoff, 1982, however).

Papoušek and Papoušek (1989) provide an intensive analysis of mother–infant vocal matching in the age range 2 to 5 months. They recorded in the laboratory, on audio and video, monthly three- to five-minute interactions of German mother–child dyads, beginning when the infants were 2 months old. They report the results of a microanalysis (using both transcription and spectrographic analysis) for the "precanonical" period (age 2, 3 and 5 months). Focusing on non-distress, voiced and egressive infant vocalizations only, they compared both sequential and simultaneous utterances by mother and child for six features: absolute pitch (which could be offset by one or two octaves), pitch contour, duration, rhythm, and vowel-like resonance or consonant-like closure.

The number of infant matches was correlated with the number of infant vocalizations (which varied considerably by infant and by session); there was no tendency for individual dyads to show a stable level of matching across sessions. The proportion of infant vocalizations produced as matches to a maternal utterance increased across the age range, from 27 percent at 2 months to 43 percent at 5 months (when infants vocalized somewhat less, "because several infants showed more interest in exploring the environment than in face-to-face vocal interchanges with their mothers" (p. 143).

As in Kessen et al. (1979), absolute pitch was the most commonly matched feature (about 70 percent of infant matches), with no significant change with age. Other features were rare at 2 months but increased over time. Of the matches involving pitch contour, fall and rise-fall contours were the most common, with an increase from less than 20 percent of the infants showing such a match at 2 months to about 80 percent at 5 months.

Papoušek and Papoušek emphasize the reciprocity of vocal matching. They found infant matches to a maternal model to be proportionately equal to maternal matches at all ages, and higher than previously reported in the literature. As these authors point out, it is impossible to disentangle the separate contributions of mother and child to these spontaneous interactional data. However,

> On a number of occasions in the present study, 3- and 5-month-old infants appeared to invest persistent efforts in order to approximate a well-integrated match to a salient maternal model from the infant's repertoire. A series of repeated trials, including voiceless articulatory movements, generalized motor activation and arousal, hyperventilation, increasing loudness, high-pitch squeals, and pleasure upon success indicated not only some level of intentional control but also an intrinsic motivation to imitate. (p. 150)[8]

The emergence of adult-like syllables

The appearance of recognizable ("canonical") syllables, each composed of a true consonant (involving complete or near-complete supraglottal closure) and a transition (timed as in adult speech) to a "fully resonant nucleus" or vowel, constitutes the most striking production milestone in the first year, easily recognized by parents with only rudimentary training (Koopmans-van Beinum and Van der Stelt, 1986). As Roug et al. (1989) remark, "The onset of this babbling type is sudden and stable, which makes it especially interesting from a clinical point of view" (p. 35; cf. also Eilers et al., 1993).

Rhythmicity and silent babbling

Oller (1980) emphasizes that "the relatively rigid timing characteristics of syllabification in natural languages" are first seen in the canonical stage (p. 99), either in single syllables or in reduplicated series. Holmgren et al. (1986) identified three independent components which contribute to the adult-syllable-like impression afforded by (reduplicated) canonical babbling: supraglottal closure, polysyllabicity, and temporal regularity of sequencing. Temporal regularity, or rhythmicity, is a product of the cyclic alternation of consonant- and vowel-like gestures which effect articulatory closure and opening, as in adult syllable production. Thelen (1981) reported that repetitive movements, or "rhythmic stereotypies," characterize a number of developing motor skills in the middle of the first year, such as movements of the limbs, fingers, and torso. She suggested that these stereotypies function as a transition between uncoordinated and coordinated movements. Thus, as Kent (1984) remarked, "reduplicated babbling . . . [may be] part of a more general developmental process in which cyclicity is used to motor advantage" (p. R891).

Given the evident importance of timing in the emergence of adult-like syllable production, Holmgren et al. (1986) developed an automatic procedure for detecting rhythmicity in the waveform of infant vocalizations. In a follow-up study, Bickley, Lindblom, and Roug (1986) reported that the automatically computed syllable rates derived from that procedure were in close correlation with hand measured vowel-onset intervals; similarly, automatic classification of rhythmicity was in good agreement with subjective judgments of rhythm. Based on these analyses, Bickley et al. concluded that temporal and rhythmic features of canonical babbling can be identified independently of complete supraglottal closure, or stop gestures, and may appear in the infant's vocal production somewhat *prior* to the time when canonical babbling is identified by adult listeners. At the same time, Roug et al. (1989) comment that "several infants have, according to the reports of some of the parents, been observed moving the jaw rhythmically up and down without phonating a few days before the onset of . . . reduplicated stop consonant babbling" (p. 34).

Thus, before producing characteristic chained sequences such as [bababa], [dadada] or [nanana], infants may produce repeated sequences of partial consonantal closure, yielding fricative- or glide-like sounds, followed by vocalic opening. They may produce such syllable-like sequences rhythmically and they may produce them silently. When full closure, phonation, and rhythmic multiple syllable production are all present, the child is perceived as babbling in the canonical sense.

Canonical vs. variegated "stages"

Most of the studies represented in figure 5.1 identify two stages in the second half of the first year, distinguishing canonical or reduplicated from variegated babbling. According to both Oller (1980) and Stark (1980), systematic variation of consonantal or vocalic elements is found from age 10 or 11 months on. Elbers (1982) traced the development from reduplicated to variegated babbling in the speech of one child acquiring Dutch, between 6 and 12 months of age. Elbers's "cognitive-continuity approach" views babbling in this period as "a systematic, continuous and largely self-directed process of exploration," in which the child constructs a phonetic "spring-board" to speech (45).

Later studies have found that the two types of babbling co-occur from the onset of canonical syllable production, although variegated sequences may not become a dominant category in the child's production until some weeks or even months later.

Thus, Roug et al. (1989) find that "variegated utterances are found throughout the study, but increase dramatically towards the end of the first year of life" (p. 34), or early in the second year (see their fig. 5: three out of four subjects).

Two studies focused specifically on the issue of the temporal relationship between reduplicated and variegated babbling. Smith, Brown-Sweeney, and Stoel-Gammon (1989) used a conservative definition of variegated babbling, involving changes of place in consonants or relatively large changes in vowels or both, based on phonetic transcription, to test the stage model against their longitudinal data. Both types of babbling productions occurred in the youngest group sampled (nine subjects aged 6 to 9 months), though reduplicated was somewhat more frequent than variegated babbling (57% vs. 43% of all multisyllabic utterances analyzed, respectively). There was virtually no change in relative frequency in the next age group (six subjects aged 10 to 13 months), but the pattern reversed in the oldest group (eight subjects aged 14 to 17 months: 34% reduplicated vs. 66% variegated babbling).

Mitchell and Kent (1990) followed eight infants longitudinally, sampling at 7, 9 and 11 months (the age range of the first two groups in Smith et al.). They defined phonetic variation on the basis of consonantal changes only, including both place and manner, and reported frequency of occurrence of all "speech-like" vocalizations (excluding "cries, whimpers, grunts, laughs" (p. 252), as well as identifiable words or protowords), whether or not they included multiple CV syllables. They supplemented perceptual coding with acoustic analysis.

The proportion of vocalizations including a consonant increased from 26% to 48% on average over the period studied; multisyllabic productions including more than one consonant doubled between 7 and 9 months (to 12%) and then remained constant. Within the category of multisyllabic productions, reduplicated vocalizations dominated the entire period, with changes in manner accounting for the next highest proportion (about a third or less) while the proportion of vocalizations showing change in place only was the smallest.

The data failed to show sequential stages of reduplicated and variegated babbling: Overall, phonetic variation accounted for 52%, 38% and 43% of all multisyllabic productions including more than one consonant at 7, 9 and 11 months. However, re-analysis of Elbers's (1982) data to yield proportionate use of the same two broad categories revealed that in that case at least there was a pattern of increasing phonetic variation over the period 6 to 12 months.

Mitchell and Kent suggest that the U-shaped curve evidenced by their group data might be understood within the framework of animal models of motor skill acquisition, such as rodent grooming sequences (Fentress, 1983). According to such a model, the considerable variation seen in the first phase would be the result of somewhat haphazard production of consonantal closure within a single vocalization. In the second phase, simpler and more accurate gestures are produced repeatedly, yielding decreased within-unit variation, while in the third phase deliberate elaboration of the gestures practiced earlier becomes possible. If we align Mitchell and Kent's subjects by level of vocal production (based on the onset of multiple syllable use as displayed in their tables 2 and 4), three conform to the U-shaped schema, showing a decrease in variation in the second period of multisyllabic production, while four, like Elbers's son, show the opposite trend of *increasing* variation over time (the remaining child produces few multisyllabic vocalizations and none before 11 months).

Interestingly, Elbers draws on Bruner's (1972, 1973) account of the development of "skilled action," as well as on Slobin's "operating principles" (1973), to arrive at the predictions of her cognitive model. Bruner sees the acquisition of a complex skill as involving, first, the mastery of individual features, then the combination of those features, while repeated production or practice of the new skill functions to develop routinization, which will permit further combination. Elbers draws from this the two "prelinguistic operating principles" of feature combination and variant exploration. Thus, Elbers's cognitive model incorporates a motor (or action) skill component; as noted in chapter 2, cognitive and "biological" approaches are not necessarily in competition, but may be seen as complementary. In the case of syllabic babbling, both models are appealing in principle and offer a good fit with at least some empirical data, unlike the earlier learning and maturational (or structuralist) theories which Elbers reviews. However, neither the highly systematic progression of Elbers's son, nor Mitchell and Kent's U-shaped schema applies to the full range of individual patterns of development.

Vowel production in the first year

Despite the salience to the adult observer of CV syllable production, once it emerges, vocalic utterances actually dominate production for most children throughout the first year. This is illustrated by the figures cited above from Mitchell and Kent, according to which, even at 11 months, less than half of the children's speech-like productions included a consonant.[9] Yet vowels have been less extensively investigated than consonants, primarily because they are particularly difficult to transcribe reliably and thus difficult to characterize. We will not review here the earlier studies in which children's vowels were transcribed, without the benefit of tape-recording, with reference to adult phonemes. Recent work on vowels in the first year include both perceptual transcription, based on high-fidelity audio recording (sometimes supplemented by video recording), and instrumental analyses.[10]

Vocal tract changes and vowel production

Buhr (1980) and Lieberman (1980) collected data from several infants with the primary purpose of testing hypotheses "that bear on the biological bases of language" (Lieberman, 1980, p. 113).

Buhr reports in some detail the findings for one infant for the period from 16 to 64 weeks, when the child was not yet producing identifiable words. Buhr and Lieberman exclude from their primary analysis vowels which could not be perceptually identified as a vowel sound of English. Even so, overall reliability reached only 73 percent for retranscription by five phonetically trained linguists of a subset of vowel sounds from the first and next-to-last sessions included in Buhr's study.

Spectrograms of vowel sounds showing nasal formants were excluded from the analysis due to the difficulty of making accurate measurements; the resulting data thus reflect only a small and not entirely representative portion of the child's actual productions.

Buhr and Lieberman are interested in discovering effects on vowel production of restructuring of the infant vocal tract, from a "one-tube system to a two-tube system" (Buhr, 1980, p. 75). Based on the findings of George (1978), Buhr expects such anatomical restructuring to be complete at some point between 3 and 9 months of age. Despite exhaustive description of the acoustic profile for each vowel over the period of the study, he finds no consistent trend of lowering (or raising) of formant values that might indicate a constant manner of production of individual vowels in the face of a lengthening vocal tract.

Buhr finds considerable acoustic overlap between perceptually different vowels in the first sessions. However, he also finds that a relatively consistent relationship between the first two formants emerges after week 38 or so for the low vowels [a, ʌ, æ]. Over time, a vowel space demarcated by the "point vowels" [i], [æ] and [u] emerges, beginning at 24 weeks and showing clearer definition by 41 weeks. In discussing his findings, Buhr cites Lindblom and Sundberg (1969) to the effect that the front vowels [i], [e], [ɛ], which occur in his data from the beginning, can be produced by action of the jaw alone. The back vowel axis, on the other hand, is poorly represented in Buhr's corpus, which may reflect the more complex production mechanism required for these vowels, involving coordinated movement of lips, tongue and jaw.

Lieberman (1980) also presents data from the infant described by Buhr and comments that the lack of change in average formant frequencies over the period of the study is not surprising, since the length of the supralaryngeal vocal tract can be expected to be correlated with the child's overall growth (only about 3 inches in this period). In addition, he includes formant frequency plots from two sessions each from four additional children aged between 9 months and 3 years. These data illustrate a continuation of the tendency toward elaboration of the acoustic vowel space as the children become older and begin to produce meaningful words. It is notable that different children at similar ages present quite different profiles, although the data from the 3-year-olds agree in displaying the emergence of an adult-like back vowel axis absent from the younger children's data.

Lieberman draws particular attention to the fact that the child's vowels resemble adult vowels by virtue of their related spectral patterning rather than any matching of absolute values for formant frequencies, which could not be expected from the child's considerably shorter vocal tract. He postulates "an innate, species-specific neural mechanism" for perceptual normalizing of "incoming speech sounds in terms of the . . . speaker's presumed supralaryngeal vocal-tract length" that also "allows the child to 'know' that it has produced an equivalent signal as it listens to its own speech" (p. 137).

Kent and Murray (1982) investigated vocalic as well as phonatory aspects of production at 3, 6, and 9 months. They focus on the acoustic and anatomical/physiological aspects of speech development and do not attempt to relate individual infant productions to adult phonetic categories by transcribing them perceptually.

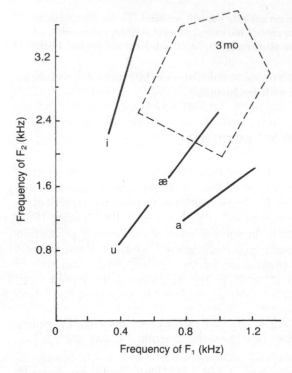

Figure 5.3 F_1–F_2 region for 3-month-olds (area bounded by broken line) compared to isovowel lines for /i æ o u/.
Source: Kent and Murray, 1982

Instead, they use a small set of descriptive features to code the spectrographic representations of utterances (e.g., for utterances with well-defined formant structure, or vowels: rate of formant change, if any, suspected presence of nasalization, duration of utterance).

Like Buhr and Lieberman, Kent and Murray find a gradually emerging vowel space over the period studied, with the range of formant frequencies of the later plots encompassing the range of the earlier plots; for all three age groups, the formant patterns fit within the range of mid-front or central vowels as produced by adults and 4-year-old children (figure 5.3). That is, they find that most vocalic utterances produced in the period 3 to 9 months are relatively mid-front or central, corresponding to a neutral or schwa vowel in adult speech.

The acquisition of control over vowel production is a slow process, as Lieberman (1980) demonstrated. The finding of a characteristic use of low and central vowels throughout the first year seems best understood with reference to the concept of a "default" vowel space, the result of a resting or passive tongue riding on an active jaw, or mandible. As Kent (1992) has pointed out, the tongue is a "muscular hydrostat":

> The tongue has no joints *per se*; it flexes by appropriate contraction of its three-dimensional network of intrinsic longitudinal, vertical, and transverse fibers. Bending a hydrostat requires that muscle fibers be shortened on one aspect simultaneously with a resistance to a change in diameter . . . If the diameter change is not resisted,

then the hydrostat will shorten on one side but will not bend. To use the tongue in speech, the child must learn to control the tongue to meet skeletal, movement, and shaping requirements, often simultaneously. (p. 72; cf. also Kent and Hodge, 1990).

Thus, mastery of the tongue as a phonetic articulator can be expected to require an extended period of experience with production.

Influence from the ambient language

Boysson-Bardies and her colleagues have been engaged in a long-term effort to identify ambient language effects in production in the prelinguistic period. They have cast this quest as a means of deciding between two theoretical perspectives on babbling. The "independence hypothesis" (e.g., Lenneberg, 1967; Locke, 1983) maintains that "babbling is simply the natural output of an immature production apparatus, with no link to perceptual mechanisms," while "the interactional hypothesis" holds "that perceptuo-motor attunements are already operating in babbling" (Boysson-Bardies et al., 1989, p. 2).[11] According to this second view, "articulatory procedures . . . are mastered step by step[,] oriented by auditory configurations" (p. 2).

Prosodic features may be the first aspect of infant vocalizations to display influence from the ambient adult language. Boysson-Bardies, Sagart, and Durand (1984) presented 15-second samples of vocal production from 8- and 10-month-old infants exposed to French, Cantonese and Arabic to adult judges (all native speakers of French), asking them to decide which samples derived from infants acquiring French. An effort was made "to obtain samples with homogeneous intonation patterns," interrupted by few pauses; thus, "most of these samples were characterized by long melodic patterns" (p. 6). Somewhat surprisingly, it proved easier to discriminate samples from younger than from older infants, and also Arabic from French than Cantonese from French. Specifically, the samples from the younger infants were discriminated for both pairs of languages, but for the older infants French and Cantonese samples were not successfully discriminated.

In a follow-up study, only French and Arabic samples were used, but vocal productions were added from 6-month-olds in each group. All listeners were again native speakers of French, but two groups of judges, one of them phoneticians, were told that the non-French samples derived from Arabic, while a third group was not told the identity of the non-French samples. Samples for the 10-month-olds were selected from "highly articulated productions of reduplicated babbling," which are "generally poor in intonation patterns" (p. 8). All three groups successfully discriminated French from Arabic in the case of the samples from 8-month-olds, only phoneticians discriminated the 6-month-old samples, and no group discriminated the samples from the 10-month-olds. The investigators concluded that discrimination in both studies resulted from non-segmental or prosodic features, such as "phonation type and organization of pitch and intensity contours" (p. 10). In particular, the Arabic infant samples showed rapidly alternated sequences of inspiratory and expiratory phonation, whereas the direction of air flow was always expiratory in the French samples; also, rhythmical weak : strong contrasts were prominent only in the Arabic samples.

Whalen, Levitt, and Wang (1991) compared the intonation patterns of reduplicated two- and three-syllable vocalizations produced by five infants each exposed to English and French, based on weekly recordings within the age-range 6 to 12 months. Complementary perceptual and instrumental analyses revealed that the falling pitch contour that Kent and Murray (1982) found to be typical of their American subjects in the first year of life was the dominant pattern for the English-learning infants in this study as well, but was balanced for the French subjects by a roughly equal proportion of simple rising patterns. For the more numerous two-syllable utterances, the difference between the two groups of infants reached significance. The pattern of early production of rising contours by the French but not the American subjects is consonant with the chief difference in the prosody of the two adult languages (cf., e.g., Delattre, 1961).

Boysson-Bardies et al. (1989) undertook a cross-linguistic study of 10-month-old infant vowels. They note that the accounts of the development of vowel space summarized above, based on infants acquiring English as a native language, converge in the finding of "evolution from a rather centralized vocalic space at the onset of babbling to a more spread-out space at the end of the first year, and the predominance of front over back vowels" (p. 4). Furthermore, these studies agree in finding a continuous course of development from birth to speech production. Cross-linguistic investigation of the constellation of vowel space in the period just preceding the usual time of onset of word production should then be particularly relevant to an investigation of the effects of the specific linguistic environment on infant production.

Boysson-Bardies and her colleagues selected a representative sample of oral vowels from the canonical babbling of five 10-month-old infants recorded in their homes in each of four linguistic communities – Algerian Arabic, Hong Kong Chinese, London English, and Parisian French. The vowels were first transcribed narrowly and classified within the matrix of intersecting categories high, mid, low and front, central, back. About fifty vowel tokens from each infant were then selected for acoustic analysis in such a way as to be representative of the distribution of that child's vowels. Only the first two formants were extracted from the instrumental analysis for comparison.

The distribution of oral vowels, based on transcription, shows a strong concentration in just three categories, low front, mid central, and low central; these classes account for the vast majority of vowels from all four groups. Acoustic analysis revealed characteristic patterns of vowel production for each group within those limits, however, with relatively more front vowels for English, for example, more mid central vowels for French, and more low central vowels for Chinese. The results for English were consistent with the findings of Buhr, Lieberman, and Kent and Murray.

Despite considerable variation among the productions of each child and across children within each language group, differences in mean formant frequencies *between* the groups were significantly greater than differences *within* any one group. In addition, these investigators calculated comparable mean formant frequencies for adult vowels, weighted by their reported distribution in running speech, and found essentially the same profile of characteristic patterns as reflected in the children's babbling. Specifically, English was found to favor vowels which are high, front, or both (/i/, /e/) while Cantonese, at the opposite extreme, favors low back vowels (/ɑ:/, /ɔ:/). The investigators interpreted these differences in vowel production as supporting the interactional hypothesis, showing that infants "set loose articulatory limits to tongue and lip movements" as a first step toward acquiring the vowel system of the ambient language (p. 14).

Canonical babbling was once viewed as primarily the result of physiological maturation, uninfluenced by exposure to the adult language. However, Oller and Eilers have reported that deaf children do not produce canonical babbling within the first year (1988; cf. also Stoel-Gammon and Otomo, 1986; Kent et al., 1987), whereas such babbling typically occurs in hearing babies by about 10 months at the latest. These findings suggest that the onset of babbling depends on auditory exposure and thus could be expected to reflect the influence of the adult language as well as physiological maturation.

The fact that stops (and nasals, or stops articulated with a lowered velum) are the earliest true consonants to be produced may be related to the natural perceptual salience of syllables with a stop onset. Stops present the sharpest possible contrast with vowels and provide the most obtrusive break in the acoustic stream of speech sounds. On the other hand, stop production is also relatively undemanding: Syllables such as [ba], [da], [na] may be articulated through action of the mandible alone (Hodge, 1989; MacNeilage and Davis, 1990a, 1993). It is likely that this production milestone represents an advance in: (1) motoric control, which is maturational or tied to natural anatomical and neuro-physiological development in the first year, (2) the (experience-based) integration of visual and auditory perception of adult sequences of open/closed mouth and voice/silence alternation, and (3) the expression of the percept of adult vocalization through global imitation. In other words, children see as well as hear stop consonants in adult speech, produce such sounds themselves, and engage in repetitive vocal production or sound play, recreating their impression of adult speech.

A number of studies have looked at the sound repertoire found in the variegated babbling of children learning different languages. These segmental repertoires are virtually indistinguishable. Locke (1983) cited the babbling repertoires for infants acquiring one of fifteen languages each. Stops and nasals form the core of each inventory and the glides and [h] occur in most cases as well, while most other sounds have a relatively low incidence. Vihman (1992) presented evidence that French infants, like infants exposed to English, Japanese, or Swedish, frequently produce [h] in babbling, in spite of the fact that adult French lacks a phoneme /h/ (except in marginal cases).[12]

Nevertheless, direct cross-linguistic comparisons of consonant production frequencies in babbling vocalizations have revealed language-specific differences already at 10 months (Boysson-Bardies and Vihman, 1991; Boysson-Bardies et al., 1992). Analysis of the place and manner of articulation of consonants produced in infant vocalizations in six sessions sampled over the period from 9 or 10 to about 17 months in English, French, Japanese and Swedish (five infants in each group) revealed significant differences in production of labials (French vs. Japanese and Swedish), reflecting a difference in incidence of labials in the adult language (Vihman, Kay et al., 1994). Labial production was higher in French and English already at the outset of the study as compared with Japanese and Swedish. This early global reflection of the higher proportion of labials in the French and English adult samples is most likely the result of the combined effects of visual and auditory cues.

Summary: Biological and social foundations

What conclusions can we draw regarding the gradual emergence of speech-like vocal production in the first year? Certain anatomical and neuromotor factors undoubtedly play a critical role in pacing the development of vocal behavior. The primary such factor is the change in vocal tract length and positioning; a second factor is development in the neuromuscular control of the tongue. The evidence of a role for vegetative adjustments as precursors to consonantal production in comfort sounds, as advanced by Stark, remains controversial.

The "stage model" of infant vocal production is useful in general outline. The timing of the stages differs somewhat from one model to another, however, and the division between stages is sharply demarcated only in the case of a clearly identifiable landmark event, such as the emergence of canonical syllables. Earlier vocal forms persist in later stages: "There is a quantal and highly salient change after the onset of a new behavior that is not accompanied by extinction of the old" (Stark et al., 1993, p. 555). Finally, the individual differences reported in every domain of vocal production are sufficient to cast doubt on any overly rigid stage model.

The role of social context in facilitating advances in vocal production is intriguing but unresolved; studies to date have raised many possible interpretations. Stark's (1993) account of the transition from the first to the second stage of vocal production provides a compelling illustration of the "coupling of early social inter-action and infant vocalization," for example. Like earlier work by Stark as well as by Kent, Laufer and others, it is focused on the development of the child's system, within the context of child capacities and child functions or goals, rather than on the acquisition of the adult system. The child "is considered to be motivated by the need to exercise abilities and to play rather than by any conscious effort to learn to talk" (Stark, 1980, p. 90). In this account, which is clearly compatible with that of K. Bloom, both anatomical and neurophysiological changes and emergent social and communicative functions contribute to the child's advances in vocal production.

"Regressions" to seemingly "earlier" forms of production or organization may be observed in conjunction with shifts in infant capacities for vocal or communicative behavior, or both. For example, the primitive vocal form known as a "grunt" occurs not only at the transition to *en face* communication, as a first step in the production of comfort sounds or cooing (Stark, 1993), but also at the onset of what Stark et al. (1993) term the "activity period," in relation to physical activity not connected with communication, shortly before the emergence of reduplicated babbling. As we will see in chapter 6, the same primitive form reaches a peak of use in conjunction with efforts at intentional vocal communication, shortly before the first generalized use of words (Vihman and Miller, 1988; McCune, 1992). It is possible to see this involuntary vocal accompaniment to effort as coming to mark the infant's marshalling of attention, first for contemplation of novel objects or events, then for communicative effort as well (McCune et al., in press). The rise in frequency of grunt production in the later period interrupts an otherwise steady trend toward an increased proportion of supraglottal consonant production over all vocalizations, reflecting the kind of non-linearity expected within a dynamic systems model as complex subsystems (vocal, communicative) come into mutual alignment.

Kessen et al. (1979) hypothesized that infants, like birds, are genetically predisposed to "respond to pitched tones" (p. 99) and, furthermore, that early pitch matching is "modified to . . . experience [with the ambient language]" through the loss of that ability in the absence of environmental support. We found the earliest evidence of ambient language influence in connection with prosodic features, affecting phonation type in Arabic by 8 months (although the precise relationship to the adult language was not specified) and leading to an earlier use of rising intonation by infants exposed to French. By 10 months some aspects of the production of both vowels and consonants appeared to reflect the child's experience with the specific language of the environment as well as general maturational factors. At the very least these findings lead to the conclusion that a voluntarily accessible link between perceptual and motor processes develops by the second half of the first year. Fry (1966) has described how such a link may be forged through proprioception in the course of babbling:

> The child is "getting the idea" of combining the action of the larynx with the movements of the articulators, of controlling to some extent the larynx frequency, of using the outgoing airstream to produce different kinds of articulation, and also the idea, which is quite important, of producing the same sound again by repeating the movements. The second important development at this time is the establishment of the auditory feedback loop. As sound-producing movements are repeated and repeated, a strong link is forged between tactual and kinesthetic impressions and the auditory sensations that the child receives from his own utterances. (p. 189)

This same account would seem to apply to earlier vocal production, based on the evidence of early vocal imitation. Indeed, based on experimental data involving both visual and auditory cues, Legerstee (1990) concluded that "infants are able to imitate vowel sounds that they themselves can produce almost as early as they begin to produce sounds resembling those of speech" (p. 352). Nevertheless, the stage of development described by Fry, in the second half of the first year, appears to include a greater degree of voluntary control or access – hence the proposed distinction between "vocal contagion" (at 3 or 4 months) and more or less intentional "matching" (after the onset of canonical babbling, at 6–8 months). Lieberman (1980) maintains that only an innate neural mechanism could explain children's production of vowels which perceptually resemble those of adults, given the anatomical differences between infant and adult vocal tracts. However, proprioception is well established as an essential biological process that operates from the beginning as part of the perceptual activities that enable a child to adapt to the environment (J. J. Gibson, 1966; E. J. Gibson, 1969; Edelman, 1987; Thelen, 1991). Since normally hearing children receive constant feedback from their own vocal productions, they are in a position to accumulate knowledge regarding the aural consequences of phonetic gestures.

It is likely that visual as well as auditory factors enter into the child's first expression, in production, of features of the ambient language. We have seen that silent gestures are reported to occur, at least in some infants, as probable precursors to vocal production in the period leading up to the emergence of both cooing, or the first vowels, and canonical babbling, or the first syllables. Such non-vocal "practice" or exercise of the articulatory gestures involved in vocalization, but without phonation and thus with no auditory effect, strongly suggests attention to the visual effects produced by talking faces. Note also Emily's use of the silent vocal gesture "wide open mouth" to express surprise (Appendix A: Focus).

The critical importance of the caretaker's face has been emphasized by psychologists interested in newborns (e.g., Field et al., 1982). Over a decade of studies of infant imitation of simple facial acts, which occurs even in newborns, led Meltzoff and Moore (1993) to propose that "it is the psychological resonance between the face that is seen and the face that is felt that makes human faces so meaningful to infants . . . The infants' self-produced movements provide a framework for interpreting the facial movements they see" (p. 211f.). That is, it is proprioception, here again, which can be said to drive surprisingly precocious infant reproduction of adult behavior.

A possible relationship of these findings to those of Boysson-Bardies and her colleagues may be proposed. The characteristic positioning of tongue and lips differs from one language to the next, yielding what is sometimes known as differing "bases of articulation" (Heffner, 1950; Malmberg, 1963).[13] This difference in facial "set" affects the phonetic detail of speech production, though not the phonological oppositions of the language system; that is, two languages could, in principle, differ in this respect while sharing essentially the same inventory of contrasting vowels and consonants. Developmentally speaking, the basis of articulation affords visual cues which must exert a powerful influence on the infant, given the critical affective bond with caretakers and the focused visual attention lavished on caretakers' faces from the earliest moments of social interaction. Thus, we can hypothesize that the mechanism that enables a child, in an experimental context, to imitate tongue protrusion or lip rounding within hours of birth (perhaps something like that which underlies "vocal contagion"?) is also operative as a cumulative tendency to model facial set on the habitual expressions of closely observed adult faces. This could be expected to contribute considerably, by 10 months, to biasing vowel production in the direction of the ambient language, although experimental efforts to test such a hypothesis have not been undertaken. The same attention to visual as well as auditory effects would account for the finding that labials are the one consonantal category to show distributional differences in infant production according to ambient language within the first year.

NOTES

1 For a review of the older literature on "pre-speech" vocalizations, see Stark (1986).

2 A still earlier account is that of the Marburg philosopher D. Tiedemann, first published in 1787; excerpts from all of these studies are reprinted in Bar-Adon and Leopold (1971).

3 The IPA is sometimes supplemented by extra diacritics to accommodate peculiarities of infant speech, such as the auditory percept of "wetness" produced by the presence of saliva during consonantal release: See Bush et al. (1973).

4 Holmgren et al. (1986) provide additional discussion and concrete analyses evaluating the relative merits and reliability for infant vocalizations of auditory transcription as compared with acoustic analysis.

5 Netsell (1981) develops an opposing view, that "vegetative and speech movements emerge in parallel, and are not sequentially dependent" (p. 142; see also the discussion that follows, pp. 153–6 as well as Lenneberg, 1967). However, Netsell's examples of infant sound production are surprisingly at odds with the chronology of other contemporary studies.

6 For an interesting debate involving cognitive vs. neuromotor or anatomical interpretations of early vocal development, with particular reference to vocal play and its characterization as "exploratory" (Eilers and Oller *contra* Kent and Kagan), see Stark (1981), pp. 122–6.

7 Lewis (1936) notes a complementary phenomenon: "The sight of a speaker's lips moving silently as in speech may evoke a vocal response from the child" (p. 81).

8 Cf. also Kessen et al., 1979: "The babies worked hard at their assignment [to imitate pitch]. They watched the experimenter closely and they vocalized to her often and energetically" (p. 96).

9 Cf. also Vihman, Ferguson, and Elbert, 1986: The ten subjects of that study also made use of "true" (supraglottal) consonants in the period before word use, and even in the first month of established word use, in less than half of their vocalizations, on average.

10 Both Lieberman (1980) and Kent and Murray (1982) discuss the particular challenges that infant vocalizations pose for acoustic analysis and the techniques they used to respond to these challenges. For an early but more extensive treatment of problems in the acoustic analysis of speech development (beginning at age 3), see Kent, 1976.

11 A more recent expression of the maturational ("independence") hypothesis can be found in Petitto (1991).

12 Note the caution expressed by Kent and Murray (1982) regarding apparent infant production of [h], however (see pp. 188–9, below). Even in the later prelinguistic period, when infant production is more speech-like and perceptual transcription is generally accepted as a basis for the analysis of child data, reliability in the transcription of the glottal consonants remains problematic (Vihman et al., 1985).

13 O'Connor (1973) offers this definition of "bases of articulation": "General differences in tension, in tongue shape, in pressure of the articulators, in lip and cheek and jaw posture and movement, which run through the whole articulatory process" (p. 289).

6 The Transition to Language

Within the first year the child develops the capacity to produce increasingly speech-like vocalizations, but deliberate attempts at word production are unlikely to be reliably identified until late in that year. The timing of turn taking is mastered early on – but there is no evidence of early infant awareness of the "verbal" (or semantic) aspect of vocal interaction. From the point of view of the nurturing caretaker, the infant's vocal and gestural production may seem highly expressive, effectively communicating the child's emotional state and focus of attention as well as responses to adult initiatives. Yet there is at first no evidence of an "intention to mean" (Pylyshyn, 1977). In short, what remains missing until late in the first year is the essence of language: the deployment of a consistent and voluntary link between sound and meaning.

The child's dawning appreciation of some of the conventional meaning units of the adult language ("word comprehension") is gradually evidenced over the last months of the first year (Lewis, 1936; Huttenlocher, 1974). At the same time, gestural expression emerges: pointing, showing and giving (exchange routines) precede the establishment of adult-based word use and are sometimes followed by the development of an extensive gestural lexicon (Bates, Camaioni and Volterra, 1975; Acredolo and Goodwyn, 1988). Most children also develop sound–meaning links of their own ("protowords"), producing more or less stable sound patterns in conjunction with relatively broad or global meanings expressive of their personal needs and interests and other affects (Menn, 1976b; Ferguson, 1978; Vihman and Miller, 1988). Finally, voluble babblers begin to produce recognizable and appropriate but situationally rooted or "context-bound" word forms in this period (Snyder, Bates and Bretherton, 1981; Vihman and McCune, 1994).

It is only in the second year that truly referential or symbolic word use is typically observed, however (Werner and Kaplan, 1984; Bates et al., 1979): This is the advance that crowns the transition period, as the child appears to discover the relationship between word types and word tokens and the vocabulary explosion of the preschool years is underway (McShane, 1980; Vihman and McCune, 1994). The critical step from phonetic to phonological structure has been identified as accompanying this defining shift in the child's word production (Vihman et al., 1994).

Beginnings of word comprehension

The first signs of language comprehension are typically reported within the first year. The precise timing is difficult to pinpoint; it appears to be highly variable across infants, no doubt depending on many factors, including differences in cultural and personal interactional styles across caretakers, the individual child's opportunities for one-on-one intercourse with adults, and the particular interests and natural proclivities of the child. As Huttenlocher (1974) points out, accurate assessment of the beginnings of word comprehension are particularly hard to verify since ordinary conversation between mother and child rarely requires that the child rely solely on the linguistic message (or phonetic form) in order to react appropriately (see also Chapman, 1981). Indeed this reflects the fundamental dynamic by which the apprehension of meaning is very gradually transferred from situation of interest plus familiar voice producing an affect-bearing intonational contour to phonetic pattern alone. In the words of Lewis (1936),

> the child responds affectively both to the intonational pattern of what he hears and to the situation in which he hears it. And at this very same time he hears a phonetic pattern, inextricably intertwined with the intonational pattern and – in many cases – linked expressively or onomatopoetically with the situation. Then his affective response fashions a new whole out of these experiences, this new whole including the intonational pattern, the situation, and the phonetic pattern . . . Finally, there comes a time when the child on hearing the particular word refers to a particular object. (p. 122)

Documentation is difficult. Lewis was explicit as to the minimum criteria for a useable report:

> It is not sufficient merely to say that at a given moment the child "understood" a given word; we need a record of the word, of the circumstances in which it was uttered and of the manner in which the child responded; and in order to trace the child's development we need a series of such instances noted of a particular child. (p. 106)

In her study of "the origins of language comprehension" nearly forty years later, Huttenlocher (1974) elaborated methodological guidelines for judging the evidence. She requires that (1) the child be faced with a range of possible choices in addition to the target object, and that (2) the choice not be dictated by the child's natural preference for that object. In addition, it is important (3) to guard against extralinguistic cues, including "tone of voice." Finally, (4) there must be within the child's repertoire a behavior capable of demonstrating comprehension to the skeptical onlooker.

Huttenlocher's conclusions regarding the general process by which words come to have meaning for the child fit closely with those of Lewis (1936), cited above: The child first becomes familiar with certain objects in the environment and with certain routines which he or she is able to perform; eventually, the sound patterns connected with these familiar objects and actions come to serve as "retrieval cues for these salient experiences" (Huttenlocher, p. 355). The "'meanings' which become linked to word-sounds formed unitary cohesive elements of experience before that linkage occurred" (p. 356).[1]

More recently, efforts have been made to develop a methodology which could tap early manifestations of receptive word learning and trace the developmental path in the first months of language use. Oviatt (1980) was the first to attempt to track responses to new words in infants less than a year old (i.e., what is known as "fast mapping" in older children: Carey, 1978). Oviatt's goal was to study "the emergence and consolidation of recognitory-comprehension ability in 9–17-month-old infants . . . in the context of object- and action-designation tasks that required recognition of a trained name" (p. 98). She specifies that "recognitory-comprehension" is "a rudimentary level of comprehension that is first evident when infants begin responding reliably and appropriately to particular words" (p. 98). It involves:

> (1) recognition of a linguistic item through perception of some organized pattern(s) within the speech stream and (2) association of the linguistic item with significant regularities in the environment, such as perceptions and action patterns, which leads to (3) awareness of the intended referent, although symbolic language understanding is not necessarily implicated. (p. 98)

Oviatt's experimental design, carried out with meticulous attention to methodological rigor and the need for subsequent quantitative analysis, was simple. Ten children at each of three age levels (9–11, 12–14 and 15–17 months) served as subjects in a cross-sectional design embedded in a longitudinal study involving biweekly visits to the child's home – which ensured child familiarity with the observer as well as observer knowledge of the child's level of ability with regard to comprehension and production of language and gesture. Nouns (animal names: *rabbit* or *hamster*) and action words (*press it*; *tap it*) were tested on consecutive visits. These real words, carefully established as previously unknown to the child, were introduced through naturalistic training (a bombardment of twenty-four repetitions: eighteen by the observer and six by the mother over a three-minute period) while the child was actively attending to the caged live animal or manipulating an apparatus which activated a moving and barking toy dog. A brief distraction period (three minutes of play with other novel toys but no adult talk with the child) was then followed by a series of probes ("where's the X?"), in which the new word was alternated with a nonsense word and a control word established as familiar to the child. A second, longer distraction period (fifteen minutes) was followed by a second probe sequence.

The results were clear-cut and striking. For both nouns and action words, children in the youngest age range seldom exhibited any word learning at all (one and two children, respectively, responded successfully after the long distraction and one more in each experiment after the short distraction only). In the middle range half the children responded after the long distraction in both cases and again one more succeeded only after the short distraction. Finally, in the oldest group eight children succeeded in recognizing the new nominal term after the long distraction and one more after the short distraction only, while all ten succeeded with the new action term after the long distraction. Thus, the experiments were able to reveal a dramatic shift in receptive word learning capacity over the period 9 to 17 months.[2]

Using a different design to test early comprehension of concrete nouns, Thomas et al. (1981) made a particular effort to rule out nonverbal cuing by mothers or observers and to allow blind coding of 11- and 13-month-old infants (sixteen per age level). Duration of looking at objects displayed at the four corners of a test apparatus was measured as each mother produced (1) a word she believed the child knew, (2) a word she believed the child did not know and (3) a phonetically similar nonsense word as a control. Here again, despite the fact that the "known" words were reported by mothers rather than newly trained as in the Oviatt study, the younger children as a group showed no evidence of comprehension while the 13-month-olds' responses confirmed their knowledge of the object words tested. However, the authors note that the mothers were required to choose the test words from a list, and many mothers of younger children expressed doubts concerning the child's knowledge of any of the proposed test words.

Oviatt remarks that efforts to achieve language comprehension in infants in her youngest group "typically required considerable time and repetition by parents and was limited to very salient objects and activities" (p. 105). We can assume that where specific parental effort to demonstrate understanding is not at issue (i.e., outside of academic studies), it is more likely to be a gradual accumulation of exposures to salient objects and events, frequently named with attention-calling prosodic support, which subtly transforms the child's growing understanding of the surrounding environment into the rudiments of language comprehension.

Word comprehension vs. word production

An asymmetry between comprehension and production was in evidence in Huttenlocher's observations of the three children in her pilot project (1974): The children generally understood many more words than they could produce. A comparable asymmetry has been reported in virtually every careful study of early lexical development, whether based on parental diaries, responses to interviews and checklists, or comprehension tests and audio or video recordings. It has been quantified in numerous studies (e.g., Benedict, 1979; Snyder, Bates and Bretherton, 1981; Reznick and Goldfield, 1992). What remains unclear is the explanation for the discrepancy.

Huttenlocher (1974) outlined two broad classes of possible explanation, based on differences in (1) the processes underlying perception as compared with production of the sound patterns of words and (2) the processes linking the forms of words with their meanings in the case of encoding as compared with decoding (or retrieval of a word form from a situational or semantic cue vs. retrieval of semantic information from an auditory (word form) cue). Her suggestions regarding the first class of explanation are currently attracting more attention than they received twenty years ago. Specifically, she proposed that children may be able to perceive sound patterns which they cannot yet produce, and "the determining factor in which words the child produces first could be the sound-patterns they involve; that is, the early words might involve only those sounds that babies make spontaneously" (p. 365; cf. also Waterson, 1971; Ferguson and Farwell, 1975; Menn, 1983). Furthermore, she observed that "the gap between receptive and productive language might derive from *incomplete storage of the sounds of the words*" (p. 365). Although Huttenlocher did not go on to make this connection, one current model hypothesizes that an "articulatory filter" acts to "screen in" as particularly salient words which resemble the child's existing motor production patterns; only those words which roughly match the child's preexisting production patterns would be represented in sufficient detail to allow early identifiable word production (Vihman, 1993c; cf. also Locke, 1986; Locke and Pearson, 1992; Vihman, 1991 – and see "Early word production," pp. 141f.).[3]

Development of intentional communication

The course of prespeech communicative development aroused a good deal of interest in the 1970s and early 1980s. Many studies appealed to Piagetian cognitive interpretations, relating advances in communication to the understanding of either means–ends relations (Bates et al., 1975) or causality (Harding and Golinkoff, 1979). Others emphasized a social, interactional perspective: "Language is acquired as an instrument for regulating joint activity and joint attention . . . Its acquisition must be viewed as a transformation of modes of assuring co-operation that are prior to language . . . both phylogenetically and ontogenetically" (Bruner, 1975, p. 2). (Cf. also Halliday, 1975; for critical analysis of this approach, see Atkinson, 1980.)

More recently there has been a renewed focus on the role of early affective resonance between mother and child and the emergence, in the course of the first year, of the "sense of a subjective self" (Stern, 1985), with concomitant growth in the capacity for intersubjectivity (Trevarthan and Hubley, 1978; Trevarthan, 1979), or the understanding of reciprocal intentions (Bretherton, 1988). Rooted in biology (Malatesta and Izard, 1984), such a capacity is seen as providing the essential foundation for the development of intentional communication. Dore (1983), for example, emphasizes "the personal relationship between mother and infant, the affective nature of prelinguistic communication, the centrality of dialogue, and the functional analyses of affective expression" and insists that "the origin of words occurs in the immediate context of affective conflict, arising as solutions to maintain and negotiate relationship through dialogue" (p. 168).[4]

Although some theorists have assumed that communicative gestures, "phonetically consistent forms" or protowords (i.e., idiosyncratic "invented words") and first adult-based words emerge in sequence (e.g., Ferguson, 1978; Fletcher and

Garman, 1979), in fact considerable individual differences may be found in their timing and balance of use. We will nevertheless take up in this order the three phenomena which characterize children's production in the transition to language: gesture, protowords, and first word use.

Gesture

The gradual nature of the transition into intentional communication was eloquently outlined and illustrated by Bates et al. (1975), based on a quasi-longitudinal study of three Italian infants. A "perlocutionary" phase, in which the child's behaviors are seen as communicative only in their *effects*, is distinguished from an "illocutionary" phase, in which the child communicates *intentionally* (the terminology derives from philosophical accounts of "speech acts": Austin, 1962; Searle, 1969). In the earlier phase (before about 10 months) the child's behaviors reveal either social goals (smiling; gazing at an adult) or object-related goals (straining toward or grasping at an object), but there is no coordination of the two. The "communicative" value of these behaviors is as yet solely in the "eye of the beholder." In the next phase the child begins to make use of gesture, with or without accompanying vocalization, to request objects by pointing ("proto-imperatives": making use of people to obtain objects) or to show or give objects ("proto-declaratives": making use of objects to gain the attention of people).

Communicative intent may be inferred from the child's use and timing of gesture and vocalization (with pauses for an expected response), coordinated with eye contact (alternating between adult and object) (Bates, 1979). Additional evidence of a maturing capacity for intentional communication may be found in the "ritualization" or increasingly consistent and conventional *form* used in communicative gestures and vocalizations. Finally, the child's responses to the interlocutor's "uptake" is relevant: Both (1) persistence and intensification of gestural or vocal expression in the absence of a response, and (2) a return to object manipulation or other ongoing activity in case of satisfactory adult acknowledgment of the child's signal, provide validation of his or her original communicative intention (Harding and Golinkoff, 1979).[5]

The considerable literature devoted to the origins of communicative intention in the past ten to fifteen years (cf., e.g., Lock, 1978; Bullowa, 1979; Golinkoff, 1983; Feagans, Garvey, and Golinkoff, 1984; Volterra and Erting, 1990) has resulted in documentation of a relatively consistent developmental sequence. The first evidence of communicative intent may be gleaned from eye gaze alone, at about 8 or 9 months (D'Odorico and Levorato, 1990). Specifically, at that age infants begin to seek out the mother's gaze in the course of activity, particularly with a new as opposed to a familiar object, and then to return to activity with the object.

The emergence of communicative gestures follows: Open-handed reaching (seen at 8 to 9 months) precedes the more explicitly communicative gestures of point, show and give, which emerge between 10 and 14 months (Masur, 1983; Leung and Rheingold, 1981). The tendency to accompany gesture by a vocalization increases steadily over this period (Masur, 1983; Carpenter, Mastergeorge and

Coggins, 1983). Vihman and Miller (1988) note that their ten subjects, aged 8–9 months at the outset of the study, all first made use of the three basic communicative gestures within the period of the study but before first word use was "established" (defined as the use of four different word types in a half-hour recording session), between age 10 and 15 months.

This apparent consistency within and across samples is particularly striking in view of the extent of individual differences reported in virtually every aspect of vocal and communicative development. Harding (1984), for example, remarks that the path to the integration of social and object goals is variable:

> Some infants . . . appeared to recognize that certain behaviors, particularly eye contact, vocalizing, and reaching, served to activate the mother and directed these behaviors toward her as intentional communication. Other infants, in contrast, appeared only to recognize that their behaviors operated as means to make things happen, and they directed their behaviors toward the desired object as if signaling to it . . . At least for some infants, it appeared that the means for communicating (i.e., the ability to signal with intention), developed prior to the recognition that signaling only works when an animate being responds to it. (p. 131)

The extent to which additional gestural communication develops in normally hearing children of hearing and speaking parents is also highly variable. Caselli (1990) reports a diary study of her son's early gestural and verbal development, for example. She distinguishes between "deictic gestures" (our "basic communicative gestures") and "referential gestures." The deictic gestures, whose "semantic content does not change . . . depending on the situational context" (p. 66), emerged as communicative signals, sometimes accompanied by preverbal vocalizations, at around 10 months, while the referential gestures began to be noted one or two months later. Caselli sees these gestures as emerging from early interactional routines through a process of gradual decontextualization. Such gestures include BRAVO "good boy" [clap hands], BYE-BYE [wave], and REQUEST RADIO [dance], all produced within the first year. Within the next month the child adds gestures for objects which he uses in conjunction with a point to specify a request: e.g., PACIFIER [sucking], SHAMPOO [ruffle hair]. Both pretend play and use of the first word forms (e.g., *bam* 'bang, boom'; [amba] *acqua* 'water') follow a similar course, first forming part of an action or routine, then developing increasing autonomy. Whereas the child's early referential gestures are generally used to supplement pointing, by 12 to 16 months he uses these gestures for a variety of different speech acts (request for object, request for action, assertion). The early words, in contrast, are first restricted to a purely social function. In a third stage the gestures are progressively replaced by spoken words, which now serve a variety of functions.

In a series of studies beginning with a descriptive account of one child's development, Acredolo and Goodwyn (1985, 1988, 1991, Goodwyn and Acredolo, 1993) have sought to establish the role and extent of such referential or, in their terms, "symbolic gestures" or "signs" (by analogy with the units of the natural sign languages of the deaf).[6] Two studies, one based on hour-long retrospective interviews with mothers of 38 toddlers, the other based on weekly diaries kept by the mothers of 16 children aged 11 to 20 months, yielded findings similar to those of Caselli. In the interviews 87 percent of the children were reported to have used symbolic gestures, mainly to name objects and make requests (mean use 3.9 gestures); the gestures were used early in the second year and were later replaced by words. In the longitudinal study, all the children produced such gestures (mean 5.1), typically beginning at 14–15 months. Individual differences in gesture use were striking: Out of the 54 children, 5 (all girls) produced between 12 and 17 gestures each, while the remaining subjects produced fewer than 9 each.

Like Caselli, Acredolo and Goodwyn find symbolic gestures to follow roughly the same developmental course as early words. As predicted by Werner and Kaplan (1984), sensorimotor or action schemes provide a ready source of communicative symbols to the child, once the notion of representation has been grasped: Old forms (well-practiced or highly familiar gestural routines) may be put to the service of a new function (naming). Gestural symbols have several advantages over verbal symbols for this purpose. First, they may bear an iconic or non-arbitrary relationship to the meaning to be represented (e.g., FLOWER [sniff], DOG [pant], STAR or CHRISTMAS TREE LIGHT [open/close fist]; FISH, HOT, BEAUTIFUL [blow], the form derived in the last case from action on a mobile]), which may provide mnemonic support to the child. "The gestures seemed to be transitional forms that served to ease the infants into the symbolic function and substitute until the 'distancing' process was complete and the articulation of specific words could be worked out" (Acredolo and Goodwin, 1988, p. 453). Second, their "articulation" or manner of formation is accessible to visual inspection and learning, which might permit lexical production in children who are cognitively prepared for language but who still lack some of the phonetic prerequisites for speech. Finally, even clumsy attempts at gestural expression may be more readily recognized by caretakers than poorly reproduced phonetic forms.

Caselli found that her son's gestures and early words, like the separate vocabularies of some bilingual subjects (Volterra and Taeschner, 1978), tended to have different referents and thus made up a single lexicon with complementary subparts. Acredolo and Goodwyn report the same finding (cf. also Volterra et al., 1979). Overlap occurred only when a newly acquired word had not yet displaced the gesture. Vihman (1985) reports two instances of such transitional gestural/ verbal synonyms in the early development of her son Raivo (acquiring Estonian and English). ALLGONE was first expressed gesturally (seen in the context of eating and drinking only at first, from 12 months on): "hands flung out before him and to the sides, palms up – for example on noting that no more cake is available, or to express surprise at the absence of a picture on the back cover of a book when a picture appeared on the front" (p. 301). Later, first *'bye* (1;8), then *allgone* (1;9) replaced the gesture. Similarly, early use of NO [a straight-arm gesture of refusal] was replaced, at 1;5, by English *no*, while the Estonian equivalent, *ei* 'no,' was used for self-prohibition (most likely derived from the expression *ei tohi* 'mustn't').

On the other hand, children often *accompany* their early words with a specific gesture: e.g., [babu] (+ clapping) *bravo* 'good girl'; [se] (+ point) *see* 'this' (Virve:

Vihman, 1976); [ş] (+ toss hand down) *viska* 'throw' (Raivo: Vihman, 1981). In addition, Raivo Vihman produced several arguably "symbolic" gestures at 13–14 months (GREETING/FAREWELL [wave], BOUNCE BALL [patting the air several times] – a request), when he was on the verge of first identifiable word use. Such gestures were often recorded as a "recognitory" response to a familiar word pattern: HOT [blow] – in response to mother's comment on a hot iron, SO BIG [raised hands] for *suur* 'big,' hitting out for *ai-ai* 'ouch,' patting or caressing in response to *pai-pai* 'nice-nice.' This kind of use may be considered intermediate in terms of decontextualization: The sound pattern evokes the associated gesture, clearly indicating recognition/comprehension of the adult word, but symbolic function need not be involved. Finally, since Raivo's early words were sometimes syllabic consonants only (Vihman and Roug-Hellichius, 1991) and thus quite difficult to identify, it is likely that his gestures and first words actually began to appear at the same time, but that more of the former could be identified by observers. See the helpful discussion in Acredolo and Goodwin (1991) of the "gestural advantage" which some have proposed (e.g., Abrahamsen, Cavallo, and McCluer, 1985; Orlansky and Bonvillian, 1988; Meier and Newport, 1990).

Protowords

Turning to vocal production in the transition period, we immediately encounter a thicket of distinct terms which correspond to different aspects of what is most likely in essence a single phenomenon. Fletcher and Garman (1979), for example, attempted to distinguish between "prewords" (based on Ferguson, 1978, who used the term "vocable," however),[7] "phonetically consistent forms" (Dore et al., 1976), "sensorimotor morphemes" (Carter, 1979) and "protowords" (Menyuk and Menn, 1979). To these we may add Werner and Kaplan's (1984) "call sounds" and the "quasi-words" of Stoel-Gammon and Cooper (1984), as well as the "acts of meaning" which make up the "protolanguage" of Halliday's son (1975, 1979). The difficulty in arriving at precise definitions with agreement across different observers may be a direct product of the transitional nature of the phenomenon itself as well as the character of the infant at this age: "An outstanding characteristic of behavior during [this] period . . . is its lability, that is, the easy movement from one activity to another, from one state of mind or mood to another, or from one form of vocalization to another" (Vihman and Miller, 1988, p. 151).

Menn (1976b) used the term "protoword" to mean any pre-referential or pre-symbolic child vocal form which has a stable meaning, regardless of the source of the form itself (invented by the child or presented or "taught" by adults). We will use the term in a slightly different sense here, to refer to relatively stable child forms with relatively consistent use which *lack* any clear connection with the form + meaning unit of a conventional adult model. Pre-referential word forms related to an adult model in both form and use will be treated in the next section as "context-bound" early words, following the usage of Bates and her colleagues (1979).

The most useful framework for understanding the phenomenon of protowords, like that of symbolic gestures, is to be found in Werner and Kaplan's *Symbol Formation* (1984). Though only fragmentary data were available to these authors, their classic account of the child's parallel development in the "motor-gestural" and vocal modalities of context-bound, transitional, and autonomous or symbolic forms ("vehicles" for making reference) provided the basic theoretical model for many of the observational studies on which we can now draw to illustrate their conceptualization. We will therefore begin our account of this phenomenon with a brief review of their model.

The essence of a symbol is its representational function: "a symbol represents a referent" (p. 43). As Werner and Kaplan elaborate,

> Whereas pointing entails only reference, the indication or denotation of a concretely present object, symbolization involves differentiation and integration of two aspects: reference to an object and representation of that object. In reference by pointing, the referent (the object) remains "stuck" in the concrete situation; in reference by symbolization, the characteristic features of the object (its connotations) are lifted out, so to speak, and are realized in another material medium (an auditory, visual, gestural one, etc.). (p. 43)

Symbol formation is taken to involve two essential developments: increasing differentiation or *distancing* of the components of symbol situations (namely speaker, hearer, symbolizing vehicle, and symbolized referent) and increasing "integrative systematization" or *autonomization* of symbolic forms. We have already exemplified these developments in our discussion of gestures, in which movements first embedded in routines or actions (blowing on hot food, tossing an object) provide highly accessible "vehicles" for reference in a first step toward symbolization. In the vocal medium, Werner and Kaplan identify "call sounds" as "the first sounds uttered in the context of object-directedness" (p. 81). These "ingredients of the straining movements of the child towards objects . . . short, scarcely modulated sequences, formed within a very small range of qualities" (p. 81) are typically first used in the course of goal-directed activities at 10–12 months (based on Tischler, 1957). In other accounts similar short, sometimes repeated vocalizations with initial glottal stop or [h] are used in the period 10–12 months to mark affect (interest, excitement, frustration) while the child's attention is directed toward an object (cf. Lewis, 1936: "The child . . . is beginning to use sounds in declarative and manipulative ways, calling upon us either to share his feelings about things, or do something for him," p. 151).[8]

From their description, the call sounds correspond to the grunts accompanying both physical effort and the effort of focal attention which we have observed in the same period (McCune et al., in submission). These physiologically based vocal forms are transformed, at about 13–14 months, into "communicative grunts," whose use appears to coincide with or to herald the first referential or symbolic use of word forms (see table 6.1).

Werner and Kaplan see call sounds, which naturally accompany straining toward an object, as parallel to reaching in the gestural domain; a shift to verbal denoting is seen as parallel to the gestural shift to pointing:

Table 6.1   Distribution of vocal categories for five subjects

Age in months	Babble %	Effort grunts %	Attention grunts %	Communic. grunts %	Words %	Total
			Alice			
9	79	9	2	0	10	98
10	70	17	3	0	10	132
11	73	4	5	0	18	117
12	61	17	14	0	8	106
13	67	3	4	13*	12	98
14	42	2	2	4	49+	179
15	28	8	7	5	52	180
16	17	4	6	22	51	189
			Aurie			
9	80	14	6	0	0	66
10	50	29	21	0	0	38
11	92	7	1	0	0	126
12	85	14	1	0	0	88
13	69	8	18	1	4	192
14	73	8	4	5*	10+	198
15	35	7	24	22	12	194
16	52	8	8	7	24	194
			Rick			
9	70	29	1	0	0	125
10	78	16	4	0	2	180
11	80	10	5	1	3	300
12	87	10	3	0	0	121
13	67	10	10	1	12	101
14	75	4	1	20*	0	125
15	59	4	16	2	19+	97
16	30	8	18	8	36	120
			Nenni			
11	79	13	4	0	4	48
12	84	5	5	3	3	37
13	90	5	5	0	0	21
14	66	7	20	2	4	116
15	64	7	11	11*	7	104
16	86	0	11	3	0	81
			Danny			
12	96	4	0	0	0	67
13	80	16	4	0	0	50
14	72	28	0	0	0	18
15	92	3	5	0	0	37
16	46	0	32	4*	18	76

*Communicative Grunt Onset
+Referential Word Onset
Source: Adapted from McCune et al. (in press)

> Although denotative utterance – a cognitive reference to something "out there" – is not derivative from any other activity, the directive character of call sounds renders them easily amenable to exploitation by the newly emerging denotative "attitude": the call-sounds undergo a *shift in function* and begin to subserve denotation. (1984, p. 82)

Specifically demonstrative vocal forms (adult-based child forms such as [da] from *that*) emerge shortly thereafter. Werner and Kaplan conclude their discussion of call sounds by emphasizing the social grounding of these developments: "These patterns gain their significance as denotative symbols only in so far as they refer to objects-of-contemplation which are shared – by the child and the other – in an interpersonal context" (p. 83).[9]

Using the classic diary method, Halliday (1975) provided a full and influential account of his son's development of a protolanguage in which several different "acts of meaning" were observed to be associated with distinct phonetic forms (age 9–12 months). Halliday identified four "semantic functions" for these productions: instrumental (i.e., request object), regulatory (request action), interactional (make social contact) and personal (share interest). It is worth noting that these functions of early vocal productions correspond closely with those expressed by the "basic communicative gestures" which we outlined earlier (point, show). The basis on which the functions or meanings of the large number of distinct prespeech forms were established is not always clear, however.

The use of audio-visual recording has allowed investigators to take up the study of transitional phenomena with new attention to such matters as interobserver agreement on phonetic transcription and the coding of intention and function. Dore et al. (1976) videotaped eight monthly hour-long observations of four children (beginning at age 11 to 16 months). These investigators identified "phonetically consistent forms" which could be "partly correlated with specifiable, recurring conditions" and were made up of "phonetic elements more stable than in babbling though less stable than in words" (p. 16). A minimum frequency of five uses per session was required, based on formal similarity in syllable structure and specified consonant and vowel parameters along with similarity in conditions of use. The criteria for identifying communicative intent were similar to those described earlier. As with Halliday's son, four distinct functions were identified: "Affect" (not typically communicative), "instrumental," "indicating" (or interest sharing), and "grouping" (affect + orientation to objects). Illustrations of both the instrumental and the indicating expressions suggest that communicative grunts (in our terms) were among the vocalizations observed. The description of grouping expressions is the least persuasive; one of the three examples given appears in fact to be an early word ([babi], used for both *bottle* and "doll" (or *baby?*)).

Dore and his colleagues conclude that reference, in addition to "singling out" some thing or event, must also involve a *choice* among alternatives or, in linguistic terms, some minimal system of lexical contrast. On that basis, they see the vocalizations they have described as containing only "germs of reference" (p. 20) and as organized, at least in some cases, on an affective rather than a cognitive (sensorimotor) basis. As they note, such an affective core meaning is also characteristic of many types of adult words, including exclamations, greetings and formulaic routines; futhermore, such meanings are a prominent feature of children's early vocabularies (Nelson, 1973a; Ninio, 1993).

Carter (1979) identifies the "sensori-motor morphemes" used by the subject of her longitudinal study, based on videotapes of the child's second year, with previous accounts of "stably significant but idiosyncratic sounds" (p. 71). These forms were recognizable as *types* with an identifiable "pragmatic significance" primarily through the "stably associated gestures" which accompanied them (p. 72). However, they appear, from Carter's description, to constitute poorly articulated early words whose phonetic shapes globally reflect one or more functionally related adult words (e.g., *this, that, there* – child deictic form, accompanied by point or show, [d]-initial; *here, where, have-one* – child exchange form, accompanied by reach towards a person, [h]-initial). Carter's account of the emergence of a range of adult words from the initially primitive shape of eight formally and functionally distinct "morphemes" is meticulous, but the forms do not actually appear to be "idiosyncratic" or "invented" by the child.

At least three recent studies have approached protowords primarily from the point of view of emergent phonological organization. Stoel-Gammon and Cooper (1984) describe "quasi-words" (with a consistent sound–meaning relationship but no adult model) for three subjects. Two children used one quasi-word each for eight to ten weeks, beginning just prior to or contemporaneously with the first word: An interest-marker ([di:] – influenced perhaps by *see*?) and a request form (marked by rising pitch). The third subject, Will, is described as using twelve such forms along with conventional words. Most of these forms are [d]-initial and consist of CV syllables. Some (e.g., a request form and an "all-purpose name," both [didi]) differ only in their accompanying gestures; others appear to be loose renderings of adult phrases ([diduba] ~ [dadaba] *stop that barking*). Will's earliest conventional words were also [d]-initial.

Menyuk and Menn (1979) emphasize the "fuzziness" of the boundary between late babble and speech. Not only do babble and speech co-occur temporally, but "individual recurrent entities in the child's production" defy easy classification as one or the other (p. 61). A range of such entities may be identified, including relatively stable "words invented by the child" (our "protowords") as well as adult words incorporated into the child's sound play and intonationally adult-like jargon sequences with no stably recurrent form (or meaning). Protowords may be characterized by greater variability in form than is usual for adult-like words.[10] Menn's subject Jacob, for example, made frequent use of a form [ioio], manifested in a very broad range of phonetic shapes, the common element of which could only be expressed in terms of phonetic gestures: "Jacob was varying the timing of front-back articulations against the timing of lowering and raising the tongue" (p. 61).

Vihman and Miller (1988) attempted to capture the range of vocal phenomena characteristic of the transition period in a series of vignettes drawn from a longitudinal study of ten children (recorded weekly from about 9–16 months). Viewing words and babble as "different expressions of a single [phonetic] system" (p. 152), these authors see both word forms and communicative functions as continuous with the prespeech period. The phenomena illustrated are ranged along two continua. Examples of the development in awareness of sound patterns include imitative and other (associative) responses to language, with no evidence of comprehension, as well as the production of word forms embedded in jargon. Development in pragmatics and reference includes a number of unstable, less-than-adult-like early sound–meaning pairings, with use of word forms both in and out of context and dummy words or forms lacking an adult model used as placeholders in an interactional setting.

Vihman and Miller also describe the use of both protowords and adult-based word forms (emptied of their adult meaning) to serve early expressive and communicative functions. These meanings are both global, or relatively undifferentiated, and essentially subjective, reflecting the lack of distance between child, expressive vehicle and expressed content (see Appendix A). It is not surprising, then, that "child-originated communicative forms are difficult for adults to recognize, given our preconceived, largely language-based notion of meaning" (Vihman and Miller, 1988, p. 167).[11]

First word use

It is evident from our account of protowords that several types of recurrent vocalizations may be identified in the period of transition into speech. We consider as "first words" only those which demonstrate both a phonetic shape and conditions of use which may be related to a specific adult word model with some consistency, preferably across several uses or tokens and across different episodes in a recorded session (Vihman and McCune, 1994; see Appendix 6.1 at the end of this chapter). These requirements reflect those of the earlier diarists as well as more recent accounts, such as the exhaustive treatment of the early words of a late talker, Jessie (Labov and Labov, 1978). We will adopt a relatively tolerant interpretation of a potential phonetic "match" (viewing as potentially adult-word-based any child vocalizations "borrowed from the adult language or influenced by its forms": Lewis, 1936, p. 124), while requiring in addition that the child's *use* of the word reflect at least partial awareness or understanding of the adult meaning (in contrast with the word-forms "cut loose from their semantic moorings" which we included in Appendix A). This maximally inclusive approach to word identification avoids overestimating the extent of "invented words" in the transition to speech. It recognizes that early phonetic accommodation, like early expressive and communicative functions, is likely to be relatively global. And it allows us to consider the "ragged beginnings" of word use (Vihman and McCune, 1994).

Our approach to word identification also corresponds to the natural response of caretakers, who often, in discourse, treat as words any child vocal forms which could possibly be intended as such, given the situational context. It is evident that the interpretation of a mother or other primary caretaker may be influential in supporting or even shaping some early word-like productions as the child's use begins to evolve toward language. Like Dore (1983), Veneziano (1981, 1988) focused on this dialogic process:

> Although it is not clear to what extent the caretaker's response to the sound is related
> to actual properties of it, we contend that, at the early stages, both the properties of

the sound and the properties ascribed to it by a familiar conversational partner constitute important and indissociable factors in determining the word-like status of a sound. (1981, p. 545)

Based on longitudinal recording of six Hebrew-speaking dyads, Veneziano found that the balance of child vs. adult accommodation in form varied considerably from one natural interactional exchange to another; mutual accommodation was common (cf. also Vihman et al., 1985, p. 406). It is to be expected that the characteristic response of the primary interlocutor will vary across dyads within a particular culture as well as across cultures (cf., e.g., Schieffelin, 1973; Heath, 1983).

Although the work of psychologists like Bates and her colleagues provides the broadest data base for the study of the first lexicon (Volterra et al., 1979, codify the first words of twenty-five children learning Italian or English, from 9 to 13 months), studies by phoneticians and phonologists (e.g., Labov and Labov, 1978) have paid closer attention to the problem of characterizing early word *forms* as they begin to crystallize out of the pool of infant vocalizations. Such words are typically simple in phonetic structure and represent attempts at comparably simple adult targets (Ferguson and Farwell, 1975; some examples, from Vihman's (1976) diary study of her daughter Virve's acquisition of Estonian: [aita] ~ [aida] *aitäh* 'thank you'; [pai] *pai* 'pat [the kitty]'; [te] *tere* 'hello'; cf. also [se] *see* 'this,' cited above).

With regard to *meaning*, Menyuk and Menn (1979) offer a succinct description of the "context-bound" or "context-limited" character of such early words:

> The first word-like objects . . . are tightly bound to specific functions . . . They are, at this early stage, essentially vocal signals, and may be compared to adult words which have very limited pragmatic range, like greetings and cries of *ouch*. The meanings of such items, for both adult and child, are best characterized as "what you say when you do X." (p. 62)

Similarly, Dore (1983) has insisted that the "widely overgeneralized word uses" on which debate about early semantic development focused in the 1970s (Clark, 1973; Nelson, 1973b; Bowerman, 1978) should be considered to be not words but precursors to words, or "indexicals": "They lack the semantically discrete, contrastive, displaced, referential features of genuine words . . . " (p. 174). Such early words reflect an "intent-to-act" rather than an "intention-to-convey," which

> presupposes the development of recognizable words whose intensional meaning features partly overlap the adult's. Their forms are phonemically stable and largely conventional; their use is displaced in time and space, detached from the immediate context and well established in memory; the choice of one over another routinely exhibits a semantic contrast among a limited set of items (p. 175)

Such adult-like word use is fully developed only by the end of the transitional period. Within that period, however, the shift to referential word use, rooted in a nascent "intention-to-convey," may be clearly identified; it is dependent on advances in representational capacity and is foreshadowed by such developments as the use of communicative grunts (McCune et al., in submission), pretend play (Bates et al., 1979; McCune-Nicolich, 1981b; McCune 1995), and "dual directional signaling" (Masur, 1983).

Referential word use

The onset of truly general or symbolic use of language is the second of what Bates (1979) identified as "two moments in the dawn of language" (p. 33) – the first developmental "moment" being the onset of communicative intentions and conventional signaling, which we have already discussed. Symbolic usage involves the completion of a two-stage shift in function from the natural use of gestures and vocal forms within the action context of a familiar routine, first to (transitional) semi-autonomous, iconic use, then to fully autonomous (or symbolic) referential use. Protowords, with their simple "whole form" relationship between vocal sign and expressed content, are possible with only limited progress in "distancing" between vehicle and referent: their expressive form is highly personal (reflecting closeness of speaker and vehicle) and their meanings are equally personal or subjective (reflecting closeness of speaker and referent). Some of the gestural forms we reviewed (*bravo*; *bye-bye*) constitute a stable, semi-autonomous expression of meaning, emerging from action contexts to refer to those limited contexts but developing relative freedom of function as they come to serve as a request for an activity, for example. Context-bound words, similarly, do not *represent* the activity to which they refer but are *part* of the activity (e.g., from Italian subjects [Bates et al., 1975]: *bam* 'boom,' used while knocking down a tower; *da* 'give' and *tieni* 'here you are,' used in the course of an exchange routine, like Estonian *aitäh* 'thank you'). Social games of naming animal sounds or uttering *peek-a-boo* at the critical moment provide the framework for equivalent purely verbal routines.

When a "performative" word such as *bam* comes to be used to announce an intention to act, prior to the act itself, we have the beginnings of symbolic function: "Such behavior is truly symbolic activity, wherein the vehicle is differentiated from its referent though simultaneously standing for, suggesting, or evoking its referents" (Bates, 1979, p. 40). Bates (1979) proposes a working developmental definition of "symbol":

> The comprehension or use, inside or outside communicative situations, of a relationship between a sign and its referent, such that the sign is treated as belonging to and/or substitutable for its referent in a variety of contexts; at the same time the user is aware that the sign is separable from its referent, that is, not the same thing. (p. 43)

According to both Piaget (1951) and Werner and Kaplan (1984), an advance in representational ability is a prerequisite for the capacity to make full, autonomous use of symbols. McCune-Nicolich (1981b) proposed a set of specific correspondences between levels of symbolic play behavior and language production, on the assumption that both play and language reflect the child's emerging ability to manipulate symbols. She suggested that "decentered play" – in which the child shows an appreciation of the general meanings of play actions and their separation from the self by applying such schemes to dolls or by "borrowing" the actions of others themselves (pretend telephone) – should correspond to a more differentiated use of language as well. McCune (1995) provides documentation of this correspondence, based on a large cross-sectional study (cf. also McCune, 1992).

The shift from context-bound to general or referential use of words is most clearly observable in the case of nominal and relational terms. When words for objects or animal sounds come to be used in a more general way, in a variety of contexts as required by Bates's definition, we see the emergence of flexible nominals. With regard to the presumed advance in mental representation, the application of a word form to different and particularly to novel exemplars reveals a capacity for making implicit comparisons: A rose is a rose is a rose. Such comparison would permit a new understanding of the naming function: Individual instances of word forms (tokens) refer to categories or classes of word meaning (types).

A moment of "nominal insight" is sometimes apparent to the observer. Vihman (1976) cites such an episode from the diary record of her daughter's development (aged 14 months):

> Seeing a picture of a monkey in a book, V shyly attempted to imitate the word *ahv* 'monkey,' which I then repeated several times. Suddenly, she ran off to get a monkey-puppet she had left on a bed some time earlier. She brought it to me, very excited, and insisted on my returning repeatedly to the page with the monkey picture. Finally she placed the puppet right on the page next to the picture. (p. 232; cf. also Kamhi, 1986)

The episode occurred after weeks of intense interest in hearing the names of things (pointing to objects one after another, poring over pictures in books, and using the deictic form *see* 'this,' with rising pitch, while turning to adults). The first generalization of a nominal term followed a week later: The child spontaneously produced the word [abe] *habe* 'beard' (imitated shortly before the monkey episode as she looked at a bearded man in a picture and then turned to her (bearded) father) on seeing a bearded playing-card king. For three or four weeks thereafter the child displayed her new understanding of the type–token relationship by collecting instances of words bearing the same name (cf. also Velten, 1943). As is often the case with children who have developed the requisite phonetic resources through babbling by the time of this symbolic advance, a rapid increase in vocabulary ensued (though the "lexical spurt" is individually variable: cf. Robb, Bauer, and Tyler, 1994, as well as table 6.1).

The first use of relational words (termed "functional" in L. Bloom, 1973), reflecting child attention to reversible perceptual events, depends upon the same emergent capacity to mentally represent a state of affairs not fully present to the speaker (McCune-Nicolich, 1981a; e.g., *allgone* and *more* express a relationship between the present vs. the past or potential future availability of some desirable item or event; *up* and *down* are typically first used as requests to relate the child's current position to a desired state; *bye-bye* may be used to describe or predict the relationship between present and absent while observing a jack-in-the-box in action). In the case of Virve Vihman, the first recorded relational word was *kinni* 'closed,' used on the day of the monkey episode while closing a wallet, then (four days later) while closing the door of the clothes drier – uses which displayed an understanding of a reversible state in two quite different contexts.

Vihman and McCune (1994) divided the word types identified in monthly samples from two longitudinal studies (at Stanford and Rutgers Universities) involving ten subjects each, aged 9 to 16 months, into three categories: flexible nominals and relationals ("flexible"), context-bound words ("other spontaneous"), and imitations (see figure 6.1). The number of words produced in the two samples begins to diverge by 12 months, with a far greater number of context-bound words as well as imitations in the Stanford sample. "Flexible" words, on the other hand, are scarce until 14 months, when there is a sudden increase in both samples. Vihman and McCune interpret the difference between the samples as reflecting a "training effect" in the Stanford study, in which weekly visits and conversations with mothers about the children's language led to an increase in prereferential routine-based language as well as imitations, but did not affect the timing or extent of the move to symbolic language use (total spontaneous flexible word production by 16 months was 104 types at Stanford, 111 at Rutgers).

Phonetic and phonological development in the transition period

In the previous chapter we traced the emergence of canonical and variegated babbling, which involve the production of adult-like syllables including a "true consonant" (that is, a consonant other than a glottal or a glide). These syllables provide the primary basis for word production, although first words may lack a true consonant (see Appendix B: *hi* and *uh-oh* occur among the first five or six English words of several children; early words in other languages include French *ouah-ouah* 'bow-wow,' Estonian *ei* 'no,' German *Wewe* 'weewee,' Japanese *hai* 'here,' *iyu* 'no,' and *wanwan* 'doggie'[12] and Swedish *oj* 'oh'; altogether, 16 percent of the words cited in Appendix B were produced in at least some variants without a true consonant).[13]

An increase in the use of true consonants is the single most striking phonetic trend in this period; it has been noted in many studies (e.g., Vihman et al., 1985; Holmgren et al., 1986; Koopmans-van Beinum and van der Stelt, 1986; Bauer, 1988; Roug et al., 1989). Incidence of consonants in prelinguistic vocalizations is the basis for most of the predictors found to be of some value in relating early phonetic progress to later verbal development (Stoel-Gammon, 1992). Let us consider some relevant data.

For five subjects who produced twenty-five or more different word types in a half-hour recorded session at 14–17 months, the proportion of true consonants rose from 43% in a prelinguistic ("0-word") session to 71% at the last session ("25-word point": Vihman et al., 1986). The trend is not linear for all of the children,

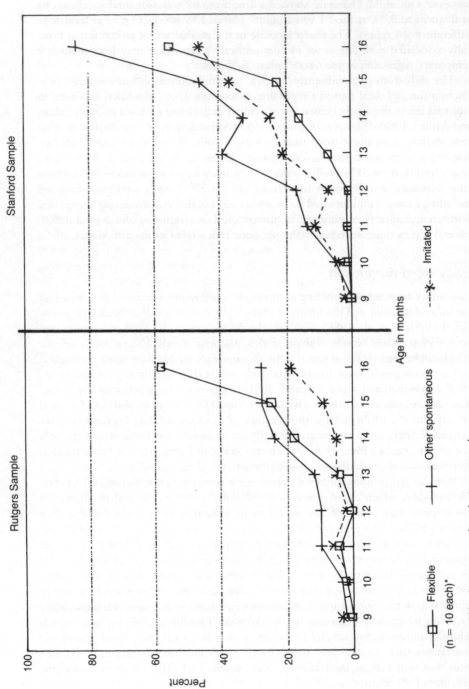

Figure 6.1 Word use over time in two samples.
Source: Vihman and McCune, 1994. Reprinted with the permission of Cambridge University Press.

however. One child, Deborah, showed a drop from 68% consonantal vocalizations at 0 words to 33% at the "4-word point" (defined by production of at least four different word types). The sharp increase in the production of glottal forms typically associated with the onset of communicative grunt use may lead to such a temporary regression in the overall phonetic trend.

The shift from predominantly "vocalic" to predominantly "consonantal" production (i.e., to vocal patterns including at least one true consonant) was seen in word tokens in one study before it was evident in babbling (4-word point: Vihman and Miller, 1988). The *overall* proportion of vocalizations with a consonant rose only slightly from the 4-word to the 15-word point in this study (based on two sessions at each point from seven subjects, age range 10–13 and 12–15 months, respectively), from 51% to 59%, since the proportion of *word* tokens including a true consonant actually decreased (from 73% to 57%) while *babble* productions including a consonant increased (from 46% to 66%). Before considering the critical qualitative change from phonetic to phonological or systematic sound production, we will review more specifically the phonetic characteristics of early words.

Early word production

Continuity between the babbling patterns or "vocal motor schemes" developed by the individual child and the forms of that child's early words has been well established (Vihman et al., 1985, 1986; see the discussion in ch. 2). Word production nevertheless entails certain changes or new phonetic trends: For example, labials, which can be seen as well as heard, provide a more secure basis for word production and are accordingly more frequent in early words than in babble (Vihman et al., 1985; Boysson-Bardies and Vihman, 1991); fricatives, whose intentional production requires relatively precise articulatory control, are considerably less frequent in early words, while stops – the product of a simple ballistic movement – are correspondingly more common. Similarly, most early word productions are only one or two syllables in length, while the incidence of longer babbling vocalizations increases over the transition period (Vihman and Miller, 1988).

With regard to phonotactic structure early words are closely matched to their adult models, which are also mono- or disyllabic and typically include at most a single consonant type, at least in the more salient syllable onset position (see Appendix B: disregarding consonant clusters, 36 percent of the early word targets include more than one consonant but only 15 percent include different consonant types in syllable onset position).[14] The children's early word productions are relatively accurate segmentally as well. For example, only about one out of five show consonant substitutions (e.g., [d] for /ð/), although omission of word-final consonants and of fricative or liquid members of clusters is common. Phonologically based preselection is suggested by the fact that the adult models for early words tend to conform to typical child production patterns, with more labial and dental consonants than velars, more stops, nasals and glides than fricatives or liquids, more low and central than high or back vowels and little variation across the syllables of the word.

The apparent "accuracy" of the early words can be taken to reflect the disproportionate influence or salience of those adult words whose phonetic pattern falls within the range of the child's babbling repertoire. That is, the child may be seen as experiencing the flow of adult speech through an "articulatory filter" which selectively enhances motoric recall of phonetically accessible words. We can assume that a subset of words have already become familiar to the child by virtue of frequent occurrence, with child-appropriate prosodic modulation, in interesting situations (Vihman, 1993a; Vihman et al., 1994). The earliest recognizable word productions would then be a product of the child's experience of a match, in familiar situational context, between a commonly produced adult form and his or her own babble forms ("vocal motor schemes"); eventually, the combined effect of these associated phonetic and situational experiences will be child production of a "context-limited" but recognizably appropriate phonetic form or "early word." Figure 6.2 illustrates the proposed development of the production filter on perception of phonetic patterns, a filter which is taken to be the product of the ongoing strengthening – due to the combined effects of proprioceptive and auditory feedback – of emergent child vocal patterns in rough accord with the sound patterns of the ambient language (Vihman and Boysson-Bardies, 1994; Vihman et al., 1994).

Emergence of phonological systematicity

Three characteristics of the early words which Ferguson and Farwell (1975) observed surprised them: Their relative accuracy at first, followed by later "reduction" or regression; the phonological selectivity evidenced by early word targets; and the extent of variability. All of these characteristics were also found in the Labovs' comprehensive case study of their daughter Jessie (1978);[15] in addition, Jessie's five-month period of early word production was notable for the ebb and flow in frequency of use of the two dominant words ("cat and mama") as well as a series of "minor" words, and for the apparent wholesale phonological reorganization which followed (hinted at but not further characterized in the 1978 account). "J . . . acquired a competence in phonological contrast, canonical forms, and consonantal articulation and . . . fully outlined the shape of the vowel space she would use later on . . . " (p. 850), but her learning in this period was less a matter of substance than of "gearing up" for word production. Like Ferguson and Farwell and in contrast with Jakobson (1941/68), Labov and Labov conclude that "the separation of phonetics and phonology must be de-emphasized . . . J's . . . selection of phonetic realizations was the product of her perception of the fit with adult forms, the canonical shape of her syllable, and some fortunate matches between articulation and meaning" (p. 849) – as well as parental perception and recognition of these forms.

More recent studies of early word forms and their relation to the vocal resources developed in babbling support this account. Beyond the earliest words we find the new developments described by these authors, specifically, an increase in variability and the loss of phonetic accuracy (regression). These characteristics have been directly implicated in the process of phonological reorganization found to follow first word use (Vihman and Velleman, 1989). Is this change related to the increase

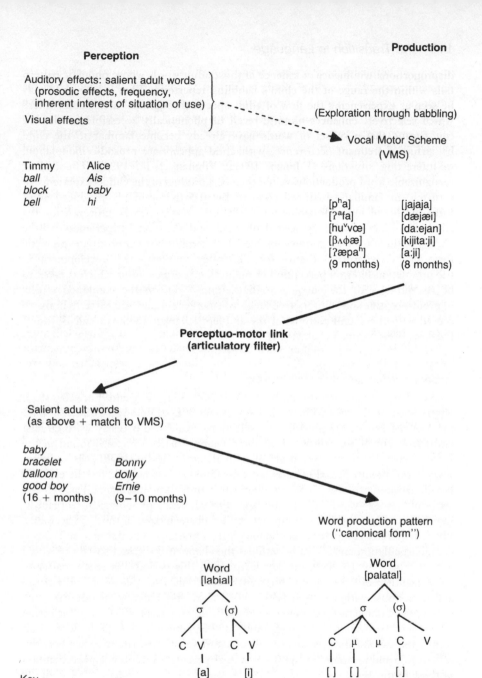

Fig. 6.2 Model of the interaction of perception and production.
Source: Vihman et al., 1994. In Yavas (ed.), *First and Second Language Phonology*.
Reprinted with the permission of Singular Publishing Group.

in representational capacity which underlies the shift to symbol use? Can the phonetic roots of the earliest words be viewed as qualitatively distinct from the phonology of later *referential* word use (in the sense defined above)? To suggest a cognitively based discontinuity of this kind *within* the period of the first words – a shift from phonetic to phonological organization – may go against the spirit of the passage cited above, yet to the extent that empirical data are available on this point such an interpretation seems plausible (Vihman et al., 1994).

The lack of inter-word organization which Jusczyk (1986b) posited for the earliest word recognition network appears to correspond to a similar lack of inter-word connections between the first word types produced (see Waterson, 1978, and Appendix B). These early unrelated vocal forms (termed "item-based phonology" in Waterson, 1971, 1978; "phonetic" matching of adult form against available child patterns in Vihman et al., 1994), develop into a first idiosyncratic holistic system (the "word-based phonology" of Ferguson and Farwell, 1975) through a highly individual process of integration of perceived adult models and accessible child forms. Based on Vihman and Velleman's (1989) account of the development of one highly verbal child (Molly), as well as a later study which briefly reviewed the early phonological development of several children (Vihman and Roug-Hellichius, 1991), the first word productions can be seen as reflecting the first, presystematic phase in a three-part process of emergent phonological systematization (see Appendix 6.2 at the end of this chapter).

The distinction made in Appendix 6.2 between "crystallization" and "controlled expansion" should not be regarded as absolute. In the case of crystallization, one or more fairly clear-cut patterns appear to come more and more sharply into focus over the three data-points presented, leaving an ever-smaller residue of "other" patterns. In the case of controlled expansion the line of progress is one of increasing diversity of relatively simple patterns rather than a single more complex pattern encompassing a variety of adult word types. Of the profiles presented in Appendix C, that of Laurent is most appropriately viewed as "mixed," showing an emergent pattern based on medial [l] alongside a reduplicated disyllabic pattern much like that of Charles.

The longitudinal profiles of Molly (Vihman and Velleman, 1989) and of Alice and Timmy (Vihman et al., 1994) suggest that further movement from a whole-word to a segment-based system involves repeated cycles of pattern matching, analysis, and reorganization along the lines of the last two phases outlined. (For Alice, see the emergent [æ]-pattern in monosyllabic production – Appendix C, 15-word point (b) and 25-word point; for Timmy, see table 6.2–15 months vs. 16 months as well as Appendix C). The timing of cycles of analysis and reanalysis is no doubt as variable as the onset of word combination and progress toward an adult-like syntactic system. It may be expected to take at least two to three years for completion in the normally developing child (that is, to age 3 or 4).

With regard to the relationship between emergent phonological organization and advances in the capacity for mental representation, Vihman et al. (1994) proposed the following: Pre-symbolic, context-limited word production may be likened to the "perceptually dependent memories" demonstrated by Rovee-Collier and her colleagues in an ongoing series of studies of infants aged 8 weeks to 6

Table 6.2 Inventory of a child's syllables (Timmy)

Age (in months)	Consonant at syllable onset									
	\<b\>	*\<t\>*	*\<k\>*	*\<β\>*	*\<s\>*	*\<ɟ\>*	*\<m\>*	*\<n\>*	*\<j\>*	*\<w\>*
9	ba									
10	ba									
11	ba		ka							
12	ba		ka							
13	ba		ka							
14	ba		ka						ja	
15[a]	ba		ka	βa		ɟa		na	ja	
15[b]	ba		ka	βa		ɟa	ma	na	ja	
16[a]	ba	ta	ka	βa	sa	ɟa	ma	na	ja	
		ti	ki							
16[b]	ba	ta	ka	βa	sa	ɟa	ma	na	ja	(wa)
	bi	ti	ki				mi	ni		
	bu	tu	ku		(dʒu)		mu			

a Earlier in month
b Later in month
Source: Vihman et al., 1994. In Yavas (ed.), *First and Second Language Phonology*. Reprinted with the permission of Singular Publishing Group.

months (e.g., Rovee-Collier et al., 1980). In these studies a trained motor response (a foot kick to activate a mobile attached by a ribbon) is re-instantiated, after a period of days or weeks, by a specific situational context. In the case of early word production, "a specific familiar event evokes an intentional state and associated vocalizations (Bloom, 1991). There is minimal differentiation among such components as speaker, hearer, physical context, and vocal motor action (Werner and Kaplan, 1963)" (Vihman et al., 1994, p. 17).

In contrast, the capacity for mental representation – "a contentful mental state distinguished from perception by its capacity to reference absent and past realities" (p. 15) – which underlies symbolic or referential use of language, as described above,

allows the elements of the speech situation to be differentiated, yet integrated. An unfamiliar event might now evoke the word associated with a related event. A given event might be referenced by one of several words. The child experiences an increasing range of potential representational meanings, whereas vocal motor skill may remain limited. Vocal expression thus comes to rely on the word production patterns [or "canonical forms"] which now evolve, made possible by the increased capacity for separating word form from situation of use and for the internal experience of relationships between linguistic elements, which facilitates the juxtaposition of one or more vocal motor schemes and a range of phonetically related adult words . . . Furthermore, once the child's vocal forms are no longer embedded in a particular situation of use, they can be compared or "superposed" (as in connectionist models . . .) as a basis for the development of a generalized word production pattern . . . At this point, something more abstract than a vocal motor scheme operating in combination with perceptual attention to particular auditory patterns has materialized. This is a phonological mental representation which may become instantiated when reference to the corresponding object or event is contemplated. (p. 17)

Influence from the ambient language

In the last chapter we reviewed evidence of ambient language influence in the pre-linguistic period. Early "positive" global influence was reflected in the effect of adult prosodic patterns on child prosody, in the effect of adaptation to adult facial postures on language-specific use of vowel space and in the combined auditory and visual effects of adult incidence of labial consonants on babbling production at 9 or 10 months. In addition, we cited apparent *loss* of use of an accessible phonetic gesture (the laryngeal positioning which yields [h]) in the absence of auditory support from an adult model. To these we may add the dramatic drop in final consonant use (from 41% at the 0-word point to 1% at the 25-word point: Vihman, 1993c) in the vocal production (both words and babble) of one child exposed to a language which makes relatively low use of final consonants (French, as compared with English and Swedish: the comparative figures for final consonants in the content words of mothers speaking each of these languages are French, 25% vs. English, 67%, Swedish, 51%: Vihman, Kay et al., 1994).

It is to be expected that the influence of the adult language will increase as the child advances in language use, acquiring a larger lexicon and thus developing a broader-based phonological system. Vihman et al. (1986) reported a drop in within-group variation over the transition period, especially in those phonetic parameters which the children control comparatively early (labials, dentals; stops, nasals). This trend was generally replicated in the findings of Boysson-Bardies and Vihman (1991) for three additional languages (French, Japanese and Swedish); Vihman (1993c) reported a drop in variability over this period for monosyllables as well, especially for French and Japanese. It is striking that these signs of within-group accommodation to the ambient language appear only within motorically accessible phonetic categories – that is, those phonetic categories which already begin to be mastered in the prelinguistic period.

Phonetic categories not available to most infants in the prespeech period ("minor categories": Vihman and Boysson-Bardies, 1994) include velars, fricatives and liquids, longer vocalizations and final consonants. Preliminary efforts to trace the "emergence" of these categories (defined as 20 percent or greater use by one or more children out of five sampled) in the production of children learning different languages within the transition period suggest that it depends on the extent to which the ambient language affords "sufficient exposure" to the category in question. "Sufficient exposure" is taken to mean a level of incidence which exceeds a "chance" distribution, based on the logic of the phonetic oppositions available to the children. For the category final consonants, for example, greater than 50 percent adult language incidence would exceed chance, since the opposition is open vs. closed (word-final) syllable; for a place category in English, French, Japanese or

Swedish, the relevant adult language incidence is over one-third, since three categories are opposed: labial, dental and velar. And for manner, the adult language incidence required would be over 25 percent (based on the opposition of four categories of consonants with supraglottal closure: stop, fricative/affricate, nasal and liquid). Emergent use of final consonants (Molly), liquids (Laurent) and fricatives (Charles) is illustrated in Appendix C. In each case, the child has incorporated a relatively prominent adult "minor category" into an early phase of phonological organization, resulting in a *specific* ambient language effect – that is, an effect sensitive to the adult-language incidence of specific phonetic categories.

Summary: Continuity and change

We reviewed development in a number of important language-related behaviors over the course of the transition period: comprehension of language, intentional communication with gesture and protowords and first word production. We saw these developments as continuous with earlier "precursor" behaviors. Language comprehension, for example, is rooted in child attention to aspects of familiar situations associated with specific prosodic and phonetic patterns, the whole bathed in affective meaning. Similarly, the origins of intentional communication go back to the first days of life, when the roots of "intersubjectivity" are laid in the child–caretaker relationship.

Intentional communication itself is typically first expressed in deictic gestures and in "protowords," relatively stable vocal forms which express a more or less consistent but global or child-derived (personal) meaning. The primitive grunt form, in particular, has been found to mark attentional focus before it is extended to communicative use; an increase in the frequency of communicative grunts appears to mark child recognition of the potential for intentional vocal expression of meaning. Early words are used contemporaneously with meaningful gestures and protowords, including grunts.

An important qualitative change is implicit in the shift to symbolic or representational behaviors, as evidenced in pretend play and the symbolic use of gestures as well as in the first generalized or referential use of language, which comes to be based on categories of meaning rather than on individual instances or action schemata. The emergence of early phonological organization, expressed in the first systematic relations between the adult words targeted or child word forms, or both, may be seen as a further consequence of the advance in mental representation: Internal comparison of newly autonomous word forms leads to the capacity for phonological system-building, based on the development of canonical forms or the application of rule-like constraints on phonological structure.

NOTES

1 Reich (1976) documents the gradual emergence, within the framework of a "game called *Where?*", of his 8-month-old son's understanding of the adult-like extension of

the word *shoe* from its first context-bound, underextended use to mean "the shoes in mommy's open closet"; Griffiths (1986) provides a useful discussion of the emergence of early word meaning in both comprehension and production.

2   The results were partially replicated in a follow-up study, at 15–17 months, of six infants who had participated at the youngest age.

3   A recent experimental fast-mapping study tested the hypothesis that something like an articulatory filter selectively enhances words resembling the child's own production patterns while leaving unenhanced words which fall outside the scope of those patterns (Kay-Raining Bird and Chapman, in submission). The results supported the hypothesis at the youngest age tested (13 months).

4   A current metaphor for this position is that, based on infants' ability to produce communicative behavior "designed to attract and direct the addressee's attention to topics of mutual interest" (Bretherton, 1988: p. 230), "infants have an [implicit] theory of mind or the ability to impute mental states to self and other" (p. 230) – although an "explicit, verbally expressible" theory of mind is thought to develop only by about age 3 (Bretherton, McNew, and Beeghly-Smith, 1981, p. 358; cf. Wellman, 1990).

5   Scoville (1984) expresses a principled doubt as to whether any truly objective basis for imputing intent to the child's preverbal communicative efforts is possible.

6   Both Caselli, and Acredolo and Goodwyn restrict their studies to gestures used communicatively, to name, request, etc., in contrast with the somewhat broader discussion of "recognitory" gestures in Bates et al., 1983 (cf. also the "enactive names" of Escalona, 1973).

7   Contrast Werner and Kaplan's use of the term "vocable," to mean a word-like child form in the period before word combination and the beginning of syntax. A vocable, functionally a "name" in the early period, "becomes a word only insofar as it fulfills a grammatical and syntactic function in an utterance" (Werner and Kaplan, 1984, p. 138).

8   Leopold (1939) included in the list of his daughter Hildegard's first vocabulary "sound-combinations with no standard equivalent . . . which developed a definite meaning" (p. 150), or in our terms, protowords; the first such item, which persisted from 0;8 to 1;6, was a grunt, [ʔəʔ], a "demonstrative interjection without model," produced with high pitch and later accompanied by pointing (p. 81f.).

9   Werner and Kaplan's balanced crediting of cognitive and social factors anticipates such criticisms as that of Halliday (1979): "Recently dominant theories among linguists and psychologists, the so-called 'nativist' and 'environmentalist' approaches . . . appear now . . . as variants on a single theme, that of the child as an island, an individual existent who has to 'acquire' some ready-made object 'out there' that we call language" (p. 181).

10   Cf. also Menn and Matthei, 1992, where the consequences of such variability for phonological theory are explored more fully.

11   See Blake and Fink (1987), who attempt to derive such forms impartially, by statistical analysis of the co-occurrence of independently coded recurrent phonetic shapes and child actions as contexts.

12   Final /n/ in Japanese is frequently realized as nasalization on the preceding vowel.

13   Ninio (1993) provides some examples of first words in Hebrew, drawn from the records of sixteen children aged 9 to 13 months, although she does not specify the phonetic shape of the child productions. Of the twenty-seven different words she cites, five – all onomatopoeic or otherwise unconventional words which she does not gloss – lack a true consonant. Of the remaining twenty-two words, seven are CV monosyllables, five are (h)VCV disyllables, and four are CVCV disyllables with a repeated C (or a change in

voicing only). Only three words have a final consonant; two additional words include a change in place of articulation across the onset consonants of successive syllables (*Michaela, kaftor* 'button').

14   Of the 139 child words cited in Appendix B only three are produced with a consonant cluster, five with a second consonant type in syllable-final position, and six with two different syllable-onset consonants.

15   The study by Labov and Labov must surely be the most detailed analysis ever afforded of a child's start on word production. It includes acoustic as well as phonetic analysis and careful description of the child's meaning-bearing gestures, both vocal and other. Based on a virtually *complete* account of everything Jessie said over the five-month period of her first word use, it effectively traces numerous paths of advance and retreat in the process of phonetic, phonological and lexical learning – all within the framework of the "grammar" of two words, *cat* and *mama*.

APPENDIX 6.1 WORD IDENTIFICATION CRITERIA

I   *Criteria based on context*
1   Determinative context: Does at least one use occur in a context which strongly suggests that word and no other?

Applies only to words with specific meanings easily identifiable in context, including most concrete nouns and many relational words. Does not apply to an imitative response to a purely verbal stimulus.

2   Maternal identification: Does the mother identify at least one instance of the form as a token of the hypothesized word?

Identification need not be explicitly intended as such; it could involve the mother acknowledging a particular word by continuing the conversation or by rejecting the child's word choice as an error.

3   Multiple use: Does the child use the word more than once?
4   Multiple episodes: Is there more than one episode of use?

Multiple uses are identified only in determinative contexts, and with similar phonological shapes across different uses.

II   *Criteria based on vocalization shape*
5   Complex match: Does the child form match more than two segments of the adult form?

Credited if three segments match, or two non-nasal segments plus nasality match a model which includes a nasal, or vowel length or an off-glide match the complex nucleus of the model, in addition to the basic two-segment match. Also applies if a second consonant matches in manner of articulation but not in place, or vice versa.

6   Exact match: Is there at least one instance that even an untrained ear would recognize as an instance of the word?

Credited if the child form neither clearly omits, adds, nor substitutes segments in relation to the model (again disregarding voicing). Reflects the probable judgment of a non-specialist that a particular word is intended.

7   Prosodic match:
(a)   to model: Is there a tuneful match with the adult target?
(b)   across tokens: Is there a characteristic tune which fits the word-meaning and which occurs across all suspected tokens?

Credited when the child uses a special vocal effect (growl, squeak) repeatedly, in pragmatically plausible contexts, for the same probable word (*lion*, *mouse*).

III   *Relation to other vocalizations*
8   Imitated tokens: Is at least one instance imitated?

Credited if imitation is produced with apparent understanding.

9   Invariant: Do all instances of the word exhibit the same phonological shape?

Phonetic identity ("invariance") evaluated by the principles applied for phonetic match in general and for "exact" in particular.

10   No inappropriate uses: Do all uses occur in contexts which plausibly suggest the same word?

Scored if candidate form is not used in conflicting contexts (no homonymy) or outside of any plausible context (no "favorite sound pattern" uses).

Each word candidate is rated for the presence or absence of each type of evidence, yielding a word status profile which provides a framework for the process of evaluation, discussion, and re-evaluation. Since a variety of irrelevant factors may influence (and even bias) the initial screening – such as the observer's familiarity with the child, the child's volubility and apparent intelligibility, or maternal evaluation and level of interaction with the observer – the word status profile and decision-making based on it maximize comparability in word identification across subjects.

Source: Vihman and McCune, 1994; reprinted with the permission of Cambridge University Press

APPENDIX 6.2 PHASES IN THE EMERGENCE OF A PHONOLOGICAL SYSTEM

I *Presystematic*: No single word production pattern is apparent; few inter-word relationships are revealed either in the child's forms or in the words attempted (see 4-word point in Appendix C).

II *First signs of organization*: Systematicity first begins to be apparent in the shapes of the adult words attempted or in the child's own word forms, or in both (see 15-word point in Appendix C). The focus of incipient patterning has been observed to include:

- words with fricatives (Charles, Deborah) or liquids (Laurent, Sean);
- words with final consonants (Molly, Sean);
- words with reduplicated stops (Timmy; J in Macken, 1978);
- other within-word consonant sequences, such as labial–dental (Si in Macken, 1979);
- nuclei involving palatal offglides and/or final /i/ (Alice).

The first manifestations of incipient patterning fall into two distinguishable types (see Appendix C for illustrative phonological profiles; children named below without further reference are represented in that Appendix)

A   Crystallization (the less common type: see Alice, Molly).

- Selective targeting of adult forms with particular phonetic characteristics.
- Increase in variability in the production of certain word shapes, suggesting "experimentation" or "work" on particular phonetic "problems" posed by a type of adult model.

B   Controlled expansion (see Charles, Deborah, Timmy and to some extent Laurent).

- Gradual relaxation of production constraints.
- Expansion in the range of adult targets attempted, resulting in an increase in the inventory of sounds and phonotactic shapes produced.

III *Emergence of system*: One or more of the child's word shapes assume the status of "canonical forms" or production templates (especially noticeable in the case of "crystallization"). These forms begin to dominate production; adult models are restructured to fit the template. At the same time, systematic treatment of problematic aspects of adult forms may result in the first regular adult-model–child-form relationships, expressible as "phonological rules" or "processes."

7 Linguistic Perception and Word Recognition

As a first step in considering what is known of the course of phonological development beyond its origins in infancy we will review here studies of linguistic perception, or the discrimination and identification of distinct meaningful patterns. We
will begin by returning again to the question posed by phonological theories of the
seventies (reviewed in ch. 2): How accurate are the underlying representations of
words as children begin to acquire a rapidly growing receptive lexicon while still
limited by a relatively restricted expressive phonological system? Next, we will turn
to studies of the understanding of running speech, a relatively new research area
which has just begun to receive attention from a developmental perspective. To
complete this picture we will take up some recent proposals regarding the role of
vocabulary growth in word recognition and its relationship to the emergence of the
segment as an "implicit perceptual unit." Finally, we will provide a brief overview
of the extensive literature on the relationship of phonological development to early
reading skills.

It is important to stress the fact that the term "linguistic perception" refers not
only to auditory discrimination, or the sensory perception of contrasts between
different sound patterns, but also to the storing and accessing for recognition of the
particular sound patterns that constitute word forms and phrases in the language
being acquired. Previously, we dealt with the child's discriminatory capacities and
growing auditory attunement to the ambient language. Here we are concerned with
the child's ability to marshall those capacities appropriately as part of a range of far
more complex tasks, which can be subsumed under two distinct processes: (1)
attending to and retaining specific sound patterns in association with specific
meanings (situations of use), in order to begin to construct a repertoire of familiar
words; (2) accessing the relevant meaning upon identifying a particular sound
pattern in the speech stream, or recognizing the word in the course of on-line
language comprehension. In short, instead of testing the child's capacity to register
a passive response to a change in auditory stimulus, as in studies of infant speech

perception, we are now interested in probing the child's internal representation of sound patterns and his or her capacity to make active use of those representations when listening to language.

Research with very young children

Given the very extensive literature on infant perception of speech (reviewed in chs 3 and 4), the relative lack of information regarding early word recognition is striking. With one notable exception, investigators have been frustrated in their attempts to ascertain the limits of linguistic perception in the period of emergence of the first word production, typically, the second year of life. The exception, a classic study by a Russian linguist (Shvachkin, 1973, originally published in Russian in 1948), was designed to determine an order of acquisition for the distinctive features used in minimal contrasts (recall the contemporaneous interest of another Russian linguist, Jakobson, in the order of acquisition of distinctive features in early production).

Shvachkin's procedure involved teaching a group of very young children (nineteen 10–18-month-olds, tested variably over a two- to eight-month period) to associate monosyllabic nonsense words with small objects.[1] All of the words conformed to Russian phonology and all phonemic contrasts were in word-initial position. For each contrast of interest, three object names were taught. Two were minimally contrastive (e.g., /mak/, /bak/) while the third differed in all three segments (/zub/). Once a child could identify the objects by name, he or she was presented with all three and asked to carry out from three to six different tasks involving the objects with minimally contrasting names. Based on these studies with Russian children, Shvachkin proposed a universal sequence of phonemic perception, beginning with the discrimination of different vowels, the presence vs. absence of consonants and the discrimination of sonorants from obstruents, and then proceeding to discrimination among sonorants, continuants and stops. The last discrimination was that of voiced from voiceless obstruents.

Shvachkin emphasized the methodological difficulties in dealing with such young children, whose relation to both words and objects may be different from that of older children and adults. According to his account, the youngest children showed a prereferential "attitude," in which words may have a diffuse or subjective relationship to objects (see the discussion of protowords in ch. 6) or may be narrowly context-bound. "Phonemic perception" could only be tested once the children had begun to form a stable verbal representation for each object. In Shvachkin's words, "The child passes through words to the phonemic perception of speech" (p. 96); once word production is established and "articulation becomes voluntary," we find "*a radical reconstruction of both articulation and speech perception*" (p. 96).

Unfortunately, Shvachkin gave little detail regarding his analysis. He implies that only 100 percent accuracy in the performance of a task was taken as evidence of successful discrimination ("If the child *always* carried out the assignment, one could attest to the presence of a phonemic distinction," p. 101), but he does not tell us how many trials were presented to individual children (in some cases, a "collective experiment" was conducted), how many different contrasts were presented within a postulated phonemic stage, and so on.

Attempts to replicate Shvachkin's method with English-speaking children in a more controlled experimental design have proven frustrating. Garnica (1973) and Edwards (1974) reported a high level of individual differences among their 2- and 3-year-old subjects; not all of the children showed evidence of having mastered the full set of phonemic contrasts tested even at these ages. Barton (1975) criticized the methods and statistical treatment of both Garnica and Edwards and questioned the acquisition orders they reported. In a reanalysis of several studies based on English, Barton (1976) found little relationship between the order Shvachkin had reported for Russian phonemic contrasts and the level of difficulty reflected in the English data. The question of an order of acquisition remains moot (Barton, 1980).

In an effort to test the idea that full perception is achieved very early (Stampe, 1969; N. V. Smith, 1973; Stemberger, 1992), Barton (1976) developed a procedure for use with children under the age of 2 or 3. He began by assessing each child's ability to identify a set of pictures and then training them on any unfamiliar labels. He then presented several pairs of cards, two at a time – each pair representing a minimal contrast – while a recorded voice instructed the child to point to one of the pictures. A wide range of contrasts was tested on children ranging in age from 2;3 to 2;11, including differences in voicing, nasality, and place of articulation, as well as /r/ vs. /l/, /w/ vs. /r/, and /tr/ vs. /ʧ/. Overall discrimination was 80 percent; errors occurred primarily in cases in which one of the pictures had been initially unfamiliar to the child.

In a second study Barton used just two minimal pairs (*pear/bear* and *coat/goat*), focusing on the contrast in voicing, which Shvachkin and Garnica had reported to be a late or difficult discrimination. He began with teaching sessions in which the children played various games with small objects that represented each of the words. After checking familiarity with the object names at least a day later, he tested the children on the minimal contrasts by repeatedly asking them to take different objects out of a bag or to place them back in it. Eight out of ten subjects (aged 1;8 to 2;0) succeeded in making one or both discriminations. Failures of discrimination due to task difficulty could not be clearly differentiated from failures due to difficulty with the linguistic discrimination of interest. Despite the methodological difficulties, Barton (1976) interpreted his data as evidence for Smith's position (1973) that full perception occurs at an early age. He concluded that discrimination was less difficult for 2-year-olds than had been reported in some earlier work.

The significance of the effect of word familiarity on children's discrimination should not be overlooked. If children make more errors in discriminating contrasts in new words, then it may be wrong to assume that they are typically able to draw on accurate internal representations of surface forms when they produce words. Instead, it seems likely that children's internal representations continue to change for some years. When first attempting a word, the child may be operating with an internal representation which is only partially correct. In time, this representation becomes more accurate as the child profits from additional exposure to the adult form. But the child may fail to notice the discrepancy between his or her initial internal representation and the adult surface form and could then persist in the perception-based error for some time.

Examples of such changing internal representations are difficult to obtain in any systematic or experimental way but may be revealed by careful analysis of longitudinal data (cf. Macken, 1980a). Specifically, when a child begins to produce a new adult sound (such as /θ/) for which he or she formerly produced a substitute sound (such as /f/), we can look to see whether, as claimed by Stampe (1969) and Smith (1973), the change occurs "across the board," in all and only the words containing the relevant phoneme. If so, we can assume that the words were correctly represented before they began to be correctly produced. On the other hand, if the child begins to use the new sound (/θ/) in some words that were formerly correctly produced with the substituting sound (*wife*, *frosty* as /waiθ/, /θrasti/), we can conclude that /θ/ words had formerly been mistakenly represented with /f/ and that the child is now faced with the problem of sorting out which are actually /θ/ words and which are /f/ words (Vihman, 1982). This process may take a matter of months or even years.

Attempts to test even younger children in an effort to obtain perception data corresponding to the period of first word production have not so far been successful (an exception is the fast mapping study mentioned in ch. 6, n. 3). Shvachkin's preliminary discussion of his search for a method and the difficulties he encountered are sobering. In addition, current research has largely abandoned the assumption that the distinctive feature of a minimally contrasting pair of segments are functional units in early perceptual acquisition. If the word or the syllable is the earliest contrasting unit of linguistic perception, as has been suggested (e.g., Menyuk et al., 1986; see The role of vocabulary growth, below), then the question "In what order are phonemic contrasts learned?" is no longer relevant.

Instead, one would like to know how global – or how specific – children's early representations of word forms actually are. Is a contrast such as /bagi/ : /gabi/ more difficult to discriminate than /babi/ : /gagi/, for example, since it requires recording the *order* of the two contrasting segments (even though the same two consonants are involved in both contrasting pairs)? Is a contrast in the order of syllables – /bagi/ : /giba/ – less difficult to discriminate than a contrast in the order of consonants only? And does position in the word affect the difficulty of discriminating a contrast, as has been suggested for both English and Russian? Or do languages differ in this respect, perhaps in relation to prosodic characteristics?

Do individual children differ? There are as yet no studies reporting *individual* discriminatory responses in studies of early perception. Tests of production and perception effects in individual children in the transition period would allow us to assess the claim that individual children "screen in" input speech differently, with specific reference to the possible effect of individual production patterns in babbling (cf. the "articulatory filter" hypothesis discussed in ch. 6). Is level of vocabulary attainment a more reliable predictor of relative discriminatory ability than chronological age? And how reliable or how significant is the relationship Shvachkin reported between an individual child's word production patterns and the sound patterns he or she appears to discriminate most easily?

Interaction of perception and production

The potential relationship between perception and production has been probed in children aged two or three, partly in an effort to determine whether inaccurate perception may be the source of at least some speech errors. Eilers and Oller (1976) tested for a relation between ease of perception of a contrast and frequency of production errors involving the contrast. Adapting a technique of Vincent-Smith, Bricker, and Bricker (1974), Eilers and Oller used paired real and nonsense words to test fourteen children aged 1;10–2;2. Familiar objects, such as *fish*, were paired with nonsense toys given minimally contrasting names, such as /θiʃ/. The paired word forms included (1) pairs in which the first element typically substitutes for the second in child production, such as [k] vs. [kʰ], [f] vs. [θ], [w] vs. [r]; (2) pairs of elements which do not typically substitute for one another, such as [pʰ] vs. [tʰ]; and (3) a non-minimal pair, [p] vs. [kʰ]. Eilers and Oller reasoned that if the substitutions were motivated by perceptual confusions, type (1) pairs should be more difficult for children to discriminate than type (2) or (3) pairs.

The hypothesis was partially confirmed. None of the children could discriminate the fricatives [θ] : [f], most (six out of ten) could discriminate the glides, and all could discriminate the non-minimal pair. Unexpectedly, however, the pair which differed in aspiration (VOT) proved easily discriminable (twelve out of fourteen subjects succeeded). Analysis of the children's imitative productions showed that, as expected, the type (1) contrasts were least often maintained in production. On the other hand, some children produced a place contrast for [pʰ] : [tʰ] although they did not demonstrate discrimination on the perception task. Thus, no simple formula could capture the observed relationship between production and perception, although there was evidence that perceptual difficulties played some role in production errors.

Zlatin and Koenigsknecht (1975, 1976) conducted two studies of the development of the voicing contrast in English, the first focused on perception only, the second comparing production and perception for the same subjects. Ten children in each of two age groups, just under 3 and 7 years (mean age, 2.8 and 6.11; the authors refer to these subjects as "two-" and "six-year-olds," respectively), participated in these studies; twenty adult subjects provided comparative data. Four minimal pairs were synthesized for testing in the perception study, *bees/pees*, *bear/pear*, *dime/time* and *goat/coat*. The younger children showed a significantly longer mean lag time for the identification of the voiceless velar stop than the older children and adults; in addition, the youngest group generally required a greater difference between voiced and voiceless stops for successful discrimination than did the older groups, while the older children differed from the adults in the same way, but only with respect to the velar pair. Zlatin and Koenigsknecht (1975) noted individual differences in the responses of the children, revealing "a disparity between chronological age and stage of phonological development for the voicing contrast" for some children (p. 548), particularly with respect to the more difficult velar pair.

Finally, the authors observed some interesting strategies in the course of the experiment: Some adults indicated their awareness of phoneme boundary areas by marking some stimuli as "nebulous" or "in-between" voicing categories. Similarly, several of the older children spontaneously repeated the word they had heard prior to pressing the response button provided;

> In some six-year-old children, actual verbal vacillation (for example, repetitions such as "bear, pear, bear . . .") was noted. These vacillations were sometimes accompanied by hand alternation between the response buttons and appeared to occur only in response to VOT stimuli associated with the child's own perceptual boundary. The verbal repetition exhibited by some of the six-year-olds additionally appeared to influence the terminal motor response selection, that is, the button pressed corresponded to the last word said by the child. Although some two-year-old children also evidenced hand vacillation between the response buttons, there were no instances of verbal vacillation. In fact, the repetition of stimuli by two-year-old children rarely occurred in response to VOT stimuli associated with the child's own phoneme boundary. Such repetitions accompanied within-category stimuli and were not consistent with the motor response selection. (p. 550)

Zlatin and Koenigsknecht interpreted these differences in response between the older and younger children as supporting Luria (1961), who believed that "there is a shift in the role of speech from an accompanying function associated with the child's physical activities [as in the case of the near-3-year-olds here] to a planning role which eventually becomes internalized as part of the thought process [as exhibited by the near-7-year-olds]" (Zlatin and Koenigsknecht, 1975, p. 550).

In the 1976 study Zlatin and Koenigsknecht recorded from every subject thirty-five or more productions of the same words used in the perception study and subjected these tokens to spectrographic analysis. Comparison of the three age-groups showed statistically significant differences. Adults showed a mean VOT in the short lead range (i.e., slight prevoicing) for voiced stops and produced voiceless stops in the moderately long lag region (i.e., with relatively strong aspiration, in traditional phonetic terms). The younger children rarely produced voiced stops with a voicing lead and both groups of children produced more voiceless stops in the short to moderate lag region than did adults (see figures 7.1 to 7.3). The percentage of within-category tokens (based on the perceptual identification categories determined in the earlier study for each subject) increased with age, particularly for the voiceless labial and velar stops.

Overall, Zlatin and Koenigsknecht reported that for perception, the phoneme boundary width required for identification narrowed with age. For production, based on a review of earlier studies (on Lebanese as well as English: see Preston, Yeni-komshian, and Stark, 1967; Kewley-Port and Preston, 1974) as well as their own data, the authors conclude that children at first produce stops primarily in the short lag region, regardless of ambient language or of the voicing of the target stop (see also Macken, 1980b). Over the next two years, "bimodal distributions characteristic of two-category languages begin to emerge; however, one prime mode for homorganic stops in the voiced range is typical for productions by children in this developmental period" (Zlatin and Koenigsknecht, 1976, p. 106). In English, development of the VOT contrast involves the gradual mastery of longer lag produc-

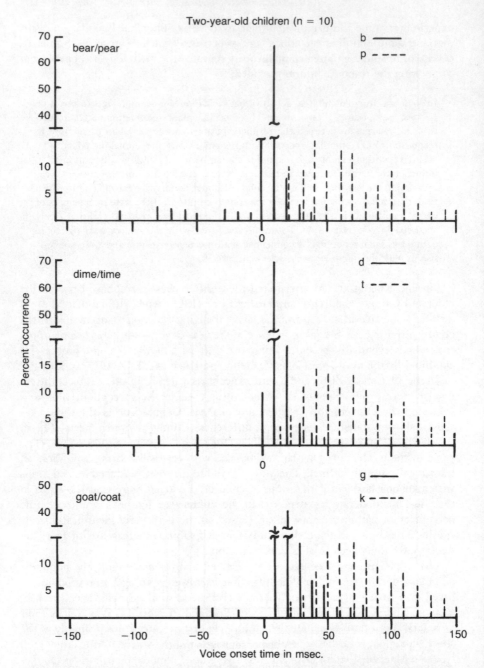

Figure 7.1 Voice onset time distributions for ten 2-year-old English-speaking children: labial, apical and velar stops. Very few productions exceeded the limits of −150 to +150 msec. included in this histogram.

Source: Zlatin and Koenigsknecht, 1976, reprinted by permission of the American Speech-Language-Hearing Association

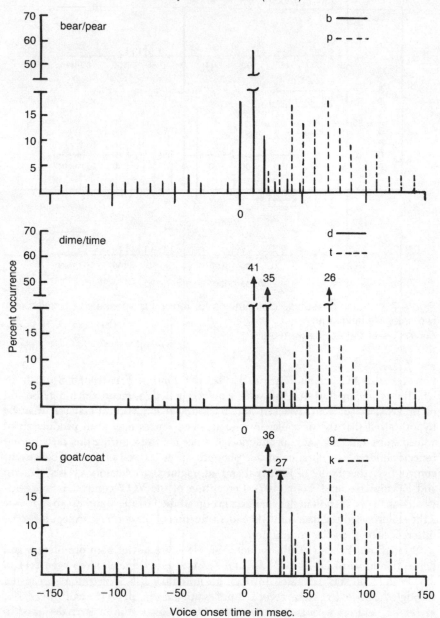

Six-year-old children (n = 10)

Figure 7.2 Voice onset time distributions for ten 6-year-old English-speaking children: labial, apical and velar stops. Very few productions exceeded the limits of −150 to +150 msec. included in this histogram.

Source: Zlatin and Koenigsknecht, 1976, reprinted by permission of the American Speech-Language-Hearing Association

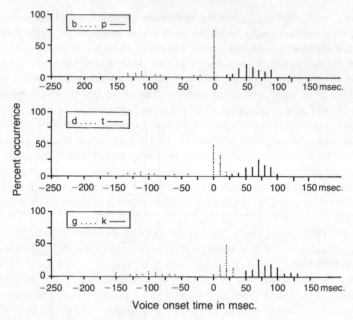

Figure 7.3 Voice onset time distributions for four adult speakers of English (a two-category language).
Source: Lisker and Abramson, 1964

tions (cf. also Macken and Barton, 1980a, and contrast French and Spanish, in which it is voicing lead that has to be acquired, a development which may be still in progress at age four: Macken and Barton, 1980b; Allen, 1985). "It may be hypothesized that the unstable, infrequent occurrences of lead in production of voiced stops and long lag in production of voiceless stops during this early period reflects children's exploration of the 'phonetic space' as well as a lack of consistent control over the timing of laryngeal and supraglottal articulatory events" (Zlatin and Koenigsknecht, 1976, p. 107). Perception of the VOT contrast is more advanced than production in the youngest group studied by these authors; by age 6 or 7 the children showed near-adult-like identification of the contrast, except for some differences on the velar continuum.

Strange and Broen (1980) conducted an elaborate test of both production and perception of word-initial /w/, /l/ and /r/ by twenty-one children aged 2;11 to 3;5. Production was examined through an imitation task. Perception was tested through the use of live voice, recorded and synthetic stimuli for the pairs *rake/lake*, *wake/rake* and (as a control), *wake/bake*. The acoustic stimuli were designed to differ in several of the criterial dimensions that distinguish the target phonemes but had identical rhyming portions (*-ake*); testing proceeded from live voice to recorded to synthetic stimuli.

In production, some of the children had not yet mastered the liquids. In perception, overall accuracy was over 90 percent; /w/ : /r/ was the most difficult contrast, /w/ : /b/ the easiest. Identification accuracy was clearly related to /r/ and /l̩/ production ability, with far more errors made by the eight children who had made the most production errors. However, there was a great deal of variability in performance among those subjects and all showed better than chance identification of all three contrasts on one or more test. Strange and Broen tentatively concluded that both perception and production of phoneme contrasts develop gradually and that perception of a contrast normally precedes its production. However, they emphasized that their test situation was highly constrained; it involved only two response alternatives and a long series of tests using the same stimuli, which could serve as training on the contrast. Thus, the study does not reflect "intentional, coordinated perception," such as ordinary life requires, in which the child-listener is actively involved in extracting the relevant phonetic cues from a complex set of stimuli in order to determine which words were intended by the speaker.

Locke (1980) developed a "speech production-perception task" in which perceptual stimuli are chosen to reflect a preliminary test of the child's productions. Of 131 children tested, ranging in age from 3 to 9 years (mean age 5.3), most had speech substitutions but not necessarily speech disorders. About one-third of the contrasts misproduced were also misperceived. However, misperception was not equally likely to be involved in all production errors. Specifically, only 49 percent of those errors consisted in the substitution of one voiceless fricative for another, yet this type of substitution accounted for fully 89 percent of the misperceived contrasts. The pair that accounted for the largest number of perception errors was /f/ : /θ/ (67 percent incidence of misperception). Of fifty-two children who substituted /f/ for /θ/ in production, the twenty-six younger subjects (mean age 3.7) were much more likely to misperceive the contrast as well than were the older subjects (mean age 6.2).

Velleman (1988) designed a study to focus on the distinction between production errors likely to be due to perceptual difficulties and those likely to be due to articulatory difficulty. She predicted that poor production of /s/ would occur in the absence of poor perception. For the /f/ : /θ/ contrast, weak and confusable acoustic signals are a likely basis for production difficulties; Velleman predicted that in this case only children with high perception scores should have high production scores.

Velleman tested twelve English-speaking children aged 3 to 5, sampling free speech production as well as imitation. To test perception, Velleman first assessed word familiarity and then used a real-word, picture-identification task. The pairs of interest were *thumb/some, thumb/fum* (as in "fee, fi, fo, –"), and *some/fum*. Velleman's results confirmed her hypotheses. Perception and production of /s/ were not correlated. Some children with poor production had good perception of contrasts involving /s/, and in general perception errors with /s/ were rare. In contrast, perception and production of /θ/ were highly correlated, with production of /θ/ better for children with perception scores of over 80 percent.

In summary, the few studies examining production and perception in the same children have all asked the question, To what extent are production errors rooted in perceptual errors? The results are in good agreement with the general conclusion that some phonemic contrasts remain difficult to discriminate perceptually as late as age 3 or older (e.g., /θ/ : /f/, /r/ : /w/), and thus that production errors involving these pairs, which typically continue to occur in the later preschool period, may originate in a lack of attention to the perceptual contrast. It should be mentioned that the /f/ : /θ/ contrast is notoriously difficult for adults as well (Miller and Nicely, 1955). Other production errors show no evident relation to perception (lack of aspiration in voiceless stops at age 2, /s/ distortions at age 3 to 5).[2]

The converse question – To what extent is the child's perceptual attention guided by his or her vocal (motoric) experience? – has received even less attention. It was discussed somewhat inconclusively by Shvachkin (1973), who conceded that "*articulation*, and not only hearing, evidently influences . . . phonemic [perceptual] development" (p. 107), based on the behavior of his preschool subjects. Shvachkin explicitly rejected the categorical position that "we hear only those speech sounds which we are able to pronounce" (Bernshteyn, 1937, p. 15, cited in Shvachkin, 1973), proposing instead the more moderate view that there is "an intimate connection" between the two processes (cf. also Studdert-Kennedy, 1991a). Straight (1980), who generally insists on the autonomy of perception and production, suggested that the child's own simplified or otherwise distorted output may in some cases lead to inaccurate internal representations which then will underlie the child's subsequent spontaneous productions; Vihman (1982) offered two illustrations of probable "feedback" from the child's own productions to his or her internal representations (cf. also Hsieh, 1972).

Understanding running speech

As the child gains fluency and begins to enter the world of discourse outside the home, the challenge arises of understanding continuous or running speech in wholly unfamiliar situations of use and reference. What factors enter into that task? Do children process spoken language differently from adults?

Under ordinary circumstances, listeners are not called on to identify isolated words but rather must retrieve a message from the unsegmented flow of speech. Recently investigators have designed a variety of research methods to investigate the complex process by which listeners interpret speech "on-line," when there is no time to make sure of what was heard, consult a lexicon of possible words, and assess the plausibility of one word or interpretation against another. A number of studies have compared adult and child responses to real-time word recognition conditions, including listening through noise and picking content words and meanings out of the ongoing flow.

Listening conditions

Even adults may find it difficult to understand speech under noisy circumstances; infrequently occurring words, monosyllables, and unpredictable words have been found to cause more problems than more common words, longer words, and words predictable from the context. Elliott et al. (1979) administered an adaptive perceptual test to 226 school children, aged 5 to 10, and to thirty-eight adults. To assure that all the words tested were very familiar ones, they first pilot-tested their response pictures against the receptive language skills of 3-year-old inner city children who tended to come from lower socio-economic backgrounds. A set of sixty-seven monosyllabic nouns (such as *dog*, *school*, *milk*) were illustrated by line drawings presented in sets of four to a page, with each of the four pictures representing a different vowel. Notice that Elliott and her colleagues were not concerned with finding minimally contrasting words since they were interested in word recognition or comprehension under differing listening conditions rather than in the discrimination of particular segmental contrasts.

Four experimental listening conditions were included, all involving tape-recorded stimuli presented through earphones. There were two tests in "quiet," one in which the subject was simply asked to repeat the word ("open set") and one in which the subject was to point to one of four pictures ("closed set"). The closed set procedure was also used in the two noisy conditions, in which either (1) the "babble" of twelve speakers or (2) electronically filtered speech-like white noise was presented to one ear as background noise or "perceptual masking" while the target stimuli were presented to the other ear. An adaptive procedure was used for each condition to estimate a 71 percent correct response level. In each case, the first test item was presented loudly enough to be easily understood and after every two correct responses, the stimulus intensity was decreased 2 dB.

The 71 percent correct level was found to be about 10 dB lower for the quiet closed set condition (the easier task) than for the quiet open set condition across all age groups. Performance on both these conditions improved significantly with age. With regard to the noisy conditions, the 71 percent correct level was achieved with a signal about 10 dB lower in intensity for the filtered noise than for the more distracting multi-talker babble. No clear age trend was apparent under noisy conditions. Ten-year-olds achieved roughly adult-like performance under all conditions. Children with language problems (about one-third of those tested) tended to require a higher intensity signal to meet the criterion in the quiet test conditions at all ages.

As Elliott et al. pointed out, their findings mean that younger children are likely to require a more intense signal level than is needed for older children and adults to understand a message spoken in a quiet environment. There are implications for children's initial representations of new or unfamiliar words as well. Where listening conditions are less than ideal, as is often the case both at home and in school, misperceptions may be expected – particularly for some of the perceptually more difficult sound contrasts (e.g., between voiceless fricatives or pairs of stops differing in voicing).

Recovering words and meanings

Some of our knowledge of the process of word recognition derives from studies using isolated words. For example, both word naming (Balota and Chumbley, 1985) and a lexical decision task (Cirrin, 1984), in which a stimulus must be identified as rapidly as possible as a word or a nonword, have been used to infer some of the factors involved in accessing the lexicon. Studies addressing the comprehension of natural, continuous speech have exploited one of two research methods: (1) *Fast reaction time* tasks, in which the listener is required to shadow the input speech (Marslen-Wilson, 1973, 1985) or to monitor the speech for occurrences of particular words ("identical monitoring"), word categories (Tyler and Marslen-Wilson, 1981), or mispronunciations deliberately included in ongoing sentences or stories (Cole and Jakimik, 1980; Cole, 1981); (2) The *gating* task, developed by Grosjean (1980), in which listeners are presented with successively longer fragments of a word (either isolated or in sentential context) and are required to respond at each new increment with a guess as to what word they are hearing.

Recognizing spoken words is thought to involve integrating two different sources of information (Tyler and Frauenfelder, 1987): (1) *sensory input*, or "bottom-up" (phonetic) information deriving from the speech signal itself, and (2) *contextual constraints*, or "top-down" information, deriving from the speaker's knowledge of what has already been said, what might plausibly follow, what semantic and syntactic structures the language allows, and what words the language makes available, given the unfolding message.

There is experimental evidence to suggest that words are typically (though not always) identified *before* sufficient acoustic-phonetic information has become available to allow all words but one to be eliminated on the basis of the sound pattern alone (Marslen-Wilson and Tyler, 1975, 1980; Grosjean, 1980; Marslen-Wilson, 1987). This finding applies particularly to content words (nouns, verbs, adjectives, adverbs – those words which are likely to be stressed, which convey the most information in a sentence, and which are least predictable from grammatical structure: Grosjean and Gee, 1987). "Early selection," or word recognition before the entire word is actually registered by the listener, means that word recognition is based on informed guessing as well as perception. That is, the listener is continually engaged in constructing an interpretation of the incoming message, so that the more predictable a particular word is – given the conversation up to that point, the preceding sentence and the phrase in which the word is located – the more rapidly a listener can guess or "recognize" it from a brief phonetic clue, such as the first sound or the first syllable.

In addition to the importance of context in arriving at a "best fit" among possible candidates for word recognition, other factors must also be taken into account. Experimental manipulations have shown that high frequency words are recognized more rapidly than low frequency words when both provide equally good matches to the initial phonetic shape of the input and each are plausible in context (Tyler, 1984; Marslen-Wilson, 1987 – but see also Wayland, Wingfield, and Goodglass, 1989).

Luce (1986) has elaborated on the nature of multiple candidate evaluation in the process of word recognition by developing a model of the "similarity neighborhood structure" of words. According to Luce, the relative ease with which a word can be identified depends on (1) the density of segmentally similar words in the listener's receptive lexicon and (2) the frequency of both the target word and words closely related to it, with which it might be confused.

To what extent do children resemble adults in the recognition of words in running speech? Each of the factors that enter into adult word recognition – ongoing (bottom-up) analysis of the acoustic-phonetic signal, (top-down) expectations based on the semantic, syntactic, and pragmatic context, and relative lexical familiarity – may potentially reflect a long period of development. Both increasing experience with language and possible changes in processing abilities may affect the child's capacity to carry out the complex task of interpreting running speech.

Adult–child differences in word recognition

A few studies have focused on adult–child differences in analysis of the phonetic signal. Elliott, Hammer, and Evan (1987) used a *forward gating procedure* to test children, teenagers and adults aged 70–85 on their recognition of highly familiar spoken monosyllabic nouns under conditions of limited acoustic information. The subjects were required to make a response (i.e., to guess, if the word had not yet been recognized) to each successive stimulus. The teenagers performed more successfully on this task than either the children or elderly adults. They recognized more words and did so more rapidly. Their guesses were usually real words which were phonetically compatible with the sounds heard, whereas the children's responses sometimes failed to match the phonetic stimuli. These results are consistent with the hypothesis, advanced by Walley (1988), that children require more acoustic information to identify stimuli than do adults. In addition, it is likely that children are less able to carry out the more complex cognitive task of integrating the signal with the unfolding semantic and pragmatic interpretation of the message.

Cole and his colleagues (Cole and Jakimik, 1980; Cole and Perfetti, 1980; Cole, 1981) used a mispronunciation task to compare the processing of continuous speech by children and adults. The subjects' reaction times are assumed to reflect the time it takes to (1) identify the intended or target word (e.g., *pajamas*) and (2) note the acoustic mismatch (e.g., /pədaməz/ or "padamas"). By manipulating both the words and their sentence context Cole has tested several hypotheses about the process of word recognition in context. Cole's work supports three major theoretical assumptions regarding the process of decoding or recognizing words in running speech:

1   Words are recognized through the interaction of auditory perception and linguistic and pragmatic knowledge.

2   Words are typically recognized in order. As each word is recognized, it allows the listener to establish word boundaries. In addition, each decoded word imposes syntactic and semantic constraints on the following words, which enables the listener to progressively narrow the field of possible interpretations. For example, after decoding the word *picnic*, the listener is well prepared for a word like *basket*. When the phonetic pattern [pʰæskət] is heard instead, a mispronunciation is quickly identified. When [pʰæskət] follows a word with which *basket* is less likely to be combined – such as *plastic* – the mispronunciation is detected less rapidly.

3   Words are decoded *sequentially*, using earlier-occurring sounds to narrow the range of possible candidates (cf. also Marslen-Wilson and Welsh, 1978). It should be noted that this aspect of the Marslen-Wilson model of adult word recognition is subject to some qualification on methodological, empirical and theoretical grounds. Huttenlocher and Goodman (1987) point out that the role of stress, typically located early in the word in English, was not controlled for in Marslen-Wilson's experiments; Nooteboom (1981) and Salasoo and Pisoni (1985) provide evidence that words can be identified from *word-final* as well as from word-initial fragments (though less efficiently), and Grosjean (1985) shows that monitoring and post-access correcting strategies also play a role in on-line word recognition. More work with languages of contrasting prosodic and phonotactic structure – such as French, say, or Japanese – would be informative. Finally, conceptualization of word recognition in terms of a parallel processing model largely eliminates the need for the assumption of "left-to-right" sequential processing: "Any system with powerful parallel features could allow for processing the signal in larger units while the smaller units are being processed. An increased probability of correct identification with increasing word-onset information, thus, might not necessarily imply that the analysis is sequential, but that the word is simply better specified" (Wayland et al., 1989, p. 484).

Nevertheless, there is a temporal effect in word recognition. Adults detect errors in second syllables more rapidly than in first syllables, presumably because the target word has already been identified when the mispronounced second syllable error is heard. Similarly, mispronunciations in the second syllable of words beginning with relatively unusual first syllables (e.g., *sham-*) are recognized more rapidly than those in words with common first syllables (*com-*), presumably because the set of possible lexical matches can more quickly be narrowed to one. On the other hand, mispronounced word-final consonants are less likely to be detected than mispronounced word-initial consonants. This probably reflects the limited attention paid to the end of a word, even under the special circumstances of a mispronunciation-detecting task.

In three experiments with 4- and 5-year-old children and adults, Cole (1981) investigated the effects of word-position, consonant substituted, and phonotactic structure, or permissible vs. impermissible consonant clusters, on the detection of mispronunciations in running speech. The children were tested on familiar songs and nursery rhymes. The main results were:

1   The children averaged about 50 percent detection in word-initial position; in medial position, detection fell to 25 percent and in final position, to 12 percent. Adult detection frequencies were 95 percent, 86 percent, and 71 percent, respectively, in the three word-positions. Thus, the children, like the adults, paid most attention to initial position and least to final position (cf. also Walley, 1987).
2   In word-initial position children were most sensitive to changes in place of articulation of stops and to changes of stop to nasal and of voiced to voiceless stop. Interchanges among nasals, fricatives, or liquids were less often detected.

Most easily detected were common articulatory substitutions of a stop for a fricative. In a follow-up study, Bernthal et al. (1987) also found that developmental substitutions were more easily detected than non-developmental substitutions by normally developing and misarticulating 4- to 6-year-old children as well as by adults.

Cole and Perfetti (1980) reported one important difference between children and adults: Though the children, like adults, detected errors more readily in words predictable from the context (an advantage of about 14 percent, across all ages), they failed to identify second syllable errors more readily than first syllable errors. This difference may mean that, unlike adults, children put off deciding which word was intended until they have heard several syllables. Such a strategy seems reasonable for listeners who to some extent lack confidence in their ability to recognize words. That is, if a great many words in adult conversation are still unfamiliar, it is easy to see why children would be slower to settle on a lexical interpretation. The same effect might be found in testing second language learners who are just attaining relatively good comprehension of fluent speech.

Other investigators have addressed differences between adults and children in the use of context. Tyler and Marslen-Wilson (1981) investigated the role of discourse and of syntactic context alone on the comprehension of running speech by children aged 5, 7 and 10 years. Children were tested on two tasks: identical monitoring, in which the occurrence of a particular word is to be noted as soon as it is spoken; and category monitoring, in which a word belonging to a particular category (body part, fruit, furniture) is to be identified when heard. The target words fell toward the end of the second of a pair of sentences of one of three kinds: Normal prose, in which the first sentence provides a normal discourse context for the second; syntactic prose, in which the sentences are anomalous in meaning but syntactically correct; and random word order, which violates both semantic and syntactic structure and thus provides no contextual support for word recognition. Examples (with the target word in italics):

John had to go back home. He had fallen out of the swing and had hurt his *hand* on the ground. (Normal)

John had to sit on the shop. He had lived out of the kitchen and had enjoyed his *hand* in the mud. (Syntactic)

The on sit shop to had John. He lived had and kitchen the out his of had enjoyed *hand* mud in the. (Random)

The results suggested that children as young as age 5 are able to make good use of discourse and even of syntactic context: Mean reaction times decreased significantly with age, but all three groups showed a marked facilitatory effect from the normal discourse, and a lesser effect from normal syntax only. The category monitoring task was considerably more difficult for the children than identical monitoring. The normal discourse context again aided recognition, but the semantically anomalous "syntactic" sentence sequences gave no significant advantage in this case.

Another study suggests that children's ability to make use of semantic knowledge continues to improve up to as late as age 15. Elliott (1979) tested twenty-four children at each of four age levels (11, 13, 15, and 17 years) on their understanding of sentences against a background of multitalker babble. The test sentences were designed to fall into two groups: "high predictability" and "low predictability," a function of the presence or absence of two or three semantically related "pointer" words that could help cue the listener as to the identity of the final (target) word, always a monosyllabic noun. The test consisted of twenty-five sentences of each type; none was longer than eight syllables. The subject's task was to repeat back the last word of the sentence.

Under just one set of conditions, when the target sentence was presented at the same intensity as the noise, a significant age trend was found, with the 11- and 13-year-olds performing less well on high-predictability sentences than the 15- and 17-year-olds, who did about as well as young adults tested earlier with written responses. No age differences were found in quiet or in comprehension of the low predictability sentences. A later test of 9-year-old children showed significantly poorer performance than that of the 11-year-olds. The age-related differences are not a direct auditory effect since only the high-predictability sentences proved easier for older subjects. Rather, the difference appears to reflect the extent to which children of different ages were able to use the semantic information in the "pointer syllables" to guess at the final, difficult-to-hear target noun.

Lexical familiarity has also been found to play a different role for children as compared with adults. Cole and Perfetti (1980) reported a significant difference between children and adults in the detection of mispronunciations in a simple, clearly articulated story: On average, preschool children (ages 4 to 5) detected about 50 percent of the mispronounced words and children in kindergarten through fifth grade caught about 60 percent, while adults detected 95 percent of the errors in the same recording. Cole and Perfetti suggested that children probably treat mispronunciations as unfamiliar words: "It seems likely that children learn to tolerate (or actively ignore) unfamiliar words, so that each occurrence of an unfamiliar word does not result in a breakdown of the comprehension process" (p. 313).

It is important to note that the children detected mispronunciations in isolated words (95 percent) far more readily than in fluent speech. The high detection rate for isolated words, due in part to their slower articulation, may also be ascribed to the cues provided by pictures that accompanied the test words. As Cole (1981) pointed out, however, this procedure is commonly used in clinical tests of phonetic discrimination, and therefore, the tests may overestimate children's ability to perceive phonetic differences in the course of conversational speech.

The importance of word familiarity has begun to receive explicit attention. Brown and Watson (1987) analyzed the effects on reaction time in word naming of spoken and written word frequency as compared with subjective estimates of "age of acquisition," an indirect way of rating word familiarity. The age of acquisition estimate proved to be the single most important predictor of the speed with which (adult) subjects could name a picture. This type of estimate has been validated by the very high correlations found with children's scores on vocabulary tests at ages 5 to 21 years (Gilhooly and Gilhooly, 1980). Brown and Watson noted that age of acquisition effects are reliably associated only with tasks requiring overt word production. Assuming that adult estimates of age of acquisition do in fact reflect how early in the child's development a word was acquired, Brown and Watson hypothesized that early words may be stored in a more complete phonological representation, reflecting the fact that the child has not yet begun to make efficient use of the phonological redundancies afforded by the language at the time of acquisition of these words. Later words would be stored more efficiently, so that for production "more time might have to be spent in generating phonological information not directly represented in the phonological lexicon" (p. 214), thus slowing the reaction time for naming later-acquired words.

Walley and Metsala (1990) directly addressed the question of word familiarity in mispronunciation tasks presented to children aged 5 and 8. Subjective age-of-acquisition ratings were used to categorize test words as "early," "current," and "late." The familiarity factor proved to be important: Young children were more likely to detect mispronunciations in early and current words. Furthermore, the children were biased toward identifying late (or for age 5, both late and "current") words as *mispronounced* – including words which were correctly pronounced ("intact" words). Thus, whereas the subjects in Cole and Perfetti (1980) were found to treat mispronounced words as unfamiliar, Walley and Metsala showed through analysis of "false alarms" that their subjects were reluctant to treat unfamiliar words as "intact," preferring to label them mispronounced. These results call to mind the biasing role of familiarity in early tests of linguistic perception (Barton, 1976; Clumeck, 1982). They are reminiscent also of several anecdotes reported in Vihman (1981, p. 248), in which pre-school children misperceived unfamiliar words as relatively more familiar ones, disregarding the fact that their interpretation was at odds with the ongoing discourse context.

The role of vocabulary growth

In a lengthy review of the literature on adult spoken word recognition and development in perception and production Walley (1993b) set forth two hypotheses regarding phonological development: (1) "The phonemic segment *emerges* first as an implicit, perceptual unit by virtue of vocabulary growth" and (2) "only later [does the segment become available] as a more accessible, cognitive unit that can be consciously deployed in reading" (p. 287). Walley grounds her developmental proposal in two models of adult spoken word recognition described above, Marslen-Wilson's Cohort model (1987) and Luce's Neighborhood Activation Model (1986). The basic argument is that as children's vocabularies grow, there is mounting pressure to develop a network of interrelated word shapes, which will allow the child to make better use of the temporal structure of on-line word recognition (Jusczyk, 1986; see ch. 9, below, and the related proposal in Studdert-Kennedy, 1987 and Lindblom, 1992, regarding the emergence of segmental structure as a basis for *production* in logical consequence of increased lexical pressure).

Assuming that word perception at the outset of language comprehension is "holistic . . . in the sense that segmental information is not used at the level of perceptual representations that are accessible in real time and relevant to word recognition" (Walley, 1993b, p. 291), Walley infers that children will gradually shift to a more adult-like reliance on partial input for recognition as the number of familiar lexical items increases. This increase is by all accounts dramatic in the first few months of testable language comprehension (Oviatt, 1980; see ch. 6, above). By age 6 a child's receptive vocabulary (in English) was estimated by Templin (1957) to include as many as 8,000 root words or 14,000 different word types, counting inflectional variants; Anglin's (1993) study, based on testing thirty-two children each in grades 1, 3 and 5 on a carefully designed representative sample from the third edition of Webster's unabridged dictionary (1981), validates that figure, estimating that over 10,000 dictionary entries were known by the first-graders, while the figure doubles for each grade level tested (i.e., nearly 40,000 entries for fifth-graders).

It is worth pausing to consider the difficulty of arriving at a useful assessment of the size of children's vocabularies. Within the first year of language use a dedicated diarist living with a child can record virtually all the words a child produces. Leopold (1939), for example, after a thoughtful discussion of the problems involved in counting words, particularly for a bilingual child, lists the new word types acquired by his daughter Hildegard month by month, from 0;8 to 1;11, arriving at a total of 377 words, only 241 of which remained in active use at the end of this period; Vihman (1985), similarly, arrives at a figure of nearly 500 words for the first nine months of word production by her son Raivo (1;1–1;10). For comparison, Fenson et al. (1993) report a productive vocabulary of about 525 words for children aged 2.5, based on a norming sample of sixty-eight children (derived from parental responses to a detailed lexical checklist, now available as the MacArthur Communicative Development Inventory).

Labov and Labov (1978), on the other hand, "undertook to record everything that [their daughter Jessie] said" (p. 818); they arrived at a figure of 12,400 word tokens for the first five months of word production. Following a similar approach, Wagner (1985) reports on the Dortmund corpus, which at the time included twelve samples, each a recording of everything said by a single child in the course of a full day (or part of a day, typically about three hours), as registered on a wireless microphone and transcribed in full. The children so recorded, over five years of research, ranged in age from 1;5 to 14;10. The two youngest children (under age 2 years) spoke notably less than the rest, averaging perhaps 10,000 to 15,000 word tokens in a day (nearly 4,000 tokens recorded in three to four hours); for the older children, word production per twelve-hour day (standardizing across the different lengths of sample) ranged from 21,000 to 25,000 words per day, if exceptionally talk-intensive recordings are excluded. The "general lexicon" for the younger children, based on these recordings, yielded a figure of 500–600 words used (types, not tokens, but with a separate count for each inflectionally distinct word form – such forms being considerably more numerous in German, the language of these recordings, than in English); for the older children the range was from 770 (age 5;4) to 3,050 (age 9;7: based on two full-day recordings). All of these instances involve *productive* vocabulary; even so, the basis on which one might extrapolate from the words used in a day to the child's complete active vocabulary remains an open question – although, as Wagner points out, "the increase in types is exponential and not a linear function. In the course of extended speech, the rate for new types being introduced decreases steadily" (p. 486).

Calculation of a comprehension vocabulary would seem to be even more challenging. Studies of "fast mapping," initiated by Carey and Bartlett (Bartlett, 1978; Carey, 1978), have begun to lead to a better understanding of the amazingly rapid accumulation of words which are at least partially represented, enough so to permit word recognition in well contextualized situations. Rice and Woodsmall (1988), for example, showed that a group of thirty-four 5-year-old children viewing an animated video program stocked with twenty new words (for a total of 114 presentations of the novel words in 12 minutes) were able to develop some understanding of these words: Comparing pre- and post-test comprehension scores, these children doubled the mean number of words they could identify (from 5 to 10 out of 20) – despite the fact that exposure to the new words was relatively brief, "in a format that allowed for minimal parsing support or time for reflection" (p. 425). A group of twenty-seven 3-year-olds exposed to the same video programs, in contrast, learned on average only 1.6 new words, based only on the immediate recognition post-test results.

Rice and Woodsmall's study gives some indication of the role of an existing knowledge base in accelerating the word learning curve. A similar lesson can be gleaned from figure 7.4 (from Anglin, 1993), which clearly shows the sharp increase in receptive vocabulary between grades 1 and 5 and also the key factor in that increase: A growing capacity to use "morphological problem solving" to analyze new morphologically complex words to derive their meaning. "Thus, learned or 'psychologically basic' vocabulary – the words for which there are distinct entries in the mental lexicon – would likely show a growth curve somewhere between the curve for root words + idioms [which have to have been learned and encoded in long-term memory] and that for total main entries known" (Anglin, 1993, p. 68). Returning to the issue of the density of word forms in the mental lexicon, we can conclude, first, that 6-year-old children have a very sizeable receptive vocabulary, most of it consisting of monomorphemic roots, and second, that the increase in new root words in the middle grammar school years is small in comparison with the increase in analytic understanding of word structure and the consequent increase in word comprehension. Only the root words would seem directly relevant to the issue of word form density in the lexicon in relation to perceptual processing or phonological representation.

Charles-Luce and Luce (1990) compare the density of similar word forms in children's vs. adults' lexicons. Defining a "similarity neighborhood" as "a set of words that differ from a given target by a one-phoneme substitution, addition, or deletion" (p. 207) – such as *bit, pot, pig, spit, it* . . . for target *pit* – Charles-Luce and Luce provide a comparative profile of the similarity neighborhoods for 3-, 4- and 5-phoneme words in a computerized lexicon (based on the spontaneous word production of 5- and 7-year-old children: Wepman and Hass, 1969) and adults (based on 20,000 entries in Webster's Pocket Dictionary). The profiles reveal a sharp contrast

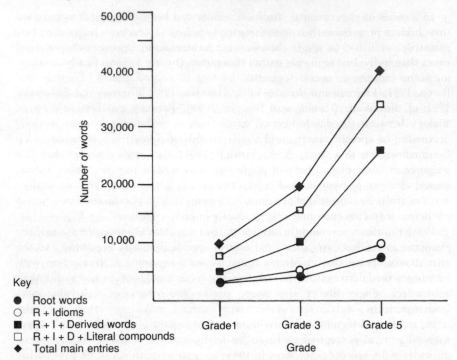

Figure 7.4 Vocabulary growth in middle childhood. Cumulative functions showing mean established number of words known at each grade for root words + idioms; root words + idioms + derived words; root words + idioms + derived words + literal compounds; and total main entries.
Source: Anglin, 1993

between the sparsely populated lexical similarity neighborhoods of 5- and 7-year-olds and those of adults. The size of the children's "representative lexicon" is unrealistically small, however: 679 entries for the 5-year-olds, 943 for the 7-year-olds.

Noting the problematic sampling in the study by Charles-Luce and Luce, Dollaghan (1994) calculated by hand similarity neighborhoods for monosyllables only on two vocabulary check lists intended to be reasonably representative of the active vocabulary of children aged 1;0 to 3;0; she helpfully provides an appendix in which all the words in each neighborhood are listed. She found a greater density for these younger children than Charles-Luce and Luce had estimated for their older children (over 80 percent of the words had one near phonological neighbor, while 18 percent had six or more, the criterion word density expected to impose a need for detailed perceptual analysis, according to Charles-Luce and Luce). Dollaghan concludes that "very young children appear to require . . . auditory perceptual skills [such as the ability to categorize, label, and order phonetic segments] quite early in their lexical development" (p. 264).

In a series of experimental studies Treiman and her colleagues demonstrated that children progress in their sensitivity to phonological structure, responding first primarily to syllables (at age 4), then showing greater facility in accessing onsets and rimes than individual segments within those units (by age 5),[3] and finally developing some capacity to access segments (by first or second grade) (Treiman and Baron, 1981; Treiman and Breaux, 1982; Treiman, 1985; Treiman and Zukowski, 1991; cf. also Walley, Smith, and Jusczyk, 1986); Treiman and Breaux draw an analogy between the developmental trend from more holistic to more analytic processing of speech patterns and similar trends in visual categorization tasks. Commenting on this work, A. E. Fowler (1991) elaborates the idea that this progression "may extend beyond phonological awareness to reflect more fundamental changes in phonological representation . . . The child's early vocabulary may originally be represented at a more holistic level, with organization in terms of phonemic segments emerging only gradually in early childhood" (p. 97).

Fowler outlines several difficulties with the once standard interpretation of the phoneme as the basic organizational unit of speech from the beginning and the related assumption that children's difficulty with segments in connection with learning to read derives from the *metacognitive* requirements of the task rather than with a lack of accessibility of segments *per se*. She reviews evidence that poor readers perform poorly in tests of short term memory, make more errors in naming tasks, and have difficulty with certain perceptual tasks. For example, poor readers with no general perceptual or language deficit have been shown to experience difficulty with speech perception in noise as well as with recall of a word list (subjects were third-graders: Brady, Shankweiler, and Mann, 1983).[4] Fowler concludes that "a failure to gain access to phonemic segments is associated not with general metacognitive inadequacies, but with a host of other subtle phonological deficits, involving the formation, retrieval and maintenance of phonological representations" (p. 101).

Walley (1993b) reviews a wide range of studies of perception and production in support of the idea of a general developmental trend from "whole to parts." Above all, she stresses the gradual nature of the restructuring of lexical representations in terms of segments: "It may not occur uniformly . . . throughout the lexicon, or even within a given word. Rather, it may be accomplished in more 'piecemeal' fashion, because it depends largely on the way in which individual lexical repertoires evolve and on those similarity relations among different words that are noticed by a given child" (p. 292). Walley suggests that perceptual development may "continue to consist of recurrent cycles in which representations of similar words (existing or new) are 'moved closer' to one another and relevant differences noted" (p. 311). As she points out, even when segmental representations have begun to develop, "segmental analysis would not necessarily be used in on-line recognition, but perhaps only when encountering unfamiliar or nonsense words" (p. 312).

Vihman (1981) offered a tentative outline of developmental changes in representational salience, based on anecdotal cross-linguistic data illustrating "mini-malapropisms" (Aitchison, 1972), or lexical errors made by children, as well as perceptual "slips." Such errors reveal something of the nature of phonological indexing in [the child's] developing lexicon. The features which appear to be most salient to adults – number of syllables and position of stress – are undoubtedly among the first to be clearly tagged in the child's storage system. Other features are weighted differently for adult and child, however: The segments that make up the stressed syllable, specifically, appear to be more salient than word-initial or -final segments, and among the latter, final position may be more important. The changes assumed here to be taking place in word-storage, first as the child models his output forms more closely on the adult's, then as he learns to read, write, and list in alphabetical order, have yet to be tapped more directly (Vihman, 1981, p. 262).

Aitchison and Straf (1981) reported very similar results from a comparison of over 400 adult and 200 child malapropisms. Both adults and children tend to preserve both syllable count and initial consonant in their misremembered words; when this pattern breaks down, however, adults are more likely to retain the consonants while children retain syllable count. Aitchison and Straf suggest that the shift to greater attention to the initial consonant may be due in part to increase in vocabulary size and the concomitant "necessity for a more parsimonious system for storage and fast retrieval, since in English, word beginnings distinguish between words more efficiently than word endings" (p. 773).

Walley (1993b) provides a useful discussion of probable differences between child and adult word recognition processes in middle childhood, as well as some suggestions for future research. She points out several reasons why reliance on partial, word-initial input would not be reliable at this age, including the continuing rapid growth of the lexicon, which presumably necessitates ongoing changes in lexical interconnections, and the relative difficulty of error recovery; to these we would add children's greater difficulty in integrating the contextual information which plays such an important role in facilitating the task of listening and comprehending for adults.

Phonology and emergent literacy

The intimate connection between phonological processing and reading skills began to be a focus of direct investigation about twenty years ago. Liberman et al. (1974) provided the first experimental evidence of children's difficulty in explicitly identifying individual segments as compared with syllables, and speculated that this metalinguistic ability may be the major hurdle to be overcome in learning to read an alphabetic script (cf. Mattingly, 1972). The burgeoning of research which followed these first findings and speculations continues unabated today.[5]

While the connection between phonology and reading is itself no longer in doubt, the directionality and nature of the postulated interaction remains controversial (see, for example, the various contributions to special issues of *Cognition* (1986) and the *Merrill-Palmer Quarterly* (1987), and reviews by Wagner and Torgesen (1987), and Bowey and Francis (1991)). A number of intertwined themes recur in this evolving story: differences in the segmentation skills of illiterate vs. newly literate adults as well as of children and adults exposed to different orthographic traditions, with a range of different relationships between speech sounds and graphic units; attempts to tap the segmentation abilities of preschoolers, alongside increasingly age-appropriate tests of their phonological sensitivities, primarily responses to rhyme, and the important discovery of the role of subsyllabic structure (onset and rime) as a precursor to the segment.[6] We will consider each of these in turn.

Cross-linguistic studies

Liberman et al. (1974) reviewed the various types of relationship possible between linguistic units and their graphic representation, distinguishing between meaningful units (morphemes, words or sentences) and units which lack meaning (syllables or phonemes, typically). Drawing on the history of writing systems, the authors remind us that the earliest forms were based on meaningful units; the Chinese logographic system (and the Japanese kanji which derive from that system) comes closest to exemplifying this type of writing today. Syllabic writing systems later developed more or less independently in different cultures (including the Japanese kana, the Native American Cherokee syllabary, and others: Gelb, 1963). The alphabet developed out of one such system (the Phoenician syllabary, which also underlies the Armenian, Arabic, Georgian, Hebrew and Indic scripts today) and was "invented" only once, by the Greeks; all present-day alphabets are derivatives of that system. It has often been pointed out that the unique historical status of the alphabetic system, in which individual sound segments are represented by individual graphemes, must reflect the relative inaccessibility of phonetic segments as compared with syllabic units.

Liberman et al. (1974) demonstrated the greater ease of access of syllables as compared with segments by presenting children aged 4–6 years (forty-odd children each in nursery school, kindergarten and first grade) with a "tapping game," in which the child was required, following some training trials, to repeat a word or sound and tap out the number of its constituent units (from one to three) with a wooden dowel. The child continued to be corrected as needed in the course of testing on forty-two items; "passing" the test involved reaching a criterion of six consecutive correct responses without demonstration. The results showed both a clear (monotonic) trend across the three groups of children and a sharp difference between segmentation into syllables vs. phonemes: 46 percent of the 4-year-olds could pass the syllable test while none could pass the phoneme test; at the end of first grade, after beginning reading instruction, 90 percent succeeded in segmenting syllables while 70 percent could now segment into phonemes. Liberman et al. noted that their experiment provided no way of determining to what extent the developmental trend reflected maturational change and to what extent it reflected instruction in reading; they suggested that developmental studies of children exposed to reading in languages such as Chinese or Japanese could provide additional insight.

A number of separate research groups have since taken up this challenge, investigating the effect on segmentation skills of differential exposure to alphabetic, syllable-based and logographic writing systems. One of the first such studies compared segmentation abilities in illiterate and formerly illiterate Portuguese adults, using the addition or deletion of a single consonant at word onset as the experimental task (Morais et al., 1979).[7] The illiterate group achieved less than 20 percent correct responses to nonword stimuli, while the adults who had attended literacy classes achieved over 70 percent correct. The authors concluded that some specific training is necessary in order to segment speech at the phonemic level (cf. also Morais et al., 1986; Morais, Alegria, and Content, 1987).

Read et al. (1986) compared segmentation abilities in adults literate in Chinese characters only and in adults who had also learned an alphabetic transcription system for Chinese (Hanyu pinyin) many years earlier. The task used for testing was that of Morais et al. (1979) and the results closely replicated those of the earlier study of illiterates vs. "ex-illiterates": Literacy in an alphabetic script appeared to be necessary to foster phonetic segmentation skills. In fact, even subjects with little remaining fluency in the use of the alphabetic system still performed well on the segmentation test.

Mann (1986) extended the investigation to a comparison of Japanese and American children as well as of Japanese children with and without some exposure to an alphabetic transcription system (Romaji). In her testing Mann used both the counting task designed by Liberman and her colleagues and a deletion task similar to that used by Morais and Read and their respective colleagues.

The results generally conformed to expectations: the Japanese first-graders found counting phonemes considerably more difficult than counting morae (a syllable-like rhythmic unit which reflects certain particularities of Japanese phonological structure): All of the children reached criterion (using Liberman et al.'s scoring system) on mora counting, while only 10% passed the phoneme counting test (recall the results for American first-graders: 90% counted syllables successfully vs. 70% for phonemes). However, the children were found to be strongly influenced by orthographic conventions in their mora counting, making errors of overcounting in the rare cases in which more than one symbol is used to write a single mora. In a test of phoneme counting in older children, 50% of third graders and 75% of fourth to sixth graders passed; the introduction of Romaji late in the fourth grade had little apparent effect.

In order to pursue further the question as to why Japanese children developed an ability to count phonemes *without* training in an alphabetic script, in contrast to the adults tested by Morais and Read and colleagues, Mann tested new groups of first graders in Japan and in the United States, using the more sophisticated deletion test. Both groups of children found deleting phonemes more difficult than syllables or morae; though the Japanese were even more successful with morae than the American children with syllables, the difference between the groups was greater in the case of phonemes, with the American children receiving higher scores. All scores were related to ratings of the children's reading ability except that of the American children on syllable deletion. In a final test, Japanese fourth-graders showed improvement over the first-graders in phoneme deletion, without the benefit of exposure to alphabetic script; Japanese sixth-graders showed further improvement, with such exposure.

The relative success of older Japanese children in counting phonemes, without training in an alphabetic script, suggests that phonological awareness must indeed have a cognitive or maturational component, independent of specific reading instruction. However, an important difference between Mann's Japanese subjects and the Portuguese and Chinese adults tested is experience with the Japanese syllabary, a relatively transparent phonologically based system. The demonstrated relationship between Japanese children's success in deleting phonemes and their fluency in reading kana also points to a role for the syllabary in heightening awareness of segments.

Finally, a study of preschool and early school-age children in Italy, designed to replicate as closely as possible the studies conducted by Liberman and colleagues in the United States, showed that the same shift from awareness of the syllable to awareness of the phoneme was evident with the onset of reading instruction in Italian, but was considerably more rapid, presumably because of the more transparent relationship between phonology and orthography in Italian (Cossu et al., 1988); the authors cite a study reporting comparable results for Spanish, with its similar sound–letter relationships (de Manrique and Gramigna, 1984).

Rhyme, alliteration, and subsyllabic structure

Although the boost which training in reading an alphabet script gives to the development of phonological awareness, particularly of phonemes, seems to be indisputable, the cross-linguistic studies provided some suggestion of a "spontaneous" or maturational evolution as well. Furthermore, numerous studies have now documented a relationship between children's sensitivity to phonological structure in the preschool period and their subsequent facility in acquiring reading skills (Bradley and Bryant, 1983; Helfgott, 1976; Lundberg, Olofsson, and Wall, 1980; Stanovich, Cunningham, and Cramer, 1984). We turn now to the remarkably productive line of research concerning this development in responses to rhyme, alliteration and subsyllabic structure – a development which leads to the more recent distinction between phonological sensitivity and metaphonological awareness (Wagner and Torgesen, 1987; A. E. Fowler, 1991).[8]

Despite long-standing concern about the effectiveness of reading instruction (see E. J. Gibson, 1965), investigators were surprisingly slow to consider the relevance of "auditory perception" – or the construction of phonological representations which permit effective manipulation of phonological units (A. E. Fowler, 1991). Bradley and Bryant (1978) identified the probable conceptual source of this oversight: "It might seem . . . that although auditory perception is essential to reading, it would not be a significant source of difficulty, for . . . most children who have difficulties with reading can hear perfectly well, and can discriminate and understand the words which they signally fail to read" (p. 746). They went on to articulate clearly the relevance of rhyming tests: "But discriminating words is not the only aspect of audition involved in reading. The child must also be able to group together words which are different but which have sounds in common" (p. 746).

Knafle (1973, 1974) was a pioneer in the successful testing of very young children on rhyme recognition. She presented over 200 kindergarteners with four test categories of triads of CVC(C) monosyllabic words, all involving a stimulus, a rhyming word and a nonrhyming word which shared the initial consonant of the stimulus (1973). The easiest category involved change in both consonants of a final cluster as compared with the test rhyme: *mend* vs. *melt/felt*, while the most difficult involved change of just the final consonant (*yarn* vs. *yard/hard*).

In a follow-up study, Knafle (1974) tested children in kindergarten through third grade; she repeated the two most difficult categories only, involving change in one or the other of the final consonants ((a) *best* vs. *belt/felt*; (b) *yarn* vs. *yard/card*), and also included a test for a subsample of kindergarteners in which the non-rhyming response agreed with the rhyming response instead of the stimulus in initial consonant (*silk* vs. *milk/mink*). As expected, the children's responses generally showed improvement with grade level. Also, at all grade levels the change of final consonant (b) was more difficult than the change of the pre-final consonant of the cluster (a). The kindergarteners tested on the alliterating responses found the test easier (81% correct: (a) 90%, (b) 71%) than the original test structure (66% correct: (a) 76%, (b) 55%).

Lenel and Cantor (1981) moved the investigation of rhyming responses back in age, testing children from preschool through first grade, and systematically varied the extent and position of phonetic contrast in CVC monosyllables between rhyme and non-rhyming foil. The test was presented both with and without pictures of the word stimuli, which were therefore restricted to concrete nouns.

All three age levels performed above chance; correct responses increased gradually with age, with a significant difference in error scores only between preschool and first-grade children. The use of pictures did not affect performance. Within the categories of pattern contrasts, those triads in which the foil differed from the stimulus by two phonemes were significantly less difficult than the others. Furthermore, it was significantly more difficult to identify the rhyming word when the consonant common to the stimulus and the non-rhyming foil was in initial position (*tent* vs. *toes/nose*) than when it was in final position (*pin* vs. *sun/gun*).

The studies of both Knafle, and Lenel and Cantor showed that small children could successfully be tested with the rhyme-recognition method. Both studies also pointed the way to further investigation of the relative difficulty of discriminating different phonetic patterns, especially based on consonant position. Finally, as Lenel and Cantor pointed out, these studies strongly suggested a need for further investigation of the relationship between rhyming ability and reading. In Oxford, England such work had in fact already begun (cf. also Lundberg et al. 1980).

Selecting children who were one to three years behind their peers in reading ability, Bradley and Bryant (1978) compared this sample with a sample of *younger* children of normal reading ability, matched to the poor readers on IQ as well as reading level. Matching for reading level was designed to eliminate the confounding factor of reading experience as a possible reason for differences in the "perceptual task" (sensitivity to phonological patterning).

Bradley and Bryant tested the children's ability to categorize sounds with an "oddity task" which involved identifying the "odd word out" from a set of four monosyllabic words, three of which matched in initial consonant (*sun, see, sock* vs.

rag), vowel (*red, fed, bed* vs. *nod*) or final consonant (*weed, need, deed* vs. *peel*). The results were striking: Overall, 92% of the poor readers made at least one error, 85% making more than one, while only 53% of the normal readers made any errors at all and only 27% made more than one – this despite the fact that the poor or "backward" readers were an average of three years older than the comparison group. Interestingly, in a finding complementary to that of Lenel and Cantor's study of rhyme detection, the children had the most difficulty with the set in which only the odd word had a different word-initial sound, even though in the example given the odd word shared *no* sounds with the other stimuli.

Bradley and Bryant (1983; Bradley, 1980) followed up their findings with a large-scale study, combining a longitudinal design with a training study in an effort to establish causality. The first step was administration of an oddity test to 4- and 5-year-olds who were not yet reading (403 children were tested initially). Tests of reading and spelling abilities over three years later showed high correlations with results on this first test of sound categorization.

The training study focused on a subset of sixty-five children who showed the lowest scores in the initial testing; these children were divided into four subgroups, matched for age, verbal IQ, and their initial sound categorization score. Two of these groups were given intensive training in sound categorization in forty sessions over a two-year period; one of these groups also received training in mapping sounds to letters. As a control, a third group was given purely conceptual categorization training, while a fourth group received no training at all. The results were unequivocal: The children who received phonological categorization training achieved significantly higher reading and spelling scores, with a greater advantage for those children who were trained in sound–letter relationships as well.[9] The two control groups were not statistically distinguishable.

The Oxford group turned next to a series of studies of rhyming abilities and knowledge of nursery rhymes in preschool children and the relationship of these to later reading skills (Maclean, Bryant, and Bradley, 1987; Bryant et al., 1989; Bryant, MacLean, and Bradley, 1990). The earlier study reported that some, but not all, 3-year-old children were able to detect rhyme and alliteration and to produce such phonetic matches spontaneously after demonstration; most of them were able to recite one or more complete lines from nursery rhymes, but the amount of knowledge varied considerably across the group of sixty-six children. Quantitative analysis showed "a highly specific relationship between a child's knowledge of nursery rhymes and his or her ability to detect rhyme" (MacLean et al., 1987, p. 271); more importantly, there was also a relationship between rhyme detection at age 3 and early signs of reading fifteen months later, independent of general intelligence and family background. The later studies followed the children to age 6, establishing a connection between early phonological awareness and later reading and spelling skills and attempting to distinguish statistically between the contributions of more general linguistic and metalinguistic capacities and "awareness of rhyme" (see also the comment by Bowey, 1990, and the authors' reply in the same issue).

We mentioned earlier the contribution of Treiman and her colleagues to the study of subsyllabic structure. In addition to her work with children, Treiman

(1983; Treiman and Danis, 1988) tested adults to assess the psychological validity of the concept that syllables have a hierarchical internal structure (Fudge, 1969, and Halle and Vergnaud, 1980, had arrived at this concept through analysis of the constraints on the distribution of segments within a syllable; MacKay, 1972, provided evidence from speech errors). Based on both "word games" and short-term memory tasks (cf. also Brady, Shankweiler, and Mann, 1983), Treiman found strong support for the validity of the division into onset and rime, but less support for the further division of the rime into "peak" and "coda." The various studies of small children's responses to tests of rhyme recognition and "oddity tests" of phonological "awareness" or sensitivity have provided further evidence that some phonological patterns are inherently more salient or memorable than others – long before reading instruction intervenes to direct the child's attention.

Kirtley et al. (1989) brought these lines of evidence together in an analysis of "Rhyme, rime and the onset of reading," in an effort to counter the argument that awareness of phonemes is a product of reading experience and is unrelated to prior sensitivity to rhyme (Morais, Alegria, and Content, 1987). They argued that recognition of similarity based on a single segment should be accessible to prereaders just in case the single segment corresponds to a natural subsyllabic unit, such as the onset, but should be difficult when it does not – as in the case of a final consonant, which is part of the rime. In an oddity test of words with 5-year-olds and both words and nonwords with 6- and 7-year-olds these authors systematically varied the commonality in the foils while testing for detection of a different initial or final consonant ("opening sound" or "end sound").

As predicted, detection of similarity in a single segment proved particularly difficult (at all age levels) when the similar words could *not* be grouped on the basis of the onset or rime as a whole in opposition to the odd word, but only on the basis of a portion of the rime, vowel or coda (*lead* vs. *mop*, *whip*: final consonant is the same; *cot* vs. *can*, *cap*: vowel is the same). In the remaining single–consonant-difference condition (same CV or VC: *lad* vs. *cap*, *can*; *tip* vs. *hid*, *lid*), the similar words always share either onset or rime while the odd word does not: The odd word was considerably less difficult to detect in these cases.

A recent study by Bowey and Francis (1991) provides both a lucid methodological critique of the existing literature and a theoretical formulation which seems to resolve the paradox involved in the finding that "phonological awareness" is both a prerequisite for and a consequence of beginning reading experience. These authors note that "it may be prereaders' sensitivity to onset and rime units that predicts subsequent reading achievement, rather than their ability to analyze spoken words at the segmental level," since

> children who can attend to units of sound structure, such as onsets and rimes, are more likely to understand early reading instruction than children who are not able to focus on sound at all . . . They are also more likely to discover sound-symbol correspondences for themselves . . . Since most English onsets are in fact singletons (e.g., /k/ in /kæt/), sensitivity to onsets and rimes, coupled with knowledge of a few sight words, could provide the point of entry into comprehension of the alphabetic principle. (p. 96)

Methodologically, Bowey and Francis insist on the point that studies examining the value of performance on phonological analysis tasks as predictors of reading achievement take scrupulous care to screen out children with some rudimentary knowledge of reading from the sample of "prereaders." The point is critical, since "being able to read just a few words appears to represent a qualitative leap in terms of phonological processing" (p. 93). They argue that when those precautions are taken, it will be found that phonemic analysis skills become available only with special environmental support, typically from learning to read (although certain other verbal games or activities may have the same effect). They conclude from the study by Kirtley and colleagues that "prereaders are sensitive to onsets and rimes but not to phonemes unless phonemic oddity coincides with onset or rime oddity," and that sensitivity to onset and rime is "a natural developmental phenomenon facilitating comprehension of reading instruction, which in turn fosters phonemic sensitivity" (p. 100).

In order to investigate this "alphabetic principle proposal," Bowey and Francis tested three groups of twenty children each in a large Australian school system: one group of older kindergarteners, carefully screened to see that none had even limited reading abilities, the other two groups both midway through the first grade year, when reading is introduced – a younger group, less than three months older than the kindergarten sample, and a group about eight months older. The children were presented with oddity tests designed to distinguish between sensitivity to onset and rime units or to phonemic units within the rime (see Appendix 7.1a–c at the end of this chapter). The authors predicted that the two groups of first-graders would not show significantly different results, and that only first-graders, but not kindergarteners, would succeed at a better than chance level on those oddity tests which required phonemic analysis. These predictions were fully borne out in the results. The kindergarteners had more limited success with the onset/rime tests than the earlier literature might have led one to expect (20 percent passed) – perhaps because of the exclusion of all children with even incipient reading ability. Of the younger first-graders – comparable to kindergarteners in general developmental level, but with six months of reading instruction – 60 percent performed above chance on these same tests. None of the kindergarteners passed the phoneme oddity tests, which were very difficult for the first-graders as well: only 10 percent performed above chance.[10] The authors conclude that

> Children who are sensitive to sound structure are more likely to understand early reading instruction than those who are not . . . It seems likely that sensitivity to multi-phonemic units such as syllables and subsyllabic onset and rime units also develops spontaneously and concomitantly with linguistic maturity . . . Nevertheless, onset and rime sensitivity is enhanced by alphabetic reading instruction . . . However, unless specifically stimulated [e.g., by alphabetic literacy instruction] . . . this metalinguistic orientation to the sound structure of language does not develop further. (p. 117)

The Oxford group has interpreted the strong connection between knowledge of nursery rhymes at three and later rhyme detection skills and reading as reflecting a direct role of experience with nursery rhymes in the children's "growing awareness that words and syllables can be broken into, and can be categorized by, smaller units of sound" (MacLean et al., 1987, p. 271). An alternative interpretation would be that children who are relatively sensitive to phonological patterning are more likely to enjoy nursery rhymes, to request their frequent repetition, and to remember parts of them; the same underlying sensitivity to speech sounds, following Bowey and Francis, would lead to faster progress in developing more detailed or more accessible phonological representations, which would also serve to facilitate reading. This is the kind of sensitivity that leads some precocious children to learn to read on their own and to develop their own spelling patterns (Read, 1975; Bissex, 1980; Mann, Tobin, and Wilson, 1987; Barton, 1992); it might also be related to individual differences in the timing of first word production, given the role of sensitivity to sound patterns in "making connections" (Bradley, 1988) between own productions and adult input (Vihman and Miller, 1988, Vihman, 1993b).

Stark, Ansel, and Bond (1988) provide some evidence of a relationship between late talking and reading difficulties, which would also support such an interpretation. These authors followed the early vocal development of forty-five children in a mixed longitudinal and cross-sectional design. One of those children failed to produce canonical babbling by 12 months and had no identifiable words by 18 months. Early in his third year the child showed a developmental spurt in language and caught up with his peers. "In first grade, however, he was considered by his teachers to 'lack motivation' and to show poor attention during reading instruction. It is probable that his difficulty with reading reflected his earlier problems with phonetic development. These problems might well have resurfaced as a difficulty with phonetic recoding" (p. 17).

Summary: Listening for meaning

Linguistic perception involves active attention to speech sound patterns in order to relate word forms to meanings, store this association, and access the appropriate lexical item at will. Not all lexical items appear to be represented fully accurately from the beginning of speech production. Despite the difficulty of testing children younger than age 2, word familiarity has been shown to play an important role, suggesting that some production errors may derive from perceptual misinterpretations, i.e., internal representations that fail to match the adult model, since initial attempts at a new word inevitably reflect an internal representation based on perception of a relatively unfamiliar word. The relationship between perception and production appears to be complex, with possible bidirectional effects.

Word recognition is a complex process as well, involving the integration of both the sensory input, or acoustic/phonetic signal, and contextual information, including both pragmatic and general knowledge-based inferences regarding the gist of the incoming message and specific structural effects relating to the phonotactic, syntactic and semantic restrictions characteristic of the language code. The listener's lexical expectations are also influenced by word frequency.

On the whole, school-age children process continuous speech in an adult-like way, making use of context to aid in the interpretation of the acoustic signal. In several respects children are different from adults, however. They appear to need more acoustic information before they commit themselves to a decision as to word identity, perhaps in part because so many words continue to be unfamiliar. Furthermore, children's use of semantic knowledge as a clue to the unfolding message is not fully developed until the teen years. Finally, school-age children, like younger children, perceive familiar words more accurately than unfamiliar words and take a cautious approach to apparent mispronunciations in running speech.

Vocabulary growth has been advanced as a primary factor in the development of adult-like word recognition. Several studies have documented a shift in children's attention or sensitivity to and memory for phonological units, from whole syllables to parts of syllables (onset and rime) and finally to individual segments. This shift is thought to pave the way to the more efficient processing of input speech characteristic of adults, who typically identify words even before the full signal has become available. The connection between increased lexical density and more detailed phonetic representations remains speculative, however. That is, to date no one has conducted a longitudinal study directly supporting a link between relative vocabulary size (independent of chronological age and associated maturational changes) and attention to detail in the phonological structure of the input.

The likely connection between phonology and reading has been appreciated for some time. Early experimental work established the intuitively plausible idea that syllables are more accessible than segments; both maturation alone and experience with reading an alphabetic script proved to be contributors to awareness of segments. Most recently, sensitivity to the phonological structure of syllables, whether inherent or trained, has been found to be related to facility in learning to read and spell. The salience of rhyme, at least in a stress-timed language such as English, is well attested by poetic tradition, yet not all English-speaking adults are equally attracted by poetry. It is plausible that individual differences in sensitivity to sound structure – so evident in the period of transition into speech – should be manifested later in life in a variety of ways, including sensitivity to sub-syllabic structure and a corresponding facility in redirecting attention down to the individual segment.

NOTES

1 For a discussion of some of the methodological considerations involved in testing children's ability to discriminate speech sounds, see Barton (1980), Vihman (1993b). Notice that for testing purposes, training an association between a nonsense word and an arbitrary referent is no different from teaching the child any other word; in either case a particular sound pattern is made to evoke a particular meaning or situation of use.

2 For a discussion of the complex interrelation between children's perceptions, misarticulations, and self-monitoring on the phonetic and phonemic level, see Locke (1979).

3 The notion that syllable structure consists of an "onset" – the initial consonant or cluster – and a "rime" (or "rhyme") was first elaborated by Fudge (1969); see also Halle and Vergnaud (1980); Selkirk (1982).

4   The qualitative analysis of the children's recall errors provides striking evidence of the role of onset/rime substructure. Good readers showed the same transposition patterns as poor readers, but produced significantly fewer errors of recall.

5   It is probably not coincidental that infant speech perception and experimental investigation into the role of phonology in learning to read should have blossomed into productive research areas at about the same time: Both have their origins in the research into adult speech perception which flourished in the 1960s, particularly at Haskins Laboratories; Haskins investigators played an important role in the launching of both of the developmental applications as well.

6   Another theme is the relevance to reading of phonological or metalinguistic "awareness" vs. phonetic "recoding" for short-term memory and the extent to which the two represent *separate* factors in reading readiness (Wagner and Torgesen, 1987; Gathercole and Baddeley, 1993); the evidence appears to be intriguing but inconclusive and we will not review it here.

7   It has since been established that this test of segmental analysis is a particularly difficult one for children (Content et al., 1984; Stanovich, Cunningham, and Cramer, 1986).

8   We will generally follow the usage of the literature we review in using the term "awareness," although the term "sensitivity" seems more appropriate: Following the arguments of A. E. Fowler (1991), it seems likely that spontaneous development in the preschool period involves improvement in detail or "definition" (in a photographic sense) in phonological representations rather than involving advances in metalinguistic "awareness"; see also Bowey and Francis (1991), whose helpful theoretical formulation and supportive findings are discussed below.

9   Long-term effects (at age 13) were later identified for both reading and spelling in the two experimental groups (Bradley, 1988).

10   Among the first graders, after exclusion of one unusually precocious child as a statistical outlier, rime and onset oddity tests presented *before* presentation of the more difficult phoneme oddity tests correlated at $p < 0.05$ with early reading achievement. No correlation was found for the sound sensitivity measures and vocabulary age, contrary to what both A. E. Fowler (1991) and Walley (1993b) might predict.

APPENDIX 7.1a   ITEMS USED FOR TESTING SENSITIVITY TO ONSET AND RIME UNITS

Rime task	Onset task
Practice	
deck neck fit	clue fray fry
zip bat hat	fly floor* crow
fish man dish	slow draw dry
top hop run	throw stew three
Test	
bed shut cut	ski glow glue
pin win look	gray star* grow
hop let bet	true try blow
rock nut sock	store* cry stay
rug cat hug	flow sky flea
log dog wish	tray tree blue

cook set book   snow clay claw
pen got dot   scar* score* pray

*In Australian English, the final /r/ is not pronounced in this context.

Source: Bowey and Francis, 1991, reprinted with the permission of Cambridge University Press

APPENDIX 7.1b ITEMS USED FOR COMPARING SENSITIVITY TO PHONEME AND RIME UNITS

Rime unit	Medial phoneme
Practice	
mop hop tap	mat mop man
hat cot pot	win wig wash
pat fit cat	cat kick kid
neck rock lock	dog dip dot
Test	
jug dog log	sit sick sad
fish wash dish	bed bit bin
fell doll bell	pin pick pet
red bed lid	cake cut cage
wag peg leg	poke peg pen
dig pig hug	hop hot hum
fun pin gun	lid leg lip
sick kick pack	set soap soak

Source: Bowey and Francis, 1991, reprinted with the permission of Cambridge University Press

APPENDIX 7.1c ITEMS USED FOR TESTING ANALYSIS OF ONSET UNITS

Initial phoneme	Medial phoneme
Practice	
blue blow glee	prow play pry
floor* sly flea	fly fray free
cry cray true	crow crew clay
sleigh flow flu	blow brow blue
Test	
clay claw snow	star* stay ski
crow try tray	slow spy spur
dry fray draw	plea plough pray
tree grow gray	claw cry clue
fry pray free	fry floor* flow
plough clue play	store* sleigh stay
throw three crew	scar* sky snow
fly glue glow	flue grow gray

*In Australian English, the final /r/ is not pronounced in this context.

Source: Bowey and Francis, 1991, reprinted with the permission of Cambridge University Press

8 Prosodic Development

As Allen and Hawkins (1980) have pointed out, prosody – or "phonological rhythm" – presents a particular challenge to investigators because

> the dimensions underlying it are often simultaneously involved in various other phonological contrasts as well. For example, greater phonetic duration not only signals the end of a spoken English phrase . . .but also serves to differentiate phonologically long from short vowels, voiced from voiceless post-vocalic consonants, and stressed from unstressed syllables; similarly, changes in the fundamental frequency of voicing not only mark many of the metrically accented syllables within the rhythmic phrase but also define the overall intonation contour; and the degree of stress-accent a syllable receives is determined partly by the rhythm of the phrase and partly by lexical, syntactic, and stylistic constraints. In investigating phonological rhythm, therefore, we are examining a set of interrelated phenomena, each of which aids in some way the sequential integration of the utterance while, at the same time, playing a number of other nonrhythmic roles. (pp. 229f.)

Despite these difficulties, an understanding of the development of prosody, and of rhythmic behavior in particular, is of considerable importance for phonological development in so far as the dual role of rhythm as a regulator of motor behavior in general and of speech production in particular (the constraints of each language defining the particular manifestations of the requirement of rhythmicity in speech)[1] may be seen to constitute an essential link between biological and linguistic structure (Kent, Mitchell, and Sancier, 1991).

Three basic components of the production of voice – laryngeal tension, timing, and air pressure (Lieberman, 1985) – can be manipulated to produce patterns involving the acoustic variables which enter into the intonation systems of adult languages (Crystal, 1969): (1) fundamental frequency (Fo), (2) duration and (3) intensity or amplitude (see table 8.1). These acoustic parameters yield the auditory percepts of pitch and melody, duration and rhythm, and loudness. Finally, language systems make phonological use of these variables in the form of accentual and intonation systems involving tone or pitch accent and stress. The development of control of the basic production variables can be traced in prelinguistic vocal behaviors to determine what "raw materials" are available to infants as they begin to shape their production in the direction of the ambient language or, somewhat later, to learn the system of contrasting prosodic values which make up the intonation and accentual systems of their language.

It has long been thought that "intonation" is the first aspect of language to develop (e.g., Fry, 1966; Lenneberg, 1967). However, such claims were based on impressionistic accounts of infant production (often associated with highly subjective interpretations of infant "meaning"), to the extent that they were empirically supported at all (for a review of the earlier literature, see Crystal, 1973). A difficulty in evaluating the claims is their relative lack of specificity: What develops early? The production of a range of distinct melodies, such as rising and falling pitch patterns? Differential use of such melodies for distinct communicative functions? Or appropriate production of language-specific prosodic features for lexical or grammatical contrast?

We begin by reviewing studies which provide information regarding the development of laryngeal control within the first year, setting the stage for the acquisition of distinct pitch contours, which are the central element in adult intonation systems. In the next section we will consider aspects of timing in prelinguistic vocalizations and early speech. Finally, we will consider separately what has been learned about the development of intonation, stress accent and tone.

Acquiring the ability to control pitch

We have already noted that the child's first vocal production, cry, draws on the same respiratory timing characteristics as speech. Lieberman (1985) points to an additional aspect of cry that resembles speech:

The alveolar air pressure function rapidly rises prior to the onset of phonation and

Table 8.1 Elements of prosodic systems

Aspects of vocal control	Acoustic variables	Percepts	Phonological effects
laryngeal tension/ rate of glottal vibration	fundamental frequency (Fo)	pitch/melody	tone/pitch accent intonation
time taken to articulate	duration	perceived duration/ rhythm	length of segments, syllables, words
subglottal pressure/ respiratory drive	intensity/ amplitude	loudness	stress accent

Source: Adapted from Allen, 1983, by permission of S. Karger AG, Basel

then falls rapidly at the end of phonation as the infant enters the inspiratory phase . . .The abrupt shift in the alveolar air pressure function at the end of phonation thus reflects a basic vegetative constraint . . .All things being equal, Fo will fall at the end of an expiration. If the larynx does not maintain its phonatory configuration until the end of phonation but instead begins to open toward its inspiratory position, the terminal fall in Fo will be enhanced as the laryngeal muscles relax. (p. 38; cf. also Langlois, Backen and Wilder, 1980)[2]

One important aspect of control of phonation that the infant does not control at birth, due to differences in rib structure between infant and adult, is the inspiratory or "hold-back" gesture of the intercostal muscles, which regulates subglottal pressure (Lieberman, 1985). Inability to perform this gesture effectively limits the permissible length of infant vocalization for at least the first three months of life.

Laufer and Horii (1977) report a longitudinal instrumental study of fundamental frequency characteristics of infant non-distress vocalization during the first twenty-four weeks, based on intensive recording of four infants. Like earlier studies (Sheppard and Lane, 1968; Delack and Fowlow, 1978), these authors found that fundamental frequency shows little change in mean value over the period studied (335 Hz, closely comparable to the mean of 355 Hz reported by Delack and Fowlow for nineteen subjects over the first year). The chief developmental changes observed in this study involved duration of vocalization and within-utterance range and variability of pitch. Although the individual profiles showed considerable differences over time, all of the infants showed a sharp decrease in within-utterance range and variability from the first to the second four-week interval (based on relatively few utterances in the first interval), followed by a fairly steady increase over the remaining weeks. Changes in duration followed a similar course, with a dramatic increase in mean length of vocalization (from 600 to nearly 1500 milliseconds [ms]) between 4 and 20 weeks.

A remarkably close correlation between pitch range and variability was observed. The growls and squeals typical of vocal play were observed for three of the four infants in the latter portion of the period studied; the fourth child, whose fundamental frequency was lower than that of any of the others, was less active in general and "appeared to process information predominantly through the visual modality throughout the first year[,] quieting to the presentation of stimuli . . ." (p. 181).

Kent and Murray (1982) also investigated "phonatory function," at 3, 6 and 9 months (seven infants at each age level). They note features of non-distress vocalizations which represent continuity with cry: The same fundamental frequency range is typical of both (350–500 Hz); abrupt changes in harmonic structure may be observed in both. An unusual laryngeal characteristic which they describe and illustrate is vocal tremor or vibrato, more common at 3 and 6 than at 9 months. In general, Kent and Murray find infant vocalizations to be "affected by nonlinearities that older speakers learn to avoid," such as "noise components, irregular vocal fold vibrations, or transient deviations from the overall Fo contour" (p. 360); "all of these characteristics may be taken as evidence of instability of laryngeal control" (p. 362). Kent and Murray caution that it is probably inappropriate to interpret transient noises and shifts in phonatory function as productions of glottal stop or [h] (as in the earlier transcriptional practice), leading to the unwarranted implication that consonant-like "control elements" are present in infant vocalization.

Although the primary characteristic of phonatory function in this age range was variability, both within and across utterances, Kent and Murray selected about 100 relatively stable vocalizations from each age group for analysis of melodic contour. For all three age levels flat, falling, and rising-falling contours predominated (accounting for 31%, 24% and 23% of the total at 3, 6 and 9 months). Kent and Murray relate this tendency toward a falling contour to *either* the decline in subglottal pressure in the course of a vocalization *or* a reduction in vocal fold length and tension as the muscles of the larynx relax. A rising pitch contour requires an increase in vocal fold length or tension at the end of the vocalization, or an increase in subglottal pressure, or both; production of such contours is reported late in the first year and is affected by the dominant patterning of the adult language (as discussed below).

Changes in pitch appeared informally to be associated with changes in the child's state of arousal in the Laufer and Horii study (increased muscular tension in the body as a whole leads to higher pitch even in adults). Attempts to characterize more specifically the effect of social context (solitary play, interaction with mother, object play) on the prosodic contour of infant vocalizations have so far proven inconclusive, however (Delack and Fowlow, 1978; D'Odorico, 1984). In a painstaking statistical analysis of the non-segmental characteristics of the vocalizations of five Italian infants, for example, D'Odorico and Franco (1991) were able to find some consistency in the production of pitch contour in context in the longitudinal record of individual infants from 4 to 8 months. Broadly speaking, they found that "vocalizations demanding some intervention by the partner . . . are likely to be marked by rising melodic patterns and high pitch" (p. 495), as was also reported in earlier studies using somewhat different contextual definitions and procedures. However, the distinctive pitch contours were no longer related to context after 9 months. The authors speculated that a new, segmental production-based organization of sound–meaning relationships may begin to emerge around that time.

Final syllable lengthening

In addition to pitch or tonal change, an aspect of accentual systems which has received some attention in both adult languages and developmental studies is timing, or the relative duration of syllables within a word or phrase. Two principles of rhythmic organization have been proposed: isochrony, or equally timed production of some designated unit (such as the rhythm group, or foot, meaning the "stretch of utterance from one stressed syllable to the next": Cruttenden, 1986), and lengthening of particular syllables in relation to others. Lengthening is often found to be associated with stress or tonal accent, but it has also been reported to occur in final or prepausal syllables independent of accent; the incidence of isochrony in adult languages is less clear (cf. Wenk and Wioland, 1982). Developmental data have been invoked as a way of resolving the question of the origin and, by implication, the function of final syllable lengthening: Is it built upon a preexisting physiological tendency, given in infancy, and thus to be considered a natural feature of speech production actively suppressed in languages which lack it? Or is it a learned behavior and thus arguably a listener-oriented function, facilitating the segmentation of utterances?

Adult languages

In 1966 Pierre Delattre presented a painstaking comparative analysis of the influence of syllable type (open vs. closed), weight (stressed vs. unstressed) and position (final vs. nonfinal) on relative syllable length in four languages, English, German, Spanish and French. He found that the first three of these languages, all of which have variable stress placement, show good agreement in absolute length in stressed non-final syllables (19–20 centiseconds [cs]) but differ in the extent of the divergence from this norm for syllables in stressed and unstressed final and in unstressed non-final position (see table 8.2). The degree of divergence correlates with the degree of intensity that is associated with stressed and unstressed syllables: English shows the greatest difference between overall amplitude (or perceived loudness) in stressed and unstressed vowels and also the widest range in syllable length under different conditions; Spanish shows the smallest differences, while German falls in between. Final stressed syllables were the longest in all three languages, while unstressed final syllables were slightly longer than stressed non-final syllables in English, on average, and slightly shorter in German and Spanish.

Table 8.2 Comparison of syllable lengths (in cs) under the effects of syllabic weight, place, and type

	English	*German*	*Spanish*	*French*
Stressed				
Final				
Closed	40.81	36.15	32.13	34.12
Open	33.45	29.75	24.50	24.57
Non-final				
Closed	25.88	24.56	25.88	
Open	19.19	19.72	20.23	
Unstressed				
Final				
Closed	25.62	27.81	23.03	
Open	21.24	17.69	18.52	
Non-final				
Closed	15.50	17.51	19.27	19.19
Open	12.02	13.22	18.16	13.74

Source: Delattre, 1966

French contrasts only final stressed and non-final unstressed syllables, since stress is always phrase-final. In addition to having fixed stress placement, French is known to have a "weak stress"; there is actually a *decrease* in intensity between the final stressed vowel and other vowels. Thus, syllable length plays a more important role as a signal of stress in French than it does in the other three languages, where stress placement is also variable. As in the other three languages, final syllables were longer in French than non-final ("unstressed") syllables.

Russian and Swedish agree with the four languages analyzed by Delattre in showing final syllable lengthening, but Finnish, Estonian and Japanese are said to "reveal little (if any) final-syllable vowel lengthening" (Oller and Smith, 1977, p. 994). It is important to note that segmental length contrasts play a prominent role in all of these latter languages. Finnish and Estonian agree in featuring fixed, word-initial stress. In Finnish, contrastive vowel length occurs in unstressed as well as stressed syllables. In Estonian, on the other hand, vowel length is contrastive only under stress;[3] the second (unstressed) syllable is phonetically longer than the first (stressed) syllable whenever the initial syllable nucleus is "light", or consists of a short vowel and no coda (Ariste, 1953; Lehiste, 1960). In Japanese, a weak, variable pitch accent serves lexical contrasts; any tendency toward final lengthening, like lengthening under accent, may be held in check by the "comparatively strict durational control" implemented in this "mora-timed" language (Hoequist, 1983: p. 228).

Developmental studies

A series of studies is now available, most of them based on English, to which one can refer to obtain some idea of a possible developmental basis for final syllable lengthening. In the first study to address the questions mentioned above, Oller and Smith (1977) analyzed 108 reduplicated utterances from six subjects aged 5 to 12 months. The number of utterances ranged from seven (for the two subjects aged 11 or 12 months) to forty (one subject aged 10 months). No attempt was made to control the perceived stress in infant syllables; for comparison with the length of final syllables all non-final syllables were combined, regardless of total number of syllables in the utterance. The study revealed "only minimal differences between final and non-final vowels" (p. 996).

Laufer (1980) reported a more extensive and more tightly controlled longitudinal study of four infants over the first six months of life (284 utterances). The "protosyllables" produced by these infants were considerably longer than adult syllables, ranging from means of 200 to nearly 400 milliseconds for the four subjects, or up to twice the length reported for stressed non-final syllables by Delattre (mean length of disyllabic utterances ranged from 650 to nearly 900 msecs; intersyllabic silent intervals were omitted from the measurement of both initial and final syllables).[4] Restricting her analysis to disyllables, Laufer reported that all four children showed final lengthening; the difference between final and nonfinal syllables was statistically significant for three of the four. There was a tendency for utterances to be longer in the second half of the period studied (12–24 weeks), when infants were entering the expansion stage of vocal production. Post-vocalic glottal stop was associated with shorter duration in both monosyllables and embedded syllables.

A study which spanned prelinguistic and linguistic stages was conducted by Robb and Saxman (1990). Seven subjects were recorded monthly for a period of thirteen months; age at the onset of the study ranged from 8 to 14 months. Only disyllables were analyzed; following Laufer, the investigators omitted any intervocalic silent intervals. Words were distinguished from non-words (babbling) and protowords. The ten-word and the fifty-word points were also identified, to allow interindividual comparison on the basis of developmental milestones. Results were clear-cut: No pattern of change in duration was observed over the time of the study, but final syllable lengthening was found for all of the children in all of the periods analyzed, in both words and nonwords and in both open and closed syllables.

Kubaska and Keating (1981) examined word duration in children's multiword productions, to determine whether the decrease in overall duration over the course of development is related entirely to such general factors as increased motor control and increased familiarity with the lexicon or is positionally dependent and thus perhaps due at least in part to progressive integration of syntactic and prosodic variables. Kubaska and Keating recorded three children biweekly over a period of about one year, beginning early in the period of combinatorial speech (Mean Length of Utterance (MLU) 1.1–1.7). Analysis was based on spontaneous production of frequent words, which allowed comparison of tokens over time. Three positions in utterance were identified: isolated, utterance-nonfinal and utterance-final, based on breath group information. No consistent increase in duration was found over time in this period, nor was there any apparent effect on duration of relative word familiarity. Durational differences were significantly correlated with position in utterance for the three words (from one child) for which a sufficient number of tokens could be found, however; furthermore, tests of non-final vs. isolated and utterance-final word tokens showed that the latter were generally longer, while the two prepausal positions were not typically distinguishable. In an intensive case study covering the same period, however, Mack and Lieberman (1985) failed to find consistent differences in prepausal and non-prepausal words; they did find that syllable-final vowels in disyllabic words were considerably longer than vowels in monosyllabic words and in non-final syllables.

Lastly, Konefal, Fokes, and Bond (1982) conducted a study of stressed vowel duration in the spontaneous speech of three older children, two boys aged 3;0 and 3;4 (MLU 2.8 and 4.2, respectively) and a 5-year-old girl. These authors contrasted three conditions: "prepausal" (or utterance-final), "monosyllabic" (including both monosyllables and word-final stressed vowels in polysyllables which were not utterance-final) and "polysyllabic," including all other stressed vowels. They found the longest vowels in prepausal position in all cases where the same vowel could be compared across conditions. Furthermore, the vowels produced in the "monosyllabic" condition proved quite similar to those of a single adult subject reading sentences (from Umeda, 1975); the prepausal vowels agreed with the adult's vowels in being relatively longer, but showed considerable variability across the three subjects and three different vowels.

A cross-linguistic perspective

Final syllable lengthening in children's vocal productions has been investigated for French and, in a preliminary way, for Japanese as well as for English. Allen (1983) reported differences in duration between final and penultimate syllable in 161 utterances recorded from six French 2-year-olds. Absolute duration was greater than adult norms, as expected, but the median non-final to final vowel ratio was strikingly similar to the adult ratio (1.59 to 1 for the children vs. 1.6 to 1 for adults, according to Benguerel, 1971 or 1.78 to 1 according to Delattre, 1966). Similarly, Konopczynski (1986) reported a mean final syllable lengthening ratio of 1.6 for four French children aged 1;4 to 2;0. In contrast to Robb and Saxman, however, Konopczynski reported isosyllabicity in the vocal production of these infants at 8–10 months.

Levitt and Wang (1991) examined reduplicated babbling sequences from five children each learning English (7–35 utterances apiece) and French (8–42 utterances). The infants were audio-recorded weekly by their parents for 10–20 minutes over a period of 2–6 months, from the onset of reduplicative production (age 5 to 9 months). The utterances analyzed (ca. 100 per group) represent "all the reduplicative babbles" of these infants, and thus may be taken to constitute an extremely small selection from the children's vocal output, as produced in brief but frequent samples over a period of several months.

Final syllable lengthening characterized the reduplicated babbling of both groups of infants, although the French children showed a greater incidence of substantial increases in final as compared with penultimate syllable length (defined as increases of 20 ms or more). In addition, the French infants produced more sequences of four or more syllables than did the American infants, which the authors interpret as ambient language influence: In adult French, four or more unaccented syllables have been shown to precede an accented final syllable in conversational speech (J. Fletcher, 1991), while English speakers rarely produce such a large number of inter-stress syllables (Crystal and House, 1990). On the other hand, American infants have been found to produce shorter utterances in the presence of an interlocutor than alone, especially in the latter part of the period sampled here (Vihman et al., 1986), while longer strings of jargon (variegated babbling with adult-like variation of pitch and vowel quality) occur in both French and English prelinguistic vocalizations (Boysson-Bardies, et al., 1981; Vihman and Miller, 1988). It would be interesting, then, to test these findings on a more representative sample of infant vocalizations, in relation to infant age, total amount of vocalization, situation (play alone or with a caretaker) and developmental indices, such as onset of word use.

Hallé, Boysson-Bardies, and Vihman (1991) analyzed prosodic aspects of disyllabic word and nonword production at the session in which twenty-five words were produced in four children each learning French and Japanese (age range 1;2–1;7 for French (497 productions), 1;3–1;11 for Japanese (458 productions)). Mean duration ratio for second to first syllable rime was 1.45 for French (range 1.23–1.58) vs. 1.15 for Japanese (range 0.83 to 1.68). Three of the four Japanese infants ended over 20 percent of final syllables with a glottal stop; the single exception, who produced only 5 percent such syllables, was the only Japanese child to show final syllable lengthening (1.68 to 1). In this study, as in the Robb and Saxman study of children acquiring English, contemporaneous words and babble showed closely similar mean duration ratios. Hallé and his colleagues concluded that "global properties of French *vs.* Japanese . . . duration patterns are present in the vocalizations of children by about 18 months *in either word or babbling forms.*" They add, on the basis of their own and other studies, that

> final lengthening eventually emerges in children's vocalizations when it is present in the adult model, as in English or French, although we are not clear as to when . . . [One] explanation is that final lengthening is potentially universal at a certain developmental stage, but later becomes exaggerated in some languages, inhibited in some others: For those languages where final lengthening is not present in adult speech, like Japanese, children may have to learn to inhibit final lengthening. A possible way is to produce terminal glottal stop. (p. 315)

The phonological use of prosody

In 1975 two landmark papers proposed an alternative to the nativist view of syntactic structure as the first significant step in language acquisition (cf. also L. Bloom, 1973). Both Bruner (1975) and Dore (1975) suggested that pragmatic development, which has clear antecedents in the prelinguistic period (Golinkoff, 1983), be seen as setting the stage for syntax by allowing the child to enter into intentional vocal communication with contrastive speech acts whose *linguistic* component may be limited to prosodic form. Specifically, Bruner suggested that in the period of transition to speech the child begins to map his or her "knowledge of action" and capacity for joint reference onto primitive linguistic structure. The formal basis for this first contrastive communicative expression is the deployment of

> a kind of prosodic envelope or matrix into which the child "knows" that morphemes go – an interrogative and vocative/demand contour, and possibly an indicative. It is as if mode were being inferred, a place-holding matrix established, and lexis then added . . . There is the possibility that distinctive "speech acts" are learned in a primitive fashion by this means . . . [although] there is little concrete evidence. (p. 10)

Since then, evidence bearing on this theoretical formulation has slowly begun to accumulate.

The development of intonation: The transition to first words

Halliday's classic study of his son's "protolanguage" (1975, 1979) has provided the conceptual base and the coding categories for numerous studies of communicative development (see ch. 6), but his diary account of the contrastive use of eight pitch ranges and four directions to differentiate several protowords has yet to be replicated in a study involving tape-recordings and instrumental or interobserver reliability controls on transcription. Other early studies, like Halliday's, rely on "ear transcription," or perceptual judgments of prosodic distinctions and impressionistic coding of child intent, based on one or two children. Nevertheless, the cumulative effect of several such studies is to provide us with some idea of individual variation in the use of prosody in the transition from the prelinguistic to the early word period.

Dore (1974) briefly describes the early communicative development of two children who pursued differing strategies: Whereas M produced more words and participated regularly in "labeling" and "repeating" routines initiated by her mother, a male subject J produced a wider range of prosodic patterns, both for a range of "primitive speech acts" such as requests and calls and for apparent "practice," outside of any interpretable context.

Clumeck (1980) reports a study of the earliest stages of the acquisition of tone, a longitudinal case study of a boy M acquiring Mandarin (aged 1;2–2;8; based on Clumeck, 1977). M vocalized little and was late in beginning to produce words. In the first few months of the study M, like Halliday's son Nigel, used contrasting pitch patterns for contrasting communicative functions: Requests for objects or action were marked by vowel production on a high, mid or rising pitch while falling pitch was used to mark interest or to accompany his own actions. After 17 months M developed a repertoire of reduplicated disyllabic protowords bearing these same tones: [mumu] and [jojo], accompanied by falling pitch, were used to refer to animals and plants, respectively, marking the child's interest in an object (accompanied by looking at the object, showing it, or reaching for it), while [(n)ʊni], with high level pitch, was used to express a request or some kind of unhappiness or discomfort. At about 1;10 M began to produce adult-based words, using reduplicated disyllables with rising pitch (the pattern most frequently used by M's parents in addressing him). The first contrasting tone was high level, which was sometimes produced with rising pitch, however. Clumeck interprets M's early use of pitch for contrasting communicative functions as intonational, and comments that the use of *lexical* tone begins no sooner than the first use of segmental lexical patterns (see the discussion of tonal accent, below).

Four recent studies have provided more objective documentation of early uses of intonational contrast for communicative purposes. In the first such study, Furrow (1984) defined both prosodic and social categories broadly, to permit reliable judgments (both interobserver and repeated intraobserver codings) of a relatively large number of subjects (six boys, six girls, aged 1;11–2;1 and with MLUs ranging from 1.3 to 3.0). Psychophysical ratings of pitch level, loudness, and pitch range on a scale of three were added together to yield scores ranging from one ("utterances . . . very quietly spoken in a relatively flat, low-pitched voice") to nine ("a loud, higher-pitched utterance with exaggerated contours": p. 206). Social context categories reflected only degree of social involvement (with the experimenter, who manipulated the video camera on a tripod), involving scores for eye contact specific to the utterance, other evidence of social orientation, and lack of any such evidence, termed "private speech." The results showed a significant tendency for private speech to *decrease* in prosodic score in relation to child language level, as reflected in MLU. Furrow interprets his finding as "consistent with Vygotsky's (1962) hypothesis that children are initially undifferentiated social beings, while egocentric speech becomes distinct with development . . . At age two . . . children are learning to take their own perspective" (p. 212), or to distinguish more clearly between utterances designed for social communication (corresponding to Halliday's "pragmatic" or interpersonal function) and those intended to accompany the child's attention or action (Halliday's "mathetic" or learning oriented function). As Furrow points out, the prelinguistic use of prosody which Halliday (and also Clumeck) reports is consistent with Furrow's findings for children about a year older, in that pragmatic utterances were associated with higher pitch.

Supplementing perceptual judgments with instrumental verification of a small random sample from her data, Galligan (1987) set out to trace the emergence of "grammatical use" of intonation in the early word period. Reliable evidence of such use would meet Halliday's (1975) stipulation that contrastive use be made of different intonations combined with the same word (or phonetic form). Galligan followed two children, a boy, Sebastian, and a girl, Leslie, from the age of 10 to 21 months; the children were chosen from a larger study involving eleven subjects for their contrasting acquisition styles – "analytic" (focusing on single words and their referent objects) vs. "holistic" (producing phrases as well as words and displaying social as well as referential language functions). Sebastian was found to use rising tones in connection with "general interest utterances" (*see, that*) from the earliest sessions, whether or not the utterance was apparently directed to his mother; when addressed, his mother consistently responded by naming the object. By 12 months Sebastian began repeating both general interest and naming utterances, typically adding a rising tone as he turned to his mother. By 15 months, when Sebastian began to acquire a larger vocabulary, repeated utterances were marked not only by an increase in (rising) pitch range but by an increase in loudness and/or duration as well. In the last three months of the study the child increasingly used falling-rising tones in eliciting naming responses.

Leslie's developmental use of intonation was strikingly different, as were her mother's responses. In the first sessions Leslie directed general interest utterances, generally on a rising tone, to her mother, who would reply by imitating the child's vocal pattern with the same intonation rather than by naming. In subsequent months the child seldom named objects; she also directed few of her general interest utterances to her mother, and from 14 to 18 months steadily decreased the proportion of rising tones used in conjunction with these utterances. At 18 months she again began to use rising tone as she turned to her mother with utterances such as *see, there*, or *here*, usually in the newly common context of book reading. However, already from 14 months on Leslie seemed to make gradually increasing use of rising or falling-rising tone as she held up objects whose names were not well established.

Whereas the two children showed contrasting developmental patterns with respect to the use of intonation for pragmatic functions, the emergence of grammatical use of intonation was largely parallel in both nature and timing. Galligan details the instances in which each child first began to make sporadic use of a contrasting intonation pattern with a particular word form, from 14 or 15 months on, to an increase in rising-tone requests for absent objects (at about 18 months) in contrast to the declarative intonation used for labeling the same objects in a descriptive context. For both children increased grammatical use of intonation could be said to coincide with the transition to syntax, although Leslie's early use of formulaic multiword utterances made it difficult to pinpoint this shift.

Marcos (1987) took an experimental approach to the development of intonation for communicative functions. Ten subjects (acquiring French) were followed in four monthly recording sessions, six from age 14 to 18 months, four from 17 to 21 months. Standardized objects were used to elicit requests and labeling; mothers were asked to participate in a relatively unstructured play session, but to elicit requests and repeated requests in specified ways. Instances of vocalizations apparently intended as requests or labeling as well as those accompanying giving and showing were coded; pitch range and direction was perceptually coded by a professional musician. No attempt was made to distinguish words from protowords or babble.

Pitch was found to be significantly higher for repeated requests than for requests at three out of five age levels, particularly at the last two ages tested (18 and 20 months). Requests tended to have higher pitch than vocalizations accompanying giving and showing, which in turn tended to have higher pitch than labeling. An attempt to relate differences in pitch direction (level, falling and rising) to communicative function (requesting, labeling) over time was less successful. The expectation that ten children would show similar patterns at similar ages may not be realistic, given individual differences in rate and style of lexical development as well as in the use of intonation across parent-child dyads, as Galligan's study illustrates.

Flax et al. (1991) undertook a study of the developmental relationship between prosody and communicative expression in three children observed at three linguistically defined points prior to syntax (based on maternal diaries, and corresponding to the 0-, 4- and 25-word points of our Appendix C): no words (age range 11–15 months), 10 words (15–17 months) and 50 words (19–22 months). The children were audio- and video-taped for one-hour play sessions with their mothers. All non-cry vocalizations were transcribed and then coded for communicative function based on the transcript, to avoid direct influence from intonation patterns; acoustic analysis was used to identify peak and range of fundamental frequency, leading to an objective description of perceptually identifiable pitch changes. Since flat and fall categories proved not to be systematically associated with particular communicative functions, only analysis of terminal rise vs. non-rise was pursued.

A significant interaction of prosodic form (terminal contour) and communicative function was found for each child and proved stable across all three sessions; these relationships differed by child, however. The one male subject, AL, used the largest proportion of rising contours (54 percent), including use for requests, yes-no responses and giving; non-rise was consistently produced for "Comment-interaction." The use of rise narrowed over time, so that in the final session most rises were used for requests. The two girls used a smaller proportion of rises, mainly for protests and requests for objects, but sometimes for comments and responses as well. Since the association between form and function was relative and could not be used to predict intended meaning from prosodic form alone, Flax et al. conclude that no "over-riding induction" could be imputed to the child as to the meaning of a rising contour (e.g., for all pragmatic functions, as in Halliday's account). Instead, these authors suggest that more specific meanings may have been inferred from input patterns by each child in a somewhat different way (cf. also Menn, 1976b).

The development of intonation: The transition to syntax

Snow and Stoel-Gammon (1994) and D. Snow (1994) have reported the results of meticulous analyses of final syllable lengthening in relation to pitch contour as they interact, in the period of transition to word combination, in the acquisition of adult English intonation. Snow and Stoel-Gammon contrast two models of the relationship between tone and timing in production. The "association model" interprets the lengthening of final syllables as a more or less mechanical consequence of limits on the speed at which the fundamental frequency of the voice can change (Lyberg, 1979). They draw from this model the prediction that intonation and timing skills would develop concurrently. Alternatively, these two features of English phrasal accent are seen as independent acquisitions: This "dissociation model" draws some support from Allen's (1983) study of French 2-year-olds, which failed to find a statistically reliable relationship between wide pitch contours and syllable lengthening (in contrast with the relationship between changes in pitch and intensity, which were strongly correlated, suggesting a lack of independence in the children's production).

In the first study, based on three children sampled at 18 and 24 months, Snow and Stoel-Gammon defined group acquisition of the final lengthening aspect of English phrasal accent as identifiable by the occurrence of a duration ratio greater than 1.0 between final and non-final accented syllables in the productions of two out of three children. Since early disyllabic English words are largely trochaic, these investigators compared monosyllables (= final accented syllable) with the first (non-final accented) and last (final unaccented) syllable of disyllables. They found that for all three children falling contours were associated with longer final than non-final syllables at both 18 and 24 months (based on group totals of 20–50 syllables in each category). For rising contours, only one child gave evidence of final lengthening at 18 months and two did so at 24 months (one child failed to produce any rising contours at that age). The three children all showed a larger pitch-change in final as compared with non-final accented syllables by 18 months.

In his later study based on nine children D. Snow (1994) addressed the same issues of association vs. dissociation between the lengthening and tonal aspects of accent acquisition. Subjects (all female) were selected on the basis of vocabulary size (30–70 words) and single word production only at the outset of the study; the age range was 12 to 20 months. Data was collected in the course of "semi-structured play activities" involving mother, investigator and child, in four sessions spaced three months apart. As in the earlier study, monosyllables were compared with trochaic disyllables, all accented words falling under phrasal stress if taken from multiword utterances (e.g., *bottle BAby*; *need SOCK*; *put SOCK on*).

Snow's findings revealed a U-shaped curve: Final lengthening appeared in early sessions, was replaced by approximate final/non-final syllable isochrony in subsequent sessions, and then reemerged – for some of the children – in a still later session. Snow presents three alternative bases for cross-child comparison, as a way of identifying the critical factor associated with the shift away from final lengthening to isochronicity: vocabulary size (approximately equivalent at the first session), age of child, and onset of combinatorial speech. In this last comparison alone a pattern common to all the children emerged: The point of greatest syllable isochrony corresponded relatively closely to the time of shift to word combination (defined as the use of at least three two–word or longer phrases within the first 100 utterances transcribed) (see figure 8.1).

As in the earlier study, Snow found that "the timing aspects of prosody seem to develop more slowly than intonation" (p. 837).

> Following a period of variability in speech timing before syntax, the children developed a consistent final/nonfinal contrast within 3 months after they had begun to combine two words in phrases. This change in rhythmic patterns took place in the children's speech without any corresponding fluctuation in the intonation contrast that had been acquired much earlier . . . Because intonation is controlled first, the tone contour difference between final and nonfinal syllables is greater than the duration difference. Thus, in the early part of the study, the rate of final syllable pitch change is about twice that of nonfinal syllables. Later, final syllables begin to lengthen without adding proportional increases in the tone contour . . . When children acquire final lengthening at about age 2, the rates of tone change that they use for final and nonfinal syllables begin to approach the proportional use of tone and timing that characterizes adult speech. (pp. 837f.)

Snow suggests that the final–syllable lengthening which was detectible in the speech of his subjects before the onset of combinatorial speech (though it was too variable to be statistically reliable) may reflect the physiological constraints present already in infancy, as proposed by Laufer (1980), namely, a general relaxation of vocal activity associated with the end of a breath group. The "regression" to isochronicity at the onset of syntax would reflect a period of reorganization, when previously passive consequences of production are brought under the child's active control.

Acquisition of stress accent

One of the specific difficulties associated with the study of children's acquisition of stress is the interaction between child variability and lack of control over the several phonetic parameters which combine to give the percept "stressed syllable," on the one hand, and the relative (un)reliability of investigator attempts to transcribe stress in child words, on the other. The less competent the child, the less reliable the adult transcription – hence the difficulty in either establishing criteria for mastery or selecting proper objects for instrumental study. The relative paucity of studies of the acquisition of stress is perhaps in part a result of this dilemma – as well as of the lack of attention to prosodic factors in adult phonological theory until

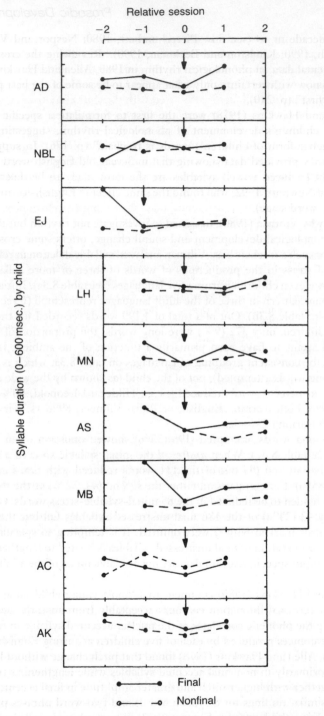

Figure 8.1 Mean duration of nuclear syllables: by child, session, and phrase position, aligned by relative session 0. Arrow marks point of greatest syllable isochrony.

Source: D. Snow, 1994, reprinted by permission of the American Speech-Language-Hearing Association

the past decade or so (see now Pierrehumbert, 1980; Nespor and Vogel, 1986; Goldsmith, 1990; Kingston and Beckman, 1990).[5] Reviewing the cross-linguistic developmental data on phonological rhythm in 1980, Allen and Hawkins admitted that "we know with certainty only what appear to be some of the best problems to approach first" (p. 240).

Allen and Hawkins (1978) were the first to formulate a specific hypothesis regarding children's development of phonological rhythm, suggesting that "the natural metric form of children's words is trochaic" (p. 176). In support of this proposal they provided data showing that in 3-year-old English word production initial light (reduced vowel) syllables are the most likely to be deleted (cf. also Echols and Newport, 1992, who found the same effect in English-learning children at the one-word stage).

A study by Vihman (1980), designed to investigate not rhythm but the relationship of phonological development and sound change, offers some cross-linguistic support for such a trochaic bias. Vihman analyzed syllable deletion in relation to the position of stress in the productions of words of three or more syllables ("long words") by eleven children learning five languages (see table 8.3a). Initial stress was the dominant pattern in three of the adult languages represented (Czech, Estonian and English: table 8.3b). Out of a total of 4,199 words recorded for these 1- to 2-year-old children, only 372 (9%) were long words; the proportion of long words attempted seems to have been primarily a function of the ambient language (as shown by the consistent grouping of languages on table 8.3a, which is ordered by percent long words attempted), not of the child (as shown by the wide intra-group variability in percent words reduced – e.g., Hildegard Leopold, 90% vs. Amahl Smith, 29%, both learning English; or Raivo Vihman, 89% vs. Virve Vihman, 37%, both learning Estonian).

Of the long words attempted, 196 (53%) showed omission of an identifiable syllable (see table 8.3c). When *unstressed* the initial syllable showed a strong tendency to be omitted (94 out of the 111 words reduced with non-initial-syllable stress, or 85%). For comparison, either the second (44: 52%) or the third syllable (35: 41%) tended to be reduced in the 85 initial-syllable-stress words. On the other hand, only 42 (24%) of the 186 final unstressed syllables (all but the ten three-syllable words marked with [c]) were omitted. It is tempting to speculate that the children's preservation of final unstressed syllables is related to lengthening of that syllable in input speech; relevant data are not available for all of the adult languages, however.

Allen and Hawkins (1980) comment that "most young children appear to express their terminal intonation contours acceptably from an early age" (p. 231). Identifying the phonetic correlates of the nuclear accented syllable in fifty conversational utterances produced by each of five children acquiring English (age range 2;2 to 3;9), Allen and Hawkins (1978) found that pitch change without lengthening occurred primarily in non-final accented syllables while lengthening typically occurred together with higher pitch and greater amplitude in final accented syllables; they cite similar findings for disyllabic words and two-word phrases produced by two Hungarian children from Fónagy, 1972). The work reviewed above by Snow and Stoel-Gammon (1994) and D. Snow (1994) lends additional empirical support

Table 8.3a Long word use and reduction in five languages: Subjects, languages, size of sample (ordered by percent of long words attempted)

Child (language; source)*	Age range**	Total	Long words	Reduced words
J (Spanish)	1;9–2;6	144	39 (27%)	28 (72%)
Si (Spanish)	1;7–2;4	152	37 (24%)	18 (49%)
Maja (Slovenian; Kolaric, 1959)	(0;6)–2;0	138	31 (22%)	19 (61%)
Tomaz (Slovenian; Kolaric, 1959)	(0;11)–2;0	320	71 (22%)	58 (82%)
Jiří (Czech; Pačesová, 1968)	(0;10)–1;8	300	56 (19%)	15 (26%)
Virve (Estonian)	(0;7)–1;10	372	40 (11%)	15 (37%)
Linda (Estonian)	1;6–1;11	364	32 (9%)	17 (53%)
Raivo (Estonian)	1;1–2;0	488	36 (7%)	32 (89%)
Hildegard (English; Leopold, 1939)	(0;10)–2;0	322	19 (5%)	17 (90%)
Amahl (English; Smith, 1973)	2;2 (one day)	225	7 (3%)	2 (29%)
Jacob (English; Menn, 1976b)	1;0–1;8	150	4 (2%)	3 (75%)
Total		4,199	372	224

* Unpublished sources: The Spanish data were collected as part of the Stanford Child Phonology project (see Ferguson et al., 1992); the same data form the basis for Macken, 1978 (J) and 1979 (Si); the Estonian data formed the basis for Vihman, 1971 (Linda), 1976 (Virve), and 1981 (Raivo), as well as 1978 and 1980, which drew on all of the data referred to here
** Child's age (in parentheses) at the beginning of diary studies typically antedates the appearance of the first words
Source: Vihman, 1980. In Traugott, Labrum and Shepard (eds), *Papers from the Fourth International Conference on Historical Linguistics*. Reprinted with the permission of John Benjamins.

Table 8.3b Long word use and reduction in five languages: Stress patterns of three- and four-syllable words produced with omission of one or more identifiable syllables (ordered by percent initial stressed words)

	Stressed syllable				
	first	*second*	*third*	*fourth*	*Total*
Czech	13 (100%)	–	–	–	13
Estonian	44 (86%)	6	1	–	51
English	11 (61%)	6	1	–	18
Slovenian	14 (19%)	50	8	–	72
Spanish	3 (7%)	21	18	–	42
Total	85	83	28	–	196

Source: Vihman, 1980. In Traugott, Labrum and Shepard (eds), *Papers from the Fourth International Conference on Historical Linguistics*. Reprinted with the permission of John Benjamins.

to the general conclusion that the linguistic use of pitch change is controlled somewhat earlier than final lengthening, but that both have begun to be mastered as the child moves into the acquisition of syntax.

Despite relatively early control of intonation, however, Allen and Hawkins find that children are slow to develop the ability to *reduce* weak syllables.[6] They suggest that early words are produced with "peripheral (non-central) vowels and rather fully articulated consonants . . . The unaccented syllables, though low in pitch, are still heavy" (1978, p. 174); this goes along with Leopold's (1947) observation that "the child begins . . . with level stress . . ., both in babbling and at the outset of speaking" (p. 24; cf also Fudge, 1969). The absence of reduced syllables in the word production of 1- or 2-year-olds results in a speech rhythm with "fewer syllables per foot, or more beats per utterance; in short, it sounds more syllable timed" (Allen and Hawkins, 1980, p. 231). As these authors note, the slower rate of 2-year-old speech will itself tend to produce a *percept* of more even timing.

The "overarticulation" of unstressed syllables in early words stands in contrast to the jargon produced by some infants in the same period, in which the alternation of full and reduced vowels, together with varied pitch patterns over a long string of syllables, yields a striking impression of conversational speech (see the comments on the children's *baragouin* in Fónagy, 1972, as well as Menn, 1976b; Peters, 1977); the examples given in Vihman and Miller (1988) characteristically show a pitch change in the last or next to last syllable, capturing the most salient aspect of English intonation (cf. also Crystal, 1986, p. 182). Boysson-Bardies et al. (1981) identify a shift from a relatively rapid rate of articulation to slower production of two- and three-syllable sequences (but not longer strings) in the jargon of a 19-month-old French child as his utterances begin to be more frequently interpretable. Boysson-Bardies and her colleagues see this change as reflecting the child's

Table 8.3c Long word use and reduction in five languages: Syllables omitted in relation to position of stress

Position of stress	Omitted syllable				3- (and 4-) syllable words	Word total
	1st	*2d*	*3d*	*4th*		
1st syllable	12 (4)	39 (5)	[b]30 (5)	– ([b]4)	72 (13)	85
2d syllable	[a]74 ([a]2)	2	[b]7	–	81 (2)	83
3d syllable	[a]6 ([a]12)	5 (16)	–	– ([b]1)	[c]10 (18)	28
Total	92 (18)	46 (21)	*37 (5)	– (*5)	163 (33)	196

Three- and four-syllable words are combined here, with the figures for three-syllable words followed in parentheses by those for four-syllable words. The number of syllables omitted exceeds the number of words, since more than one syllable may be omitted.
[a] Unstressed initial syllables
[b] Unstressed final syllables
[c] Stressed final syllables
* Omitted unstressed final syllables
Source: Vihman, 1980. In Traugott, Labrum and Shepard (eds), *Papers from the Fourth International Conference on Historical Linguistics*. Reprinted with the permission of John Benjamins.

attempts to reach precise articulatory targets, in other words, to match particular adult words, in contrast to the *global* matching of ambient language prosodic and segmental patterns which is assumed to underlie jargon production (Boysson-Bardies, Sagart, and Bacri, 1981; Leroy, 1975, provides examples of jargon-like imitations in the production of a French child aged 2;2).

Allen and Hawkins (1978, 1980) report that the 3-year-olds they recorded varied widely in the extent to which they used light syllables appropriately (table 1, 1978). In function words and polysyllabic content words alike, the proportion of accurately reduced syllables ranged from 33 to 70 percent; individual children showed roughly the same level of syllable reduction in both word types. According to Allen and Hawkins, speech rate increases, along with greater numbers of reduced syllable nuclei, will yield an adult-like rhythm only by the age of 4 or 5 years. Nittrouer (1993) reports instrumental evidence of over-long productions of the unstressed article *a* (/ə/) as late as 7 years of age (see ch. 9).

A few studies have focused specifically on the acquisition of lexical stress placement. Klein (1984) analyzed the spontaneous and unelicited imitative word tokens of a boy learning English, aged 1;9–1;10; this child's MLU of 1.04–1.37 places him in the period preceding the onset of word combination ("session 0") as defined by D. Snow (1994). Using phonetically transcribed data, Klein identified distinct groups of words based on consistency of stress placement:

1 Words consistently (13 words) or predominantly (9 words) stressed as in the adult model: All of these were produced more often spontaneously than as imitations;
2 Words usually produced with "misplaced primary stress" (4 words): All were disyllables ending in a syllabic liquid, which the child produced with [u(:)] for /l/ (3 out of 4 words) or [ɚ] (*water*). "Final /r/ . . . was not yet mastered and may have been associated with an increase in articulatory effort [leading to] greater tension and longer duration" (385); the increased effort itself may be the source of the adult percept of stress on the final syllable.[7]
3 Words which appeared to be predominantly produced with level stress (6 words, 63 tokens) or which exhibited no clear stress placement pattern across different tokens (5 words): More of these tokens were imitated (58 percent) than spontaneous.

Klein concluded that stress placement, like consonant production in early words, is learned word-by-word ("lexical primacy"). The words which the child knew best – and thus often produced spontaneously – had relatively consistent and accurate stress placement, while less familiar words showed instable production of stress. Words ending in a syllabic liquid, in which the struggle for articulatory mastery seems to have conflicted with control of the parameters capable of producing a percept of stress on the first syllable, constituted exceptions.

The nature of stress learning – whether it is wholly lexically based or involves rule learning – was taken up by Hochberg (1988b) in a study of Spanish stress involving both picture naming and imitation of nonsense words by Mexican-American children aged 3, 4 and 5 years. Hochberg found that "the rule learning process was essentially complete by age 3" (p. 694). More specifically, at all three ages there was a significant increase in imitation errors in relation to increasing irregularity of stress placement in the adult models, from nonsense words with regular stress (i.e., final stress on consonant-final words, penultimate for vowel-final words) to those with irregular stress (including such relatively commonly occurring patterns as either final or antepenultimate stress on vowel-final words: cf. *mamá* 'mother,' *fásforo* 'match'), and finally to those with an impermissible stress pattern (**cátapana*). The errors tended strongly to go in the direction of regularizing the stress pattern. In spontaneous production, similarly, irregular words prompted more errors, although there was evidence that the children were familiar with the more common exceptions to the regular stress system. Hochberg concludes that children do learn stress rules even though "doing so was neither necessary nor straightforward" (p. 704), since "with few exceptions, all words that children use, they have heard correctly stressed" (p. 684). Furthermore, Hochberg notes that whereas her 3-year-olds had evidently already mastered the stress system, they were still making errors on difficult individual segments such as /r/ as well as on irregular morphological forms, producing **sábo* for *sé* 'I know,' for example (cf. *sabes* 'you know,' *sabe* 'he knows').[8]

With regard to the question of rule use vs. "word-by-word" learning it is important to notice that "segmental" phonology is whole-word based only at the outset (as demonstrated by Ferguson and colleagues: see chs. 2, 6 and 9), whereas prosodic features necessarily have the whole word as their domain (if not a longer unit, such as a phrase), since it is only in the context of a sequence of syllables that a particular syllable can be perceived as longer, louder, or the bearer of a change in pitch. The earlier acquisition of the prosodic patterns of a language as compared with the complete inventory of segments, then, may be a consequence of at least two independent factors. First, prosodic features are salient to infants from early in life and also appear to be available relatively early for voluntary manipulation in production. Second, even in a language like Spanish, which actually permits stress on any one of the three last syllables of a word, regardless of the final segment (see table 1 in Hochberg, 1988b), the number of possible patterns is far more limited than the number of segments. The evident progression from whole word to segment which we observe in production and perhaps in perception as well would in itself lead to earlier mastery of prosodic patterns. It is a separate question whether the "structure-changing errors" which Hochberg identified in the children's productions must be interpreted as "rule learning," or whether a more theoretically neutral term such as "familiarity with language-specific constraints or patterns" (in line with the current line of thinking embodied in optimality theory, for example) would not account just as well for these findings.

Hochberg (1988a) drew on the early word production of four children learning Spanish in a Mexican-American neighborhood in California to challenge Allen and Hawkins's notion of a universal trochaic bias in children's speech. The subjects, aged 1;7–1;9 at the outset, were recorded weekly for ten months (one of the children is J in table 8.3a). Hochberg found that the percent correct stress overall was approximately the same on penultimate- (ranging from 52% to 74% in spontaneous productions) and final-stressed words (57–63%) for her subjects, contrary to the "trochaic bias" prediction that final-stressed words will be more difficult. Furthermore, the most commonly produced words had penultimate stress (*cása* 'house,' *zapáto* 'shoe') and thus should have provided favorable targets for exercising an inherent trochaic production bias, yet initial accuracy of stress placement in spontaneous production was close to chance (37–44%) for three subjects (aged 1;7–1;9); the fourth began with 80% accuracy (at 1;10) and showed little development over time.

Finally, Pollock, Brammer, and Hageman (1993) conducted a carefully controlled experimental study of the ability of 2-, 3- and 4-year-olds to imitate novel disyllabic words designed to contrast in stress placement. The experimental word shapes were [bʌfi], [fibʌ] and [bodɑ], [dɑbo], each with initial and final stress; six subjects in each age group produced up to four tokens of each word. Peak fundamental frequency and peak intensity of each syllable and absolute duration of each vowel were measured instrumentally; statistical analysis of the results showed increased pitch and intensity peaks on stressed syllables for the 3- and 4-year-olds but not the 2-year-olds, who appeared to mark stress highly inconsistently. Longer vowels were associated with final position as well as with stress at all ages; however, unstressed syllables were significantly longer in 2-year-old productions than in those of the older children, supporting Allen and Hawkins's suggestion that the younger children find it difficult to reduce unstressed syllables.

Based on perceptual judgments, the 2-year-olds produced accurate matches to the stress pattern of the model only 55% of the time (vs. 89% at age 3, 99% at age 4). There was no evidence that initial-stressed targets were produced more accurately than final-stressed targets, a result similar to Hochberg's findings regarding her subjects' production of Spanish penultimate and final stress words. The only evidence of a possible trochaic bias was the younger children's tendency to delete initial unstressed syllables (there was only one instance of final unstressed syllable deletion).

In the face of these results, then, how are we to regard the trochaic bias, which seemed to Allen and Hawkins to explain a good many independent phenomena of early prosodic development? First the age and stage of development of the various children studied needs to be considered. We learned from the studies reviewed earlier that final syllable lengthening can be considered a natural early tendency, made "biologically" available. Nevertheless, as children move beyond their first (vocal-motor-scheme-based) words to less familiar word shapes, they are faced with the difficulty of planning and integrating segmental and prosodic aspects of two- or three-syllable sequences; as a result, they may produce each syllable with attention, effortfully (Elbers and Wijnen, 1992), yielding a percept of "level stress." In the case of imitation of unfamiliar word forms, ill controlled production of the different correlates of stress may result in seemingly random variation between accurate, inaccurate, and "untranscribable" stress placement (Klein, 1984; Pollock et al., 1993).

It is not clear from the literature to what extent the finding of relative isochronicity reflects the challenge of early attempts at word combination within a single prosodic contour (as suggested by D. Snow, 1994) or – given the apparent variability across children in the "one-word stage" – whether it is, for some children at least, already a concomitant of the move away from a small set of familiar templates toward a wider range of phonological shapes and attempts at production of novel words. Robb and Saxman's (1990) report of final syllable lengthening for the entire period of their study – from before the onset of word production through the months following acquisition of a fifty-word vocabulary – reflects only the "central tendency" for open and closed nonwords and words; it is not clear how much individual variation is masked by this measure. On the other hand, in an impressionistic account of the prosodic effects of the transition to syntax in two French children Leroy (1975) provides another indication that it is the onset of word combination and the particular challenge this presents which leads to the "intonational regression" identified by Snow (cf. also Fónagy, 1972). As children become able to plan a syntactically complex utterance, prosodic parameters should begin to be independently controlled, first pitch contour, then lengthening (Snow, 1994).

A preponderance of initial over final unstressed syllable deletions need not reflect a preference for initial over final stressed words as well, as implied by the term "trochaic bias." Instead, the children may simply be showing a greater tendency to retain final (and thus generally longer) as compared with initial unstressed syllables in multisyllabic words; this appears to be the same kind of data that gave rise to the Allen and Hawkins hypothesis in the first place. Thus, Hochberg's younger subjects seem to be beginning where Snow's subjects began, with apparently "level" stress ("isochrony"). As they come to control stress in familiar words their accuracy increases – and words like *zapáto* are produced as [pwatʊ] (Macken, 1979), with loss of initial unstressed syllable yielding a trochee. The subjects of Pollock and colleagues, on the other hand, seem to be responding at a close to chance level in attempting to repeat the stress pattern of unfamiliar words. Pollock et al. suggest that the difficulty may be perceptual. Another possibility is that longer exposure to the input is needed before a younger child is able to represent a word form in a sufficiently stable way to be able to marshall and integrate the various production parameters needed to yield an acceptable stress percept on a single syllable; Klein's subject appeared to experience the same difficulty with imitated tokens.

Acquisition of pitch accent and lexical tone

Fewer studies have so far focused on the acquisition of tone and pitch accent than stress, so that only a rather broad sketch of the developmental pattern to be expected can be offered. What information is available on tone provides a useful supplement to the research on final lengthening and stress reviewed above, however, providing a broader basis for interpreting the earlier acquisition of pitch change than final lengthening, for example, as each of these enter into an adult-like accentual system. Furthermore, the increase in interest in the origins of prosodic systems generally now allows a richer interpretation of the data available for the acquisition of tone.

Two studies have directly addressed ambient language influence on prosodic organization in the period immediately preceding the transition to syntax (based on use of twenty-five words or more in a half-hour recording session, reflecting a cumulative lexicon of at least fifty words). Hallé et al. (1991) compared pitch contours on the disyllabic vocal productions of four infants each exposed to French (which has a preponderance of rising contours) and Japanese (with its typically level and falling contours): All of the French infants produced a majority of rising contours (73 percent), taking both words and babble into account, while all of the Japanese infants produced a majority of falling or level contours (74 percent); no significant difference in these results was found when words and babble were analyzed separately. Thus, a global effect of the dominant adult intonation patterns were found in the children's vocalizations.

In Japanese, lexical tone plays a contrastive role. In order to determine the extent to which the infants learning Japanese had acquired the appropriate tone pattern for the words they attempted, target words were divided into those with a rising pattern (36%, plus 2% rise-fall) vs. those with a falling pattern (62%). At the 25-word point approximately 60% of the children's vocalizations could be identified as words. Of those intended to match an adult word with a rising contour, 43% were produced with a rising Fo, while of those with a falling contour in the adult model, only 18% were produced with a rising contour. These data suggest that word tone is just beginning to be acquired by the Japanese infants at this point (age range 15 to 23 months).

In a parallel study, Engstrand, Williams, and Strömqvist (1991) compared the production of Fo contours at the 25-word-point in the disyllabic vocalizations (both words and babble) of ten children, five each acquiring English and Swedish. The study focuses on the acquisition of a salient tonal word accent used in Swedish, the "grave accent," which is expressed as a "two-peaked contour resulting from (1) a falling sequence High–Low, associated with the primary stressed syllable, and (2) a subsequent rising sequence Low–High, associated with the secondary stressed syllable" (p. 190). The authors note that the second-syllable rise is optional, being primarily a correlate of sentence stress, while the first-syllable fall provides the critical cue to grave accent for adult listeners.

Despite considerable individual variation and overlap between the two language groups, a statistically significant difference was found in production of the second syllable rise (measured as the Fo difference between the first vowel offset and the second vowel maximum) but not in the production of a first syllable fall. Similarly, when "grave word candidates" (or attempts to produce words bearing the grave accent in the adult model) were compared with all other vocalizations for the Swedish children only, the second syllable rise was found to occur significantly more often on the grave word candidates than on the others, while the first syllable fall failed to show a significant difference.

As in the case of Japanese lexical tone, then, it appears that Swedish word accent has just begun to be produced on appropriate words at the 25-word-point (about age 17 months). It is interesting that despite the importance for adults of the fall in the first syllable, it is the rise in the second syllable which appears to be the focus of the children's early attempts to produce this characteristic accent. It is possible, as the authors suggest, that the rise is produced in a more exaggerated way in child-directed speech. Alternatively, child production of an exaggerated difference on the second syllable may correspond in some sense to the "overarticulation" of unstressed syllables typical of children's early words in English or Hungarian, for example, as discussed earlier. In any case, the interaction between global attunement to the adult language, as demonstrated in both the French/Japanese and the Swedish/English comparisons, and the incipient use of intonation for pragmatic or grammatical meaning remains to be investigated.

Our knowledge of children's acquisition of lexical tone remains disappointingly meager. Only three published studies, all dating back to the 1970s, have provided some kind of systematic analysis of the initial period of acquisition, based on Mandarin and Cantonese.[9] In the first such study, Li and Thompson (1977) set forth the key issues for the study of tone acquisition:

(a) In what ways do the child's utterances deviate from the adult's with respect to tone during the acquisition process?
(b) What is the duration of the tone acquisition process?
(c) What is the chronological relationship between the acquisition of tones and the acquisition of segmental units?
(d) What explanations can be offered for the patterns of errors which are found and for the relative speed with which tone seems to be acquired? (p. 187)

Li and Thompson collected data from seventeen children of Mandarin-speaking families in Taipei (aged 18 to 36 months) by eliciting naming responses to pictures; ten of these children were followed over a period of about seven months (the ages are not specified). Unfortunately, this landmark paper lacks most of the detail expected of a data-based study, failing to complement the clarity and focus of presentation with an overview of results from either individual children or designated groups. Nevertheless, the study does provide a framework which can be used for comparative study of any tone language.

The authors begin with a brief account of the tone system of Mandarin, which contrasts four tones, high [-], rising (mid to high) [ˊ], dipping (roughly, a falling-rising contour in the mid range) [ˇ], and falling (high to low) [ˋ]. In addition, there is a neutral tone associated with unstressed syllables (the tone of certain suffixes and particles, the second syllables of many compound words and syllables reduced in connected speech); neutral tone takes on a characteristic pitch following each of the contrastive tones. Four stages of tone acquisition are identified:

Stage I. The child's vocabulary is small. High and falling tones predominate irrespective of the tone of the adult form.

Stage II. The child is still at the one-word stage, but he has a larger vocabulary. The correct 4-way adult tone contrast has appeared, but sometimes there is confusion between rising and dipping tone words.

Stage III. The child is at the 2- or 3-word stage. Some rising and dipping tone errors remain. Tone sandhi is beginning to be acquired.

Stage IV. Longer sentences are being produced. Rising and dipping tone errors are practically non-existent. (p. 189)

Li and Thompson illustrate a number of findings from their data, but provide no specific information about the individual child's age or level of lexical or grammatical development. Thus, as one example of the early mastery of tone in relation to the comparatively undeveloped segmental system, they cite the following (from a child at Stage II):

Child form   Adult form
ipi [- ˇ]   cyenbi [- ˇ] 'pen'
dziyu [- ´]   jünren [- ´] 'soldier'

(that is, the child correctly reproduces the tone, but not the segmental content, of two words, the first with a sequence high–dipping, the second with a sequence high–rising).

More specific to Mandarin is the finding that "high and falling tones are acquired earlier and more easily than the rising and dipping tones" (p. 189); confusion between the rising and dipping tones is not resolved until after stage III (the authors note evidence of this confusion in the lexicon which Chao, 1951, provides for Canta at age 2;4). In addition, of the two subjects who lacked these tones at the start of the study, one failed to produce contour tones at all in the earliest stage, substituting low for falling or dipping and high for the rising tones, which suggests that the easiest Mandarin tone is high level, followed by falling, and then the two confusable tones with a rising component. Production of the rising and dipping tones emerged at about the same time for these two children.

In an attempt to account for these findings, the authors note that the tones with a rising component have also been found to cause trouble in perception tests of both adults learning Mandarin and native speakers responding to synthetically produced tones whose frequency range was systematically reduced. The lesser difficulty of falling tones is further suggested by their wider incidence in the world's languages and by the fact that sandhi rules are more likely to assimilate rising to non-rising tones than vice versa. To these observations we can add that speech production naturally involves a falling pitch movement, whether it is a gradual declination over the entire utterance or a fall toward the end (Lieberman, 1985); children learning the intonation of English as well as a tonal accent system such as that of Mandarin must learn to produce a rise when it is called for, while in the absence of a voluntary rise, they will naturally tend to produce a fall (Kent and Murray, 1982; Snow and Stoel-Gammon, 1994).

Finally, Li and Thompson report that "the neutral tone is often misinterpreted as a full tone" (p. 189), which they take to relate to overproduction of stress in the infant-directed prosody of input speech. Since, as discussed earlier, there is now ample evidence that learning to reduce the unstressed syllable is a major task in the acquisition of stress-accent systems, the treatment of neutral tone in Mandarin falls under the general case rather than standing out as an exception. Demuth's (1993) case study of tone acquisition in Sesotho provides another parallel to overuse of stress, in that the phonologically marked high tone is also overproduced in early stages. The idea that the source of the children's error lies in the prosody of caretaker speech can be related to the issue of a trochaic bias underlying infant maintenance of word-final unstressed syllables: Little study has so far been addressed to these fine points of infant-directed prosody, particularly in the period of first evidence of language comprehension and the production of the first words.

Tse (1978) reports a longitudinal diary study of the acquisition of tone in

Cantonese by his son, Y.L. Tse provides anecdotal evidence regarding the first word comprehension (at 9 months). By experimenting with both the segmental content and the tonal pattern of the first word to elicit comprehension out of context (/təŋ təŋ/ 'light,' with "upper even," a high level tone, on both syllables), Tse found that Y.L. responded equally readily to the tonal pattern alone or to tone plus segments, responded with hesitation to the segmental pattern with other tones, and failed to respond when both tonal and segmental pattern were changed. When the child began to respond with comprehension to other objects and at least one nursery-rhyme routine (at 11 months), Tse pursued the experiment further, again finding that change of tone was more detrimental to comprehension than change of segmental pattern.

With regard to the production of tone, Tse's findings support those of Li and Thompson, showing relatively rapid acquisition (over an eight-month period), beginning with the high and low level tones (first three months of the single-word stage: 1;2–1;4), then the first contour tones and the mid tone (still within the single word stage: 1;5–1;8), and adding the two remaining contour tones only after the onset of word combination (1;9, corresponding to the period of acquisition of tone sandhi in Mandarin). By 1;10 Y.L. seldom made errors in the use of lexical tones, while his segmental inventory remained incomplete. Final unreleased /-p/ and /-t/ were replaced by /-k/, /l/ was replaced by /j/ or (in harmony with a final nasal) by /n/; and the low-rounded front vowel was replaced by a back vowel. Some of these errors were still in evidence several months later. Tse also reports the child's attempts to imitate English words (meaningless to him) at age 2. Y. L. accurately reproduces the English pitch pattern by choosing the closest approximation within the tonal system of Cantonese, but exhibits difficulty in reproducing the foreign segments and in retaining the order of segments. Thus, Tse's data provide additional evidence that pitch patterns are relatively more accessible to the child than segmental patterns.

Making biweekly audio recordings, Clumeck (1977) followed two children acquiring Mandarin in monolingual homes in the San Francisco Bay Area: a boy, P., aged 2;3 to 3;5, and a girl, J., aged 1;10 to 2;10. Like Li and Thompson's subjects, these children mastered the non-rising tones early (before the onset of the study). Over the entire period, based on analysis of words produced utterance-finally or in isolation only (to avoid the complexities of tonal interaction in other positions), P. correctly produced over 83% of the rising tones he attempted; the other tones showed even fewer errors. The younger child, J., correctly produced 61% of her rising tones and 74% of her low-dipping tones (the remaining tones were over 95% accurate). Interaction of the two rising tones accounted for most of the errors. Despite the similarity in the order of tonal acquisition for the few children acquiring Mandarin for whom we have data, however, Clumeck cautions that it is not possible to draw general conclusions about an order of acquisition of tones.

Summary: The tune before the words?

The natural salience of prosody and its possible role in paving the way to linguistic structure was discussed under the general rubric of developmental change in infant speech perception (ch. 4). In this chapter we reviewed the origins of prosodic control in production and the structuring of prosody into the accentual systems of adult languages. We organized our account "from the bottom up," beginning with the elements which appear to be naturally available to the infant in the prelinguistic period – the voluntary modulation of pitch and final syllable lengthening, culminating in the rudiments of an intonational system which appear late in the prelinguistic period but which begin to coalesce only with the first steps in syntactic structure (beyond the one-word stage).

With regard to infant vocalizations, we found that control of pitch increases and stabilizes throughout the first year of life. The natural tendency for pitch to fall at the end of an utterance may be counteracted, in the production of rising contours, both under the influence of global prosodic patterns of the ambient language (e.g. more rising contours in French than in English) and in response to particular interactional experiences (leading to the reported variability in the use of rising contours for communicative function).

Our review of the role of final lengthening suggested that the phenomenon is well rooted in an early, presumably neuro-physiological tendency. The developmental profile of lengthening in child vocalizations seems clearly to be a function of the degree of lengthening in the adult language, however, and thus this too is a production variable which must be learned or "reorganized" as it comes under voluntary control. Acquisition of prepausal lengthening appears to interact with syntactic learning and may not be fully in place until the early school years. As Lindblom (1978) tentatively concluded, multiple factors ("indirect phonetic causation") must be called on to account for the origin and function of final lengthening: "Being phonetically natural [such] a process is easy to learn and to use and therefore stands a good chance of becoming a characteristic feature of how sound patterns are structured as well as used in individual speech acts" (p. 98).

We considered separately the available evidence regarding the developmental profile of the two major types of accentual system, stress accent and tone. Although there continues to be relatively little data regarding the early stages in the acquisition of a tonal accent system, some similarity in accentual development was apparent for stress and tone, in that *unaccented* syllables pose a greater production problem to the child than do the (perceptually more salient) accented syllables in both cases. Furthermore, the relationship between developmental trends and aspects of the adult input appears to constitute a potentially important but heretofore relatively unexplored area. Specifically, the much debated "trochaic bias" may be a reflection of the greater salience of final (as compared with initial) unaccented syllables due to phrase-final lengthening in the input. Similarly, the unexpected precedence of second-syllable rise over first-syllable fall in children's productions of Swedish grave accent may be derivable from prosodic modulations in infant-directed speech.

Finally, we found considerable support for the long-standing view that pitch variables are controlled relatively early. The predominant prosodic characteristics of the adult system are reflected in infant productions within the one-word period at the latest, when only a subset of the adult segmental inventory may be used; acquisition of the full adult system is not typically achieved until after the child has begun to master the syntactic system, however.

NOTES

1   Cf. Studdert-Kennedy, 1979: "Like other motor behaviors, speech is compelled, by natural constraints on the relative timing of components, to be rhythmic" (p. 61).
2   Stark et al. (1975) dispute Lieberman's (1967) interpretation of the rising-falling pitch contours of early vocalizations as a product of subglottal air pressure change; in their data, "such contours were noted within individual cry segments even where these were followed by breath holding and by another expiratory cry segment, rather than by an inspiratory gasp" (p. 218). These authors consider changes in vocal fold tension more likely to be responsible for the pitch contours.
3   Loan words sometimes constitute exceptions to the initial syllable stress rule, but vowel length remains associated with the stressed syllable: cf. *büroo* 'study' < French *bureau*.
4   A correlation between rate of articulation and child age is commonly reported: cf. Smith (1978) (2- and 4-year-olds), Kent and Forner (1980) (4-, 6- and 12-year-olds), and also Starkweather's (1980) thoroughgoing review of speech rate in both adults and children in relation to nonfluencies (pauses and hesitations) and length of utterance. In addition, Hulme et al. (1984) document a close relationship throughout childhood between speech rate and short-term memory span.
5   Liberman and Prince (1977) represents perhaps the first extensive attempt to incorporate rhythmic principles into phonological theory.
6   Kassai (1988) reports the same phenomenon for the prosody of a Hungarian child in the "one-word utterance stage" (p. 72); see also Fónagy (1972).
7   Hochberg (1988a) adds examples from Leopold (1947) and from her own data of both phonetic and *semantic* sources of extra attention to the "normatively unstressed" syllable, resulting in apparently misplaced or level stress. An example of the apparent use of misplaced stress in association with an effort to achieve contrast within a tightly constrained segmental system is given in Vihman et al., 1994 (p. 28): [ba'bi] *bottle* (4 tokens) vs. [ba'bü] *bubble* (27 tokens: Timmy, aged 1;4).
8   With regard to her data from a single child acquiring Sesotho, a grammatical tone language with a rich set of sandhi rules, Demuth (1993) concludes that "the underlying tone of verb roots appears to be acquired gradually over time, on an item-by-item basis" (p. 299), together with the acquisition of some of the most pervasive tone sandhi effects (by about age 3), while the rule-assigned tone of certain functional morphemes such as subject markers is acquired earlier (by 2;1).
9   In a classic diary study of his granddaughter "Canta," Chao (1951) provided an early impressionistic account of a child's use of tone in Mandarin.

9 Advances in Phonological Development

We have seen that identifiable word use is the product of months of preparation in the form of both (auditory and visual) perceptual exposure to ambient speech (ch. 4) and vocal expression, which affords proprioceptive experience of selected auditory patterns (ch. 5); furthermore, the first systematic word use emerges, within a supportive social and affective framework, as one of several communicative and cognitive advances in the first eighteen months of life (ch. 6). We have emphasized these developments in infancy because we believe that they will ultimately provide a way out of the celebrated theoretical impasse between the "impossible and the miraculous" (ch. 2). Once the child has taken the first steps toward developing referential language and the organization of a simple phonological system, analogies with infrahuman communicative systems are quickly superceded as we enter the complex realm of linguistic contrast, which implies a category-based network of mutually defining elements and hierarchical structures.

Recent studies of phonological development have focused largely on the earliest period; with respect to later advances recent work is more programmatic than conclusive. Our goal in the present chapter will be, first, to review the evidence from *production* regarding the "emergence of the segment," on the premise that the word is the first unit of organization (see also ch. 7). We will begin by recalling some of the findings of the 1970s with regard to the development of "rule-based" phonology, on the one hand, and the importance of production constraints and "word templates," on the other. We will then consider current work involving instrumental analyses of children's productions as a way of identifying changes in coarticulation. Finally, we will sample promising new avenues of research concerning the role of prosody in the development of morphosyntactic structure.

The emergence of segments

Explicit concern with the size of the first production unit may be traced back to Moskowitz (1973), who specifies that a "unit" is the smallest section of the speech chain which the child uses distinctively. It is not defined by the investigator's recognition of distinction, but rather by the child's evidencing in some significant way that he has achieved an ability to organize his grammar on the basis of that unit. (p. 49; cf. also Ferguson et al., 1973)

Whereas Moskowitz postulated the syllable as a universal first phonological unit and reduplication as a universal early stage, Ferguson and his colleagues suggested that children may differ, some basing their first phonological organization on the "entire lexical unit," or word (e.g., Jacqueline Bloch: cf. Bloch, 1913; Ferguson, 1963), while others begin with the syllable (e.g., Leslie Weeks, the subject of Ferguson et al., 1973; cf. also Andrew in French, 1989; Timmy in Vihman, 1992, Vihman et al., 1994). In subsequent work Ferguson (e.g., Ferguson and Farwell, 1975, Ferguson, 1978, Macken and Ferguson, 1983) emphasized the priority of the word as a unit of contrast in the child's developing phonological system (cf. also Menn, 1971, 1983; Menyuk et al., 1986).

If the whole word is, in some sense, a basic production unit for the child, where do segments come from? And when do they begin to play a role in the child's phonological organization? MacNeilage and Davis (1990a) stated succinctly that "serial ordering errors in normal adult speech that involve single speech segments moving around in an otherwise correct utterance tell us beyond doubt that the individual segment is an independent unit in the control of adult speech (p. 55; cf. Kent, 1983; Studdert-Kennedy, 1987; Levelt, 1989)." They propose that in the "highly variegated pattern in successive cycles [of jaw opening and closing]" which characterizes adult speech, "variegation is achieved by placement of independently controlled '*content*' elements in syllable '*frames*'." Since "there is no evidence that when infants first sound as if they are producing speech segments with speech-like durations, they already have segmental units under independent control," they raise the question: "How do infants achieve this segmental independence?" (p. 55). Adopting a strict motor approach to linguistic organization, they argue that the first speech-like production – that of canonical babbling – may be viewed as a "motor correlate of the syllable frame" (p. 57). Similarly, the variegated babbling which soon follows reflects only a limited capacity to insert selected patterns or *content* into these frames (modulation of the degree of opening of the jaw yields changes in manner only across the vocal production unit: Davis and MacNeilage, 1994). In other words, the frames constitute a rhythmic base or carrier for specific segment sequences or syllables; independent motor control of these elements emerges only gradually from the tongue/jaw synergy with which the child enters into adult-like vocal production (see also Hodge, 1989).

A recent report of silent babbling production by both deaf and hearing children over the age range 8 to 13 months (Meier, Willerman, and Zakia, 1994) lends support to the MacNeilage and Davis characterization of vocal organization in this period. The "jaw wagging" these authors observed, typically involving labial closure, occurred *after* the onset of canonical babbling, sometimes mixed with voiced production within a single sequence (for example, from a hearing child at 10 months, [ma.ma.JW.JW.JW.JW.JW.JW], where "." indicates a syllable break or the start of a new oscillatory cycle and "JW" represents the silent jaw wagging).

Silent babbling may be viewed as a "pure frame" which incorporates the *timing* element of vocal production without phonation. In contrast, such non-canonical vocal elements as syllabic fricatives or clicks, for example, represent incomplete attempts at speech-like vocal production of another kind, in which phonation and/ or supraglottal closure is produced in the *absence* of the rhythmic frame (or timing) of canonical sequences (such non-syllabic elements also sometimes serve as the basis for early word production: See French, 1989; Matthei, 1989; Vihman and Roug-Hellichius, 1991; for an example of such production by a 2-year-old child with developmental verbal dyspraxia, see Velleman, 1994).

MacNeilage, and Davis's interpretation of early phonetic patterns fits well with the "vocal motor schemes" of McCune and Vihman (1987; see ch. 6 above) as well as with Kent's proposal that early words are represented as "gestural scores" (1992: see ch. 2 above). Studdert-Kennedy (1987) has argued that the shift from the word, an "articulatory routine" which is also "a unit of meaning that mediates the child's entry into language" (p. 67), to the segment is the result of vocabulary growth, which leads "recurrent patterns of sound and gesture" to "crystallize into encapsulated phonemic control units," resulting in emergence of a full repertoire of phonemes by the middle of the third year. Similarly, Lindblom's functional model (1992) suggests that the segments of a later stage of the child's phonological organization emerge through the "interaction of subsystems" in the form of an accumulation of distinct word forms (or gestural scores) involving somewhat different activity patterns for the various articulators. Because the structuration resulting from this interaction is self-organizing, "children are never aware of having acquired phonemic coding. It appears to emerge in a completely automatic and implicit manner" (Lindblom, MacNeilage, and Studdert-Kennedy, 1984, p. 185).[1]

Despite these impressive formulations, there is as yet little evidence regarding the actual developmental course from articulatory routine or whole-word unit to "phoneme control unit" or segment. An indirect source is provided by accounts of children's use of "phonological processes" or "rules" at various ages and stages of lexical development (but N. V. Smith, 1973, for example, begins at a relatively late stage, when his son is already aged 2;2). Macken (1979) traces a single child's production from whole-word templates to the emergence of a nearly complete inventory of adult segments, while a handful of less thorough case studies offer a further glimpse of the process. Taken together, such studies reveal a gradual qualitative shift from a predominance of processes affecting the structure of whole words (consonant harmony, reduplication, final consonant deletion) to those affecting specific segments or classes of segments (stopping of fricatives, gliding of liquids). The shift itself can be understood as a reflection of the progressive emergence of segments as control units for the child. Evidence of the very gradual nature of the change may be gleaned from studies which attempt to compare the degree of coarticulation in the speech of younger and older children and adults.

Rule-based child phonology

Phonological systematicity has its origins in the period *following* first word production (see ch. 6). First words are identified when the child begins to produce existing vocal motor schemes (or phonetic patterns developed through babbling) in situations appropriate to similar ("matching") adult word patterns. The first words of early talkers may not appear to be phonologically related; each is the product of an idiosyncratic match between a prelinguistic gestural score or articulatory routine and a salient adult word. Early in the second year the child experiences an expanded capacity for internal representation; it is hypothesized that this maturational change provides the necessary basis for phonological systematization, in which one or more word templates are formed and used to assimilate growing numbers of adult word forms (Vihman, 1993c; Vihman et al., 1994). It is in this second stage of phonological organization that the child begins to accommodate adult forms which go beyond his or her production constraints by making systematic changes in the reproduction of adult segments, sequences and syllable or word shapes.[2] These adjustments have been termed (child) phonological rules (Menn, 1971; Ingram, 1974, 1976; N. V. Smith, 1973) or processes (Stampe, 1969; Oller, 1975), despite the fact that the relationship to the rules of *adult* phonology is more apparent than real (cf. Kiparsky and Menn, 1977): While adult phonological rules relate variant shapes of morphemes affected by phonological or morphological context, the purported child rules describe the discrepancy between children's forms and the adult model, which is taken to be equivalent to underlying forms for children's words (Ingram, 1974).

In one of the first attempts to characterize a range of typical child rules based on cross-linguistic data, Ingram (1974) emphasizes the systematic nature of child phonological behavior (cf. also Oller, 1975). This emergent systematicity was noted also by linguists of an earlier day:

> As the child gets away from the peculiarities of his individual "little language," his speech becomes more regular, and a linguist can in many cases see reasons for his distortions of normal words. When he replaces one sound by another there is always some common element in the formation of the two sounds . . . There is generally a certain system in the sound substitutions of children, and in many instances we are justified in speaking of "strictly observed sound-laws." (Jespersen, 1922, pp. 106f., quoted in Ingram, 1986, p. 223).

As Ingram (1974) points out, the adult forms may or may not be taken to be represented as such in the child's mental lexicon (see ch. 2). Ingram allows for a distinction between adult pronounced form, child's perceived form, child's underlying form, and child's spoken form. Subsequent treatments of child phonological rules have often failed to take account of these various alternatives, however.

Ingram (1986) provides examples of various common rule types or "processes" from several different languages, distinguishing between syllable structure processes, in which the complexity of the adult syllable or syllable sequence is reduced in the child form (cluster reduction, final consonant deletion, unstressed syllable deletion, and reduplication), assimilatory processes, in which sounds are affected by their phonetic environment (voicing,[3] consonant harmony), and substitution processes, in which a sound segment which is within the child's productive inventory substitutes for an adult sound which is not (stopping, fronting, gliding, vocalization).[4]

Table 9.1 presents Grunwell's (1982) Profile of Phonological Development, which includes a profile of the typical development of stable consonants from first word use to the end of the preschool period (age 0;9 to 4;6+) as well as a chronology of expected phonological process use over the same time course (capital letters are used to indicate processes usually present at a given stage while parentheses indicate processes likely to be optional, or in declining use). Grunwell assigns the first apparently systematic use of rules, in which the beginning of phonological organization is manifested in uniform treatment of similar adult word forms, to the second stage (age 1;6–2;0) – after the period of the first words, when individual variation across children and considerable cross-word phonetic variability are expected. In Grunwell's list of processes those affecting syllable structure appear on the left while the segment substitution processes are on the right. This organization allows us to see clearly that the processes which take the word or syllable as their domain are common only up to about age 3 (e.g., syllable deletion, reduplication, harmony, cluster reduction), after which only those which affect individual segments continue to be observed with some regularity.

Examples of processes taken from three hours of recording of ten 3-year-old English-speaking children are presented in Appendix 9.1 at the end of this chapter.[5] A three-point scale was used to score observed frequency of use, ranging from "sporadic" (1: less than 25% of the child's words are affected) to "inconsistent" (2: 25%–75% are affected) to "regular" (3: more than 75% are affected); the mean frequency for the group as a whole is indicated for each process. Usage follows Grunwell's estimate rather closely: The least used process for these three-year-olds was velar fronting (predicted to be rare by age 2;0–2;6); (unstressed) syllable deletion and cluster reduction involving consonant + /r/ and /s/ + consonant were relatively uncommon; final consonant deletion, consonant harmony and reduction of consonant + /l/ clusters occurred to a moderate extent, while stopping (including affricate reduction), palatal fronting and gliding (still expected to be typically present at 3;0–3;6) and substitution for interdental fricatives (still present in Grunwell's last stage, at 4;6) were the most common.

From templates to segments: Melodies

Macken (1979) provides a rare longitudinal account of one child's phonological development from an early period of high variability and predominant use of a specific word template to a later stage in which most of the adult segment inventory is in use. In terms drawn from nonlinear phonology, Macken (1992) refers to this template as a melody (cf. also Alice's palatal pattern and Laurent's CVIV pattern in Appendix C), in contrast with the harmony patterns to be described in the next section.

The subject, Si, acquiring Mexican Spanish in Northern California, was recorded weekly for 15–30 minutes for ten months; her speech was narrowly transcribed by two independent transcribers and her developmental speech patterns informally compared to those of the other subjects of the larger study (see Macken, 1978, and table 8.3, above). Si was 1;7 at the beginning of the study but produced only twelve different words in the first month of recording, so that this early period

Table 9.1   Profile of phonological development

Stage	Labial	Lingual		
Stage I (0;9–1;6)	Nasal Plosive Fricative Approximant		First Words tend to show: – individual variation in consonants used; – phonetic variability in pronunciations; – all simplifying processes applicable.	

Stage II (1;6–2;0)	m n
	p b t d
	w
			Reduplication
			Consonant Harmony
			FINAL CONSONANT
			  DELETION
			CLUSTER REDUCTION
				FRONTING of velars
				STOPPING
				GLIDING /r/ → [w]
				CONTEXT SENSITIVE
				  VOICING

Stage III (2;0–2;6)	m n (ŋ) p b t d (k g) w h		Final Consonant Deletion CLUSTER REDUCTION	(FRONTING of velars) STOPPING GLIDING r → w CONTEXT SENSITIVE VOICING
Stage IV (2;6–3;0)	m n ŋ p b t d k g		Final Consonant Deletion CLUSTER REDUCTION	STOPPING /v ð z ʧ ʤ/ /θ/ → [f] FRONTING /ʃ/ → [s] GLIDING /r/ → [w] Context Sensitive Voicing
Stage V (3;0–3;6)	f s j h w (l)		Clusters appear obs. + approx. used; /s/ clusters: may occur	STOPPING /v ð/ (/z/) /θ/ → [f] FRONTING of /ʧ ʤ ʃ/ GLIDING /r/ → [w]

Stage VI (4;0–4;6) (3;6–4;0)	m n ŋ
	p b t d ʧ ʤ k g
	f v s z ʃ
	w l (r) j h
			Clusters established:
			obs. + approx. : approx
			  "immature"
			/s/ clusters: /s/ →
			  FRICATIVE
			
			obs. + approx. acceptable
			s clusters: 's type'
			  FRICATIVE
				/θ/ → [f]
				
				ð → [d] or [v]
				(PALATALIZATION of
				  /ʧ ʤ ʃ/)
				GLIDING r → w

Stage VII (4;6,)	m n ŋ p b t d ʧ ʤ k g f v θ ð s z ʃ ʒ w l r j h		(/θ/ → f) (ð → [d] or [v]) (r → [w] or [ʋ])	

Source: Adapted from Grunwell, 1982

can be taken to correspond to the period of first words (Grunwell's Stage I). Her sound inventory roughly corresponded to that defined by Grunwell for Stage II, although the voicing contrast of the adult language is missing: Si made use of labial and dental voiceless stops [p, t] and nasals [m, n] and the glides [w, j]. Si's early phonology is not well captured by a set of substitution rules, even including such "word-based" rules as consonant harmony and weak syllable deletion. Instead, it can be understood as the product of production constraints which commonly obtain in early stages of phonological development. These constraints affect the permitted types of within-word (across-syllable) consonantal sequences, possible syllable shapes and the maximum number of syllables per word.[6]

The perspective which affords the most complete understanding of Si's developing phonological system is one which posits a word template as the chief organizing principle. Following the approach of Ferguson and Farwell (1975), Ferguson (1978) and Menn (1978), Macken provides detailed illustration and argument for the word and "word pattern" as the basic unit which allows Si's flexible use of syllable deletion, harmony, metathesis and sometimes surprising lexical blends or coalescence to fall into place as manifestations of a single underlying phonological organization.

From 1;7 to 1;9 Si's words adhered to a strict true consonant co-occurrence constraint which permitted only sequences of the form [labial–dental] (glides could combine freely with stops and nasals) – e.g., *zapato* 'shoe' [pwat:o], *Fernando* [wan:o], 1;8. Over the period 1;9 to 2;2 Si gradually relaxed the constraint, expanding her range of possible two- and three-syllable word patterns. After 1;10 two new developments were observed: The range of occurring consonants increased to permit sequences of /m_s_/, /f_n_/ and (at 1;11) /p_l_/, /b_ŋ_/; on the other hand, from 1;11 on velars were permitted in the initial slot, expanding the range of possibilities to include /k_t_/, /k_s_/ and even /ŋ_n_/ or /ŋ_t_/ (though adult Spanish does not allow /ŋ/ in syllable-initial position). By age 2;1 Si had expanded her pattern to include most of the consonant co-occurrence possibilities which her language afforded.

Si's manipulation of syllable reduction and metathesis to derive a labial–dental pattern from an adult word provides eloquent evidence of the organizing role of the word template: When the adult word is labial-initial followed by one or more dental-initial syllables, the medial syllable is deleted (*manzana* 'apple' [mənna], 1;7). When a labial occurs only medially, an initial syllable may be deleted (*Ramón* [mən], 1;8). Words which "contained labial and dental consonants in the 'wrong' order" might be subjected to metathesis (*sopa* 'soup': [p'wæt'a], 1;8), while words which "lacked one of the pattern-criterial consonants" were harmonized (gato 'cat': [kako], 1;9; 1979, p. 28). Substitution patterns for consonants which the child had not yet mastered were similarly subject to the influence of the word template. Thus, Spanish [r] was variably substituted by [d] (*perro* 'dog': [bɛdə]) or [b] (*reloj* 'watch': [bʊd'do]). Some semantically salient words proved particularly resistant to the child's attempts to assimilate them to an existing word pattern; in such cases, an unusually high degree of variability is observed (*elefante* 'elephant': [batte], ['hwantuti], [pfantindi], [panti], 1;9; [pwanti], 1;10; [bwante], [ʧante], [fante], 1;11: Compare the similar struggle of an English-learning child, Alice, to assimilate the similarly uncongenial word shape *elephant* to her palatal pattern: Vihman et al., 1994).

By 2;2 we observe a gradual disappearance of the word templates which exerted such a powerful "pattern force" (p. 34) on the child's early phonological organization. In the early period we see (1) assimilation of an increasing range of different adult word forms to a single word pattern and (2) a slowly expanding range of phonetic exponents of these patterns, or possible consonant segments, resulting in the ongoing "learning of contrasts between individual sounds and the equivalences between similar sounds in different environments (i.e. phonemic contrasts and allophonic relationships)" (p. 20), even while the word templates continue to hold sway. In the later period, the child's phonetic productions are in more systematic relationship to the adult phonemes in different positions in words and phrases, although "how the transition precisely came about is not . . . so clear, primarily because the two developments [i.e., (1) and (2) above] overlapped considerably" (p. 20).

Macken details the gradual appearance of segmental contrast over the period of her study. In the early period, labial : dental contrast in stops and nasals could be identified first, followed by velar : dental contrast in stops in the second month of observation. The gradual emergence of voicing contrast is largely completed for labial stops by 2;1 but remains incomplete for other places of articulation even by 2;5. Fricatives begin to be produced at 1;10–1;11; the voiceless fricatives and affricate /f, s, ʧ/ are all contrastive by 2;1. Liquids, which are highly variable in production throughout this period, remain emergent at the end of the study. In the last three months of the study, however, all the idiosyncracies of Si's phonology fade, leaving only a relatively orderly residue of substitutions characterizable by processes such as stopping (for [ð], the intervocalic allophone of Spanish /d/) and gliding (for both the tap and the trilled /r/ phonemes). At the same time, the earlier co-occurrence constraints were fully superceded: "All sequences of consonants occurred" (p. 41).

Although there are other detailed longitudinal accounts of one child's phonological development (including Leopold, 1939, N. V. Smith, 1973),[7] no other study has so clearly traced the path from the "word as a prosodic unit" (cf. Waterson, 1971) to a more adult-like system based on the principle of phonemic contrast. Macken's study also provides what is probably the single most persuasive set of arguments for a "whole word stage" in early phonology (see Ferguson, 1978; Menyuk et al., 1986; Studdert-Kennedy, 1987). Although comparable longitudinal accounts of the changing units of other children's phonological systems are not so far available, studies focusing on particular idiosyncratic patterns and their "resolution" in favor of more adult-like production suggest that evidence of a shift from whole word to segmental unit varies from one child to the next, with individual differences in the nature and timing of such a shift as well as in the difficulty of identifying or describing it.

Macken's study itself amply illustrates the importance of individual differences in phonology. Macken points out several aspects of Si's word production that were unusual in addition to the particular choice of word template. These include a high level of imitation, with patterns differing considerably from her spontaneous production; frequent use of an onset (or "filler") vowel prefixed to her words; consolidation of routine phrases into shorter word-like units; and malapropism-like "misperceptions" of adult words as revealed in her imitations: *Fernando* (her brother's name) for *Armando*, *avión* "airplane" for *León*, etc. (for related examples from a number of different children and languages, see Vihman, 1981). Macken sees these tendencies as possibly reflecting "a global, only partly differentiated auditory processing . . . paralleled by [Si's] loose, prosodic treatment of words . . . Si [may be viewed] as a child whose preferred processing mode is a global one rather than a detail or analytic one" (p. 47; cf. Peters, 1977, 1983; Ferguson, 1979; Vihman and Greenlee, 1987).

On the other hand, Macken also suggests that the one- to two-syllable production constraint reflected in Si's phonology is "probably universal" in early stages. However, further data collection across a wider number of languages has shown that "universal" is too strong a term for this common constraint on word length. Of five children acquiring Japanese, an agglutinative language which typically presents multisyllabic content words to the child, one "specialized" in long word production, achieving identifiable words of three to five syllables by 15 months, when she had about a fifty-word vocabulary (Vihman, 1991). Many of these long words included the morpheme *-san* (/ʧan/ in "baby talk" register), an honorific, produced by the child as [tan]: e.g. *hebi(-chan)* 'Mr snake' [hɛbita(n)], *penginsan* 'Mr penguin' [be:mit'aʔ] (imit.), *tombochan* 'Mr dragonfly' [tɔnmɛtæn] (imit.) (1;3.16); *bebi(-chan)* 'Miss baby' [bɛbitan], *oningyochan* 'Miss dolly' [ɔnɪʧa:n] (1;3.28); both *oumachan(chan)* 'Mr horsie' [ɔʊmʌtɔmata] and *mimi(chan)* 'Mr ear' [mɪmɪta] include an additional *-chan* which was not in the adult model (1;3.28).

As we saw in the case of Macken's subject Si, the holistic patterns of the early period survive into somewhat later stages of phonological development as well, sometimes taking on new importance for a short period as a response to new challenges posed by the ambient language. That is, once the child has mastered a small set of words resembling the production patterns developed in the prelinguistic period and has begun to actively assimilate new words and new sounds and sequences (as illustrated in Appendix C), he or she can be expected to progress through new cycles of systematization (with assimilation of new types of word targets to existing patterns) and expansion (or accommodation to new features of the adult language). We will consider a few such cases.

Priestly (1977) reports a word pattern even more unusual in its make-up than Si's sequential labial–dental pattern, involving such unexpected adult:child correspondences as *berries* [bɛjas], *rabbit* [rajap], *tiger* [tajak], *whistle* [wijas].[8] His son Christopher embarked on what Priestly refers to as "something not only amusing but systematic" at about age 1;10, when he already had a sizeable lexicon (no vocabulary estimate is offered, but over 150 bisyllabic words are analyzed in the study). The "idiosyncratic strategy" which Priestly described lasted for just over three months, to age 2;1. Although the child produced over sixty "bisyllabic ordinary forms" by 1;11, when his father took inventory, many of these (25 percent) derived from forms with a medial /j/ in the input form (a Southern British English variety "very close to Received Pronunciation," p. 47): *lion* [lajən], *fire* [fajə]. The high frequency of such forms is one possible source of the medial [j] template; substitution of the glide for liquids is another.

Priestly analyzes the child's strategy as reflecting underlying forms with generally accurate representation of the first (usually stressed) syllable, one other "noticeable" consonant (either the medial or the final consonant of the adult form) and the fact of bisyllabicity. In order to form these elements "into a phonological whole" for production, the child made use of "one of a number of component strategies, or ruses," including the insertion of a second vowel, sometimes the second vowel of the input, sometimes a neutral (low or mid central) vowel. By the end of the period in question the child had developed "ordinary replacement forms" for virtually all of the words in question (cf. *berries* ['bɛrijs], *rabbit* ['ræbit], *tiger* ['tajgə], *whistle* ['wisu]). Thus, although Priestly does not attempt to trace the transition, focusing instead on an exhaustive analysis of the template itself, this study parallels Macken's in revealing the role of the child's active and creative phonological experimentation on the threshold of adult-like production of disyllables.

From templates to segments: Harmonies

The use of consonant harmony is perhaps the best documented and most discussed phenomenon of early child phonology (Menn, 1971; Cruttenden, 1978; Macken, 1978 (Spanish); Berg, 1992 (German); Fikkert, 1994 (Dutch); Stoel-Gammon and Stemberger, 1994). N. V. Smith (1973) assumed, based on his own case study as well as on earlier reports in the literature, that consonant harmony is a "universal" function of early child rules. However, a slight increase in the sample of systematically analyzed child phonologies was enough to reveal very extensive individual differences in its occurrence: Vihman (1978), based on thirteen children, finds consonant harmony to range in use from 1 percent for a Chinese-speaking child to 32 percent for Amahl Smith. Although it may be difficult to find a child who fails to produce any forms at all which seem to exhibit assimilation of non-contiguous consonants, our summary of Macken's analysis of Si is perhaps sufficient to make the point that consonant harmony, though occurrent in her case as well, may play a negligible role in some children's phonological development. Drawing on Appendix C to illustrate the early period of phonological organization, similarly, we see that some children exhibit scarcely a trace (Alice, Molly), while for others, harmony seems likely to become established as a cornerstone of the developing system (Charles; cf. also Daniel Menn (Menn, 1971) and Daniel in Stoel-Gammon and Cooper, 1984). Vihman and Roug-Hellichius (1991) document for Vihman's son Raivo the parallel emergence (at 1;3) of consonant harmony ([dada] *head aega* /hea'taeka/ 'goodbye,' [muma] *muna* 'egg') and a "melodic" template, involving a shift from syllabic consonant production ([ʂ] *viska* 'throw,' *vesi* 'water') to monosyllabic, closed-syllable productions with a schwa nucleus ([məs] as an imitation of both *müts* 'hat' and *musi* 'kiss'; [nən] as a spontaneous form for *lind* 'bird,' *rind* 'breast,' *king* 'shoe' and *kinni* 'closed'; for further examples, see Vihman, 1981).

This suggests that children are not necessarily limited to "harmony grammars" or "melody grammars" alone, as suggested by Macken (1992), but may exhibit templates characteristic of both types.

Of the thirteen subjects of Vihman (1978), Virve produced the second-highest proportion of harmonized words (25 percent).[9] Together with Amahl Smith, her data provided "nearly half of the total harmony corpus" (p. 307). The fact that the largest proportion of harmonized forms derives from two children whose data are due to parental diary report rather than recorded sessions transcribed by independent observers raises a legitimate methodological concern:

> Both Smith and I may have tended to write down all the phonologically "interesting" forms while disregarding some of the forms which were uninterestingly close to their adult models. At the same time, one assumes that there are also limitations inherent in an experimental situation such as that used in the Spanish studies, with a restricted range of stimuli and observers not intimately familiar with the children. (p. 307)

These doubts are to a great extent allayed by the relatively close correspondence between the findings of Macken (1979: outside observer) and Priestly (1977: diary study) with regard to an unusual melodic pattern, on the one hand, and those of Macken (1978: "J" – renamed Jesus in Vihman, 1978: 21 percent harmony) and Vihman (1978: Virve) with regard to harmony, on the other.

Vihman reports that Virve's first use of consonant harmony was recorded at 15 months, when she had a cumulative lexicon of about thirty words (see Vihman, 1976, for Virve's first fifty words); frequent use of the process continued for about seven months. Within the first fifty words (to age 1;6) two constraints obtained: maximum word length was two syllables and consonants agreed in either place or manner within a word. The child's inventory included three stops, two nasals, [s] and [j]. Liquids had not yet been produced and adult /v/ did not occur word-initially. By 1;4 manner harmony was applied only optionally (*kiisu* 'kitty' [ʃiːsu], [tiːt̪u], 1;3, [tiːsu], 1;6) while place harmony continued to play an active role through 1;10 (*padi* 'pillow' [papi], 1;4; *kamm* 'comb' [pamː], 1;5; *sööma* '(let's go) eat' [föːma], 1;7; *prügi* 'trash' [küki], 1;8; *tuba* 'room' [pupa], 1;10).[10]

At 17 months the child first began to produce trisyllabic forms, soon developing a pattern which could be characterized, like that of Christopher Priestly, as "not only amusing but [relatively] systematic" (age is indicated on the left; all forms were produced spontaneously):

1;5	*banaani* 'banana, obj.'	[ˈpaːnini]
	nii moodi 'this way'	[ˈmiːmona]
	tagasi '(go, put, take) back'	[ˈtasisi]
	lennukit 'airplane, obj.'	[ˈnanunu]
	maasikas 'strawberry'	[ˈmaːsini]
1;6	*porgandit* 'carrot, obj.'	[ˈpɔnini]
	raamatut 'book, obj.'	[ˈmaːnunu]
	rosinad 'raisins'	[ˈoːsini]
1;7	*magustoit* 'dessert'	[ˈmasusu]
	mesilane 'bee'	[ˈmesini]

	pikkali 'lying down'	['pik:akai]
	vikerkaar 'rainbow'	['vik:akai]
1;9	*joonista* 'draw'	['nonini]
	mõistatus 'puzzle'	['misusu]
	Viviane	['mimian]

Like Priestly's son, Virve maintained "the syllable count and overall syllabic structure of the adult word, while abandoning any attempt at segmental fidelity for all but one of the unstressed syllables" (Vihman, 1978, p. 318).[11] As illustrated above, the syllable shape used for the unstressed syllables drew on the consonants of the adult model in a flexible manner reminiscent of Si and Christopher Priestly. Instead of a melodic template, this child seems to have drawn on a small set of preferred syllables (chiefly [ni], [si], [nu], [su]) to fill out the trisyllabic skeleton derived from her adult models. The specific consonant and vowel segments of the model seemed to "prompt" or "prime" one or the other of these choices in each case. Reduplication usually served to fill in the third syllable (Lleó, 1991), although two syllables with different initial consonants were chosen in cases where both /s/ and a nasal occurred as onset consonants in syllables of the adult model (*maasikas, mesilane, rosinad*). Interestingly, in the two cases in which the child resorted to the syllable [su] (*magustoit, mõistatus*), neither /s/ nor /n/ occurred in a syllable onset slot in the model; [su] is arrived at by mõtathesis of the rime, /us/.

From 1;8 on "Virve produces more and more long words . . . which fail to be adapted to the pattern" (p. 318): e.g., *pidžama* 'pajama' ['pisama], *uudiseid* 'news' ['u:tisi]. However, some of Virve's consonant harmony forms persisted for a long time, with new forms continuing to appear as her inventory of segments and syllable shapes grew. The word [*valmis*] 'ready,' for example, which she produced between 1;5 and 1;10 in the variant (metathesized) shapes [mais], [mas'] and [masi], later developed the form [malmis], which Virve went on using well into her fourth year, after initial *v* was otherwise well established.

Finally, from 1;7 on Virve began to include in her production the final consonants which in Estonian mark case inflections on the noun and person on present tense forms of the verb. Use of harmony for the invariant plural marker -*d* was recorded only for three forms (all with medial *k*: *jänkud* 'rabbits' ['jæŋkuk]), but the third person marker -*p* was harmonized to the medial consonant and then mistakenly represented as [-t] over a period of four months (note that the second person marker is -*t*, which likely added to the confusion: "Virve may have interpreted the adult alternation between /-t/ and /-p/ as phonological rather than semantic," p. 320):[12] *töötab* 'works' [tö:tat], *kannab* 'carries' [kaɲ:ak],[13] *proovib* 'tries' [po:pip] (1;7); *annab* 'gives' [an:at], *hüppab* 'jumps' [hüpat] (1;9); *töötavad* '(they) work, are working' [tö:tatat] (1;10).

Lleó (1990) describes the phonological development of her daughter Laura over the period 1;7 (when she had fifteen words) to 2;11 (nearly 400 words). Laura is trilingual in Catalan, Spanish and German, but only the data from Catalan, her mother's native language, are presented in this analysis. As Lleó illustrates, Laura produced a high proportion of reduplicated bisyllabic words in the early period of word production (25% at 1;7, 17% at 1;9, and 7% or less thereafter). Like Spanish,

Catalan presents the child with a large number of words of more than two syllables, however. Up to 2;3 Laura had produced only five such "long words"; as she begins to produce them in larger numbers (five at 2;3, twenty-one at 2;5, and slightly more at each two-month interval thereafter), the proportion of (partially) reduplicated forms increases as well, from 7% of trisyllables at 2;7 to 20% at 2;11.

Examples of Laura's reduplicated long forms (all taken from the last month of the study and based on both three- and four-syllable models) resemble Virve's "harmonized" long words, with allowance made for the difference in accentual pattern in Estonian vs. Catalan.

arrecada 'earring'	[kaʀ'aʀa]
bicicleta 'bicycle'	[blebl'ɛka]
Patufet	[fɔfɔf'ɛt]
sabates 'shoes'	[pap'atəs]
taronja 'orange'	[ʒɔʒ'ɔnta]
tovallola 'towel'	[β'ɔβ'ɔla]
vegada 'time'	[bəg'aga]

Virve, like Christopher Priestly (also acquiring a predominantly initial-syllable-stress language), generally faithfully reproduced the first syllable as a whole. Laura, on the other hand, in most cases accurately renders only the *vowel* of the stressed antepenultimate syllable in her reduplicative pattern while flexibly choosing a "noticeable" consonant for the stressed-syllable onset slot from anywhere in the word; this "constructed" syllable then serves as the base for reduplication, which may fill either the first two syllables of her trisyllabic skeleton, preaccentual and accented (*sabates*, *taronja*), or the last two, accented and postaccentual syllables (*arrecada*, *vegada*). The final syllable retains the target rime in each case. Notice that Laura, who is a year older than Virve at the developmental point of interest and has a considerably larger vocabulary, shows a far more varied set of syllable choices, some of them highly marked in terms of segmental content ([ʀɔ], [ʒɔ], [βɔ]) or syllable structure ([blɛ]).[14]

Analysis of the phonological patterns of any of the four children, Si, Christopher, Virve or Laura, in terms of process application would be relatively unenlightening, although some processes could certainly be said to apply in many cases (weak syllable deletion, consonant harmony, and a number of segment substitutions). In so far as no complete account would be possible in those terms, we conclude with Macken that it is the children's word templates that are guiding their phonological production here, filtering adult words which present a challenge (such as "long words") through the screen of their operating production patterns. Strict consistency was observed in none of these cases; instead, a general pattern was realized with some degree of flexibility, making use of the options presented or "inspired" by a rough match with the adult model.

The relative freedom of the children's implementation of their production plans results in creative approximations reminiscent of adult behavior in cases of accessing difficulty. That is, when attempting to recall a new name or a foreign word, adults may move segments about, reproducing the gist of the target word's prosodic skeleton while missing many of the segmental details, and being channelled in this performance by familiar patterns. When the result is an inadvertently erroneous real word choice, it counts as a malapropism (e.g., *Givenchy* as the name of the artist Monet's home in his latter years – actually *Giverny*; see Fay and Cutler, 1977; Zwicky, 1982).

Aitchison and Chiat (1981) have made a similar point, arguing that the "natural processes" of child phonology "may be memory filters – that is, processes applied when there is too much pressure on the memory to recall recently acquired lexical items accurately. They reveal themselves where perception and production problems can be shown to be absent, but where memory overload is guaranteed" (p. 311). Based on the results of their experimental teaching of a number of unfamiliar animal names to British children aged 4 to 9 years, Aitchison and Chiat suggest further that "faulty recall may reflect a hierarchical ordering of perceptual features in memory; that is, those phonetic features that are most perceptually salient may also be those that are most salient in auditory memory" (p. 322). We would argue that familiar production patterns *enter into* "perceptual salience"; that is, familiarity with the articulatory pattern is part of what makes an auditory pattern memorable, not only for 1-year-olds (whose articulatory routines influence their first word attempts: fig. 6.2) and 2-year-olds (whose existing word templates shape the patterns applied to new and difficult adult targets) but also for the older children of Aitchison and Chiat's study, as the authors suggest (see, for example, the production of *lemon* for *lemming*, *cocoon* for *raccoon*).

In order to test Aitchison and Chiat's results with adults, Smith, Macaluso, and Brown-Sweeney (1991) taught a set of new words to forty adult subjects. They report that longer words (three or four syllables) accounted for a disproportionate share of the errors. Furthermore, metathesis was relatively common in the "misproductions," or recall errors which were phonologically related to the target, while initial consonant (85%), stressed initial vowel (79%), and overall syllable count (68%) tended to be retained in instances of inaccurate recall. In short, the errors resembled malapropisms (though erroneous recall of a related real word was specifically excluded from the analysis); the adults' errors were not notably similar to children's phonological processes, but they do seem to have resembled the "long word" productions we have been describing.

Lleó (1990) was particularly interested in showing that the word may play a central role even in later stages of phonological development, since in her daughter's use of reduplication in the production of words of three or more syllables, for example, "a general outline of the word prevails over a linear analysis of its segments."

> There is a certain reluctance to attribute a crucial role to the lexical item in phonological acquisition . . . based on the assumption that the phoneme and its oppositions play an exclusive role. But child phonology is committed to both, to oppositions and to patterns, that is, to segments, but to syllables and to lexical items too. Adult phonology is also committed to both, although the segment plays a more important role than in child phonology. Within this framework, the transition from child phonology into adult phonology . . . involves a quantitative rather than a qualitative step, from a stage in which the word and the syllable play an essential role – and a lot of features are autosegmentalized – into a stage in which segments take a more important role,

although not an exclusive one – and autosegmentalization is restricted . . . As the
child's phonology evolves, "patterns" . . . lose weight, while segments become more
autonomous. (pp. 275f.)

In short, the transition to segments is gradual and may never be "complete"; adults,
like children, continue to represent words as lexical wholes as well as in terms of
syllables, segments, and perhaps also features. Phonological organization, like syntax, is nonlinear and hierarchical.

Developmental change in coarticulation

In a review of issues involving the segmental organization of speech, Kent (1983)
defines the central problem as that of relating a linguistic or (abstract) notional
construct, the phoneme, to its behavioral realization in "clock time . . . the time in
which we record muscle contractions, structural movements, and acoustic patterns" (p. 59).

> The phoneme, or something very similar to it . . . appears in many studies of machine
> speech recognition and speech synthesis. If nothing else, the phoneme has come to
> serve a basic pragmatic function in speech research because it is the highly serviceable
> tool by which we describe our speech samples. The paradox of coarticulation is that
> its behavioral definition often hinges on a segment-oriented analysis of speech pat-
> terns. In a sense, coarticulation is defined as a failure to observe a transparent
> phonemic organization of speech. (p. 59)

Kent specifies further that "close examination of articulatory patterning will show
many instances of apparent 'coproduction'. Moreover, this coproduction seems to
occur not only because different muscles are used, but also when common muscles
can be used to effect a movement parsimoniously adapted to the sequential articulation of two segments" (p. 65).

Speech commonly involves the programming of related articulatory movements
as "coordinated structures," resulting in synchronous movements of tongue, lips,
velum and jaw. Drawing on data from 4–year-old children, Kent suggested that
"young children may show less extensive coarticulation than adult speakers" (p.
72). Specifically, adults anticipate the syllable-closing consonant gesture while
producing the vowel nucleus (*box*) and undershoot the preaccentual vowel of *you* in
the sentence *We saw you hit the cat*: "One reason for the faster speaking rates of
adults may be that their production patterns are more highly coarticulated, that is,
more motorically fluent" (p. 72).

A different perspective has been taken by Nittrouer and her colleagues in a
series of studies of the perception and production of the syllables /si/, /su/, /ʃi/
and /ʃu/ designed to determine differences in degree of coarticulation across
speakers of different ages. Drawing on evidence such as that which we have
reviewed which suggests that the word (or formulaic phrase) provides the earliest
element of systematic (linguistic) contrast, Nittrouer, Studdert-Kennedy,
and McGowan (1989) propose "to derive segments rather than assume them.
We regard [articulatory] gestures as the primitive units to be coordinated,

phonemes and their featural descriptors as the abstract, systemic products of establishing routines of coordination" (p. 121). They summarize the findings of studies focused on the earliest period of child phonology (Waterson, Ferguson, Menn) as follows:

> As long as the child has only a few words, only one or two articulatory routines are needed. Initially, the child exploits those routines by adding to his or her repertoire only words composed of gestural patterns similar to those already "solved," and by avoiding words with markedly different patterns. Once the initial routines have been consolidated, new routines begin to emerge under pressure from the child's accumulating vocabulary. New routines emerge either to handle a new class of adult words not previously attempted, or to break up and redistribute the increasing cohort of words covered by an old articulatory routine. (p. 120)

Their study was intended to test these findings

> by examining patterns of articulatory organization as evidenced in the acoustic records of young children's utterances. We hypothesized that, if the account has any merit, young children whose phonological development was not yet complete would contrast phonemic minimal pairs less effectively and would show more evidence of intrasyllabic coarticulation than older children or adults. (p. 121)

Nittrouer et al. (1989) collected speech samples from eight adults and four groups of eight children each at the ages of 3, 4, 5 and 7 years; all of these subjects had previously completed a perception experiment (Nittrouer and Studdert-Kennedy, 1987). Subjects responded to pictures with the previously taught labels /sisi/, /ʃiʃi/, /susu/, and /ʃuʃu/, in which reduplicated disyllables were used to maximize opportunities for consonant-vowel coarticulation. The results confirmed the prediction of greater within-syllable coarticulation in younger children as compared with older children and adults for both fricatives. The consonants themselves were increasingly well differentiated with age, apparently due to improvement in control over the shape of the fricative constriction; on the other hand, the lip rounding associated with the palatal fricative in English and with the vowel /u/ was already within the articulatory repertoire of the youngest children (cf. also Sereno et al., 1987). The greater within-syllable coarticulation in child vs. adult productions was ascribed to overlap between consonant and vowel gestures, "that is, to greater fronting of the tongue body before /i/ and greater backing of the tongue body before /u/" (p. 130).

Nittrouer and her colleagues relate these findings to those of their earlier perceptual study, in which the children's syllable identification judgments were found to be more strongly influenced by fricative-vowel transitions, and less strongly by the steady-state spectrum characteristic of each fricative, than were the adults' judgments. "Taken together, the two studies suggest that a child's phonology is grounded in both perceptual and motoric constraints. Certainly, perceptual capacity is logically prior to and must lead productive capacity, but perhaps the two are never far apart" (p. 131).

The question of the timing of the child's motoric "discovery" of the segment remains open:

The initial domain of perceptuomotor organization is a meaningful unit of one or a few syllables, a coherent acoustic structure formed by the interleaved actions of partially independent articulators. As the number and diversity of the words in a child's lexicon increase, words with similar acoustic and articulatory patterns begin to cluster. From these clusters there ultimately precipitate the coherent units of sound and gesture that we know as phonetic segments. Precipitation is probably a gradual process[,] perhaps beginning as early as the second to third year of life when the child's lexicon has no more than 50–100 words. But the process is evidently still going on in at least some regions of the child's lexicon and phonological system as late as 7 years of age. (p. 131)

Studdert-Kennedy (1991b) suggested that "some form of segmental phonology, affording at least a modest lexicon, would seem necessarily to have evolved before syntax began to take shape, and *we still observe this sequence in development*" (p. 9; emphasis added) – implying a considerably earlier "precipitation" or "crystallization" of the segment than seems to be postulated in Nittrouer et al. (1989). Empirical studies have provided mixed results, however. Goodell and Studdert-Kennedy (1990) report evidence of between-vowel coarticulation of tongue-height across disyllables of the form [bə'ba], [bə'bi], using all three places of articulation of stops, in children aged 19–27 months but not in adults.[15] In a small production study involving himself and his two daughters aged 4;8 and 9;5, Repp (1986) found strong intrasyllabic contextual effects of vowel on the constriction noise of the preceding consonant for the younger child and the adult, but not for the 9-year-old, and intersyllabic ("vowel-to-vowel") anticipatory coarticulation for the older child and the adult only. In a study of perception of monosyllables and disyllables Nittrouer (1992) concluded that children's judgments in the age range 3 to 7 years focus preferentially on "an articulatorily defined CV syllable," showing less sensitivity than adults to transition effects *across* syllable boundaries.

Most recently, Nittrouer (1993) has found differing degrees of coproduction in disyllables of the form /ə#Ca/, /ə#Ci/ or /ə#Cu/ (i.e., *a tea(bag)*, *a "two"*, *a key*, *a "coo"*) in the production of children aged 3, 5 and 7 years and adults. Articulatory gestures involving tongue movement (e.g., in production of the syllable /tu/) showed more marked vowel effects for the children than for adults, whereas those involving the jaw only (/ta/, /da/) showed little age-related difference. These results are consistent with MacNeilage and Davis's (1990a) proposal that jaw movements provide the initial syllabic frame on which segmental content is eventually overlaid: "Children appear to acquire adult-like skill for jaw movements sooner than they do for tongue movements" (Nittrouer, 1993, p. 970).

It is possible that some kind of phonological reorganization should be invoked to explain these somewhat paradoxical findings and interpretations (assuming that the methodological issues can be satisfactorily resolved). That is, the "tighter" coarticulatory patterns of the 1- to 2-year-olds of Goodell and Studdert-Kennedy's study may reflect production at a relatively holistic level, with word-sized articulatory packages deployed wherever possible. As motoric skills develop and, concomitantly, attention to details of adult patterns improves, providing local goals for further motoric advances, the child may come to separate the syllables of a word more sharply than does the adult (see Kent, 1983, as well as the findings for Repp's

4-year-old daughter). By the early school years a new advance toward the "under-shooting" and articulatory fluency of adults would begin. Hawkins (1984) outlined a U-shaped curve of this kind, involving first a shift from the "timing-dominant" speech production basis of babbling to a segment-tied "articulatory-dominant" system, which results in slower and more variable segment production than is seen in adults, and then, at age 7 to 9 years, a return to a timing-dominant system such as has been described by Ohala (1970) for English (see B. L. Smith, 1978; Nittrouer, 1993). Further instrumental research on the heretofore relatively little examined development in speech production in school-age children certainly seems warranted.

Prosody and morphosyntax

An unanticipated finding of Nittrouer's (1994) study of coarticulation in adults and children was that children's productions of the schwa syllable which preceded the target monosyllables in the carrier phrase, "it's a ___, Bob" were consistently *longer* than those of adults, though these simple open syllables should have presented little difficulty from the point of view of motoric organization. Nittrouer suggests that the children may have treated the function word as a stressed syllable. Such an interpretation would agree with (and extend) the findings of Allen and Hawkins (1978, 1980) regarding the very gradual course of appropriate reduction of un-stressed syllables (see ch. 8). In addition, however, Nittrouer's suggestion raises the question of the interrelation between prosodic variables – such as the development of control of language-specific timing patterns or "phonological rhythm" – and growth in the knowledge of grammar. Recently, Gerken (1991; 1994; Gerken, Landau, and Remez, 1990; Gerken and McIntosh, 1993) and Peters (1995; Peters and Strömqvist, in press) have begun to address such issues directly.

In their series of experimental studies Gerken and her colleagues have pursued answers to the question of (1) the extent of children's knowledge of function words in early stages of language acquisition and (2) the basis for their frequent omission (see Gerken, 1994 for an overview). Gerken et al. (1990) addressed the question of the extent of children's attention to or awareness of function morphemes in the period when many such morphemes are omitted in spontaneous production. They presented children aged 1;11–2;6 with four-word strings to be imitated, of the form *Peter pushes the dog.* To test sensitivity to the inflectional affix *-es* and the article *the* they constructed target sentences which substituted a nonsense syllable (1) for both functors, creating an unstressed sequence /ou nɑ/, (2) for both content words or (3) for both content words and functors. Children identified as having a low MLU (1.3–2.0) omitted more English functors (37 percent) than nonsense functors (27 percent) – thereby revealing their awareness of the distinction and hence their knowledge of the functors, which they frequently omit in spontaneous produc-tion.[16] Since content words, real or nonsense, were rarely omitted and were pro-duced with relatively high accuracy, it seems clear that it was the accent pattern which distinguished them from functors, not lexical familiarity or referential mean-ing; the tendency to omit known functors more often than equally unstressed nonsense syllables suggests an additional role for morphosyntactic complexity, which is implicated only in the English functors.

In a further experiment Gerken et al. manipulated the shape of the nonsense syllables used to substitute for functors, including either full vowels (as in the first experiment and unlike English functors) or schwa and either consonants typically found in English functors or not (the nonsense "functor" sequences were /əglə/, /uzðə/, /uglɑ/). The results showed that low MLU children (but not the other children) more often omitted the functors containing fricatives than the other nonsense sequences and omitted more English functors than nonsense sequences. These findings "indicate that children have the ability to represent functors with some segmental detail, and not simply as reduced vowels" (p. 212), despite the fact that early production often involves schwa only. This lends plausibility to the suggestion (made by Maratsos and Chalkley, 1980, among others) that children make use of functors, even before they have begun reliably producing them, to identify and distinguish between such syntactic units as noun phrases and verb phrases: "The functors serve as a kind of frame for perceiving and producing content words" (Gerken et al., 1990, p. 213). Gerken and McIntosh (1993) elaborated on this conclusion by showing that children of the same age and level of syntactic development had better comprehension of imperative sentences of the form *Find ___ N for me* when the blank was filled by the definite article than when either the auxiliary *was* or a nonsense syllable *gub* was substituted for the article – thereby demonstrating children's awareness of grammatically relevant distinctions *among* the English functors.

Gerken (1991) considers several competing explanations for the missing functors of early child speech. These include "competence" accounts, which assume "that children omit sentential elements because their immature grammar either does not represent these elements at all or treats them as optional" and "performance" accounts, which take the position "that children have limits on the complexity of the utterances that they can plan and produce" (Gerken, 1991, p. 431). With regard to competence accounts, such as Hyams's (1986) pro-drop hypothesis, Gerken points out that the omission of subject pronouns is part of a "developmentally unified phenomenon" involving the omission of function morphemes in general, whose common properties notably include their weak stress. No explanation which singles out just one subset of these morphemes is likely to prove satisfactory. Similarly, semantic "bootstrapping" accounts, according to which children initially produce only content words learned in association with real world referents (Pinker, 1984), fail to explain the finding that children comprehend functors before they begin to produce them (e.g., Shipley, Smith, and Gleitman, 1969; Macnamara, 1982). There is thus little reason to assume that children's productions reflect the full extent of their knowledge or internal representations of speech. Gerken argues instead for a multilevel performance constraint model, involving limits on complexity at each level of representation (see figure 9.1): "Because the model is sequential in nature, an utterance that requires resource expenditure at higher levels (e.g., syntax and morphology) will have fewer resources remaining at the phonological level than an utterance that has no represen-

Linguistic Level

Message
⇓

Semantic rules and templates
⇓   S → Agent Action

Syntactic rules and templates
⇓   S → Subject Verb

Morphological rules and templates
⇓ |M 1 | M 2|

Foot formation rules and templates
⇓ | Σ1 | (Σ2) | | Σ1 | (Σ2) |
    Σ1 or Σ2 must be strong

Head location rules and templates
⇓ | s | (w) |

Phonological rules and templates

| C | V | (C) |

Key

M	Morpheme
Σ	Syllable
s	Strong
w	Weak

Figure 9.1 Template model of speech production.
Source: Adapted from Gerken, 1991

tation at higher levels (e.g., an utterance encoded only as a string of syllables)" (1994, p. 280; for supporting evidence, see Waterson, 1978; Kamhi, Catts, and Davis, 1984; Nelson and Bauer, 1991).

The single most consistent property of elements omitted in early child speech is their lack of prosodic salience, or stress, at least in English (R. Brown, 1973). Beyond that, Pye (1983) has provided critical complementary evidence from Quiché Mayan that unstressed verb roots are omitted while clause-final stressed inflections are not. Gerken's examination of the metrical patterns involved in the omission of function words affords a further test of the "trochaic hypothesis" of Allen and Hawkins (1980), originally based on children's omission patterns in single multisyllabic word production (as discussed here in ch. 8; see also Wijnen et al., 1994). Gerken (1991) proposes the following principles to describe the hypothesized production template favoring Strong–Weak over Weak–Strong rhythmic sequences:

(1)   A metrical foot contains one and only one strong syllable;
(2)   Create maximally binary left–to–right feet;
(3)   Metrical structure is independent of syntactic structure. (p. 437)

In the experiment reported in Gerken (1991), children of the same age range and stages as before were asked to imitate a set of sentences designed to manipulate the realization of subjects and object noun phrases (NP pronouns, common nouns with the definite article, and proper nouns with no article – e.g., *Pete kissed the lamb, the bear kissed her*). Incorrect imitations (58 percent of the children's attempts) included omissions of the entire noun phrase, article omissions, and substitutions. Subject NPs were omitted more often than objects; pronouns were omitted more than nouns. Both in the imitations and in the children's spontaneous speech the article was more often omitted from the subject NP (or, in spontaneous production, from isolated NPs), in which it is part of an iambic foot with the noun, than from the object NP, in which it is analyzed (according to Gerken's principles) as part of a trochaic foot with the (monosyllabic) verb. Furthermore, weak syllables were omitted from iambic feet with nearly equal frequency across the various functor types (articles in subjects or objects, subject pronouns).

The source of the trochaic metrical preference remains to be explained. As the painstaking analysis by Wijnen et al. (1994) of the manifestation of this same metrical pattern in two children learning Dutch reminds us, however, the nature of the resulting production pattern in the case of long word production and omission of function words is not typically the same: In the case of multisyllabic targets, but not phrases, the segmental or "melodic" content from one or more syllables of the model is often conflated.[17]

Stemberger (1988) reports an exceptional instance of such a long word strategy being used as a "between word process": In her first utterance-initial function words (at about 1;11) his daughter Gwendolyn alternated relatively accurate production with partial reduplication of the following stressed syllable (i.e., of the content word):

It's (a) root.	[ʔiʔ wɑː]	[wəwɑː]
It's mama's.	[ʔi mama]	[məmama]
It (obj.) more.	[ʔiʔ moːu]	[mimoːu]
It (obj.) away.	[ʔiʔ waija]	[wiwai], [wiʔ wai]
It (obj.) snap.	[ʔiʔ n̪ap]	[n̪ən̪ap]

As Stemberger explains, "closed class lexical items presented the first unavoidable instance where initial unstressed syllables had to be pronounced, and reduplication was part of Gwendolyn's response to the difficulty so created" (p. 56).

For the two children acquiring Dutch, the preferred metrical pattern appeared to be traceable to input frequencies. We suggested in chapter 8 that the perceptual effect of final syllable lengthening in input speech may more generally account for the apparent trochaic bias found in many languages. On that account, the initial tendency to omit functors – due to a limit on morphosyntactic complexity, as Gerken suggests – may be guided, additionally, by the lexical template developed earlier, within the one-word stage, as a response to the greater prosodic salience of final syllables, to the dominant pattern of early content words addressed to the child, or to both. (This hypothesis could readily be tested with data from appropriate cross-linguistic data collection – from English, French, and Japanese, for example.) Such a template would then gradually fade as the child acquired the specific rhythmic structures of the target language (as suggested by Wijnen et al., 1994) as well as greater knowledge of and facility with morphosyntactic structure.

A few investigators have suggested that production planning or phonological constraints – in addition to limited knowledge of semantic relations or syntactic structure – may play a role in the timing and nature of first word combinations. Branigan (1979), for example, found acoustic evidence that successive single word utterances (recorded for three children in the age range 1;5–1;11) – defined as word productions separated by pauses of 100–400 msec – were "planned as a single unit, at least on the measures of duration and intonation contour" (p. 418); these disfluent attempts at multiword production "arise from the more or less successful integration of syntactic form and semantic content with segmental and suprasegmental specifications at an underlying level of organization and planning" (p. 419; see also Fónagy, 1972; Scollon, 1979). In an interesting illustration of the process of developing or "reorganizing" articulatory plans to reflect syntactic and semantic information, Donahue (1986) reports that her son's first attempts at combining relational words with nouns (*bye daddy*, *no kitty*: 1;3) were abandoned when an active consonant harmony rule led to an explosion in lexical acquisition; at 1;6 two-word utterances reappear, governed by the same harmony constraint (*baby on bike* [bebiʌbaip], *bye Katie* [gai keki]). In addition, Donahue observes that the productive use of vocalic "pivot" words (*where*, *wa(nt)*, *uh-oh*) – which do not constrain the choice of consonants in what follows – may be a factor in the common use of presyntactic devices such as schwa fillers (e.g., Ramer, 1976), "free[ing] resources for marking semantic relations by working around phonological constraints" (p. 217).[18]

Peters (1995) provides a useful overview of what is currently understood about the role of perception and production in the acquisition of grammatical morphemes. At about age 2, at the outset of grammatical development,

> familiarity with the prosodic structure of the language . . . particularly with the likely placement within an utterance of open-class items, combined with [the] ability to recognize a growing number of open-class items even when embedded in a stream of speech, now allows [children] to begin to focus on what occurs *between* these open-class items. Second, their expanding awareness of the sorts of functions language can accomplish leads them to look for the linguistic means to express these functions . . . Exactly how a given learner proceeds seems to vary, depending on an interaction between the kinds of linguistic information the child is predisposed to pay attention to, and the prosodic and morphosyntactic characteristics of the language being learned. (p. 463)

Cross-linguistic study is especially critical to provide greater insight into the role of prosody in the child's path from first words to grammatical structure. For example, Peters and Strömqvist (in press) have proposed that language-specific phrasal rhythms may serve to direct children's attention to aspects of grammatical structure early in language development: "Perceptually salient prosodic patterns, including pitch contours, rhythm, and increased duration, may serve as 'spotlights' on any phonological forms that are regularly associated with these patterns; if such forms happen to be grammatical morphemes, learners will focus on them earlier than on morphemes not so spotlighted". They provide evidence of such a "spotlight effect" from a longitudinal case study of a child, Markus, acquiring Swedish, with its two pitch accents, grave and acute. Swedish accent, though lexically assigned, is intertwined with morphosyntactic factors as well as with informational focus. The more marked grave accent is two-peaked under focus (or sentence stress), which tends to appear late in the sentence; the second-syllable rise of the grave accent, further enhanced by final-syllable lengthening, is the first characteristic aspect of the Swedish accentual system to be reproduced by children, within the one-word period (at about 17 months, as noted in ch. 8: Engstrand et al., 1991). Several important inflections occur on the second syllable, highlighted by the second peak of the grave accent.

Sentence position and the inherent salience of the grave accent's second-syllable rise thus interact to boost early use of the grave pattern and, correspondingly, attention to word-final inflectional markers. Markus's developmental profile illustrates the role that such a salient prosodic marker may play in directing the child's attention to critical elements of grammatical structure. Word combinations appear sporadically between 1;3 and 1;8, when a vocabulary spurt occurs; mean length of utterance increases steadily thereafter, with the first appearance of inflectional morphemes at 1;9–1;10 (marking definite singular, indefinite plural and present tense). Prosodic development foreshadows this grammatical development: Recognizable grave contours are first noted at about 17 months and are overgeneralized in comparison with the adult norm in the early period of production of multisyllabic inflected forms (1;9–1;11). In the largely one-word productions of this period all of Markus's inflections are utterance-final. At age 2 a reorganization is evident in the dramatic *increase* in inflectional morpheme use, now primarily in sentence-medial position, along with a *reversal* of the role of the two accents, with overgeneralization of the acute accent – suggesting a new awareness on the child's part of the less salient member of the accent system. The authors conclude that "Swedish tonal word accent contrast is acquired . . . as a gradual integrative build-up process with dynamic developmental properties" (cf. also Peters and Menn, 1993).

Summary: Integrating frame and content

The idea that phonological organization may begin with a unit other than the phoneme was first advanced in the 1970s; it has since been validated in a number of independent studies, although the possibility remains open that some children – particularly those who make a somewhat later start on word production (both chronologically and in relation to other aspects of their development) – may begin with the syllable rather than the word. The nature of prosodic development in the first few years of life also began to be seriously investigated in the 1970s; however, the likely relationship between prosodic and segmental advances – involving the integration into a biologically given rhythmic base (shaped by exposure to the patterns of a specific adult language) of the syllables and longer sequences which make up the vocal motor schemes of a given child – did not receive explicit research attention until the 1990s.

The "phonological rules" which were at the center of attention in the seventies continue to play an important role in the analysis of phonological disorders (see Fey, 1985), but in the study of child phonology (as in linguistic theory) they have recently been largely replaced by an interest in constraints on production. The two perspectives are clearly complementary: "Induction rules" are postulated to account for the systematic patterns by which adult forms are rendered accessible to children with a limited motoric repertoire and as yet emergent phonological organization; these patterns may be described equally well, in theoretical metaphor, as first-order organizational scaffolding for satisfying constraints. If, in addition, we accept the idea that initial representations of adult forms may not be fully accurate, particularly where the adult form is remote from the child's production possibilities, we anticipate the kinds of variability and occasional "regression" (or reorganization) which most commonly mark early phonology. Finally, nonlinear phonology has prepared the way for linguists to conceive of phonology as multitiered, perhaps also chronologically multilayered, as conceptualized by Ferguson and Farwell in 1975 when they referred to the "phonic core of remembered lexical items and articulations . . . [which] is the foundation of an individual's phonology, and remains so throughout his entire linguistic lifetime" (p. 437).

Direct study of the effects of developmental level of articulatory planning on motoric patterns, as assessed through instrumental study, is largely an innovation of the eighties. Findings from this exciting line of research have so far served to highlight the complexity of the issues involved and indicate the interest of continued investigation. It does seem clear, however, that fully mature segmental organization is not complete until well into the grammar school years.

Explicit research on the interrelationship of phonology and morphosyntax is even more recent a phenomenon. It has long been observed that many children acquiring English make use of schwa-vowel fillers as "presyntactic devices" and chain successive single-word utterances, separated by noticeable pauses, for some time before they produce word combinations recognizable as such. Only in the past few years have investigators explicitly drawn the conclusion that phonological organization is an important element in the transition to syntax. Extending her earlier interest in individual differences in the use of single words vs. jargon or formulaic phrases as an entry to language, Peters has proposed that prosody plays an important role in this process. Since prosodic patterning varies independently from the morphosyntax of different languages, a great deal of careful cross-linguistic investigation will be needed to tease apart the facilitating or complicating contributions of each of these domains for the developing child.

APPENDIX 9.1   PHONOLOGICAL PROCESSES IN USE AT AGE 3

I   *Processes affecting syllable or word structure*
Segments or syllables of the target word are rearranged, assimilated or omitted in the child's production. Segmental *position* is the relevant factor here, rather than segment *identity*.

syllable deletion (0.9): An unstressed syllable of the target word is omitted in the child's production.

Thomas	*dessert*	[zɻt]
	animals	[ˈæmz]
	ambulance	[ˈæmʌns]

final consonant deletion (1.0): The final consonant of the target word is omitted in the child's production.

| Andrew | *because* | [piˈkʌ] |
| | *thought* | [fɔ] |

consonant harmony (1.0): In the child's production a consonant takes on the place and/or manner of articulation of a noncontiguous consonant in the same word.

Jonah	*yellow*	[ˈlɛloʊ]
Molly	*slimy*	[ˈsaimi]
	mailboxes	[ˈmeilmaksɨz]

cluster reduction: A sequence of two consonants in the target word is replaced by a single consonant in the child's production.

consonant + r (0.8):

Timmy	*pretty*	[ˈpiɾi]
Andrew	*Grover*	[ˈgoʊvɻ]
Sean	*thread*	[sɛd]

s + consonant (0.8):

Jonah	*monster*	[ˈmãtɻ]
Susie	*smile*	[saɪl]
Sean	*stinker*	[ˈsɪŋkɻ̥]

consonant + 1 (1.2):

| Emily | *flower* | [ˈfawɻ̥] |
| Sean | *blocks* | [baks] |

II   *Segment substitution processes*
Specific target segments are replaced by other segments in the child's production.

velar fronting (0.3): Velars are replaced by alveolars, which have a more advanced place of articulation.

Jonah	*cow*	[taʊ]
	called	[tald]
	gophers	[ˈdoʊfɻ̥z]

stopping (1.4): Fricatives (or affricates) are replaced by stops at the corresponding place of articulation.

| Sean | *move* | [muːb] |
| Deborah | *shoes* | [ʃuːt] |

Jonah	*some*	[tʌm]
Timmy	*cheese*	[tiːz]
	juice	[duːsʹ]
	orange	[ʹɔrnd]

palatal fronting (1.6): Palatals are replaced by alveolars, which have a more advanced place of articulation.

Jonah	*show*	[soʊ]
	fish	[fɪs]
Molly	*shy*	[saɪ]

gliding and vocalization (1.6): Liquids /l/ and /r/ are replaced by glides or vowels.

Camille	*love*	[jʌv]
	red	[wɛd]
Andrew	*share*	[ʹsejəʊ]

interdental fricative substitutions (2.6): Interdentals are replaced by other consonants.

Sean	*thing*	[siŋ]
Susie	*think*	[siŋk] ~ [fɪŋk]
Molly	*other*	[ʌɾɹ̩]

Source: Based on Vihman and Greenlee, 1987, reprinted by permission of the American Speech-Language-Hearing Association

NOTES

1   With regard to the ontogenetic emergence of phonological structure, the child may be viewed, in a conscious laboratory metaphor, as "a partly random, partly stimulus-controlled sampler of the universal phonetic space in the presence of performance constraints" (Lindblom et al., 1984, p. 200). The authors go on to ask,

> to what extent are the phoneme and the feature *explicitly present* in the speech signals that the child experiences? There seems to be no quantitative empirical measurements that could help us answer that question right away and fully satisfactorily . . . [but] we nevertheless suggest that phonemic segments and features are *not* explicitly present in the input to the child. Although often slightly overarticulated and characterized by a maximization of cues, baby talk presents the acoustic phonetician with the same central issues as adult speech: those of segmentation and invariance (p. 200).

2   Menn's intensive account of the phonological development of her son Daniel (1971) already makes this distinction between early, presystematic phonology and the later stages: "While phonotactic rules have not yet crystallized in stage 1, something vaguely systematic, from which the rules will develop, is at work" (p. 232; cf. also Waterson, 1971).

3   (Context-sensitive) voicing will not be illustrated here, since it appears to be something of a misnomer: "The evidence from careful acoustic analyses . . . suggests that the observed contrast between early word-initial voicing of stops and word-final 'devoicing' derives from adult (mis)interpretation of a single child phonetic type – voiceless unaspirated stop – used in both positions" (Vihman, 1993b, p. 123; cf. Macken, 1980b).

4   Vihman (1993b) also provides an account of process use taken from a number of different studies of children developing normally.

5   These data involve the same "Stanford children" as are represented in Appendix C (see Vihman and Greenlee, 1987, in which phonological behaviors at age 1 and age 3 are compared).

6   See Branigan (1976): "The constraints may be the result of an interaction of physiological, perceptual-cognitive, and linguistic factors and are best characterized as the output of a set of conspiratorial rules . . . [or] rules functionally related to produce some specified output" (p. 118; cf. Kisseberth, 1970, and recent formulations of optimality theory).

7   Leopold's 1939 study of his daughter has been reanalyzed by several writers, including Moskowitz (1971) and Ferguson and Farwell (1975); N. V. Smith's 1973 account, similarly, was subjected to reanalysis in part by Macken (1980a).

8   Priestly notes stress on the later "ordinary replacement forms" but not on the idiosyncratic productions, commenting that one syllable (always the first) was only rarely "more obviously stressed than the other" (p. 47).

9   For a time Virve also exhibited a "vowel melody" ([low] . . . [high]), which required metathesis of the adult model to produce such critical lexical items as [amɨ] *ema* 'mother' and [asɨ] *isa* 'father' (cf. also [adi] *liha* 'meat': Vihman, 1976). She thus provides another example of coexisting harmony and melody templates.

10 Whereas in Vihman (1978) a phonemic writing system developed by E. Vihman (1974) was adopted, here Estonian orthography, which is close to a phonemic transcription, is used instead. There is no voicing contrast, but the two-way segmental length contrast available for virtually all vowels and consonants – to which a third degree of length, properly associated with the stressed syllable as a whole (Prince, 1980), is added under certain morphophonological conditions – is manifested in stops as a lax vs. tense opposition rendered with "voiced vs. voiceless" members of the stop system in the orthography. Thus, the medial stop of *tuba* 'room' and the final stop of *toad* 'rooms' are both voiceless and lax and the final stop of *porgandit* 'carrot, obj.' is voiceless and tense.

11 The only adult form with non-initial stress, *banaani* (stressed on the long vowel of the second syllable), is restructured by the child to match the template; the one four-syllable model, *mesilane*, is reduced to three syllables.

12 This is an example of what Peters and Menn (1993) have termed a 'phonological toehold' on morphosyntax.

13 Like Spanish, adult Estonian lacks [ŋ] except as a variant of /n/ before velars. Thus, Virve's [ŋ], like Si's, is an innovation.

14 Wijnen, Krikhaar, and Den Os (1994) provide examples of the conflation of unstressed syllables in long word production by two children acquiring Dutch.

15 However, Hodge (1989) has raised questions concerning the proper interpretation of instrumental findings comparing adult and child productions. She has proposed alternative methods for normalizing across spectra resulting from vocal tracts differing greatly in size, in order to more fairly estimate age-related differences in the *organization* of speech movements. See Nittrouer (1993) for additional discussion of these issues.

16 It is important to note that from one-third to one-half of the children tested in the various experiments reported in this study and in Gerken (1991) failed to imitate a sufficient number of strings to be included in the study; these children were younger, on average, than the group of children who met criterion. It is fair to conclude that there is a critical threshold of syntactic knowledge below which the awareness of functors demonstrated in these experiments cannot be said to obtain. Specifically, we do not so far have evidence of knowledge or representation of functional morphemes

within the single word production period (i.e., *before* the first word combinations).

17 Note Laurent's incorporation of the /l/ of French functors to construct the disyllabic template of his early words (Appendix C): *la brosse* [bəla], *la cuillère* [kola]. This presumably antedates even incipient representation of adult morphosyntax, however.

18 Matthei (1989), similarly, reports the carry-over to first word combinations of both a limit on length (disyllables only) and a strict consonant sequence constraint, requiring the second of two syllable-onset consonants to be at the same or a lower level of sonority in comparison with the first.

Appendix A
Protoword use of child- and adult-derived forms

1 FOCUS Expression of interest (often with an element of surprise).
Distribution of use: 4/10 subjects.
Timing: Appears before communicative intent is demonstrated (9–10 months).

Subject: *Deborah*
Form: [pwi] (often whispered); quiet body, alert gaze.
Conditions of use: Focused attention.
  – response to unfamiliar visitor;
  – response to salient sound pattern (e.g., *baa* 'sheep sound');
  – response to Mother's return to the room after a brief absence.
Duration: 9 weeks (0;9.17–0;11.11); later replaced by [haɪ], [aha], [ha::] or [haha], with show/give gestures (12–15 months).

Subject: *Jonah*
Form: [huʰ] (whistle-like)
Conditions of use:
  – upon hearing a dog bark;
  – upon hearing phone ring;
  – watching a wind-up penguin flap its wings;
  – while gazing at observer in first month of visits.
Duration: 3–4 months (from 9 to 11/12 months)
  Sometimes accompanied by point from 10 months on. By 12 months replaced by "interest-marking" (communicative) [t/d]-initial forms taken to be precursors of *this*, *that*, *there*.

Subject: *Emily*
Form: [oʊ] (based on adult *oh?*). Alternates with silent facial gesture: Wide-open mouth.
Conditions of use: Attention to new events.

Duration: 3–4 months (from 9 to 11/12 months)
  Peak use at 10 months: 15–20 instances in a session.
  Accompanied by point from 11 months on.

2 DEIXIS Sharing of interest.
  Subject: *Timmy*
  Form: [ʔʌgæ] Derived from *Great Gable* (drawing of a mountain, often labeled for child).
  Accompanied by pointing.
  Conditions of use: First used to point to pictures; generalized to "all purpose name" for objects not yet within the child's productive vocabulary (whale, seal, turtle, checker).
  Duration: 2 months (11–13 months)

3 AFFECT

  Subject: *Jonah*
  Form: <dada>; very high pitch on first syllable, mid level on second syllable. Derives from name of family dog, *Edgar*.
  Conditions of use: Generalized from "Edgar/doggy" to expression of excitement or delight
  – in response to hearing the dog's name;
  – when hearing a dog bark;
  – while standing at window overlooking dog's yard;
  – while watching mother build block towers;
  – crawling to green light on video transformer.

4 REQUEST

  Coordination with gesture: Gestures first used alone, especially reaching or pointing with eye-checks to adults; later accompanied by grunts.

  Subject: *Thomas*
  Form: single clap; alternates with pointing in case of repeated use, urgency.
  Duration: 2+ months (from 12 months)

  Subject: *Jonah*
  Form: rotating open fist (derived from pantomime accompanying French song about puppets dancing); combined with pointing in case of repeated use, urgency.
  Conditions of use: Request song; generalized to all requests.
  Duration: 4+ months (from 11 months)

  Subject: *Timmy*
  Form: nod + [hə] (derived from *unh-hunh* 'yes')
  Conditions of use: First use as response to questions, including "Do you want me to do it?"; generalized to serve as request for action.
  Duration: 2 weeks (from 14 months)

  Source: Based on Vihman et al. (1985) and Vihman and Miller (1988)

Appendix B
Early words: Adult targets and child forms

Key: Age (in months) at first word use and source of data follow child name. *consonant
       substitution. †word type lacking a supraglottal consonant or produced as a no-
       consonant word token.

1   DUTCH
Thomas (15 months: Elbers and Ton, 1985)

auto, o:to	[a(u)tə], [o:t(o)]
hap(jə) 'a bite'	[ba(ba)]
part(jə) 'horse'	[pa:tə]
pus(jə) 'cat'	[pəx], [pux]

2   ENGLISH
Leslie (11 months: Ferguson, Peizer, and Weeks, 1973)

bye–bye	[ba:ˌba]
daddy	[dædæ]
doggie	*[gaga]
mommy	[mama]
patty(–cake)	*[bæbæ]

Jonathan (15 months: Braine, 1974)

† hi	[ʔɑi]
juice	*[du]
no	*[do]
see	*[di]
that, there	*[dæ], [dʌ], [da], [dɛ]

T (11 months: Ferguson and Farwell, 1975)

daddy	*[dæji], [dæɪ]
dog	[dɔ]
† hi	[(h)aɪ]
† see	*[hɪ]

thankyou   [kʰju]

Jessie (15 months: Labov and Labov, 1978)
† apple   [æ æ], [æp] (+ lateral tongue gesture)
† cat   [ʔæ(ʔ)], [ʔæʔæ]
† dada   [æʔæ], [dædæ]
† hi   [hai]
mama   [mama], [æmæ], [mæmæ], [mami], [mɛm]
there   *[dɛ]

Daniel (12 months: Stoel–Gammon and Dunn, 1985)
banana   [næŋæ]
light   *[(d)ai]
† uh–oh   [ʔʌʔoʔ]
what's that   [wəsæ]

Sarah (11 months: Stoel–Gammon and Dunn, 1985)
baby   [bebi]
bye–bye   [baɪbaɪ]
doggie   [dɔgi]
juice   *[dus]
mama   [mama]

Will (12 months: Stoel–Gammon and Dunn, 1985)
all–done   [(d)ada]
down   [dæ], [dʌ], [dau]
light   *[di]
shoes   *[tsis], [θiz]
† uh–oh   [ʌʔo], [hʌho]

Timmy (10 months: Vihman, 1992)
ball   [pʰə], [bæ], [bwæ], [bæp]
block   [pʻæː], [vːæ], [pʻæ]
car   [kaə], [akːaʰ]
kitty   [kʰə], [kʰa], [kaka], [ʔuka], etc.
quack–quack   [kʰə], [ka], [kaka], [gaga], [gakaəʰ], etc.

Deborah (10 months: unpublished data, Stanford Child Phonology Project)
baa   [bæː]
baby   [pipe], [be(be)]
† hi(ya)   [(h)ai(e)], [eː], [aː]
monkey   *[mamːɛ]
†uh–oh   [ʔʌʔɛ]

Jonah (12 months: unpublished data, Stanford Child Phonology Project)
all done   [ʔaʊdɛ]
bow (wow)   [ba], [bʊa]
bye–bye   [babaɪ]
Edgar   *[dada]
no   [nʌʊ]
rock–rock   *[baba]

Molly (10 months: unpublished data, Stanford Child Phonology Project)

baby	[pep]
cracker	*[pakæ], [kwa]
moo	[mu:–ǀ]
night–night	[ʌnʌ]
oops	[ʔʌp]

Sean (13 months: unpublished data, Stanford Child Phonology Project)

bird	[briʰ]
dog	[ɗɔ]
down	[dæ]
† flower	*[pæ], [wæ]

3   ESTONIAN

Virve (10 months: Vihman, 1976)

aitäh 'thanks'	[aita]
† hi	[haⁱ]
isa 'daddy'	[sa]
see 'this'	[se]
tere 'hello'	*[tete]

Raivo (13 months: unpublished data)

aitäh 'thanks'	[ta]
† ei 'no'	[ei:]
päh 'yuck'	[pæ]
pomm 'boom'	[bm]
viska 'throw'	[s], [is], [il], [l̩]

4   FRENCH

Laurent (10 months: Vihman, 1993c)

allo	[(h)ailo], [(h)aljo], [alo]
donne (le) 'give (it)'	[d(l)ə], [ldɛ], [heldɔ]
lolo 'bottle'	[ljoljo]
non	[ne]
tiens 'here'	[ta]

Carole (11 months: unpublished data, Stanford Child Phonology Project and Laboratoire de Psychologie, CNRS, Paris)

balle 'ball'	[ba(ba)]
bébé 'baby'	[bebe]
nounours 'teddy'	[ne(ne)]
Mickey	[kə]
papa	[papa]

Charles (11 months: unpublished data, Stanford Child Phonology Project and Laboratoire de Psychologie, CNRS, Paris)

† au revoir 'bye-bye'	[awa], [haɥa]
boum 'boom'	[ba], [bœm]
beau 'beautiful, nice'	[bo]
donne/tiens 'give/here'	[dæ]
mama	[mama]

| non | [nɛ] |
| † ouah-ouah 'bowwow' | [wɔʊ] |

5 GERMAN

Hans (14 months: Lindner, 1898, Ferguson, 1978)

Birne 'pear'	*[bap]
das 'that'	[da(da)], [dat]
Gasse 'street'	*[gak]
Mama	[mama]
Papa	[papa]
† Wewe 'weewee'	[we:we:]

Hildegard (10 months: Leopold, 1939; Ferguson and Farwell, 1975)

ball; open	[pa]
Blumen 'flower'	[pu]
Papa	[papa]
pretty	[prəti]
there	*[dɛi]
(tick)tock	[tak]

6 JAPANESE

Emi (14 months: unpublished data, Stanford Child Phonology Project)

atta 'here it is!'/ haitta 'put it in/on'	[(ha)ta]
ba 'peek-a-boo'	[pa]
bu: 'vroom'	[bu::]
† hai 'here!'	[ha?]
mama	[mam:a:]
nenne 'sleep'	[nen:e]
† wanwan 'doggie'	[wawa]

Haruo (15 months: unpublished data, Stanford Child Phonology Project)

bubu 'car'	[bubu]
† iya 'no'	[ɪjæ?]
kore 'this'	[gɔɛ]
oisho 'oof!'	[(oɪ)ʃɔ?]

Kazuko (14 months: unpublished data, Stanford Child Phonology Project)

ba 'peek-a-boo'	[bɑ?]
bubu 'car'	[βa?pa]
ju:su 'juice'	[ʒuʃu]
† yaru 'do it!'	[ja(ɣ)u]

Kenji (12 months: unpublished data, Stanford Child Phonology Project)

dore 'which (?)'	[dɔ:li]
kore 'this'	[koje], [kole], [koɾe]
nainai 'no-no, all gone'	[nja:naja], [na(i)na(i)]
nyannyan 'kitty, meow'	[njə?njə?]

7 SWEDISH

Stig (16 months: Vihman and Roug-Hellichius, 1991)

| blomma 'flower' | *[pɔ:bo] |
| buss 'bus' | [bo] |

där 'there'	[dæ]
klocka 'clock, watch'	[gɔːka]
tacktack 'thanks'	*[gaːgaː]
titta 'look'	[titæ]

Hanna (11 months: unpublished data, Stanford Child Phonology Project and Institute of Linguistics, Stockholm University)

bok 'book'	[bβuʔ]
där 'there'	[dæʔ]
tacktack 'thank you'	[dada]
titta 'look'	[ditːa]
tittut 'peek-a-boo'	[dædːæ]

Lina (10 months: unpublished data, Stanford Child Phonology Project and Institute of Linguistics, Stockholm University)

blomma 'flower'	[bɔmbə]
boll 'ball'	[ba]
brum 'vroom'	[bɛ]
bulle 'bun'	[bʊl]
† oj 'oh!'	[ʔɔj]
titta 'look'	[titːa]

Appendix C
Beginnings of phonological organization

The data given below are drawn from five half-hour sessions for each of the children. Data were collected on a weekly (Stanford English data), bi-weekly (French data) or monthly basis (Rutgers English). In order to bring out the developmental changes in the children's phonology these sessions are selected from the approximate beginning of lexical use (4-word point: two sessions within the month in which spontaneous child attempts at producing at least four different adult word types could first be identified), a later point in which some rudimentary organization can be discerned (15-word point: two sessions), and a single session from the period when lexical advance has begun to be more rapid and the lines of the child's incipient phonological system have become clearer (25-word point). This latter point, which reflects the end of data collection for the Stanford and French data, typically corresponds to a parental cumulative vocabulary record of at least fifty words. In all cases the data presented are exhaustive for the sessions in question as far as adult-based word types are concerned, both spontaneous and imitated, with the exception of some onomatopoeic forms with unstable adult models. The child tokens given are intended to be representative of the degree and type of within-word variability.

Each of the phonological profiles presented below is based on data collected or transcribed and analyzed within the framework of the Stanford Child Phonology Project between 1980 and 1988. Sixteen-month session data from each of the children learning English are presented in Vihman and McCune (1994). Additional references to published accounts involving these data are given below; this presentation includes some heretofore unpublished data for each of the children.

The child's age is given in months; imitated words or tokens are noted (im.); adult words restructured to fit the child's production template, including instances of consonant and vowel harmony as well as of wholesale phonotactic reorganization, are marked with an asterisk. Voiced and voiceless stops are not necessarily in correspondence with the adult model; transcription may not be reliable on this point, nor are the children thought to control voicing in a consistent way at this developmental stage (Macken, 1980b).

Alice – acquiring English (Rutgers) (See Vihman, 1992; Vihman et al., 1994; Vihman and McCune, 1994)

I   4–word point (two sessions: 9–10 months)

baby	[pɛpɛ:], [əpʰæ:pʹæ], [tɛɪti:], [teʹtɛ]
daddy	[əda:da], [dæ:]
* *hello*; *hiya*	[hije], [(hə)hæ] (im, *hello*); [ʔa:jɛ], [haɪje], [ha:i], [ʔa:dje]
* *mommy*	[m̩:an:ə]
* *no*	[njæ]
* *pretty* (im.)	[pi], [peə]
psh! (im.)	[pʰə̥ʰə]

II   15–word point (a) (14 months)

monosyllabic targets		disyllabic targets	

Palatal pattern

bye	[baɪ]	*baby*	[be(ɪ)bi]
eye	[ʔaɪ]	* *blanket*	[bæŋ:i], [bəpʊi]
			[bæ:pʹoʊ]
hi	[ʔa:i]		
clean	[kʕin:]	*Bonnie*	[baɲi], [baŋi], [ba]
whee	[wi:]	* *bottle*	[baɟi], [batʃi],
			[batji]
		bunny	[bæŋ:i]
		* *daddy*	[tæɟi], [ta:(i)di], [jæiji]
		* *dolly*	[da:ɪki], [ta:ji|ti], [da:ə]
		Ernie	[ʔə:ɲi] (im.), [æɲi],
			[ʔʌɲi]
		* *hiya*	[ha:ji]
		* *lady*	[jɛiji], [jeidji]
		* *mommy*	[ma:ɲi]

Other

bear	[bɛ::]	*hammer* (im.)	[həv:a]
man	[m̩mæ̃:]	*Oscar*	[ʔa]
		thank you	[hæ:ŋkm̩]

15–word point (b) (15 months)

monosyllabic targets		polysyllabic targets	

Palatal pattern

bye	[pai]	(*a*) *baby*	[beɪbi], [(hə)bebi]
* *bang*	[bæŋ:i],	** *blanket*	[baji], [hn̩ba]
	[pʕæi]		
clean	[kʕi:n]	* *bottle*	[pa:(j)i], [pʕa]
oink	[ʔai]	* *bunny*	[bæɲi], [bʌ̃ji],
			[pʌ̃ʔi]
(*o*)*kay*	[kʰei]	* *daddy*	[taji], [tadi]
tea	[ti]	* (*a*) *dolly*	[(ʔʌ:)daji]
* *toys*	[tʰahiz]	* *elephant*	[ʔæɪnu], [ʔaijʌ̃]

		* *Ernie*	[ʔa(i)n̩i]
		* *mommy*	[mãji]
		* *(night) night* (im.)	[naːji], [naiʔnai]
		Other	
hat	[ʔæʔ], [hæː] (im.)	*glasses* (im.)	[kæ]
		hammer (im.)	[ʔæmʌ]
		peek-a-boo (im.)	[pʼæːbə]

III   25-word point (16 months)

Palatal pattern

C(V)i		CVCi	
* *bang*	[pãi]	(a) *baby*	[(ə)beɪbi]
belly	[vei]	* (a) *bottle*	[(ə)badi], [badiç̩]
bye	[baɪ]	* *bunny*	[beiŋji], [bʌn̩ːi]
* *egg*	[ʔeɪ], [heːi]	* *clean*	[tiːni], [tʰind]
eye	[ʔaɪ]	*daddy*	[daːdi]
* *key*	[çi]	* *elephant*	[ʔaiː(n)jʌ], [ʔeĩjĩ]
meat	[miʔ]	* *iron*	[ʔaiŋː], [ʔaĩji]
plate	[pʼɛi]	* *flowers*	[pʼaːji]
* *shoe*	[çi]	* *lady*	[jɛːji], [ijei]
tea	[tiː]	* *mommy*	[(ə)maːn̩i]
		* *shiny*	[taːji]

Other (all monosyllabic)

Cæ		Other	
apple	[ʔæ]	*blanket*	[kʼɛt]
* *duck*	[tæʔ]	*down*	[daʊ]
man	[mæː]	*hat*	[ʔa]
* *milk*	[m̥æ]	*hello* (im.)	[loʊ]
* *no*	[næ̃]	*Oscar*	[ʔaʔ]
* *nose*	[nːæ]	*(grand)pa*	[pʼa]
		up	[ʔaːp]
		yum	[ʔm̩ː]

Charles – acquiring French (See Vihman and Boysson-Bardies, 1994)

I   4-word point

11 months		12 months	
au revoir 'goodbye'	[(h)awa]	*au revoir* 'goodbye'	[awa]
bébé (im.) 'baby'	[beːbe]	*(c'est) beau* '(that's) nice, beautiful'	[bœ]
boum 'boom'	[bə], [ba]		
non (im.) 'no'	[nẽ]	*boum* 'boom'	[bœm]

ça / donne / tiens   [da]
   'that/here'
maman 'mama'   [mama]
ouah-ouah
   'woof-woof'   [wɔu]

II   15-word point (14 months: two sessions)

[p/b]

bah 'yuck'	[pa::]
beau 'beautiful'	[bo]
bébé / poupée	[papa], [bɛpa]
'baby/doll'	
bravo	[(b)abo], [baɢo],
	[bavo]
boire 'drink'	[ba]
boum 'boom'	[bɔm]
chapeau 'hat'	[pɔ:], [ʃapɨ]
(im.)	
* lapin 'rabbit'	[pœpa]
papa	[pəpa]

[w]

au revoir	[awa]
'goodbye'	
* miaou	[mɔwɔ]
'meow'	
(im.)	

[t/d]

ça 'that'	[ta]
*gateau 'cake'	[toto]
tiens 'here'	[tɛ], [ta]

[s/ʃ]

assis 'seated'	[ætçɛ](im.); [a:ʃ], [a:s]
chaud 'hot'	[oso]
(im.)	
chaussures/	[ketʃu],
chaussettes	[tʃetʃu],
'shoes/socks'	
	[ʒoʒo]
* ours 'bear'	[ɔs], [ɔf],
	[ʒo], [tço]

Other

allo 'hello'	[alo]
canard 'duck'	[ka:na]
maman 'mama'	[mama]
myam 'eat/yum'	[(h)ɛm]
non 'no'	[nɛno], [nɔno]

III   25-word point (15 months)

<aβa>,		<aβo>	<(a)vwa>		<wawa>
c'est beau 'it's		[(h)abo]	*au revoir*		[(a)vwa]
beautiful'			'goodbye'		
c'est bon 'it's good'		[habõ]	*boire* 'drink'		[vwa]

chapeau 'hat'	[(h)apo]	*ouah–ouah*	[wawɛ]
		'woof-woof'	
lapin 'rabbit'	[apa]	*(tu veux) voir*	[(a)vwa]
		'(want to)	
		see?'	
* *oiseau* 'bird'	[abɔ]		
(im.)			
papa	[papa]		
poupée 'doll'	[(b)apa]		
va pas	[hapa] (im.),		
'doesn't fit'	[apa]		

<(a)ta>, <ato>, <toto>   <(a)ʃo>, <(a)ʃa>, <ʒaʒo>

attend 'wait'	[atæ]	*assis* 'seated'	[æs:a]
auto 'car' (im.)	[a:to], [hɔto]	*ça* 'this'	[ʃa], [tʃa]
		chaud 'hot'	[ʃo]
coucou 'peek-a-boo'	[toto]	* *chaussures*	[ɛdʒo], [ʒaʒo]
		'shoes'	
tiens 'here'	[ta]		
		garçon (im.)	[haʒœ]
		'boy'	
		* *les yeux* (im.)	[aʒo]
		'eyes'	
		ranger (im.)	[hæʒæ]
		'put away'	

<alo>, <lolo>   Other

allo 'hello' (im.)	[al:o]	*boum* 'boom'	[bœm]
* *l'eau* 'water'	[ljoljo],	*ham/myam*	[(h)am]
		'eat/yum'	
	[biʌ]	*maman*	[mama]
		non(non)	[(n)ɔnɔ̃], [hənɔ̃], [nə]
		'no, no'	

Deborah – acquiring English (Stanford)

I   4-word point (11 months: two sessions)

ah (im.)	[ha]
baby	[be(be)], [bebi], [p'e], [ʔebe:]
hi(ya)	[hai], [ʔai], [ʔaɪa],
hu-hu-hu (music)	[ʔuhu], [ʔuʔu]
monkey	[mam:æ], [mam:e], [mam:ɪ]
uh-oh	[ʔʌʔʔɛ]
yay (im.)	[əha::ə]

II   15-word point (13 months: two sessions)

	[p/b]		[t/d]
baby	[pe:bi]	*daddy*	[tata], [tætæ]
ball	[bβʊ]	*duck*	[ta]

bird	[həpə], [pɣ::-lə]	** patty-cake*	[taʌti]
book	[(m)bʊ], [pʊə], [bθ]	*turtle* (im.)	[tʰɣtəweweæi]
* bunny (im.)	[ᵐpa:mi]		
byebye	[paba], [baba], [papa]		
patty-cake (im.)	[pʻæikʻepwaɛ]		
peek (im.)	[pi:], [p̃ijɛ̃]		

[k/g]

[s/ç/tˢ]

* corn (im.)	[kʷowi]	** scratchy* (im.)	[tˢitˢi]
* rowrow	[gwolwaᵒ]	** Sesame Street*	[si:si]
		*shoe	[hiç] (im.), [çi], [tçiç] (im.), [hi], [ʃjʊ]
		three (im.)	[si], [ʂi]

[ʔ/h]

Other

ah	[ʔa]	*kitty sound*	[ɸ̌:-l] (voiceless labial trill)
hi	[ʔaɪ], [haɪ]		
uh-oh	[ʔʌʔ:ʔo], [ʔəʔə]	*mama*	[maʊwa], [bowe], [ʰmaʊwi], [mawigwʊi]
woof-woof	[ʔʊʔʊ]		
yay	[ʔe:-l], [he::-l]	*no*	[nɔ:]

III   25-word point (15 months)

[p/b]

[t/d]

baby	[pʻe:bi]	*down*	[ta:], [tæ]
ball	[bɔ]	*duck*	[tæ:]
bird	[bwa]		
bottle	[pʻa]		
bye	[pʻaɪ]		
moo	[bo:-l], [bɔ:wa]		

[k/g]

[s/tˢ]

carrot (im.)	[kʰeiwi]	*cheese*	[si:]
corn	[kʰɔ:]	*three*	[si::]
cow (im.)	[kʰɛ:]	*two*	[tˢi], [tʰi]
kitty	[kʰiwe] (im.), [tʔetʔ:i], [kʔekʔi]		

[ʔ/h]

Other

A	[ʔe:]	*monkey*	[hm̥mæ:]
ear	[ʔi:]	*water*	[wa(wa)], [bobæ]
eyes/hair	[ʔa], [ʔe]		

hi	[ʔai],	*(rock crash)*	[kx̱ː]
	[(ə)hai]	(im.)	
up	[ʔaː]		
yum	[ʔm̩ː]		

Laurent – acquiring French (See Vihman, 1993)

I   4-word point (10 months: two sessions)

allo	[hailo], [(h)aljɔ], [alœ]
lolo 'bottle'	[ljoljo]
donne (le) 'give (it)'	[d(l)ə], [həldɔ], [tlɛ]
tiens 'here'	[ta]
non 'no'	[ne]

II   15-word point (14 months: two sessions)

C1 = C2　　　　　　　　　　　　C2 = 1

bébé/poupée 'baby'	[baba], [əba]	*allo*	[ələ]
bouton 'button'	[tʉtʉtlɷ]	* *(voi)là* 'here'	[(la)la]
cocotte 'hen'	[gogo]	* *balle* 'ball'	[baːla], [bəjoe]
coucou 'peek-a-boo'	[kukku],	*pas là* 'not there'	[pala]
	[gɣgɣ]		
		parti 'gone'	[pɝ·dli]
Didier (im.)	[tyty]		
Koki (penguin)	[kok(k)o]		
maman 'mama'	[mamɛ]		
* *miam* 'yum'	[mʌmɛ], [ham]		
ouah-ouah　'bowwow'	[wawa]		
papa (im.)	[paˑ;pa]		
petits trous 'little　holes'	[tʰitʰɔ]		

Other

banane 'banana'	[mena]
donne (le)　'exchange'	[da], [dɔ], [dɛ]
non 'no'	[nɛ]
vroom	[bɷːː],　[bɷbɷbɷ . . .]

III   25-word point (15 months)

　(A) *Disyllables*

C1 = C2　　　　　　　　　　　　C2 = 1
(reduplicated)

bébé 'baby'	[bəbə]	*allo*	[alo]
caca 'poopoo'	[kaka]	*ballon* 'big ball'	[palõ]
* *chapeau* 'hat'	[bobo]	* *canard* 'duck'	[kɔla]
coucou 'peek-a-　boo'	[kuku]	* *chapeau* 'hat'	[bolo]

dodo 'sleep'	[dodo]	* *coin-coin* 'quack-quack'	[kwalakwala]
maman 'mama'	[mama]	*dans l'eau* 'in the water'	[dalo]
papa	[papa]	*de l'eau* 'some water'	[dəlo]
		* *Koki* (penguin)	[kola]
		* *(la) brosse* '(the) brush'	[bəla]
		* *(la) cuillère* '(the) spoon'	[kola]
		voilà	[wala], [ba:la]

(with vowel change)

chaussette/chaussure 'sock/shoe'	[ʃoʃy]
coucou 'peek-a-boo'	[kuko:]
Didier	[dədjɨ]
gateau 'cake'	[tato]
kekette 'penis'	[kake]
Nano (blanket)	[nano]

(B) *Monosyllables*

aie 'ouch'	[ʔa:i:]
mjam 'yum/eat/ food'	[mam]
moi 'me'	[(a)ma]
non 'no'	[nã], [noc]
tiens 'here (exchange)'	[ta]

(C) *Longer forms*

* *chaussette/chaussure* 'sock/shoe'	[ʒəʃa:tiʒə], [bɛ̃ʒɨʒəʒəje]
la dame là 'that lady'	[lələdala]

Molly – acquiring English (Stanford) (See Vihman and Velleman, 1989)

I 4-word point (10 months: two sessions)

baby (im.)	[baba], [pʿab(a)]
cracker	[paka], [tækʿʌ] (im.), [wæʰk], [kækʿ] (im.), [pækwa], [kʌk], [kwa]
* *moo* (im.)	[u:mə]
vroom	[β̆], [ʔm̥β̆m̥β̆:]
woof	[ʔu]
yum	[əmənəm]

II   15-word point (13 months: two sessions)

Final consonant targets   Other

* *button* (im.)	[pan:ə]	*baby*	[pʲapʲa]
bang	[bæ̃:n],	*chair* (im.)	[ʧəʔ]
	[pæ:],		
	[bæŋ]		
		daddy	[haʰdɔti]
boat (im.)	[be]	*hi* (im.)	[hæ], [haɪ]
box (im.)	[ba]	*ho-ho-ho*	[hoho]
burp	[ap], [pʲapʲ]	*moo*	[mʊ]
	(im.)		
cat	[kʰæ]	*nigh'-nigh'*	[ninʌ] (im.), [næ̃]
* *clock* (im.)	[kak:ʰj̥]	*no-no*	[nʌnʌ]
dog	[ta]	*one, two, three*	[hʌtʲuti]
* *down* (im.)	[tæ:n],	*pretty*	[pʲi]
	[dæ:n(ə)],		
	[tæʔ] ,		
	[da:unə]	*rockie*	[(h)ati], [haʧi]
* *good girl*	[gʊgʊk], [gugʌ]	*vroom* (im.)	[βəmβəm]
hat (im.)	[hæʔ]		
horse	[hæ:t]		
hot	[hat']		
peek	[pʰj] (im.), [pe ǀ kˣe]		
* *round*	[han:ə]		
* *squeak*	[kʰʊkʰʌ], [kʌk] (im.)		
* *teeth*	[tit:ʰi], [tiʧ]		
* *tick* (im.)	[tj̥tə]		
up	[æ:pʲ]		

II   25-word point (14 months)

Final consonant targets

stops   nasals

book (im.)	[pʲʊkʲ]	* *Brian*	[pan:ɵ], [pa:ni]
bus (im.)	[pat']	* *down*	[tʲa:nə]
* *cheese*	[a(i)ʧ], [iʧ]	* *hand* (im.)	[han:ɛ]
* *coat*	[kʊk], [ko]	*Ernie*	[hʌn:ə]
* *foot*	[tʲatʲ]		
nose	[nu:]		
* *stuck*	[tʲʌtʲ], [tæ:kʲ]		
up	[ʔʌpʲ]		

Other

apple	[ʔapu], [(h)æpə], [ʔapʲə]
baby	[pi:b], [pipi], [pʲɛbi] (im.)
ball	[pa:], [pʰoʊ]
byebye	[pʲapʲa]
daddy (im.)	[tæti]
diaper	[tʲæpʲœ], [tɛpɔ]

eye	[ʔai]
girl	[gəʊ]
* *gran'ma*	[næm:ʌ], [hɛn:ə]
hair	[heæ:]
Hooper	[ʌput], [hʌpə]
store (im.)	[tˤə], [tˤʌʊ]
uh-oh	[ʔʌo]
vroom	[βmβmæ]
woof	[ʊwʊ]

Timmy – acquiring English (Stanford): (See Vihman, 1992; Vihman et al., 1994)

I   4-word point (11 months: two sessions)

ball, block, box	[pʰə], [b⁽ʷ⁾æ], [bæp], [pˤæ:], [ʔʌβ:æ], [əpʰæ]
basket (im.)	[pˤæ:]
boat (im.)	[pˤæ], [ʔəpˤæ]
book (im.)	[pæ], [ʔmbβa]
car	[ka:ə], [ak:a], [hək:ʰa], [kˤʌ]
* *duck* (im.)	[ga:]
hi	[ʔa]
key (im.)	[hək:ʰa], [hakˤa]
kitty, quack	[kʰə], [kʰa], [kaka], [ʔuka], [haəka:ᵏ], [kakaka], [kʰə], [ka], [kaka], [gaga], [gakaə], [kʰəkʰə], [kakaga]
mama	[m̥mama]

II   15-word point (a) (15 months)

	\<ba\>
baa	[pa], [pˤæpˤæ], [bapa]
ball, bird	[bæ:], [bʌ], [pa], [ʔəbʌʔ], [həβæ]
bunny (im.)	[bæ:]
(good)bye	[pˤa], [pʰæ] (im.), [ʔɪkˤəpˤæ]
	\<ga\>, \<kaka\>
cow (im.)	[gɛ:]
cup	[ka], [kʌ], [əʔgʌ]
* *dog* (im.)	[gæ:]
* *duck* (im.)	[k'ʌ]
girl	[kʌ:], [ga:]
* *kitty*	[kʊka]
	\<βa\>
flower	[ʔəᵇβæ], [ʔebæ], [hɛβæ]
* *Ruth*	[æᵇβæ]
	\<ja\>
ear (im.)	[ʔʌijʌ]
* *eye*	[æijæ:]
	Other
moo, moon	[ʔəm:a], [m̩::mæ], [m::œ::-ǀ]
Nana (im.)	[ʌn::ʌ]
nose	[ɛn:æ]

15–word–point, (b) (1;4.0)

<ba>

baby, bracelet	[pæ], [(ə)pˤæpˤæ], [əbaba], [ʔepˤɵpˤæ]
block, peg	[pæ], [bæ], [əbæ], [pˤæpæ]
boat (im.)	[pæ]
boy (im.), *balloon*	[bʌi], [ʌbəi], [bə:→], [bæji]
please (im.)	[pai:]

<ga(ga)>, <gaba>

car	[kʰəi]
cookie (im.)	[kˤakʰi]
goodbye (im.)	[kʰæʔbæ]

<βa>

fire, * *Ruth*	[æβwæi], [hʌβæ]
flower (im.)	[ʔʌɸæ]

<ja>

hiya	[ai:jæ]

<ma>

mummy	[mʌmæ]
* *Simon*	[nʌmæ], [næɪmæ]

<na>

Nana	[nɛn:æ]

<dada>, <di>

daddy	[tʰaədæ], [tˤatˤæ]
D	[di:-ǀ]

Other

eye	[ʔai]
* *fish*	[əs:æ]

III   25–word point (1:4.22)

<ba>, <bi>, <babi>, <baby>

ball, balloon, boat, *peg, plum*	[pæ::], [bɛ], [ʔæbæ], [əv:æ::]
bee (im.)	[bi]
bottle/"bobby"	[babi], [əbab:i]
bubble	[bab:y], [bæv:y], [bæby(:)],

<ga>, <gi>, <gabi>, <gagi>, <gugi>, <gibi>

bicycle (im.)	[əgɛg:u]
car (im.)	[ka], [ga]
coffee (im.)	[gagŋ̩,ga:gi]
computer (im.)	[kˤugi]
good boy (im.)	[gɨb:i:]
key	[gɪ]

light	[ɪkæ], [iga], [jæːgæ]
quack-quack	[ʔakʿaːkʰa]

<(d)adi>

daddy (im.)	[dadːiː]
Heidi (im.)	[ʔadːiː]

<du>

Drew	[du]
juice	[du], [ədːu]
* *toe* (im.)	[du]
toot-toot	[du], [dudu], [(ə)dudːu]

<a>,<ja>   <va>

hi	[ʔaiː]	*flower*	[əvːæ]

hot (im.)	[ʔaʔ]
lizard ('caterpillar')	[(iː)jaijai]

<ma>, <mi>, <mu>

money ('coin')	[mamːi]
moo	[mʊːː]
moon/sun	[mʉːː], [mɛːuːm]

<na>, <ni>, <nimi>

knee ('knee', 'fingers/toes')	[ni], [əniː]
Nana (im.)	[nanːː]
* *neck*	[ɪnæ]
* *Simon*	[ʔənɪmːiː]
* *sun*	[(ɪ)næ]

References

Abrahamsen, A. A., Cavallo, M. M., and McCluer, J. A. (1985). Is the sign advantage a robust phenomenon? From gesture to language in two modalities. *Merrill-Palmer Quarterly*, 31, 177–209.

Abramson, A. S. (1977). Laryngeal timing in consonant distinctions. *Phonetica*, 34, 295–303.

Abramson, A. S. and Lisker, L. (1970). Discriminability along the voice continuum: Cross-language tests. *Proceedings of the Sixth International Congress of Phonetic Sciences*, 1967. Prague: Academia.

Abramson, A. S. and Lisker, L. (1973). Voice-timing perception in Spanish word-initial stops. *Journal of Phonetics*, 1, 1–8.

Acredolo, L. and Goodwyn, S. W. (1985). Symbolic gesturing in language development: A case study. *Human Development*, 28, 40–9.

Acredolo, L. and Goodwyn, S. W. (1988). Symbolic gesturing in normal infants. *Child Development*, 59, 450–466.

Acredolo, L. and Goodwyn, S. W. (1991). Sign language in babies: The significance of symbolic gesturing for understanding language development. In R. Vasta (ed.), *Annals of Child Development*, 7. Greenwich, CN: JAI Press.

Aitchison, J. (1972). Mini-malapropisms. *British Journal of Communication Disorders*, 7, 38–43.

Aitchison, J. and Chiat, S. (1981). Natural phonology or natural memory? The interaction between phonological processes and recall mechanisms. *Language and Speech*, 24, 311–26.

Aitchison, J. and Straf, M. (1981). Lexical storage and retrieval: A developing skill? In A. Cutler (ed.), *Slips of the Tongue and Language Production*. Amsterdam: Mouton. Also printed in *Linguistics*, 19, 751–95.

Allen, G. D. (1983). Some suprasegmental contours in French two-year-old children's speech. *Phonetica*, 40, 269–92.

Allen, G. D. (1985). How the young French child avoids the pre-voicing problem for word-initial voiced stops. *Journal of Child Language*, 12, 37–46.

Allen, G. D. and Hawkins, S. (1978). The development of phonological rhythm. In A. Bell and J. B. Hooper (eds), *Syllables and Segments*. Amsterdam: North-Holland Publishing Company.

Allen, G. D. and Hawkins, S. (1980). Phonological rhythm: definition and development. In G. H. Yeni-Komshian, J. F. Kavanagh, and C. A. Ferguson (eds), *Child Phonology, 1: Production*. New York: Academic Press.

Anderson, S. R. (1985). *Phonology in the Twentieth Century: Theories of rules and theories of representations*. Chicago: University of Chicago Press.

Anglin, J. M. (1993). *Vocabulary Development: A morphological analysis*. Monographs of the Society for Research in Child Development, 58, 10.

Ariste, P. (1953). *Eesti keele foneetika [Estonian Phonetics]*. Tallinn: Eesti Riiklik Kírjastus.

Aslin, R. N. and Pisoni, D. B. (1980a). Effects of early linguistic experience on speech discrimination by infants: A critique of Eilers, Gavin, and Wilson (1979). *Child Development*, 51, 107–12.

Aslin, R. N. and Pisoni, D. B. (1980b). Some developmental processes in speech perception. In G. H. Yeni-komshian, J. H. Kavanagh, and C. A. Ferguson (eds), *Child Phonology, 2: Perception*. New York: Academic Press.

Aslin, R. N., Pisoni, D. B., Hennessy, B. L., and Perey, A. J. (1981). Discrimination of voice onset time by human infants: New findings and implications for the effects of early experience. *Child Development*, 52, 1135–45.

Aslin, R. N., Pisoni, D. B., and Jusczyk, P. W. (1983). Auditory development and speech perception in infancy. In P. H. Mussen (ed.), *Handbook of Child Psychology* (4th edn), 2: M. M. Haith and J. J. Campos (eds), *Infancy and Developmental Psychobiology*. New York: Wiley.

Aslin, R. N. and Smith, L. B. (1988). Perceptual development. In M. R. Rozenzweig and L. W. Porter (eds), *Annual Review of Psychology*, 39, 435–73.

Atkinson, M. (1980). Review of A. Lock (ed.), *Action, Gesture and Symbol. Journal of Child Language*, 7, 579–90.

Austin, J. (1962). *How to Do Things with Words*. Oxford: Oxford University Press.

Bahrick, L. E. and Pickens, J. N. (1988). Classification of bimodal English and Spanish language passages by infants. *Infant Behavior and Development*, 11, 277–96.

Balota, D. A. and Chumbley, J. I. (1985). The locus of word frequency effects in the pronunciation task: Lexical access and/or production? *Journal of Memory and Language*, 24, 89–106.

Bar-Adon, A. and Leopold, W. F. (eds) (1971). *Child Language: A book of readings*. Englewood Cliffs, NJ: Prentice Hall.

Bartlett, E. (1978). The acquisition of the meaning of color terms: A study of lexical development. In R. Campbell and P. Smith (eds), *Recent Advances in the Psychology of Language, IV*. New York: Plenum Press.

Barton, D. (1975). Statistical significance in phonemic perception experiments. *Journal of Child Language*, 2, 297f.

Barton, D. (1976). The role of perception in the acquisition of phonology. Unpublished doctoral dissertation, University of London. (Reprinted by the Indiana University Linguistics Club, 1978.)

Barton, D. (1980). Phonemic perception in children. In G. Yeni-komshian, J. Kavanagh, and C. A. Ferguson (eds), *Child Phonology, 2: Perception*. New York: Academic Press.

Barton, D. (1992). The emergence of sounds: Parallels between learning to read and learning to speak. In C. A. Ferguson, L. Menn, and C. Stoel-Gammon (eds), *Phonological Development: Models, Research, Implications*. Timonium, MD: York Press.

Baru, A. V. (1975). Discrimination of synthesized vowels [a] and [i] with varying parameters in dog. In G. Fant and M. A. A. Tatham (eds), *Auditory Analysis and the Perception of Speech*. London: Academic Press.

Bates, E. (1979). Intentions, conventions and symbols. In E. Bates, L. Benigni, I. Bretherton, L. Camaioni, and V. Volterra (eds), *The Emergence of Symbols: Cognition and Communication in Infancy*. New York: Academic Press.

Bates, E., Benigni, L., Bretherton, I., Camaioni, L., and Volterra, V. (eds) (1979). *The Emergence of Symbols: Cognition and communication in infancy*. New York: Academic Press.

Bates, E., Bretherton, I., Shore, C., and McNew, S. (1983). Names, gestures and objects: Symbolization in infancy and aphasia. In K. E. Nelson (ed.), *Children's Language*, 4. Hillsdale, NJ: Lawrence Erlbaum.

Bates, E., Bretherton, I., and Snyder, L. (1988). *From First Words to Grammar: Individual differences and dissociable mechanisms*. New York: Cambridge University Press.

Bates, E., Camaioni, L. and Volterra, V. (1975). The acquisition of performatives prior to speech. *Merrill Palmer Quarterly*, 21, 205–24. Reprinted in E. Ochs and B. B. Schieffelin (eds) (1979), *Developmental Pragmatics*. New York: Academic Press.

Bauer, H. (1988). The ethologic model of phonetic development: I. *Clinical Linguistics and Phonetics*, 2, 347–80.

Bellugi, U. and Studdert-Kennedy, M. (1980). *Signed and Spoken Language: Biological constraints on linguistic form*. Dahlem workshop. Weinheim: Verlag Chemie.

Benedict, H. (1979). Early lexical development: Comprehension and production. *Journal of Child Language*, 6, 183–200.

Benguerel, A.-P. (1971). Duration of French vowels in unemphatic stress. *Language and Speech*, 14, 383–91.

Berg, T. (1992). Phonological harmony as a processing problem. *Journal of Child Language*, 19, 259–285.

Berko, J. (1958). The child's learning of English morphology. *Word*, 14, 150–77.

Berlin, B. and Kay, P. (1969). *Basic Color Terms*. Berkeley: University of California Press.

Berman, R. (1977). Natural phonological processes at the one-word stage. *Lingua*, 43, 1–21.

Bernhardt, B. (1994). The prosodic tier and phonological disorders. In M. Yavas (ed.), *First and Second Language Phonology*. San Diego: Singular Publishing Group.

Bernhardt, B. & Stoel-Gammon, L. (1994). Nonlinear phonology: Introduction and clinical application. *Journal of Speech and Hearing Research*, 37, 123–43.

Bernshteyn, S. I. (1937). *Voprosy obucheniya proiznosheniyu*. ("On the training of pronunciation").

Bernstein-Ratner, N. (1987). The phonology of parent-child speech. In K. E. Nelson and A. van Kleeck (eds), *Children's Language*, 6. Hillsdale, NJ: Lawrence Erlbaum.

Bernthal, J. E., Greenlee, M., Eblen, R., and Marking, K. (1987). Detection of mispronunciations: A comparison of adults, normal speaking children and children with articulation errors. *Applied Psycholinguistics*, 8, 209–22.

Bertoncini, J., Bijeljac-Babic, R., Kennedy, L. J., Jusczyk, P. W., and Mehler, J. (1988). An investigation of young infants' perceptual representation of speech sounds. *Journal of Experimental Psychology: General*, 117, 21–33.

Bertoncini, J. and Mehler, J. (1981). Syllables as units in infant speech perception. *Infant Behavior and Development*, 4, 247–60.

Best, C. T. (1994). The emergence of language-specific phonemic influences in infant speech perception. In J. C. Goodman and H. C. Nusbaum (eds), *The Development of Speech Perception: The transition from speech sounds to spoken words*. Cambridge, MA: MIT Press.

Best, C. T., McRoberts, G. W., and Sithole, N. M. (1988). Examination of perceptual reorganization for nonnative speech contrasts: Zulu click discrimination by English speaking adults and infants. *Journal of Experimental Psychology: Human Perception and*

Performance, 14, 345–60.

Bickerton, D. (1981). *Roots of Language*. Ann Arbor: Karoma.

Bickerton, D. (1990). *Language and Species*. Chicago: University of Chicago Press.

Bickley, C., Lindblom, B., and Roug, L. (1986). Acoustic measures of rhythm in infants' babbling, or "all God's children got rhythm". Paper presented at the 12th International Congress on Acoustics, Toronto, Canada, July (*Proceedings*, 1).

Bissex, G. L. (1980). *GNYS AT WRK: A child learns to write and read*. Cambridge, MA: Harvard University Press.

Blake, J. and Fink, R. (1987). Sound–meaning correspondences in babbling. *Journal of Child Language*, 14, 229-53.

Bloch, O. (1913). Notes sur le langage d'un enfant. *Mémoires de la Société Linguistique de Paris*, 18, 37–59.

Bloom, K. (1975). Social elicitation of infant vocal behavior. *Journal of Experimental Child Psychology*, 20, 51–8.

Bloom, K. (1977). Patterning of infant vocal behavior. *Journal of Experimental Child Psychology*, 23, 367–77.

Bloom, K. (1988). Quality of adult vocalizations affects the quality of infant vocalizations. *Journal of Child Language*, 15, 469–80.

Bloom, K. and Esposito, A. (1975). Social conditioning and its proper control procedures. *Journal of Experimental Child Psychology*, 19, 209–22.

Bloom, K., Russell, A., and Wassenberg, K. (1987). Turn taking affects the quality of infant vocalizations. *Journal of Child Language*, 14, 211–27.

Bloom, L. (1973). *One Word at a Time*. The Hague: Mouton.

Bloom, L. (1983). Of continuity and discontinuity, and the magic of language development. In R. M. Golinkoff (ed.), *The Transition from Prelinguistic to Linguistic Communication*. Hillsdale, NJ: Lawrence Erlbaum.

Bloom, L. (1991). Representation and expression. In N. A. Krasnegor, D. M. Rumbaugh, R. L. Schiefelbusch, and M. Studdert-Kennedy (eds), *Biological and Behavioral Determinants of Language Development*. Hillsdale, NJ: Lawrence Erlbaum.

Blumstein, S. E. and Stevens, K. N. (1981). Phonetic features and acoustic invariance in speech. *Cognition*, 10, 25–32.

Boehm, C. (1992). Vocal communication of *Pan Troglodytes*: "Triangulating" to the origins of spoken language. In J. Wind, B. Chiarelli, B. Bichakjian, and A. Nocentini (eds), *Language Origin: A multidisciplinary approach*. NATO Advanced Science Institutes Series, D, 61. Dordrecht: Kluwer Academic.

Boomer, D. S. and Laver, J. D. M. (1968). Slips of the tongue. *British Journal of Disorders of Communication*, 3, 2–12. Reprinted in V. A. Fromkin, *Speech Errors as Linguistic Evidence*. The Hague: Mouton. 1973.

Bosma, J. F. (1972). Form and function in the infant's mouth and pharynx. In J. F. Bosma (ed.), *Third Symposium on Oral Sensation and Perception: The mouth of the infant*. Springfield, IL: Charles C. Thomas.

Bosma, J. F. (1975). Anatomic and physiologic development of the speech apparatus. In D. B. Tower (ed.), *Human Communication and its Disorders*, 3. New York: Raven Press.

Bowerman, M. (1978). Systematizing semantic knowledge: Changes over time in the child's organization of word meaning. *Child Development*, 49, 977–87.

Bowerman, M. (1982). Reorganizational processes in lexical and syntactic development. In E. Wanner and L. R. Gleitman (eds), *Language Acquisition: The state of the art*. Cambridge: Cambridge University Press.

Bowey, F. (1990). On *Rhyme, language, and children's reading. Applied Psycholinguistics*, 11, 439–48.

Bowey, J. A. and Francis, J. (1991). Phonological analysis as a function of age and exposure to reading instruction. *Applied Psycholinguistics*, 12, 91–121.

Boysson-Bardies, B. de (1993). Ontogeny of language-specific syllabic productions. In B. de Boysson-Bardies, S. de Schonen, P. Jusczyk, P. MacNeilage, and J. Morton (eds), *Developmental Neurocognition: Speech and face processing in the first year of life*. Dordrecht: Kluwer Academic.

Boysson-Bardies, B. de, Bacri, N., Sagart, L., and Poizat, M. (1981). Timing in late babbling. *Journal of Child Language*, 8, 525–39.

Boysson-Bardies, B. de, Hallé, P., Sagart, L., and Durand, C. (1989). A crosslinguistic investigation of vowel formants in babbling. *Journal of Child Language*, 16, 1–17.

Boysson-Bardies, B. de, Sagart, L., and Bacri, N. (1981). Phonetic analysis of late babbling: A case study of a French child. *Journal of Child Language*, 8, 511–24.

Boysson-Bardies, B. de, Sagart, L., and Durand, C. (1984). Discernible differences in the babbling of infants according to target language. *Journal of Child Language*, 11, 1–15.

Boysson-Bardies, B. de and Vihman, M. M. (1991). Adaptation to language: Evidence from babbling and first words in four languages. *Language*, 67, 297–319.

Boysson-Bardies, B. de, Vihman, M. M., Roug-Hellichius, L., Durand, C., Landberg, I., and Arao, F. (1992). Material evidence of infant selection from target language: A cross-linguistic phonetic study. In C. A. Ferguson, L. Menn, and C. Stoel-Gammon (eds), *Phonological Development: Models, research, implications*. Timonium, MD: York Press.

Bradley, L. (1980). *Assessing Reading Difficulties*. London: Macmillan Education.

Bradley, L. (1988). Making connections in learning to read and to spell. *Applied Cognitive Psychology*, 2, 3–18.

Bradley, L. and Bryant, P. E. (1978). Difficulties in auditory organisation as a possible cause of reading backwardness. *Nature*, 271, 746f.

Bradley, L. and Bryant, P. E. (1983). Categorizing sounds and learning to read – a causal connection. *Nature*, 301, 419–21.

Brady, S. and Shankweiler, D. (eds) (1991). *Phonological Processes in Literacy*. Hillsdale, NJ: Lawrence Erlbaum.

Brady, S., Shankweiler, D., and Mann, V. (1983). Speech perception and memory coding in relation to reading ability. *Journal of Experimental Child Psychology*, 35, 345–67.

Braine, M. D. S. (1974). On what might constitute learnable phonology. *Language*, 50, 270–99.

Braine, M. D. S. (1976). Review of N. V. Smith, *The Acquisition of Phonology*. *Language*, 52, 489–98.

Branigan, G. (1976). Syllabic structure and the acquisition of consonants: The great conspiracy in word formation. *Journal of Psycholinguistic Research*, 5, 117–33.

Branigan, G. (1979). Some reasons why successive single word utterances are not. *Journal of Child Language*, 5, 411–21.

Bretherton, I. (1988). How to do things with one word: The ontogenesis of intentional message making in infancy. In M. D. Smith and J. L. Locke (eds), *The Emergent Lexicon: The child's development of a linguistic vocabulary*. New York: Academic Press.

Bretherton, I., McNew, S., and Beeghly-Smith, M. (1981). Early person knowledge as expressed in gestural and verbal communication: When do infants acquire a "theory of mind"? In M. E. Lamb and L. R. Sherrod (eds), *Infant Social Cognition*. Hillsdale, NJ: Lawrence Erlbaum.

Browman, C. P. and Goldstein, L. (1989). Articulatory gestures as phonological units. *Phonology*, 6, 201–51.

Browman, C. P. and Goldstein, L. (1991). Gestural structures: Distinctiveness, phonological processes, and historical change. In I. G. Mattingly and M. Studdert-

Kennedy (eds), *Modularity and the Motor Theory of Speech Perception*. Hillsdale, NJ: Lawrence Erlbaum.

Browman, C. P. and Goldstein, L. (1992). Articulatory phonology: An overview. *Phonetica*, 49, 155–80.

Brown, G. D. A. and Watson, F. L. (1987). First in, first out: Word learning age and spoken word frequency as predictors of word familiarity and word naming latency. *Memory and Cognition*, 15, 208–16.

Brown, R. (1958). *Words and Things*. Glencoe, Illinois: Free Press.

Brown, R. (1973). *A First Language: The early stages*. Cambridge, MA: Harvard University Press.

Bruner, J. S. (1972). Nature and uses of immaturity. *American Psychologist*, 27, 1–22.

Bruner, J. S. (1973). Organization of early skilled action. *Child Development*, 44, 1–11.

Bruner, J. (1975). The ontogenesis of speech acts. *Journal of Child Language*, 2, 1–19.

Bryant, P. E., Bradley, L., Maclean, M., and Crossland, J. (1989). Nursery rhymes, phonological skills and reading. *Journal of Child Language*, 16, 407–28.

Bryant, P. E., Maclean, M., and Bradley, L. (1990). Rhyme, language, and children's reading. *Applied Psycholinguistics*, 11, 237–52.

Buhr, R. (1980). The emergence of vowels in an infant. *Journal of Speech and Hearing Research*, 23, 73–94.

Bullowa, M. (ed.) (1979). *Before Speech: The beginning of interpersonal communication*. Cambridge: Cambridge University Press.

Burdick, C. K. and Miller, J. D. (1975). Speech perception by the chinchilla: Discrimination of sustained /a/ and /i/. *Journal of the Acoustical Society of America*, 58, 415–27.

Burnham, D. K. (1986). Developmental loss of speech perception: Exposure to and experience with a first language. *Applied Psycholinguistics*, 7, 207–40.

Bush, C. N., Edwards, M. L., Luckau, J. M., Stoel, C. M., Macken, M. A., and Petersen, J. D. (1973). On specifying a system for transcribing consonants in child language: A working paper with examples from American English and Mexican Spanish. Committee on Linguistics, Stanford University: Child Language Project.

Carey, S. (1978). The child as word learner. In M. Halle, J. Bresnan, and G. A. Miller (eds), *Linguistic Theory and Psychological Reality*. Cambridge, MA: MIT Press.

Carlisle, J. F. (1988). Knowledge of derivational morphology and spelling ability in fourth, sixth, and eighth graders. *Applied Psycholinguistics*, 9, 247–66.

Carpenter, G. A. and Grossberg, S. (1987). Discovering order in chaos: Stable self-organization of neural recognition codes. In S. H. Koslow, A. J. Mandell, and M. F. Shlesinger (eds), *Perspectives in Biological Dynamics and Theoretical Medicine*. New York: New York Academy of Sciences.

Carpenter, R. L., Mastergeorge, A. M., and Coggins, T. E. (1983). The acquisition of communicative intentions in infants eight to fifteen months of age. *Language and Speech*, 26, 101–16.

Carter, A. L. (1979). Prespeech meaning relations: An outline of one infant's sensorimotor morpheme development. In P. Fletcher and M. Garman (eds), *Language Acquisition: Studies in first language development*. Cambridge: Cambridge University Press.

Caselli, M. C. (1990). Communicative gestures and first words. In V. Volterra and C. J. Erting (eds), *From Gesture to Language in Hearing and Deaf Children*. Berlin: Springer-Verlag. Originally published in Italian as Gesti comunicativi e prime parole. *Età Evolutiva*, 16 (1983), 36–61.

Cazden, C. (1968). The acquisition of noun and verb inflections. *Child Development*, 39, 433–38.

Chang, H.-W. and Trehub, S. E. (1977). Auditory processing of relational information by young infants. *Journal of Experimental Child Psychology*, 24, 324–31.

Chao, Y. R. (1951). The Cantian idiolect: An analysis of the Chinese spoken by a twenty-eight-month-old child. In W. J. Fischel (ed.), *Semitic and Oriental Studies*. Berkeley: University of California Press. Reprinted in C. A. Ferguson and D. I. Slobin (eds) (1973), *Studies of Child Language Development*. New York: Holt, Rinehart & Winston.

Chapman, R. S. (1981). Cognitive development and language comprehension in 10- to 21-month-olds. In R. F. Stark (ed.), *Language Behavior in Infancy and Early Childhood*. New York: Elsevier/North-Holland.

Charles-Luce, J. and Luce, P. A. (1990). Similarity neighbourhoods of words in young children's lexicons. *Journal of Child Language*, 17, 205–15.

Chomsky, N. (1957). *Syntactic Structures*. The Hague: Mouton.

Chomsky, N. (1959). Review of B. F. Skinner, *Verbal Behavior. Language*, 35, 26–58. Reprinted in J. A. Fodor and J. J. Katz (1964), *The Structure of Language*. Englewood Cliffs, NJ: Prentice Hall.

Chomsky, N. (1965). *Aspects of the Theory of Syntax*. Cambridge, MA: MIT Press.

Chomsky, N. (1981a). Discussion of Putnam's comments. In N. Block (ed.), *Readings in the Philosophy of Psychology*, 2. Cambridge, MA: Harvard University Press.

Chomsky, N. (1981b). *Lectures on Government and Binding*. New York: Foris publications.

Chomsky, N. and Halle, M. (1968). *The Sound Pattern of English*. New York: Harper and Row.

Chomsky, N. and Miller, G. A. (1963). Introduction to the formal analysis of natural languages. In R. D. Luce, R. R. Bush, and E. Galanter (eds), *Handbook of Mathematical Psychology*, 2. New York: Wiley.

Cirrin, F. M. (1984). Lexical search speed in children and adults. *Journal of Experimental Child Psychology*, 37, 158–75.

Clark, E. V. (1973). What's in a word? On the child's acquisition of semantics in his first language. In T. Moore (ed.), *Cognitive Development and the Acquisition of Language*. New York: Academic Press.

Clumeck, H. (1977). Studies in the acquisition of Mandarin phonology. Unpublished doctoral dissertation, University of California, Berkeley.

Clumeck, H. (1980). The acquisition of tone. In G. H. Yeni-komshian, J. F. Kavanagh, and C. A. Ferguson (eds), *Child Phonology, 1: Production*. New York: Academic Press.

Clumeck, H. (1982). The effects of word-familiarity on phonemic recognition in children aged 3 to 5 years. In C. E. Johnson and C. L. Thew (eds), *Proceedings of the Second International Congress for the Study of Child Language*, 1. Lanham, MD: University Press of America.

Cole, R. A. (1981). Perception of fluent speech by children and adults. In H. B. Winitz (ed.), *Native Language and Foreign Language Acquisition*. New York: New York Academy of Sciences.

Cole, R. A. and Jakimik, J. (1980). A model of speech perception. In R. A. Cole (ed.), *Perception and Production of Fluent Speech*. Hillsdale, NJ: Lawrence Erlbaum.

Cole, R. A. and Perfetti, C. A. (1980). Listening for mispronunciations in a children's story: The use of context by children and adults. *Journal of Verbal Learning and Verbal Behavior*, 19, 297–315.

Colombo, J. and Horowitz, F. D. (1986). Infants' attentional responses to frequency modulated sweeps. *Child Development*, 57, 287–91.

Content, A., Kolinsky, R., Morais, J., and Bertelson, P. (1986). Phonetic segmentation in pre-readers: Effect of corrective information. *Journal of Experimental Child Psychology*, 421, 47–72.

Cooper, F. S., Delattre, P. C., Liberman, A. M., Borst, J. M., and Gerstman, L. J. (1952). Some experiments on the perception of synthetic speech sounds. *Journal of the Acoustical Society of America*, 24, 597–606. Reprinted in I. Lehiste (ed.) (1967), *Readings in Acoustic Phonetics*. Cambridge, MA: MIT Press.

Cooper, R. P. and Aslin, R. N. (1990). Preference for infant-directed speech in the first month after birth. *Child Development*, 61, 1584–95.

Cossu, G., Shankweiler, D., Liberman, I. Y., Katz, L., and Tola, G. (1988). Awareness of phonological segments and reading ability in Italian children. *Applied Psycholinguistics*, 9, 1–16.

Cowan, N., Suomi, K., and Morse, P. A. (1982). Echoic storage in infant perception. *Child Development*, 53, 984–90.

Cruttenden, A. (1970). A phonetic study of babbling. *British Journal of Disorders of Communication*, 5, 110–17.

Cruttenden, A. (1978). Assimilation in child language and elsewhere. *Journal of Child Language*, 5, 373–8.

Cruttenden, A. (1986). *Intonation*. Cambridge: Cambridge University Press.

Crystal, D. (1969). *Prosodic Systems and Intonation in English*. Cambridge: Cambridge University Press.

Crystal, D. (1970). Prosodic systems and language acquisition. In P. R. Leon, G. Faure and A. Rigault (eds), *Prosodic Feature Analysis*. Montreal: Librairie Didier.

Crystal, D. (1973). Non-segmental phonology in language acquisition: A review of the issues. *Lingua*, 32, 1–45.

Crystal, D. (1986). Prosodic development. In P. Fletcher and M. Garman (eds), *Language Acquisition: Studies in First Language Development* (2nd edn). Cambridge: Cambridge University Press.

Crystal, T. and House, A. (1990). Articulation rate and the duration of syllables and stress groups in connected speech. *Journal of the Acoustical Society of America*, 88, 101–12.

Cutler, A. and Mehler, J. (1993). The periodicity bias. *Journal of Phonetics*, 21, 103–8.

Davis, B. L. and MacNeilage, P. F. (1990). Acquisition of correct vowel production: A quantitative case study. *Journal of Speech and Hearing Research*, 33, 16–27.

Davis, B. L. and MacNeilage, P. F. (in press). The articulatory basis of babbling. *Journal of Speech and Hearing Research*.

DeCasper, A. J. and Fifer, W. P. (1980). Of human bonding: Newborns prefer their mothers' voices. *Science*, 208, 1174–6.

Delack, J. B. and Fowlow, P. J. (1978). The ontogenesis of differential vocalization: Development of prosodic contrastivity during the first year of life. In N. Waterson and C. Snow (eds), *The Development of Communication*. New York: Wiley.

Delattre, P. C. (1961). La leçon d'intonation de Simone de Beauvoir, étude d'intonation déclarative comparée. *The French Review*, 35, 59–67.

Delattre, P. (1966). A comparison of syllable length conditioning among languages. *International Review of Applied Linguistics*, IV/3, 183–98.

Demuth, K. D. (1993). Issues in the acquisition of the Sesotho tonal system. *Journal of Child Language*, 20, 275–301.

Dinnsen, D. A., (ed.) (1979). *Current Approaches to Phonological Theory*. Bloomington, IN: Indiana University Press.

Dinnsen, D. A. (1984). Phonology: Implications and trends. In. R. C. Naremore, *Language Science: Recent Advances*. San Diego, CA: College Hill.

D'Odorico, L. (1984). Non-segmental features in prelinguistic communications: An analysis of some types of infant cry and non-cry vocalizations. *Journal of Child Language*, 11, 17–27.

D'Odorico, L. and Franco, F. (1991). Selective production of vocalization types in different communication contexts. *Journal of Child Language*, 18, 475–99.

D'Odorico, L. and Levorato, M. C. (1990). Social and cognitive determinants of mutual gaze between mother and infant. In V. Volterra and C. J. Erting (eds), *From Gesture to Language in Hearing and Deaf Children*. Berlin: Springer-Verlag.

Dollaghan, C. A. (1994). Children's phonological neighbourhoods: half empty or half full? *Journal of Child Language*, 21, 257–71.

Donahue, M. (1986). Phonological constraints on the emergence of two-word utterances. *Journal of Child Language*, 13, 209–18.

Donegan, P. J. and Stampe, D. (1979). The study of natural phonology. In D. A. Dinnsen (ed.), *Current Approaches to Phonological Theory*. Bloomington, IN: Indiana University Press.

Dore, J. (1974). A pragmatic description of early language development. *Journal of Psycholinguistic Research*, 3, 343–50.

Dore, J. (1975). Holophrases, speech acts and language universals. *Journal of Child Language*, 2, 21–40.

Dore, J. (1983). Feeling, form, and intention in the baby's transition to language. In R. M. Golinkoff (ed.), *The Transition from Prelinguistic to Linguistic Communication*. Hillsdale, NJ: Lawrence Erlbaum.

Dore, J., Franklin, M. B., Miller, R. T., and Ramer, A. L. H. (1976). Transitional phenomena in early language acquisition. *Journal of Child Language*, 3, 13–28.

Echols, C. H. and Newport, E. L. (1992). The role of stress and position in determining first words. *Language Acquisition*, 2, 189–220.

Edelman, G. M. (1987). *Neural Darwinism: The theory of neuronal group selection*. New York: Basic Books.

Edelman, G. M. (1989). *The Remembered Present*. New York: Basic Books.

Edwards, M. L. (1974). Perception and production in child language: The testing of four hypotheses. *Journal of Child Language*, 1, 205–19.

Eilers, R. E. (1977). Context-sensitive perception of naturally produced stop and fricative consonants by infants. *Journal of the Acoustical Society of America*, 61, 1321–36.

Eilers, R. E. (1980). Infant speech perception: History and mystery. In G. H. Yeni-komshian, J. H. Kavanagh, and C. A. Ferguson (eds), *Child Phonology, 2: Perception*. New York: Academic Press.

Eilers, R. E., Gavin, W. J., and Wilson, W. R. (1979). Linguistic experience and phonemic perception in infancy: A cross-linguistic study. *Child Development*, 50, 14–18.

Eilers, R. E., Gavin, W. J., and Wilson, W. R. (1980). Effects of early linguistic experience on speech discrimination by infants: A reply. *Child Development*, 51, 113–17.

Eilers, R. E. and Minifie, F. D. (1975). Fricative discrimination in early infancy. *Journal of Speech and Hearing Research*, 18, 158–67.

Eilers, R. E., Morse, P. A., Gavin, W. J., and Oller, D. K. (1981). Discrimination of voice onset time in infancy. *Journal of the Acoustical Society of America*, 70, 955–65.

Eilers, R. E. and Oller, D. K. (1976). The role of speech discrimination in developmental sound substitutions. *Journal of Child Language*, 3, 319–29.

Eilers, R. E., Oller, D. K., Levine, S., Basinger, D., Lynch, M. P., and Urbano, R. (1993). The role of prematurity and socioeconomic status in the onset of canonical babbling in infants. *Infant Behavior and Development*, 16, 297–315.

Eilers, R. E., Wilson, W. R., and Moore, J. M. (1977). Developmental changes in speech discrimination in infants. *Journal of Speech and Hearing Research*, 20, 766–80.

Eilers, R. E., Wilson, W. R., and Moore, J. M. (1979). Speech discrimination in the language-innocent and language-wise: A study in the perception of voice onset time. *Journal of Child Language*, 6, 1–18.

Eimas, P. D. (1974). Auditory and linguistic processing of cues for place of articulation by infants. *Perception and Psychophysics*, 16, 513–21.

Eimas, P. D. (1975a). Auditory and phonetic coding of the cues for speech: Discrimination of the [r-l] distinction by young infants. *Perception and Psychophysics*, 18, 341–7.

Eimas, P. D. (1975b). Speech perception in early infancy. In L. B. Cohen and P. Salapatek (eds), *Infant Perception, 2: From sensation to cognition*. New York: Academic Press.

Eimas, P. D. (1982). Speech perception: A view of the initial state and perceptual mechanisms. In J. Mehler, E. C. T. Walker, and M. Garrett (eds), *Perspectives on Mental Representation: Experimental and theoretical studies of cognitive processes and capacities*. Hillsdale, NJ: Lawrence Erlbaum.

Eimas, P. D. (1985). Constraints on a model of infant speech perception. In J. Mehler and R. Fox (eds), *Neonate Cognition: Beyond the blooming buzzing confusion*. Hillsdale, NJ: Lawrence Erlbaum.

Eimas, P. D. and Corbit, J. D. (1973). Selective adaptation of linguistic feature detectors. *Cognitive Psychology*, 4, 99–109.

Eimas, P. D. and Miller, J. L. (1980). Discrimination of the information for manner of articulation of young infants. *Infant Behavior and Development*, 3, 367–75.

Eimas, P. D., Siqueland, E. R., Jusczyk, P. W., and Vigorito, J. (1971). Speech perception in infants. *Science*, 171, 303–6.

Elbers, L. (1982). Operating principles in repetitive babbling: A cognitive continuity approach. *Cognition*, 12, 45–63.

Elbers, L. and Ton, J. (1985). Play pen monologues: The interplay of words and babble in the first words period. *Journal of Child Language*, 12, 551–65.

Elbers, L. and Wijnen, F. (1992). Effort, production skill, and language learning. In C. A. Ferguson, L. Menn, and C. Stoel-Gammon (eds), *Phonological Development: Models, research, implications*. Timonium, MD: York Press.

Elliott, L. L. (1979). Performance of children aged 9–17 years on a test of speech intelligibility in noise using sentence material with controlled word predictability. *Journal of the Acoustical Society of America*, 66, 651–3.

Elliott, L. L., Connors, S., Kille, E., Levin, S., Ball, K., and Katz, D. (1979). Children's understanding of monosyllabic nouns in quiet and in noise. *Journal of the Acoustic Society of America*, 66, 12–21.

Elliott, L. L., Hammer, M. A., and Evan, K. E. (1987). Perception of gated, highly familiar spoken monosyllabic nouns by children, teenagers, and older adults. *Perception and Psychophysics*, 42, 150–7.

Elman, J. L., Diehl, R. L., and Buchwald, S. E. (1977). Perceptual switching in bilinguals. *Journal of the Acoustical Society of America*, 62, 971–4.

Engstrand, O., Williams, K., and Strömqvist, S. (1991). Acquisition of the Swedish tonal word accent contrast. *Phonetic Experimental Research, Institute of Linguistics, University of Stockholm*, 12, 189–93.

Ervin, S. (1964). Imitation and structural change in children's language. In E. H. Lenneberg (ed.), *New Directions in the Study of Language*. Cambridge, MA: MIT Press.

Escalona, S. (1973). Basic modes of social interaction: Their emergence and patterning during the first two years of life. *Merrill-Palmer Quarterly*, 19, 205–32.

Fant, G. (1973). *Speech Sounds and Features*. Cambridge, MA: MIT Press.

Fay, D. and Cutler, A. (1977). Malapropisms and the structure of the mental lexicon. *Linguistic Inquiry*, 8, 505–20.

Feagans, L., Garvey, C., and Golinkoff, R., (eds) (1984). *The Origins and Growth of Communication*. Norwood, NJ: Ablex.

Fee, E. J. (in press). Segments and syllables in early language acquisition. To appear in *The Acquisition of Nonlinear Phonology*. Hillsdale, NJ: Lawrence Erlbaum.

Fenson, L., Dale, P. S., Reznick, J. S., Thal, D., Bates, E., Hartung, J. P., Pethick, S., and Reilly, J. S. (1993). *MacArthur Communicative Development Inventories: User's guide and technical manual*. San Diego: Singular Publishing.

Fentress, J. (1983). Hierarchical motor control. In M. Studdert-Kennedy (ed.), *Psychobiology of Language*. Cambridge: MIT Press.

Ferguson, C. A. (1963). Contrastive analysis and language development. *Georgetown University Monograph Series*, 21, 101–12.

Ferguson, C. A. (1964). Baby talk in six languages. *American Anthropologist*, 66, 103–14.

Ferguson, C. A. (1975). Fricatives in child language acquisition. In L. Hellmann (ed.), *Proceedings of the Eleventh International Congress of Linguists*. Bologna: Mulino. Also printed in V. Honsa and M. H. Hardman-Bautista (eds) (1977), *Papers on Linguistics and Child Language*. The Hague: Mouton.

Ferguson, C. A. (1978). Learning to pronounce: the earliest stages of phonological development in the child. In F. D. Minifie and L. L. Lloyd (eds), *Communicative and Cognitive Abilities: Early behavioral assessment*. Baltimore: University Park Press.

Ferguson, C. A. (1979). Phonology as an individual access system: Some data from language acquisition. In C. J. Fillmore, D. Kempler, and W. S.-Y. Wang (eds), *Individual Differences in Language Ability and Language Behavior*. New York: Academic Press.

Ferguson, C. A. (1986). Discovering sound units and constructing sound systems: It's child's play. In J. S. Perkell and D. H. Klatt (eds), *Invariance and Variability in Speech Processes*. Hillsdale, NJ: Lawrence Erlbaum.

Ferguson, C. A. and Farwell, C. B. (1975). Words and sounds in early language acquisition. *Language*, 51, 419–39. Reprinted in W. S.-Y. Wang (1977), *The Lexicon in Phonological Change*. The Hague: Mouton.

Ferguson, C. A. and Garnica, O. K. (1975). Theories of phonological development. In E. H. Lenneberg and E. Lenneberg (eds), *Foundations of Language Development*. NY: Academic Press.

Ferguson, C. A. and Macken, M. A. (1983). The role of play in phonological development. In K. E. Nelson (ed.), *Children's Language*, 4. Hillsdale, NJ: Lawrence Erlbaum.

Ferguson, C. A., Menn, L., and Stoel-Gammon, C. (eds) (1992). *Phonological Development: Models, research, implications*. Timonium, MD: York Press.

Ferguson, C. A., Peizer, D. B., and Weeks, T. A. (1973). Model-and-replica phonological grammar of a child's first words. *Lingua*, 31, 35–65.

Ferguson, C. A. and Slobin, D. I. (eds) (1973). *Studies of Child Language Development*. New York: Holt, Rinehart & Winston.

Fernald, A. (1984). The perceptual and affective salience of mothers' speech to infants. In L. Feagans, C. Garvey, and R. Golinkoff (eds), *The Origins and Growth of Communication*. Norwood, NJ: Ablex.

Fernald, A. (1985). Four-month-old infants prefer to listen to Motherese. *Infant Behavior and Development*, 8, 181–95.

Fernald, A. (1989). Intonation and communicative intent in mothers' speech to infants: Is the melody the message? *Child Development*, 60, 1497–510.

Fernald, A. (1991). Prosody in speech to children: Prelinguistic and linguistic functions. In R. Vasta (ed.), *Annals of Child Development*, 8. London: Jessica Kingsley.

Fernald, A. (1992). Human maternal vocalizations to infants as biologically relevant signals: An evolutionary perspective. In J. H. Barkow, L. Cosmides, and J. Tooby (eds), *The Adapted Mind: Evolutionary psychology and the generation of culture*. Oxford: Oxford University Press.

Fernald, A. and Kuhl, P. K. (1987). Acoustic determinants of infant preference for motherese speech. *Infant Behavior and Development*, 10, 279–93.

Fernald, A. and Mazzie, C. (1991). Prosody and focus in speech to infants and adults. *Developmental Psychology*, 27, 209–21.

Fernald, A. and Simon, T. (1984). Expanded intonation contours in mothers' speech to newborns. *Developmental Psychology*, 20, 104–13.

Fernald, A., Taeschner, T., Dunn, J., Papoušek, M., Boysson-Bardies, B. de., and Fukui, I. (1989). A cross-language study of prosodic modifications in mothers' and fathers' speech to preverbal infants. *Journal of Child Language*, 16, 477–501.

Fey, M. (1985). Phonological assessment and treatment in articulation and phonology: Inextricable constructs in speech pathology. *Human Communication Canada*, 9, 7–16. Reprinted in *Language, Speech, and Hearing Services in Schools*, 23, 225–32.

Field, T. M., Woodson, R., Greenberg, R., and Cohen, D. (1982). Discrimination and imitation of facial expressions by neonates. *Science*, 218, 179–81.

Fikkert, P. (1994). *On the Acquisition of Prosodic Structure*. The Hague: Holland Academic Graphics.

Fillmore, C. J., Kempler, D., and Wang, W. S.-Y. (eds) (1979). *Individual Diffferences in Language Ability and Language Behavior*. New York: Academic Press.

Firth, J. R. (1948). Sounds and prosodies. *Transactions of the Philological Society*, 127–52.

Flax, J., Lahey, M., Harris, K., and Boothroyd, A. (1991). Relations between prosodic variables and communicative functions. *Journal of Child Language*, 18, 3–19.

Fletcher, J. (1991). Rhythm and final lengthening in French. *Journal of Phonetics*, 19, 193–212.

Fletcher, P. and Garman, M. (1979). Introduction to Part I. In P. Fletcher and M. Garman (eds), *Language Acquisition: Studies in first language development*. Cambridge: Cambridge University Press.

Fletcher, S. G. (1973). Maturation of the speech mechanism. *Folia Phoniatrica*, 25, 161–72.

Fodor, J. A. (1983). *The Modularity of Mind*. Cambridge, MA: Bradford/MIT Press.

Fodor, J. A. and Pylyshyn, Z. W. (1988). Connectionism and cognitive architecture: A critical analysis. *Cognition*, 28. Reprinted in S. Pinker and J. Mehler (eds) (1988) *Connections and Symbols*. Cambridge, MA: MIT Press.

Fónagy, I. (1972). A propos de la genèse de la phrase enfantine. *Lingua*, 30, 31–71.

Fowler, A. E. (1991). How early phonological development might set the stage for phonological awareness. In S. Brady and D. Shankweiler (eds), *Phonological Processes in Literacy: A tribute to Isabelle Y. Liberman*. Hillsdale, NJ: Lawrence Erlbaum.

Fowler, C. A. (1986). An event approach to the study of speech perception from a direct realist perspective. *Journal of Phonetics*, 14, 3–28.

Fowler, C. A. and Rosenblum, L. D. (1991). The perception of phonetic gestures. In I. G. Mattingly and M. Studdert-Kennedy (eds), *Modularity and the Motor Theory of Speech Perception: Proceedings of a conference to honor Alvin M. Liberman*. Hillsdale, NJ: Lawrence Erlbaum.

Franke, C. (1899). Sprachentwicklung der Kinder und der Menschheit. In W. Rein (ed.), *Encyclopädisches Handbuch der Pädagogik*, 6, 751–94, 7, 742–90.

Frauenfelder, U. H. and Tyler, L. K. (1987). *Spoken Word Recognition*. Cambridge, MA: MIT Press.

French, A. (1989). The systematic acquisition of word forms by a child during the first-fifty-word stage. *Journal of Child Language*, 16, 69–90.

Friederici, A. D. and Wessels, J. M. I. (1993). Phonotactic knowledge of word boundaries and its use in infant speech perception. *Perception and Psychophysics*, 54, 287–95.

Fry, D. B. (1966). The development of the phonological system in the normal and the deaf child. In F. Smith and G. Miller (eds), *The Genesis of Language: A Psycholinguistic Approach*. Cambridge, MA: MIT Press.

Fudge, E. C. (1969). Syllables. *Journal of Linguistics*, 5, 253–86.

Furrow, D. (1984). Young children's use of prosody. *Journal of Child Language*, 11, 203–13.

Galligan, R. (1987). Intonation with single words: Purposive and grammatical use. *Journal of Child Language*, 14, 1–21.

Garnica, O. K. (1973). The development of phonemic speech perception. In T. Moore (ed.), *Cognitive Development and the Acquisition of Language*. New York: Academic Press.

Garnica, O. K. (1977). Some prosodic and paralinguistic features of speech to young children. In C. E. Snow and C. A. Ferguson (eds), *Talking to Children: Language input and acquisition*. Cambridge: Cambridge University Press.

Gathercole, S. E. and Baddeley, A. D. (1993). *Working Memory and Language*. Hove: Lawrence Erlbaum.

Gelb, I. J. (1963). *A Study of Writing*. Chicago: University of Chicago Press.

George, S. L. (1978). A longitudinal and cross-sectional analysis of the growth of the post-natal cranial base angle. *American Journal of Physical Anthropology*, 49, 141–78.

Gerken, L. (1991). The metrical basis for children's subjectless sentences. *Journal of Memory and Language*, 30, 431–51.

Gerken, L. (1994). Sentential processes in early child language. In J. C. Goodman and H. C. Nusbaum (eds), *The Development of Speech Perception: The transition from speech sounds to spoken words*. Cambridge, MA: MIT Press.

Gerken, L., Landau, B., and Remez, R. E. (1990). Function morphemes in young children's speech perception and production. *Developmental Psychology*, 27, 204–16.

Gerken, L. and McIntosh, B. J. (1993). The interplay of functional morphemes and prosody in early language. *Developmental Psychology*, 29, 448–57.

Gibson, E. J. (1965). Learning to read. *Science*, 148, 1066–72.

Gibson, E. J. (1969). *Principles of Perceptual Learning and Development*. New York: Appleton-Century-Crofts.

Gibson, E. J. (1984). Perceptual development from the ecological approach. In M. E. Lamb, A. L. Brown, and B. Rogoff (eds), *Advances in Developmental Psychology*. Hillsdale, NJ: Lawrence Erlbaum.

Gibson, J. J. (1966). *The Senses Considered as Perceptual Systems*. Boston: Houghton Mifflin.

Gibson, J. J. (1979). *The Ecological Approach to Visual Perception*. Boston: Houghton Mifflin.

Gilhooly, K. J. and Gilhooly, M. L. M. (1980). The validity of age-of-acquisition ratings. *British Journal of Psychology*, 71, 105–10.

Givón, T. (1979). *On Understanding Grammar*. New York: Academic Press.

Gleitman, L. R. and Wanner, E. (1982). Language acquisition: The state of the state of the art. In E. Wanner and L. R. Gleitman (eds), *Language Acquisition: The state of the art*. Cambridge: Cambridge University Press.

Goad, J. L. (1991). Learnability and inventory specific underspecification. Paper presented at the meeting of the Linguistic Society of America, Philadelphia.

Goad, J. L. and Ingram, D. (1987). Individual variation and its relevance to a theory of phonological acquisition. *Journal of Child Language*, 14, 419–32.

Goldman Eisler, F. (1968). *Psycholinguistics: Experiments in spontaneous speech*. London: Academic Press.

Goldsmith, J. A. (1976). An overview of autosegmental phonology. *Linguistic Analysis*, 2, 23–68.

Goldsmith, J. A. (1979). The aims of autosegmental phonology. In D. A. Dinnsen (ed.), *Current Approaches to Phonological Theory*. Bloomington, IN: Indiana University Press.

Goldsmith, J. A. (1990). *Autosegmental and Metrical Phonology*. Oxford: Blackwell.

Golinkoff, R. M. (ed.) (1983). *The Transition from Prelinguistic to Linguistic Communication*. Hillsdale, NJ: Lawrence Erlbaum.

Goodell, E. W. and Studdert-Kennedy, M. (1990). From phonemes to words, or from words to phonemes: How do children learn to talk? Poster presented at the International Conference on Infant Studies, Montreal.

Goodsit, J. V., Morse, P. A., Ver Hoeve, J. N., and Cowan, N. (1984). Infant speech recognition in multisyllabic contexts. *Child Development*, 55, 903–10.

Goodwyn, S. W. and Acredolo, L. P. (1993). Symbolic gesture vs. word: Is there a modality advantage for onset of symbol use? *Child Development*, 64, 688–701.

Grammont, M. (1902.) Observations sur le langage des enfants. In *Mélanges linguistiques offerts à A. Meillet*. Paris.

Grégoire, A. (1937). *L'apprentissage du langage*. Bibliothèque de la Faculté de Philosophie et Lettres de L'Université de Liège, 73.

Grieser, D. L. and Kuhl, P. K. (1988). Maternal speech to infants in a tonal language: Support for universal prosodic features in motherese. *Developmental Psychology*, 24, 14–20.

Grieser, D. and Kuhl, P. K. (1989). Categorization of speech by infants: Support for speech-sound prototypes. *Developmental Psychology*, 25, 577–88.

Griffiths, P. (1986). Early vocabulary. In P. Fletcher and M. Garman (eds), *Language Acquisition: Studies in first language development* (2d edn). Cambridge: Cambridge University Press.

Grosjean, F. (1980). Spoken word recognition and the gating paradigm. *Perception and Psychophysics*, 28, 267–83.

Grosjean, F. (1985). The recognition of words after their acoustic offset: Evidence and implications. *Perception and Psychophysics*, 28, 267–83.

Grosjean, F. and Gee, J. P. (1987). Prosodic structure and spoken word recognition. *Cognition*, 25, 135–55.

Grunwell, P. (1982). *Clinical Phonology*. London: Croom Helm.

Haith, M. M. (1980). *Rules that Babies Look By: The organization of newborn visual activity*. Hillsdale, NJ: Erlbaum.

Halle, M. and Vergnaud, J. (1980). Three dimensional phonology. *Journal of Linguistic Research*, 1, 83–105.

Hallé, P. and Boysson-Bardies, B. de. (1994a). Early receptive lexicons: Representations of word-sounds. Paper presented at the 9th International Conference on Infant Studies, Paris.

Hallé, P. and Boysson-Bardies, B. de. (1994b). Emergence of an early receptive lexicon: Infants' recognition of words. *Infant Behavior and Development*, 17, 119–29.

Hallé, P., Boysson-Bardies, B. de, and Vihman, M. M. (1991). Beginnings of prosodic organization: Intonation and duration patterns of disyllables produced by French and Japanese infants. *Language and Speech*, 34, 299–318.

Halliday, M. A. K. (1975). *Learning How to Mean*. London: Edward Arnold.

Halliday, M. A. K. (1979). One child's protolanguage. In M. Bullowa (ed.), *Before Speech: The beginning of interpersonal communication*. Cambridge: Cambridge University Press.

Harding, C. G. (1984). Acting with intention: A framework for examining the development of the intention to communicate. In L. Feagans, C. Garvey, and R. Golinkoff (eds), *The Origins and Growth of Communication*. Norwood, NJ: Ablex.

Harding, C. G. and Golinkoff, R. M. (1979). The origins of intentional vocalizations in prelinguistic infants. *Child Development*, 50, 33–40.

Hart, B. (1991). Input frequency and first words. *First Language*, 11, 289–300.

Hawkins, S. (1984). On the development of motor control in speech: Evidence from studies of temporal coordination. In N. J. Lass (ed.), *Speech and Language: Advances in basic research and practice*, 11. New York: Academic Press.

Heath, S. B. (1983). *Ways with Words: Language, life, and work in communities and classrooms*. Cambridge: Cambridge University Press.

Heffner, R. M. S. (1950). *General Phonetics*. Madison: The University of Wisconsin Press.

Helfgott, J. (1976). Phonemic segmentation and blending skills of kindergarten children: Implications for beginning reading acquisition. *Contemporary Educational Psychology*, 1, 157–69.

Hewes, G. (1992). History of glottogonic theories. In J. Wind, B. Chiarelli, B. Bichakjian, and A. Nocentini (eds), *Language Origin: A multidisciplinary approach*. NATO Advanced Science Institutes Series, D, 61. Dordrecht: Kluwer Academic.

Hillenbrand, J. M. (1983). Perceptual organization of speech sounds by infants. *Journal of Speech and Hearing Research*, 26, 268–82.

Hillenbrand, J. M. (1984). Speech perception by infants: Categorization based on nasal consonant place of articulation. *Journal of the Acoustical Society of America*, 75, 1613–22.

Hillenbrand, J. M., Minifie, F. D., and Edwards, T. J. (1979). Tempo of spectrum change as a cue in speech-sound discrimination by infants. *Journal of Speech and Hearing Research*, 22, 147–65.

Hirsh-Pasek, K., Kemler Nelson, D. G., Jusczyk, P. W., Wright Cassidy, K., Druss, B., and Kennedy, L. (1987). Clauses are perceptual units for young infants. *Cognition*, 26, 269–86.

Hochberg, J. A. (1988a). First steps in the acquisition of Spanish stress. *Journal of Child Language*, 15, 273–92.

Hochberg, J. A. (1988b). Learning Spanish stress. *Language*, 64, 683–706.

Hockett, C. F. (1960). The origin of speech. *Scientific American*, 203, 88–96.

Hodge, M. (1989). A comparison of spectral-temporal measures across speaker age: Implications for an acoustic characterization of speech maturation. Unpublished doctoral dissertation, University of Wisconsin-Madison, Madison, WI.

Hoequist, C. J. (1983). Syllable duration in stress-, syllable- and mora-timed languages. *Phonetica*, 40, 203–37.

Holmgren, K., Lindblom, B., Aurelius, G., Jalling, B., and Zetterström, R. (1986). On the phonetics of infant vocalization. In B. Lindblom and R. Zetterström (eds), *Precursors of Early Speech*. Basingstoke, Hampshire: Macmillan Press.

Hsieh, H.-I. (1972). Lexical diffusion: Evidence from child language acquisition. *Glossa*, 6, 89–104.

Hulme, C., Thomson, N., Muir, C., and Lawrence, A. (1984). Speech rate and the development of short-term memory span. *Journal of Experimental Child Psychology*, 38, 241–53.

van der Hulst, H. and Smith, N. (1982). An overview of autosegmental and metrical phonology. In H. van der Hulst and N. Smith (eds), *The Structure of Phonological Representations*, 1. Dordrecht: Foris Publications.

Huttenlocher, J. (1974). The origins of language comprehension. In R. L. Solso (ed.), *Theories in Cognitive Psychology*. Hillsdale, NJ: Lawrence Erlbaum.

Huttenlocher, J. and Goodman, J. (1987). The time to identify spoken words. In A. Allport, D. MacKay, W. Prinz, and E. Scheerer (eds), *Language Perception and Production: Relationships between listening, speaking, reading and writing*. London: Academic Press.

Hyams, N. (1986). *Language Acquisition and the Theory of Parameters*. Dordrecht: Reidel.

Ingram, D. (1974). Phonological rules in young children. *Journal of Child Language*, 1, 49–64.

Ingram, D. (1976). *Phonological Disability in Children*. New York: Elsevier.

Ingram, D. (1986). Phonological development: Production. In P. Fletcher and M. Garman (eds), *Language Acquisition: Studies in First Language Development* (2d edn). Cambridge: Cambridge University Press.

Irwin, O. C. (1957). Phonetical description of speech development in childhood. In L. Kaiser (ed.), *Manual of Phonetics*. Amsterdam: North-Holland.

Iverson, G. and Wheeler, D. (1987). Hierarchical structures in child phonology. *Lingua*, 73, 243–57.

Jacobson, J. L., Boersma, D. C., Fields, R. B., and Olson, K. L. (1983). Paralinguistic features of adult speech to infants and small children. *Child Development*, 54, 436–42.

Jakobson, R. (1968). *Child Language, Aphasia, and Phonological Universals*. The Hague: Mouton. (Tr. into English by A. R. Keiler; originally published in 1941 as *Kindersprache, Aphasie und allgemeine Lautgesetze*.)

Jakobson, R. (1949). Les lois phoniques du langage enfantin et leur place dans la phonologie générale. In N. S. Trubetzkoy, *Principes de phonologie*. (Tr. into French by J. Cantineau.) Paris: Editions Klincksieck.

Jakobson, R. (1960). Why "Mama" and "Papa"? In B. Kaplan and S. Wapner (eds), *Perspectives in Psychological Theory: Essays in honor of Heinz Werner*. New York: International Universities Press.

Jakobson, R. (1971). *Studies on Child Language and Aphasia*. The Hague: Mouton.

Jakobson, R. and Halle, M. (1956). *Fundamentals of Language*. The Hague: Mouton.

James, W. (1890). *The Principles of Psychology*. New York: Dover Publications.

Jeng, H.-H. (1979). The acquisition of Chinese phonology in relation to Jakobson's laws of irreversible solidarity. *Proceedings of the Ninth International Congress of Phonetic Sciences*, 2. Copenhagen.

Jespersen, O. (1922). *Language: Its nature, development and origin*. New York: Holt.

Jones, N. K. (1991). Development of morphophonemic segments in children's mental representations of words. *Applied Psycholinguistics*, 12, 217–39.

Jusczyk, P. W. (1977). Perception of syllable-final stop consonants by 2-month-old infants. *Perception and Psychophysics*, 21, 450–4.

Jusczyk, P. W. (1981). The processing of speech and nonspeech sounds by infants: Some implications. In R. N. Aslin, J. R. Alberts, and M. R. Petersen (eds), *Development of Perception: Psychobiological perspectives, 1: Audition, somatic perception, and the chemical senses*. New York: Academic Press.

Jusczyk, P. W. (1985). On characterizing the development of speech perception. In J. Mehler and R. Fox (eds), *Neonate Cognition: Beyond the blooming buzzing confusion*. Hillsdale, NJ: Lawrence Erlbaum.

Jusczyk, P. W. (1986a). A review of speech perception research. In L. Kaufman, J. Thomas, and K. Boff (eds), *Handbook of Perception and Performance*. New York: Wiley.

Jusczyk, P. W. (1986b). Toward a model of the development of speech perception. In J. S. Perkell and D. H. Klatt (eds), *Invariance and Variability in Speech Processes*. Hillsdale, NJ: Lawrence Erlbaum.

Jusczyk, P. W. (1992). Developing phonological categories from the speech signal. In C. A. Ferguson, L. Menn, and C. Stoel-Gammon (eds), *Phonological Development: Models, research, implications*. Timonium, MD: York Press.

Jusczyk, P. W. (1993). From general to language-specific capacities: The WRAPSA model of how speech perception develops. *Journal of Phonetics*, 21, 3–28.

Jusczyk, P. W. and Aslin, R. N. (1995). Infants' detection of the sound patterns of words in fluent speech. *Cognitive Psychology*, 29, 1–23.

Jusczyk, P. W. and Bertoncini, J. (1988). Viewing the development of speech perception as an innately guided learning process. *Language and Speech*, 31, 217–38.

Jusczyk, P. W., Bertoncini, J., Bijeljac-Babic, R., Kennedy, L. J., and Mehler, J. (1990). The role of attention in speech perception by young infants. *Cognitive Development*, 5, 265–86.

Jusczyk, P. W., Copan, H., and Thompson, E. J. (1978). Perception by 2-month-old infants of glide contrasts in multisyllabic utterances. *Perception and Psychophysics*, 24, 515–20.

Jusczyk, P. W., Cutler, A., and Redanz, N. J. (1993). Infants' preference for the predominant stress patterns of English words. *Child Development*, 64, 675–87.

Jusczyk, P. W. and Derrah, C. (1987). Representation of speech sounds by young infants. *Developmental Psychology*, 23, 648–54.

Jusczyk, P. W., Friederici, A. D., Wessels, J., Svenkerud, V. Y., and Jusczyk, A. M. (1993). Infants' sensitivity to the sound patterns of native language words. *Journal of Memory and Language*, 32, 402–20.

Jusczyk, P. W. and Kemler Nelson, D. G. (in press). Syntactic units, prosody, and psychological reality during infancy. In J. L. Morgan and K. D. Demuth, (eds), *Signal to Syntax: Bootstrapping from speech to grammar in early acquisition*. Hillsdale, NJ: Erlbaum.

Jusczyk, P. W., Kemler Nelson, D. G., Hirsh-Pasek, K., Kennedy, L., Woodward, A., and Piwoz, J. (1992). Perception of acoustic correlates of major phrasal units by young infants. *Cognitive Psychology*, 24, 252–93.

Jusczyk, P. W., Luce, P. A., and Charles-Luce, J. (1994). Infants' sensitivity to phonotactic patterns in the native language. *Journal of Memory and Language*, 33, 630–45.

Jusczyk, P. W., Murray, J., and Bayly, J. (1979). Perception of place of articulation in fricatives and stops by infants. Paper presented at Biennial Meeting of Society for Research in Child Development, San Francisco.

Jusczyk, P. W., Pisoni, D. B., Walley, A., and Murray, J. (1980). Discrimination of relative onset time of two-component tones by infants. *Journal of the Acoustical Society of America*, 67, 262–70.

Jusczyk, P. W. and Thompson, E. J. (1978). Perception of a phonetic contrast in multisyllabic utterances by two-month-old infants. *Perception and Psychophysics*, 23, 105–9.

Kalmár, I. (1985). Are there really no primitive languages? In D. R. Olson, N. Torrance, and A. Hildyard (eds), *Literacy, Language and Learning*. Cambridge: Cambridge University Press.

Kamhi, A. (1986). The elusive first word: The importance of the naming insight for the development of referential speech. *Journal of Child Language*, 13, 155–61.

Kamhi, A., Catts, H., and Davis, M. (1984). Management of sentence production demands. *Journal of Speech and Hearing Research*, 27, 329–38.

Kaplan, E. (1969). The role of intonation in the acquisition of language. Unpublished doctoral dissertation, Cornell University, Ithaca, New York.

Karzon, R. G. (1985). Discrimination of polysyllabic sequences by one- to four-month-old infants. *Journal of Experimental Child Psychology*, 39, 326–42.

Kassai, I. (1988). Prosodic development of a Hungarian child: The one-word utterance stage. In T. Szende (ed.), *From Phonology to Applied Phonetics*, Hungarian Papers in Phonetics, 19. Budapest: Linguistics Institute of the Hungarian Academy of Sciences.

Katz, J. and Jusczyk, P. W. (1980). Do six-month-olds have perceptual constancy for phonetic segments? Paper presented at the International Conference on Infant Studies, New Haven, CT.

Kay-Raining Bird, E. and Chapman, R. S. (in submission). Partial representations and phonological selectivity in the comprehension of 13- to 16-month-olds.

Kaye, J. (1989) *Phonology: A Cognitive View*. Hillsdale, NJ: Lawrence Erlbaum.

Kemler Nelson, D. G., Hirsh-Pasek, K., Jusczyk, P. W., and Wright Cassidy, K. (1989). How the prosodic cues in motherese might assist language learning. *Journal of Child Language*, 16, 55–68.

Kent, R. D. (1976). Anatomical and neuromuscular maturation of the speech mechanism: Evidence from acoustic studies. *Journal of Speech and Hearing Research*, 19, 421–47.

Kent, R. D. (1981). Articulatory-acoustic perspectives on speech development. In R. E. Stark (ed.), *Language Behavior in Infancy and Early Childhood*. New York: Elsevier/ North-Holland.

Kent, R. D. (1983). The segmental organization of speech. In P. F. MacNeilage (ed.), *The Production of Speech*. New York: Springer Verlag.

Kent, R. D. (1984). Psychobiology of speech development: Coemergence of language and a movement system. *American Journal of Physiology*, 246, R888–94.

Kent, R. D. (1992) The biology of phonological development. In C. A. Ferguson, L. Menn, and C. Stoel-Gammon (eds), *Phonological Development: Models, research, implications*. Timonium, MD: York Press.

Kent, R. D. and Bauer, H. R. (1985). Vocalizations of one-year olds. *Journal of Child Language*, 13, 491–526.

Kent, R. D. and Forner, L. L. (1980). Speech segment duration in sentence recitations by children and adults. *Journal of Phonetics*, 8, 157–68.

Kent, R. D. and Hodge, M. (1990). The biogenesis of speech: Continuity and process in early speech and language development. In J. F. Miller (ed.), *Progress in Research on Child Language Disorders*. Austin, TX: Pro-Ed.

Kent, R. D., Mitchell, P. R., and Sancier, M. (1991). Evidence and role of rhythmic organization in early vocal development in human infants. In J. Fagard and P. H. Wolff (eds), *The Development of Timing Control and Temporal Organization in Coordinated Action*. Oxford: Elsevier Science.

Kent, R. D. and Murray, A. D. (1982). Acoustic features of infant vocalic utterances at 3, 6, and 9 months. *Journal of the Acoustic Society of America*, 72, 353–63.

Kent, R. D., Osberger, M. J., Netsell, R., and Hustedde, C. G. (1987). Phonetic development in identical twins who differ in auditory function. *Journal of Speech and Hearing Disorders*, 52, 64–75.

Kessen, W., Levine, J., and Wendrich, K. A. (1979). The imitation of pitch in infants. *Infant Behavior and Development*, 2, 93–9.

Kewley-Port, D. and Preston, M. S. (1974). Early apical stop production: A voice onset time analysis. *Journal of Phonetics*, 2, 195–210.

Kim, C.-W. (1982). The rise and rite of non-linear phonology. In The Linguistic Society of Korea (ed.), *Linguistics in the Morning Calm: Selected papers from SICOL – 1981*. Seoul, Korea: Hanshin.

Kingston, J. and Beckman, M. E. (1990). *Papers in Laboratory Phonology I: Between the grammar and physics of speech*. Cambridge: Cambridge University Press.

Kiparsky, P. (1965). Phonological change. Unpublished doctoral dissertation, MIT, Cambridge, MA.

Kiparsky, P. (1968). Linguistic change and linguistic universals. In E. Bach and R. T. Harms (eds), *Universals in Linguistic Theory*. New York: Holt, Rinehart and Winston.

Kiparsky, P. (1989). Phonological change. In F. J. Newmeyer (ed.), *Linguistics: The Cambridge Survey, 1: Linguistic Theory: Foundations*. Cambridge: Cambridge University Press.

Kiparsky, P. and Menn, L. (1977). On the acquisition of phonology. In J. Macnamara (ed.),

Language Learning and Thought. New York: Academic Press.

Kirtley, C., Bryant, P., MacLean, M., and Bradley, L. (1989). Rhyme, rime and the onset of reading. *Journal of Experimental Child Psychology*, 48, 224–45.

Kisseberth, C. W. (1970). On the functional unity of phonological rules. *Linguistic Inquiry*, 1, 291–306.

Klatt, D. H. (1979) Speech perception: A model of acoustic phonetic analysis and lexical access. *Journal of Phonetics*, 7, 279–312. Also printed in R. A. Cole (ed.) (1980), *Perception and Production of Fluent Speech*. Hillsdale, NJ: Lawrence Erlbaum.

Klein, H. (1984). Learning to stress: A case study. *Journal of Child Language*, 11, 375–90.

Klima, E. and Bellugi, U. (1979). *The Signs of Language*. Cambridge, MA: Harvard University Press.

Klinnert, M., Campos, J. J., Sorce, J. F., Emde, R. N., and Svejda, M. (1983). Emotions as behavior regulators: Social referencing in infancy. In R. Plutchik and H. Kellerman (eds), *Emotion in Early Development, 2: The emotions*. New York: Academic Press.

Kluender, K. R., Diehl, R. L., and Killeen, P. R. (1987). Japanese quail can learn phonetic categories. *Science*, 237, 1195–97.

Knafle, J. D. (1973). Auditory perception of rhyming in kindergarten children. *Journal of Speech and Hearing Research*, 16, 482–7.

Knafle, J. D. (1974). Children's discrimination of rhyme. *Journal of Speech and Hearing Research*, 17, 367–72.

Kolaric, R. (1959). Slovenski otroški govor. *Jahrbuch der Philosophischen Fakultät in Novi Sad*, 4.

Konefal, J. A., Fokes, J., and Bond, Z. S. (1982). Children's syntactic use of vowel duration. *Journal of Phonetics*, 10, 361–6.

Konopczynski, G. (1986). Vers un modèle développemental du rythme français: problèmes d'isochronie reconsidérés à la lumière des données de l'acquisition du langage. *Bulletin de l'Institut de Phonétique de Grenoble*, 15, 157–90.

Koopmans-van Beinum, F. J. and Van der Stelt, J. M. (1986). Early stages in the development of speech movements. In B. Lindblom and R. Zetterström (eds), *Precursors of Early Speech*. Basingstoke, Hampshire: Macmillan Press.

Kornfeld, J. (1971). Theoretical issues in child phonology. Papers from the Seventh Regional Meeting, Chicago Linguistic Society, 454–68.

Kubaska, C. A. and Keating, P. A. (1981). Word duration in early child speech. *Journal of Speech and Hearing Research*, 24, 615–21.

Kuhl, P. K. (1980). Perceptual constancy for speech-sound categories in early infancy. In G. H. Yeni-komshian, J. F. Kavanagh, and C. A. Ferguson (eds), *Child Phonology, 2: Perception*. New York: Academic Press.

Kuhl, P. K. (1983). Perception of auditory equivalence classes for speech in early infancy. *Infant Behavior and Development*, 6, 263–85.

Kuhl, P. K. (1985). Categorization of speech by infants. In J. Mehler and R. Fox (eds), *Neonate Cognition: Beyond the blooming buzzing confusion*. Hillsdale, NJ: Lawrence Erlbaum.

Kuhl, P. K. (1986a). Reflections on infants' perception and representation of speech. In J. S. Perkell and D. H. Klatt (eds), *Invariance and Variability in Speech Processes*. Hillsdale, NJ: Lawrence Erlbaum.

Kuhl, P. K. (1986b). Theoretical contributions of tests on animals to the special-mechanisms debate in speech. *Experimental Biology*, 45, 233–65.

Kuhl, P. K. (1987). Perception of speech and sound in early infancy. In P. Salapatek and L. Cohen (eds), *Handbook of Infant Perception*, 2. New York: Academic Press.

Kuhl, P. K. (1991). Human adults and human infants show a "perceptual magnet effect" for the prototypes of speech categories, monkeys do not. *Perception and Psychophysics*, 50, 93–107.

Kuhl, P. K. and Hillenbrand, J. M. (1979). Speech perception by young infants: Perceptual constancy for categories based on pitch contour. Paper presented at Biennial Meeting of Society for Research in Child Development, San Francisco.

Kuhl, P. K. and Meltzoff, A. N. (1982). The bimodal perception of speech in infancy. *Science*, 218, 1138–41.

Kuhl, P. K. and Meltzoff, A. N. (1984). The intermodal representation of speech in infants. *Infant Behavior and Development*, 7, 361–81.

Kuhl, P. K. and Meltzoff, A. N. (1988). Speech as an intermodal object of perception. In A. Yonas (ed.), *Perceptual Development in Infancy*. The Minnesota Symposia on Child Psychology, 20. Hillsdale, NJ: Lawrence Erlbaum.

Kuhl, P. K. and Miller, J. D. (1975a). Speech perception in early infancy: Discrimination of speech-sound categories. *Journal of the Acoustical Society of America*, 58, Suppl. 1, S56.

Kuhl, P. K. and Miller, J. D. (1975b). Speech perception by the chinchilla: Voiced-voiceless distinction in alveolar plosive consonants. *Science*, 190, 69–72.

Kuhl, P. K. and Miller, J. D. (1978). Speech perception by the chinchilla: Identification functions for synthetic VOT stimuli. *Journal of the Acoustical Society of America*, 63, 905–17.

Kuhl, P. K. and Miller, J. D. (1982). Discrimination of auditory target dimensions in the presence or absence of variation in a second dimension by infants. *Perception and Psychophysics*, 31, 279–92.

Kuhl, P. K. and Padden, D. M. (1982). Enhanced discriminability at the phonetic boundaries for the voicing feature in macaques. *Perception and Psychophysics*, 32, 542–50.

Kuhl, P. K. and Padden, D. M. (1983). Enhanced discriminability at the phonetic boundaries for the place feature in macaques. *Journal of the Acoustical Society of America*, 73, 1003–10.

Kuhl, P. K., Williams, K. A., Lacerda, F., Stevens, K. N., and Lindblom, B. (1992). Linguistic experience alters phonetic perception in infants by 6 months of age. *Science*, 255, 606–8.

Labov, W. (1963). The social motivation of a sound change. *Word*, 19, 273–309.

Labov, W. and Labov, T. (1978). The phonetics of *cat* and *mama*. *Language*, 54, 816–52.

Ladefoged, P. (1971). *Preliminaries to Linguistic Phonetics*. Chicago: University of Chicago Press.

Langlois, A., Backen, R. J., and Wilder, C. N. (1980). Pre-speech respiratory behavior during the first year of life. In T. Murry and J. Murry (eds), *Infant Communication: Cry and Early Speech*. Houston: College Hill.

Lasky, R. E., Syrdal-Lasky, A., and Klein, R. E. (1975). VOT discrimination by four to six and a half month old infants from Spanish environments. *Journal of Experimental Child Psychology*, 20, 215–25.

Laufer, M. Z. (1980). Temporal regularity in prespeech. In T. Murry and A. Murry (eds), *Infant Communication: Cry and early speech*. Houston, TX: College Hill Press.

Laufer, M. Z. and Horii, Y. (1977). Fundamental frequency characteristics of infant non-distress vocalization during the first 24 weeks. *Journal of Child Language*, 4, 171–84.

Lecanuet, J.-P. (1993). Fetal responsiveness to voice and speech. In B. de Boysson-Bardies, S. de Schonen, P. Jusczyk, P. F. MacNeilage, and J. Morton (eds), *Developmental Neurocognition: Speech and face processing in the first year of life*. Dordrecht: Kluwer Academic.

Legerstee, M. (1990). Infants use multimodal information to imitate speech sounds. *Infant*

Behavior and Development, 13, 343–54.

Lehiste, I. (1960). Segmental and syllabic quantity in Estonian. *American Studies in Uralic Linguistics*. Bloomington, IN: Indiana University Publications.

Lenel, J. C. and Cantor, J. H. (1981). Rhyme recognition and phonemic perception in young children. *Journal of Psycholinguistic Research*, 17, 367–72.

Lenneberg, E. (1967). *Biological Foundations of Language*. New York: Wiley.

Leonard, L. B., Newhoff, M., and Mesalam, L. (1980). Individual differences in early child phonology. *Applied Psycholinguistics*, 1, 7–30.

Leopold, W. F. (1939). *Speech Development of a Bilingual Child, 1: Vocabulary Growth in the First Two Years*. Evanston: Northwestern University Press.

Leopold, W. F. (1947). *Speech Development of a Bilingual Child, 2: Sound-learning in the First Two Years*. Evanston: Northwestern University Press.

Leopold, W. F. (1949a). *Speech Development of a Bilingual Child, 3: Grammar and General Problems*. Evanston, Northwestern University Press.

Leopold, W. F. (1949b). *Speech Development of a Bilingual Child, 4: Diary from Age Two*. Evanston, Northwestern University Press.

Leopold, W. F. (1953). Patterning in children's language learning. *Language Learning*, 5, 1–14. Reprinted in A. Bar-Adon and W. F. Leopold (1971), *Child Language: A book of readings*. Englewood Cliffs, NJ: Prentice Hall.

Lcroy, C. (1975). Intonation et syntaxe chez l'enfant français à partir de dix-huit mois. *Langue française*, 27, 24–37.

Leung, E. H. L. and Rheingold, H. L. (1981). Development of pointing as a social gesture. *Developmental Psychology*, 17, 214–20.

Levelt, W. J. M. (1989). *Speaking: From intention to articulation*. Cambridge, MA: MIT Press.

Levitt, A. G., Jusczyk, P. W., Murray, J., and Carden, G. (1988). Context effects in two-month-old infants' perception of labiodental/interdental fricative contrasts. *Journal of Experimental Psychology: Human Perception and Performance*, 14, 361–368.

Levitt, A. G. and Wang, Q. (1991). Evidence for language-specific rhythmic influences in the reduplicative babbling of French- and English-learning infants. *Language and Speech*, 34, 235–49.

Lewis, M. M. (1936). *Infant Speech: A study of the beginnings of language*. New York: Harcourt, Brace. Reprinted 1975, New York: Arno Press.

Li, C. N. and Thompson, S. A. (1977). The acquisition of tone in Mandarin-speaking children. *Journal of Child Language*, 4, 185–99.

Liberman, A. M., Cooper, F. S., Shankweiler, D. P., and Studdert-Kennedy, M. (1967). Perception of the speech code. *Psychological Review*, 74, 431–61.

Liberman, A. M., Harris, K. S., Eimas, P. D., Lisker, L., and Bastian, J. (1961). An effect of learning on speech perception: The discrimination of durations of silence with and without phonemic significance. *Language and Speech*, 4, 175–95.

Liberman, A. M., Harris, K. S., Hoffman, H. S., and Griffith, B. C. (1957). The discrimination of speech sounds within and across phoneme boundaries. *Journal of Experimental Psychology*, 54, 358–68.

Liberman, A. M. and Mattingly, I. (1985). The motor theory of speech perception revised. *Cognition*, 21, 1–36.

Liberman, I. Y., Shankweiler, D., Fischer, F. W., and Carter, B. (1974). Explicit syllable and phoneme segmentation in the young child. *Journal of Experimental Child Psychology*, 18, 201–12.

Liberman, I. Y., Shankweiler, D., Fowler, C., and Fischer, F. W. (1977). Phonetic segmentation and recoding in the beginning reader. In A. S. Reber and D. L. Scarborough (eds),

Toward a Psychology of Reading. New York: Lawrence Erlbaum.

Liberman, M. and Prince, A. (1977). On stress and linguistic rhythm. *Linguistic Inquiry*, 8, 249–336.

Lieberman, P. (1967). *Intonation, Perception and Language*. Cambridge, MA: MIT Press.

Lieberman, P. (1980). On the development of vowel production in young children. In G. H. Yeni-komshian, J. F. Kavanagh, and C. A. Ferguson (eds), *Child Phonology, 1: Production*. New York: Academic Press.

Lieberman, P. (1984). *The Biology and Evolution of Language*. Cambridge, MA: Harvard, University Press.

Lieberman, P. (1985). The physiology of cry and speech in relation to linguistic behavior. In B. Lester and C. F. Z. Boukydis (eds), *Infant Crying: Theoretical and research perspectives*. New York: Plenum Press.

Lieberman, P. (1991). *Uniquely Human: The evolution of speech, thought and selfless behavior*. Cambridge, MA: Harvard University Press.

Lieberman, P., Crelin, E. S., and Klatt, D. H. (1972). Phonetic ability and related anatomy of the newborn and adult human, Neanderthal man, and the chimpanzee. *American Anthropologist*, 84, 287–307.

Lindblom, B. (1978). Final lengthening in speech and music. In E. Gårding, G. Bruce, and R. Bannert (eds), *Nordic Prosody: Papers from a Symposium*. Lund, Sweden: Department of Linguistics.

Lindblom, B. (1983). Economy of speech gestures. In P. F. MacNeilage (ed.), *Speech Production*. New York: Springer-Verlag.

Lindblom, B. (1991). The status of phonetic gestures. In I. Mattingly and M. Studdert-Kennedy (eds), *Modularity and the Motor Theory of Speech Perception: Proceedings of a conference to honor Alvin M. Liberman*. Hillsdale, NJ: Lawrence Erlbaum.

Lindblom, B. (1992). Phonological units as adaptive emergents of lexical development. In C. A. Ferguson, L. Menn, and C. Stoel-Gammon (eds), *Phonological Development: Models, research, implications*. Timonium, MD: York Press.

Lindblom, B., MacNeilage, P. F., and Studdert-Kennedy, M. (1984). Self-organizing processes and the explanation of phonological universals. In B. Butterworth, B. Comrie, and Ö. Dahl (eds), *Explanations for Language Universals*. Berlin: Mouton.

Lindblom, B. and Sundberg, J. (1969). A quantitative method of vowel production and the distinctive features of Swedish vowels. *Quarterly Progress Status Report*, Speech Transmission Laboratory, Royal Institute of Technology, Stockholm, 1, 1432.

Lindner, G. (1898). *Aus dem Naturgarten der Kindersprache*. Leipzig: Th. Grieben's Verlag.

Lisker, L. and Abramson, A.S. (1964). A cross-language study of voicing in initial stops: Acoustical measurements. *Word*, 20, 384–422.

Lleó, C. (1990). Homonymy and reduplication: On the extended availability of two strategies in phonological acquisition. *Journal of Child Language*, 17, 267–78.

Lleó, C. (1991). A parametrical view of harmony and reduplication processes in child phonology. Paper presented at the DFG Conference, Crossing Boundaries, Tübingen, Germany.

Lock, A. (ed.) (1978). *Action, Gesture and Symbol: The emergence of language*. New York: Academic Press.

Locke, J. L. (1979). The child's processing of phonology. In W. A. Collins (ed.), *Minnesota Symposium on Child Psychology*, 12. Hillsdale, NJ: Lawrence Erlbaum.

Locke, J. L. (1980). The inference of speech perception in the phonologically disordered child. Part II: Some clinically novel procedures, their use, some findings. *Journal of speech and Hearing Disorders*, 4, 445–68.

Locke, J. L. (1983). *Phonological Acquisition and Change*. New York: Academic Press.

Locke, J. L. (1985). The role of phonetic factors in parent reference. *Journal of Child Language*, 12, 215–20.

Locke, J. L. (1986). Speech perception and the emergent lexicon: An ethological approach. In P. Fletcher and M. Garman (eds), *Language Acquisition: Studies in first language development* (2d edn). Cambridge: Cambridge University Press.

Locke, J. L. (1988). Variation in human biology and child phonology: A response to Goad and Ingram. *Journal of Child Language*, 15, 663–68.

Locke, J. L. (1990). Structure and stimulation in the ontogeny of spoken language. *Developmental Psychobiology*, 23, 621–43.

Locke, J. L. (1993). *The Child's Path to Spoken Language*. Cambridge, MA: Harvard University Press.

Locke, J. L. (1994). Gradual emergence of developmental language disorders. *Journal of Speech and Hearing Research*, 37, 608–16.

Locke, J. L. and Pearson, D. (1992). Vocal learning and the emergence of phonological capacity: a neurobiological approach. In C. A. Ferguson, L. Menn, and C. Stoel-Gammon (eds), *Phonological Development: Models, research, implications*. Timonium, MD: York Press.

Luce, P. (1986). A computational analysis of uniqueness points in auditory word recognition. *Perception and Psychophysics*, 39, 155–9.

Lundberg, I., Olofsson, A., and Wall, S. (1980). Reading and spelling skills in the first school years predicted from phonemic awareness skills in kindergarten. *Scandinavian Journal of Psychology*, 21, 159–73.

Luria, A. (1961). *The Role of Speech in the Regulation of Normal and Abnormal Behavior*. New York: Liveright.

Lyberg, B. (1979). Final lengthening – partly a consequence of restrictions on the speed of fundamental frequency change? *Journal of Phonetics*, 7, 187–96.

Lynch, M. P., Eilers, R. E., Oller, D. K., and Urbano, R. C. (1990). Innateness, experience, and music perception. *Psychological Review*, 74, 431–61.

Lynip, A. (1951). The use of magnetic devices in the collection and analysis of the preverbal utterances of an infant. *Genetic Psychology Monograph*, 44, 221–62.

Mack, M. and Lieberman, P. (1985). Acoustic analysis of words produced by a child from 46 to 149 weeks. *Journal of Child Language*, 12, 527–50.

McCarthy, D. (1930). *The Language Development of the Preschool Child*. Institute of Child Welfare Monographs Series, no. 4. Minneapolis: University of Minnesota Press.

McCarthy, D. (1954). Language development in children. In L. Carmichael (ed.), *A Manual of Child Psychology* (2nd edn). New York: Wiley.

McCarthy, J. (1989). Linear order in phonological representation. *Linguistic Inquiry*, 20, 71–99.

McCarthy, J. J. and Prince, A. S. (in press). *Prosodic Morphology I: Constraint interaction and satisfaction*. Cambridge, MA: MIT Press.

McClelland, J. L. and Elman, J. L. (1986). Interactive processes in speech perception: The TRACE model. In D. E. Rumelhart, J. L. McClelland, and the PDP Research Group (eds), *Parallel Distributed Processing: Explorations in the microstructure of cognition*. Cambridge, MA: MIT Press.

McCune, L. (1992). First words: A dynamic systems view. In C. A. Ferguson, L. Menn, and C. Stoel-Gammon (eds), *Phonological Development: Models, research, implications*. Timonium, MD: York Press.

McCune, L. (1995). A normative study of representational play at the transition to language. *Developmental Psychology*, 31, 198–206.

McCune, L. and Vihman, M. M. (1987). Vocal motor schemes. *Papers and Reports on Child*

Language Development, 26, 72–9.

McCune, L., Vihman, M. M., Roug-Hellichius, L., and Delery, D. (in press). Grunt communication in human infants (*Homo sapiens*). *Journal of Comparative Psychology*.

McCune-Nicolich, L. (1981a). The cognitive bases of early relational words. *Journal of Child Language*, 8, 15–36.

McCune-Nicolich, L. (1981b). Toward symbolic functioning: Structure of early pretend games and potential parallels with language. *Child Development*, 52, 785–97.

McDonough, J. and Myers, S. (1991). Consonant harmony and planar segregation in child language. Unpublished manuscript, University of Texas, Austin, TX.

MacKain, K.S. (1982). Assessing the role of experience on infants' speech discrimination. *Journal of Child Language*, 9, 527–42.

MacKain, K. S. and Stern, D. N. (1985). The concept of experience in speech development. In K. E. Nelson (ed.), *Children's Language*, 5. Hillsdale, NJ: Lawrence Erlbaum.

MacKay, D. (1972). The structure of words and syllables: Evidence from errors in speech. *Cognitive Psychology*, 3, 210–27.

Macken, M. A. (1978). Permitted complexity in phonological development: One child's acquisition of Spanish consonants. *Lingua*, 44, 219–53.

Macken, M. A. (1979). Developmental reorganization of phonology: A hierarchy of basic units of acquisition. *Lingua*, 49, 11–49.

Macken, M. A. (1980a). The child's lexical representation: The "*puzzle-puddle-pickle*" evidence. *Journal of Linguistics*, 16, 1–17.

Macken, M. A. (1980b). Aspects of the acquisition of stop systems: A cross-linguistic perspective. In G. Yeni-komshian, J. F. Kavanagh, and C. A. Ferguson (eds), *Child Phonology, 1: Production*. New York: Academic Press.

Macken, M. A. (1986). Phonological development: A cross-linguistic perspective. In P. Fletcher and M. Garman (eds), *Language Acquisition: Studies in first language development* (2d edn). Cambridge: Cambridge University Press.

Macken, M. A. (1987). Representation, rules and overgeneralization in phonology. In B. MacWhinney (ed.), *Mechanisms of Language Acquisition*. Hillsdale, NJ: Lawrence Erlbaum.

Macken, M. A. (1992). Where's phonology? In C. A. Ferguson, L. Menn, and C. Stoel-Gammon (eds), *Phonological Development: Models, research, implications*. Timonium, MD: York Press.

Macken, M. A. (1995). Phonological acquisition. In J. Goldsmith (ed.), *The Handbook of Phonological Theory*. Cambridge, MA: Blackwell.

Macken, M. A. and Barton, D. (1980a). A longitudinal study of the acquisition of the voicing contrast in American-English word-initial stops, as measured by Voice Onset Time. *Journal of Child Language*, 7, 41–74.

Macken, M. A. and Barton, D. (1980b). The acquisition of the voicing contrast in Spanish: a phonetic and phonological study of word-initial stop consonants. *Journal of Child Language*, 7, 433–58.

Macken, M. A. and Ferguson, C. A. (1981). Phonological universals of language acquisition. In H. Winitz (ed.), *Native Language and Foreign Language Acquisition*. New York: New York Academy of Sciences.

Macken, M. A. and Ferguson, C. A. (1983). Cognitive aspects of phonological development: Model, evidence and issues. In K. E. Nelson (ed.), *Children's Language*, 4. Hillsdale, NJ: Lawrence Erlbaum.

MacLean, M., Bryant, P., and Bradley, L. (1987). Rhymes, nursery rhymes, and reading in early childhood. *Merrill–Palmer Quarterly*, 33, 255–81.

Macnamara, J. (1982). *Names for Things: A study of human learning*. Cambridge, MA: MIT Press.

MacNeilage, P. F. (1979). Speech production. Report to the Ninth International Congress of Phonetic Sciences, Copenhagen.

MacNeilage, P.F. (1991). Comment: The gesture as a unit in speech perception theories. In I. Mattingly and M. Studdert-Kennedy (eds), *Modularity and the Motor Theory of Speech Perception: Proceedings of a conference to honor Alvin M. Liberman*. Hillsdale, NJ: Lawrence Erlbaum.

MacNeilage, P. F. (in press). The frame/content theory of evolution of speech production. *Behavioral and Brain Sciences*.

MacNeilage, P. F. and Davis, B. L. (1990a). Acquisition of speech production: Frames, then content. In M. Jeannerod (ed.), *Attention and Performance XIII: Motor representation and control*. Hillsdale, NJ: Lawrence Erlbaum.

MacNeilage, P. F. and Davis, B. L. (1990b). Acquisition of speech production: The achievement of segmental independence. In W. J. Hardcastle and A. Marchal (eds), *Speech Production and Speech Modelling*. Dordrecht: Kluwer Academic.

MacNeilage, P. F. and Davis, B. L. (1993). Motor explanations of babbling and early speech patterns. In B. de Boysson-Bardies, S. de Schonen, P. Jusczyk, P. MacNeilage, and J. Morton (eds), *Developmental Neurocognition: Speech and face processing in the first year of life*. Dordrecht: Kluwer Academic.

McShane, J. (1980). *Learning How to Talk*. Cambridge: Cambridge University Press.

Maddieson, I. (1984). *Patterns of Sounds*. Cambridge: Cambridge University Press.

Malatesta, C. Z. and Izard, C. E. (1984). The ontogenesis of human social signals: From biological imperative to symbol utilization. In N. A. Fox and R. J. Davidson (eds), *The Psychobiology of Affective Development*. Hillsdale, NJ: Lawrence Erlbaum.

Malkiel, Y. (1968). The inflectional paradigm as an occasional determinant of sound change. In W. P. Lehmann and Y. Malkiel (eds), *Directions for Historical Linguistics: A symposium*. Austin: University of Texas Press.

Malmberg, B. (1963). *Phonetics*. New York: Dover Publications.

Mandel, D. R., Jusczyk, P. W., and Pisoni, D. B. (1994). Do $4\frac{1}{2}$-month-olds know their names? Paper presented at 127th Meeting of the Acoustical Society of America. Cambridge, MA.

Mann, V. A. (1986). Phonological awareness: The role of reading experience. *Cognition*, 24, 65–92.

Mann, V. A., Tobin, P., and Wilson, R. (1987). Measuring phonological awareness through the invented spellings of kindergarten children. *Merrill-Palmer Quarterly*, 33, 365–91.

de Manrique, A. M. B. and Gramigna, S. (1984). La segmentación fonológica y silábica en niños de prescolar y primero grado (Phonological and syllabic segmentation in preschool and first grade children.). *Lectura y Vida*, 5, 4–13.

Maratsos, M. and Chalkley, M. A. (1980). The internal language of children's syntax: The ontogenesis and representation of syntactic categories. In K. E. Nelson (ed.), *Children's Language*, 2. New York: Gardner Press.

Marcos, H. (1987). Communicative functions of pitch range and pitch direction in infants. *Journal of Child Language*, 14, 255–68.

Marr, D. (1982). *Vision*. San Francisco: Freeman.

Marslen-Wilson, W. D. (1973). Linguistic structure and speech shadowing at very short latencies. *Nature*, 244, 522–3.

Marslen-Wilson, W. D. (1985). Speech shadowing and speech comprehension. *Speech Communication*, 4, 55–73.

Marslen-Wilson, W. D. (1987). Functional parallelism in spoken word-recognition. In U. H. Frauenfelder and L. K. Tyler (eds), *Spoken Word Recognition*. Amsterdam: Elsevier Science. Also printed in *Cognition*, 25.

Marslen-Wilson, W. D. and Tyler, L. K. (1975). Processing structure of sentence perception. *Nature*, 257, 784–6.

Marslen-Wilson, W. D. and Tyler, L. K. (1978). Processing interactions and lexical access during word recognition in continuous speech. *Cognitive Psychology*, 10, 29–63.

Marslen-Wilson, W. D. and Tyler, L. K. (1980). The temporal structure of spoken language understanding. *Cognition*, 8, 1–71.

Marslen-Wilson, W. D. and Welsh, A. (1978). Processing interactions during word-recognition in continuous speech. *Cognitive Psychology*, 10, 29–63.

Martin, J. G. (1970). On judging pauses in spontaneous speech. *Journal of Verbal Learning and Verbal Behavior*, 9, 75–8.

Martinet, A. (1955). *Économie des changements phonétiques*. Berne: Franck.

Masataka, N. (1992). Pitch characteristics of Japanese maternal speech to infants. *Journal of Child Language*, 19, 213–23.

Masataka, N. (1993). Effects of contingent and noncontingent maternal stimulation on the vocal behaviour of three-to four-month-old Japanese infants. *Journal of Child Language*, 20, 303–12.

Massaro, D. W. (1988). *Speech Perception by Ear and by Eye: A paradigm for psychological inquiry*. Hillsdale, NJ: Lawrence Erlbaum.

Masur, E. F. (1983). Gestural development, dual-directional signaling, and the transition to words. *Journal of Psycholinguistic Research*, 12, 93–108. Reprinted in V. Volterra and C. J. Erting (eds) (1990), *From Gesture to Language in Hearing and Deaf Children*, Berlin: Springer-Verlag.

Matthei, E. (1989). Crossing boundaries: More evidence for phonological constraints on early multi-word utterances. *Journal of Child Language*, 16, 41–54.

Mattingly, I. G. (1972). Reading, the linguistic process, and linguistic awareness. In J. F. Kavanagh and I. G. Mattingly, *Language by Ear and by Eye*. Cambridge, MA: MIT Press.

Mattingly, I. G. (1973). Phonetic prerequisites for first-language acquisition. Status report on speech research. SR 341–5. Haskins Laboratories.

Mattingly, I. and Liberman, A. (1988). Specialized perceiving systems for speech and other biologically significant sounds. In G. Edelman, W. Gall, and W. Cowan (eds), *Auditory Function: The neurological basis of hearing*. New York: Wiley.

Mehler, J., Bertoncini, J., Barrière, M., and Jassik-Gerschenfeld, D. (1978). Infant recognition of mother's voice. *Nature*, 7, 491–7.

Mehler, J., Jusczyk, P., Lambertz, G., Halsted, N., Bertoncini, J., and Amiel-Tison, C. (1988). A precursor of language acquisition in young infants. *Cognition*, 29, 143–78.

Meier, R. and Newport, E. L. (1990). Out of the hands of babes: On a possible sign advantage. *Language*, 66, 1–23.

Meier, R. P., Willerman, R., and Zakia, R. A. E. (1994). Look Ma, no voicing! Jaw wags and lip smacks in silent babbling. Unpublished manuscript, University of Texas, Austin, TX.

Meltzoff, A. N. and Moore, M. K. (1977). Imitation of facial and manual gestures by human neonates. *Science*, 198, 75–8.

Meltzoff, A. N. and Moore, M. K. (1983). Newborn infants imitate adult facial gestures. *Child Development*, 54, 702–9.

Meltzoff, A. N. and Moore, M. K. (1993). Why faces are special to infants: On connecting the attraction of faces and infants' ability for imitation and cross-modal processing. In B. de Boysson-Bardies, S. de Schonen, P. Jusczyk, P. MacNeilage, and J. Morton (eds),

Developmental Neurocognition: Speech and face processing in the first year of life. Dordrecht: Kluwer Academic.

Menn, L. (1971). Phonotactic rules in beginning speech. *Lingua*, 26, 225–51.

Menn, L. (1974). A theoretical framework for child phonology. Paper presented at the Fiftieth Annual Summer Meeting of the Linguistic Society of America.

Menn, L. (1976a). Evidence for an interactionist-discovery theory of child phonology. *Papers and Reports in Child Language Development*, 12, 169–77.

Menn, L. (1976b). Pattern, control and contrast in beginning speech: A case study in the development of word form and word function. Unpublished PhD thesis, University of Illinois at Urbana-Champaign. Reprinted by the Indiana University Linguistics Club (Bloomington, IN, 1978).

Menn, L. (1978). Phonological units in beginning speech. In A. Bell and J. B. Hooper (eds), *Syllables and Segments*. Amsterdam: North-Holland.

Menn, L. (1979). Transition and variation in child phonology: Modeling a developing system. *Proceedings of the Ninth International Congress of Phonetic Sciences*, 2. Copenhagen.

Menn, L. (1983). Development of articulatory, phonetic, and phonological capabilities. In B. Butterworth (ed.), *Language Production*, 2. London: Academic Press.

Menn, L., Markey, K., Mozer, M., and Lewis, C. (1993). Connectionist modeling and the microstructure of phonological development: A progress report. In B. de Boysson-Bardies, S. de Schonen, P. Jusczyk, P. F. MacNeilage, and J. Morton (eds), *Developmental Neurocognition: Speech and face processing in the first year of life.* Dordrecht: Kluwer Academic.

Menn, L. and Matthei, E. (1992). The "two-lexicon" account of child phonology: Looking back, looking ahead. In C. A. Ferguson, L. Menn, and C. Stoel-Gammon (eds), *Phonological Development: Models, research, implications*. Timonium, MD: York Press.

Menyuk, P. and Menn, L. (1979). Early strategies for the perception and production of words and sounds. In P. Fletcher and M. Garman (eds), *Language Acquisition: Studies in first language development*. Cambridge: Cambridge University Press.

Menyuk, P., Menn, L., and Silber, R. (1986). Early strategies for the perception and production of words and sounds. In P. Fletcher and M. Garman (eds), *Language Acquisition: Studies in first language development* (2nd edn). Cambridge: Cambridge University Press.

Miller, C. L. (1983). Developmental changes in male-female voice classification by infants. *Infant Behavior and Development*, 6, 313–30.

Miller, C. L. and Morse, P. A. (1976). The "heart" of categorical speech discrimination in young infants. *Journal of Speech and Hearing Research*, 19, 578–89.

Miller, C. L., Morse, P. A., and Dorman, M. F. (1977). Cardiac indices of infant speech perception: Orienting and burst discrimination. *Quarterly Journal of Experimental Psychology*, 29, 533–45.

Miller, G. A. and Nicely, P. E. (1955). An analysis of perceptual confusions among some English consonants. *Journal of the Acoustical Society of America*, 27, 338–52. Reprinted in I. Lehiste (ed.) (1967), *Readings in Acoustic Phonetics*. Cambridge, MA: MIT Press.

Miller, J. D., Wier, C. C., Pastore, R. E., Kelly, W. J., and Dooling, R. J. (1976). Discrimination and labeling of noise-buzz sequences with varying noise-lead times: An example of categorical perception. *Journal of the Acoustical Society of America*, 60, 410–17.

Miller, J. L. and Eimas, P. D. (1979). Organization in infant speech perception. *Canadian Journal of Psychology*, 33, 353–67.

Miller, J. L. and Eimas, P. D. (1983). Studies on the categorization of speech by infants. *Cognition*, 13, 135–65.

Mitchell, P. R. and Kent, R. D. (1990). Phonetic variation in multisyllabic babbling. *Journal of Child Language*, 17, 247–65.

Miyawaki, K., Strange, W., Verbrugge, R., Liberman, A. M., Jenkins, J. J., and Fujimura, O. (1975). An effect of linguistic experience: The discrimination of [r] and [l] by native speakers of Japanese and English. *Perception and Psychophysics*, 18, 331–40.

Moffitt, A. R. (1971). Consonant cue perception by twenty- to twenty-four-week-old infants. *Child Development*, 42, 717–31.

Mohanan, K. P. (1992). Emergence of complexity in phonological development. In C. A. Ferguson, L. Menn, and C. Stoel-Gammon (eds), *Phonological Development: Models, research, implications*. Timonium, MD: York Press.

Moon, C. and Fifer, W. P. (1990). Syllables as signals for two-day-old infants. *Infant Behavior and Development*, 13, 377–90.

Moore, J. M., Thompson, G., and Thompson, M. (1975). Auditory localization of infants as a function of reinforcement conditions. *Journal of Speech and Hearing Disorders*, 40, 29–34.

Moore, J. M., Wilson, W. R., and Thompson, G. (1977). Visual reinforcement of head-turn responses in infants under 12 months of age. *Journal of Speech and Hearing Disorders*, 42, 328–34.

Morais, J., Alegria, J., and Content, A. (1987). The relationship between segmental analysis and alphabetic literacy: An interactive view. *Cahiers de Psychologie Cognitive*, 7, 415–38.

Morais, J., Bertelson, P., Cary, L., and Alegria, J. (1986). Literacy training and speech segmentation. *Cognition*, 24, 45–64.

Morais, J., Cary, L., Alegria, J., and Bertelson, P. (1979). Does awareness of speech as a sequence of phones arise spontaneously? *Cognition*, 7, 323–31.

Morgan, J. L. (1986). *From Simple Input to Complex Grammar*. Cambridge, MA: MIT Press.

Morgan, J. L. and Demuth, K. D. (eds) (in press). *Signal to Syntax: Bootstrapping from speech to grammar in early acquisition*. Hillsdale, NJ: Lawrence Erlbaum.

Morse, P. A. (1972). The discrimination of speech and nonspeech stimuli in early infancy. *Journal of Experimental Child Psychology*, 14, 477–92.

Moskowitz, [B.] A. I. (1970). The two-year-old stage in the acquisition of English phonology. *Language*, 46, 426–41. Reprinted in C. A. Ferguson and D. I. Slobin (eds) (1973), *Studies of Child Language Development*, New York: Holt, Rinehart, & Winston.

Moskowitz, [B.] A. I. (1971). The Acquisition of Phonology. Unpublished doctoral dissertation, University of California, Berkeley.

Moskowitz, [B.] A. I. (1973). The acquisition of phonology and syntax: a preliminary study. In K. J. J. Hintikka, J. M. E. Moravcsik, and P. Suppes (eds), *Approaches to Natural Language*. Dordrecht: Reidel.

Moskowitz, B. A. [I.] (1978). The acquisition of language. *Scientific American*, 239, 92–108.

Mowrer, O. H. (1952). Speech development in the young child: The autism theory of speech development and some clinical applications. *Journal of Speech and Hearing Disorders*, 17, 263–8.

Mowrer, O. H. (1960). *Learning Theory and Symbolic Processes*. New York: Wiley.

Murai, J. (1963). The sounds of infants, their phonemicization and symbolization. *Studia Phonologica*, 3, 18–34.

Nakazima, S. (1962). A comparative study of the speech developments of Japanese and American English in childhood: 1. A comparison of the developments of voices at the prelinguistic period. *Studia Phonologica*, 3, 17–43.

Nakazima, S. (1970). A comparative study of the speech developments of Japanese and American English in childhood: 3. The reorganization process of babbling articulation mechanisms. *Studia Phonologica*, 5, 20–42.

Nakazima, S. (1980). The reorganization process of babbling. In T. Murry and J. Murry (eds), *Infant Communication: Cry and early speech*. Houston, TX: College Hill.

Nelson, K. (1973a). *Structure and Strategy in Learning to Talk*. Monographs of the Society for Research in Child Development, 38, 1–2.

Nelson, K. (1973b). Some evidence for the cognitive primacy of categorization and its functional basis. *Merrill-Palmer Quarterly*, 19, 21–39.

Nelson, K. (1981). Individual differences in language development. *Developmental Psychology*, 17, 170–87.

Nelson, L. and Bauer, H. (1991). Speech and language production at age 2: Evidence for tradeoffs between linguistic and phonetic processing. *Journal of Speech and Hearing Research*, 34, 879–92.

Nespor, M. and Vogel, I. (1986). *Prosodic Phonology*. Dordrecht: Foris Publications.

Netsell, R. (1981). The acquisition of speech motor control: A perspective with directions for research. In R. E. Stark (ed.), *Language Behavior in Infancy and Early Childhood*. New York: Elsevier/North-Holland.

Newport, E. L. and Meier, R. P. (1985). The acquisition of American Sign Language. In D. I. Slobin (ed.), *The Crosslinguistic Study of Language Acquisition*. Hillsdale, NJ: Lawrence Erlbaum.

Ninio, A. (1993). On the fringes of the system: Children's acquisition of syntactically isolated forms at the onset of speech. *First Language*, 13, 291–313.

Nittrouer, S. (1992). Age-related differences in perceptual effects of formant transitions within syllables and across syllable boundaries. *Journal of Phonetics*, 20, 351–82.

Nittrouer, S. (1993). The emergence of mature gestural patterns is not uniform: Evidence from an acoustic study. *Journal of Speech and Hearing Research*, 36, 959–1172.

Nittrouer, S. and Studdert-Kennedy, M. (1987). The role of coarticulatory effects in the perception of fricatives by children and adults. *Journal of Speech and Hearing Research*, 30, 319–29.

Nittrouer, S., Studdert-Kennedy, M., and McGowan, R. S. (1989). The emergence of phonetic segments: Evidence from the spectral structure of fricative-vowel syllables spoken by children and adults. *Journal of Speech and Hearing Research*, 32, 120–32.

Nooteboom, S. G. (1981). Lexical retrieval from fragments of spoken words: Beginnings vs. endings. *Journal of Phonetics*, 9, 407–24.

O'Connor, J. D. (1973). *Phonetics*. Middlesex, England: Penguin Books.

Ohala, J. J. (1970). Aspects of the control and production of speech. *UCLA Working Papers in Phonetics*, 15, 1–192.

Ohala, J. J. (1986). Phonological evidence for top-down processing in speech perception. In J. S. Perkell and D. H. Klatt (eds), *Invariance and Variability in Speech Processes*. Hillsdale, NJ: Lawrence Erlbaum.

Öhman, S. E. G. (1966). Coarticulation in VCV utterances: Spectrographic measurements. *Journal of the Acoustical Society of America*, 39, 151–68.

Oller, D. K. (1975). Simplification as the goal of phonological processes in child speech. *Language Learning*, 24, 299–303.

Oller, D. K. (1980). The emergence of the sounds of speech in infancy. In G. Yeni-komshian, J. F. Kavanagh, and C. A. Ferguson (eds), *Child Phonology, 1: Production*. New York: Academic Press.

Oller, D. K. (1981). Infant vocalizations: Exploration and reflexivity. In R. E. Stark (ed.), *Language Behavior in Infancy and Early Childhood*. New York: Elsevier/North-Holland.

Oller, D. K. (1986). Metaphonology and infant vocalizations. In B. Lindblom and R. Zetterström (eds), *Precursors of Early Speech*. Basingstoke, Hampshire: Macmillan Press.

Oller, D. K. and Eilers, R. E. (1988). The role of audition in infant babbling. *Child Development*, 59, 441–9.

Oller, D. K. and Lynch, M. P. (1992). Infant vocalizations and innovations in infraphonology: Toward a broader theory of development and disorders. In C. A. Ferguson, L. Menn, and C. Stoel-Gammon (eds), *Phonological Development: Models, research, implications*. Timonium, MD: York Press.

Oller, D. K. and Smith, B. L. (1977). Effect of final-syllable position on vowel duration in infant babbling. *Journal of the Acoustic Society of America*, 62, 993–7.

Oller, D. K. and Steffens, M. L. (1994). Syllables and segments in infant vocalizations and young child speech. In M. Yavaş (ed.), *First and Second Language Phonology*. San Diego: Singular Publishing Group.

Oller, D. K., Wieman, L. A., Doyle, W. J., and Ross, C. (1976). Infant babbling and speech. *Journal of Child Language*, 3, 1–11.

Olmsted, D. (1966). A theory of the child's learning of phonology. *Language*, 42, 531–5. Reprinted in A. Bar-Adon and W. F. Leopold (eds) (1971), *Child Language: A book of readings*, Englewood Cliffs, NJ: Prentice Hall.

Olmsted, D. (1971). *Out of the Mouths of Babes*. The Hague: Mouton.

Orlansky, M. D. and Bonvillian, J. D. (1988). Early sign language acquisition. In M. D. Smith and J. L. Locke (eds), *The Emergent Lexicon: The child's development of a linguistic vocabulary*. New York: Academic Press.

Oviatt, S. (1980). The emerging ability to comprehend language: An experimental approach. *Child Development*, 50, 97–106.

Oyama, S. (1989). Ontogeny and the central dogma. In M. R. Gunnar and E. Thelen (eds), *Systems and Development*. The Minnesota Symposia on Child Psychology, 22. Hillsdale, NJ: Lawrence Erlbaum.

Pačesová, J. (1968). *The Development of Vocabulary in the Child*. Brno, Czechoslovakia: Universita J. E. Purkyne.

Palmer, F. R. (ed.) (1970). *Prosodic Analysis*. London: Oxford University Press.

Palthe, T. Van W. and Hopkins, B. (1984). Development of the infants' social competence during early face-to-face interactions: A longitudinal study. In H. F. R. Prechtl (ed.), *Continuity of Neural Functions from Prenatal to Postnatal Life*. Spastics International Medical Publications, Philadelphia: J. B. Lippincott.

Papoušek, H. and Papoušek, M. (1987). Intuitive parenting: A dialectic counterpart to the infant's integrative competence. In J. D. Osofsky (ed.), *Handbook of Infant Development* (2nd edn). New York: Wiley.

Papoušek, M. and Hwang, S.-F. C. (1991). Tone and intonation in Mandarin babytalk to presyllabic infants: Comparison with registers of adult conversation and foreign language instruction. *Applied Psycholinguistics*, 12, 481–504.

Papoušek, M. and Papoušek, H. (1981). Musical elements in the infant's vocalization: The significance for communication, cognition and creativity. In L. P. Lipsett (ed.), *Advances in Infancy Research*, 1. Norwood, NJ: Ablex.

Papoušek, M. and Papoušek, H. (1989). Forms and functions of vocal matching in interactions between mothers and their precanonical infants. *First Language*, 9, 137–58.

Paradis, C. (1988). On constraints and repair strategies. *The Linguistic Review*, 6, 71–97.

Passy, P. (1890). *Étude sur les changements phonétiques*. Paris: Librairie Firmin-Didot.

Perkell, J. S. and Klatt, D. H. (1986). *Invariance and Variability in Speech Processes*. Hillsdale, NJ: Lawrence Erlbaum.

Peters, A. M. (1977). Language learning strategies: Does the whole equal the sum of the parts? *Language*, 53, 560–73.

Peters, A. M. (1983). *The Units of Language Acquisition.* Cambridge: Cambridge University Press.

Peters, A. M. (1995). Strategies in the acquisition of grammatical morphemes. In P. Fletcher and B. MacWhinney (eds), *Handbook of Child Language.* Oxford: Blackwell.

Peters, A. M. and Menn, L. (1993). False starts and filler syllables: Ways to learn grammatical morphemes. *Language,* 69, 742–77.

Peters, A. M. and Strömqvist, S. (in press). The role of prosody in the acquisition of grammatical morphemes. In J. Morgan and K. Demuth (eds), *From Signal to Syntax.* Hillsdale, NJ: Lawrence Erlbaum.

Peterson, G. E. and Barney, H. L. (1952). Control methods used in a study of the vowels. *Journal of the Acoustical Society of America,* 24, 175–84. Reprinted in I. Lehiste (ed.) (1967), *Readings in Acoustic Phonetics.* Cambridge, MA: MIT Press.

Petitto, L. A. (1991). Babbling in the manual mode: Evidence for the ontogeny of language. *Science,* 251, 1493–6.

Piaget, J. (1951). *Play, Dreams and Imitation in Childhood* (translated by C. Gattegno and F. M. Hodgson). London: Heinemann.

Pierrehumbert, J. (1980). The phonology and phonetics of English intonation. Unpublished doctoral dissertation, MIT, Cambridge, MA.

Pinker, S. (1984). *Language Learnability and Language Development.* Cambridge, MA: Harvard University Press.

Pinker, S. and Bloom, P. (1990). Natural language and natural selection. *Behavioral and Brain Sciences,* 13, 707–84.

Pinker, S. and Mehler, J. (1988). Introduction. In S. Pinker and J. Mehler (eds), *Connections and Symbols.* Cambridge, MA: MIT Press.

Pinker, S. and Prince, A. (1988). On language and connectionism: Analysis of a parallel distributed processing model of language acquisition. *Cognition,* 28. Reprinted in S. Pinker and J. Mehler (eds) (1988), *Connections and Symbols,* Cambridge, MA: MIT Press.

Pisoni, D. B. (1977). Identification and discrimination of the relative onset time of two component tones: Implications for voicing perception in stops. *Journal of the Acoustical Society of America,* 61, 1352–61.

Pollock, K. E., Brammer, D. M., and Hageman, C. F. (1993). An acoustic analysis of young children's productions of word stress. *Journal of Phonetics,* 21, 183–203.

Poole, L. (1934). Genetic development of articulation of consonant sounds in speech. *Elementary English Review,* 11, 157–61.

Preston, M. S., Yeni-komshian, G., and Stark, R. (1967). Voicing in initial stop consonants produced by children in the prelinguistic period from different language communities. *Annual Report,* 2, 305–23. Neurocommunications Laboratory, Baltimore, MD: Johns Hopkins University School of Medicine.

Priestly, T. M. S. (1977). One idiosyncratic strategy in the acquisition of phonology. *Journal of Child Language,* 4, 45–66.

Prince, A. S. and Smolensky, P. (in press). *Optimality Theory: Constraint interaction in generative grammar.* Cambridge, MA: MIT Press.

Prince, A. S. (1980). A metrical theory for Estonian quantity. *Linguistic Inquiry,* 11, 511–62.

Pye, C. (1983). Mayan telegraphese. *Language,* 59, 583–604.

Pylyshyn, Z. (1977). What does it take to bootstrap a language? In J. Macnamara (ed.), *Language Learning and Thought.* New York: Academic Press.

Queller, K. (1988). Review of N. Waterson, *Prosodic Phonology. Journal of Child Language,* 15, 463–7.

Querleu, D. and Renard, K. (1981). Les perceptions auditives du foetus humain. *Médicine et Hygiène,* 39, 2102–10.

Querleu, D., Renard, K., Versyp, F., Paris-Delrue, L., and Crepin, G. (1988). Fetal hearing. *European Journal of Obstetrics & Gynecology and Reproductive Biology*, 29, 191–212.

Ramer, A. L. H. (1976). Syntactic styles in emerging language. *Journal of Child Language*, 3, 49–62.

Ramsay, D. S. (1982). Unimanual handedness and duplicated syllable babbling in infants (Abstract). International Conference on Infant Studies, Austin, Texas.

Read, C. (1975). *Children's Categorizations of Speech Sounds in English*. Urbana, IL: National Council of Teachers of English.

Read, C., Zhang, Y.-F., Nie, H.-Y., and Ding, B.-Q. (1986). The ability to manipulate speech sounds depends on knowing alphabetic writing. *Cognition*, 24, 31–44.

Reich, P. A. (1976). The early acquisition of word meaning. *Journal of Child Language*, 3, 117–23.

Repp, B. H. (1984). Categorical perception: Issues, methods, findings. In N. J. Lass (ed.), *Speech and Language: Advances in Basic Research and Practice*, 10. New York: Academic Press.

Repp, B. H. (1986). Some observations on the development of anticipatory coarticulation. *Journal of the Acoustical Society of America*, 79, 1616–19.

Repp, B. H. and Crowder, R. G. (1990). Stimulus order effects in vowel discrimination. *Journal of the Acoustical Society of America*, 88, 2080–90.

Reznick, J. S. and Goldfield, B. A. (1992). Rapid change in lexical development in comprehension and production. *Developmental Psychology*, 28, 406–13.

Rice, K. (1992). Review of J. A. Goldsmith, *Autosegmental and Metrical Phonology*. *Language*, 68, 149–56.

Rice, M. L. and Woodsmall, L. (1988). Lessons from television: Children's word learning when viewing. *Child Development*, 59, 420–9.

Robb, M. P., Bauer, H. R., and Tyler, A. A. (1994). A quantitative analysis of the single-word stage. *First Language*, 14, 37–48.

Robb, M. P. and Saxman, J. H. (1990). Syllable durations of preword and early word vocalizations. *Journal of Speech and Hearing Research*, 33, 583–93.

Robins, R. H. (1989). *General Linguistics* (4th edn). London: Longman.

Romanes, G. J. (1888). *Mental Evolution in Man*. London.

Rosch, E. (1975). Cognitive reference points. *Cognitive Psychology*, 7, 532–47.

Rosch, E. and Mervis, C. B. (1975). Family resemblances: Studies in the internal structure of categories. *Cognitive Psychology*, 7, 573–605.

Roug, L., Landberg, I., and Lundberg, L.-J. (1989). Phonetic development in early infancy: A study of four Swedish children during the first eighteen months of life. *Journal of Child Language*, 16, 19–40.

Rovee-Collier, C., Sullivan, M. W., Enright, M. Lucas, D., and Fagen, J. W. (1980). Reactivation of infant memory. *Science*, 208, 1159–62.

Rumelhart, D. E., McClelland, J. L., and the PDP Research Group (eds) (1986). *Parallel Distributed Processing: Explorations in the microstructure of cognition*. Cambridge, MA: MIT Press.

Sachs, J. (1977). The adaptive significance of linguistic input to prelinguistic infants. In C. E. Snow and C. A. Ferguson (eds), *Talking to Children: Language input and acquisition*. Cambridge: Cambridge University Press.

Salasoo, A. and Pisoni, D. G. (1985). Interaction of knowledge sources in spoken word identification. *Journal of Memory and Language*, 24, 210–31.

Samuel, A. G. (1981a). Phonemic restoration: Insights from a new methodology. *Journal of Experimental Psychology: General*, 110, 474–94.

Samuel, A. G. (1981b). The role of bottom-up confirmation in the phonemic restoration illusion. *Journal of Experimental Psychology: Human perception and performance*, 7, 1124–31.

Sapir, E. (1921). *Language: An Introduction to the study of speech*. New York: Harcourt, Brace & World.

Schieffelin, B. B. (1973). Getting it together: An ethnographic approach to the study of the development of communicative competence. In E. Ochs and B. B. Schieffelin (eds), *Developmental Pragmatics*. New York: Academic Press.

Schultze, F. (1880). *Die Sprache des Kindes: eine Anregung zur Erforschung des Gegenstandes*. Leipzig: Gunter. Samples translated as "The speech of the child," in A. Bar-Adon and W. F. Leopold (eds) (1971), *Child Language: A book of readings*, Englewood Cliffs, NJ: Prentice Hall.

Scollon, R. (1979). A real early stage: An unzippered condensation of a dissertation on child language. In E. Ochs and B. B. Schieffelin (eds), *Developmental Pragmatics*. New York: Academic Press.

Scoville, R. (1984). Development of the intention to communicate: The eye of the beholder. In L. Feagans, C. Garvey, and R. Golinkoff (eds) (1984), *The Origins and Growth of Communication*. Norwood, NJ: Ablex.

Searle, J. (1969). *Speech Acts*. Cambridge: Cambridge University Press.

Selkirk, E. O. (1982). The syllable. In H. Van der Hulst and N. Smith (eds), *The Structure of Phonological Representations, Part 2*. Dordrecht: Foris Publications.

Sereno, J. A., Baum, S. R., Marean, G. C., and Lieberman, P. (1987). Acoustic analyses and perceptual data on anticipatory labial coarticulation in adults and children. *Journal of the Acoustical Society of America*, 81, 512–19.

Sheppard, W. C. and Lane, H. L. (1968). Development of the prosodic features of infant vocalizing. *Journal of Speech and Hearing Research*, 11, 94–108.

Shibamoto, J. S. and Olmsted, D. L. (1978). Lexical and syllabic patterns in phonological acquisition. *Journal of Child Language*, 5, 417–56.

Shipley, E., Smith, C., and Gleitman, L. (1969). A study in the acquisition of language. *Language*, 45, 322–42.

Shvachkin, N. K. H. (1973). The development of phonemic speech perception in early childhood. In C. A. Ferguson and D. I. Slobin (eds), *Studies of Child Language Development*. New York: Holt, Rinehart & Winston. (Originally published in 1948 as Razvitie fonematicheskogo vospriyatiya rechi v rannem vozraste, *Izvestiya Akademii Pedagogicheskikh Nauk RSFSR*, 13, 101–32.)

Siqueland, E. R. and De Lucia, C. A. (1969). Visual reinforcement of nonnutritive sucking in human infants. *Science*, 165, 1144–6.

Slobin, D. I. (1973). Cognitive prerequisites for the development of grammar. In C. A. Ferguson and D. I. Slobin (eds), *Studies of Child Language Development*. New York: Holt, Rinehart & Winston.

Slobin, D. I. (1977). Language change in childhood and in history. In J. Macnamara (ed.), *Language Learning and Thought*. New York: Academic Press.

Smith, B. L. (1978). Temporal aspects of English speech production: A developmental perspective. *Journal of Phonetics*, 6, 37–67.

Smith, B. L., Brown-Sweeney, S., and Stoel-Gammon, C. (1989). A quantitative analysis of reduplicated and variegated babbling. *First Language*, 9, 175–90.

Smith, B. L., Macaluso, C., and Brown-Sweeney, S. (1991). Phonological effects shown by normal adult speakers learning new words: Implications for phonological development. *Applied Psycholinguistics*, 12, 281–98.

Smith, N. V. (1973). *The Acquisition of Phonology: A case study*. Cambridge: Cambridge University Press.

Smith, N. V. (1974). The acquisition of phonological skills in children. *British Journal of Disorders of Communication*, 9, 17–23.

Smith, N. V. (1978). Lexical representation and the acquisition of phonology. In B. B. Kachru (ed.), *Linguistics in the Seventies: Directions and prospects*. Special issue of *Studies in the Linguistic Sciences*, 8, 259–73.

Snow, C. E. (1988). The last word: Questions about the emerging lexicon. In M. D. Smith and J. L. Locke (eds), *The Emergent Lexicon: The child's development of a linguistic vocabulary*. New York: Academic Press.

Snow, D. (1994). Phrase-final syllable lengthening and intonation in early child speech. *Journal of Speech and Hearing Research*, 37, 831–40.

Snow, D. and Stoel-Gammon, C. (1994). Intonation and final lengthening in early child language. In M. Yavaş, *First and Second Language Phonology*. San Diego: Singular Publishing Group.

Snow, K. (1963). A detailed analysis of articulation responses of "normal" first grade children. *Journal of Speech and Hearing Research*, 6, 277–90.

Snyder, L. S., Bates, E., and Bretherton, I. (1981). Content and context in early lexical development. *Journal of Child Language*, 6, 565–82.

Spelke, E. S. (1988). Where perceiving ends and thinking begins: The apprehension of objects in infancy. In A. Yonas (ed.), *Perceptual Development in Infancy*. The Minnesota Symposia on Child Psychology, 20. Hillsdale, NJ: Lawrence Erlbaum.

Spencer, A. (1986). Towards a theory of phonological development. *Lingua*, 68, 3–38.

Spring, D. R. and Dale, P. S. (1977). Discrimination of linguistic stress in early infancy. *Journal of Speech and Hearing Research*, 20, 224–32.

Stampe, D. (1969). The acquisition of phonetic representation. Papers from the Fifth Regional Meeting of the Chicago Linguistic Society, Chicago, IL. Reprinted in D. Stampe (1979), *A Dissertation on Natural Phonology*, New York: Garland.

Stampe, D. (1979). *A Dissertation on Natural Phonology*. New York: Garland.

Stanovich, K. E., Cunningham, A. E., and Cramer B. B. (1984). Assessing phonological awareness in kindergarten children: Issues of task comparability. *Journal of Experimental Child Psychology*, 38, 175–90.

Stark, R. E. (1978). Features of infant sounds: The emergence of cooing. *Journal of Child Language*, 5, 379–90.

Stark, R. E. (1980). Stages of speech development in the first year of life. In G. Yeni-komshian, J. F. Kavanagh, and C. A. Ferguson (eds), *Child Phonology, 1: Production*. New York: Academic Press.

Stark, R. E. (ed.) (1981). *Language Behavior in Infancy and Early Childhood*. Amsterdam: Elsevier/North-Holland.

Stark, R. E. (1986). Prespeech segmental feature development. In P. Fletcher and M. Garman (eds), *Language Acquisition* (2nd edn). Cambridge: Cambridge University Press.

Stark, R. E. (1989). Temporal patterning of cry and non-cry sounds in the first eight months of life. *First Language*, 9, 107–36.

Stark, R. E. (1993). The coupling of early social interaction and infant vocalization. Paper presented at the Biennial Meeting of the Society for Research in Child Development, New Orleans.

Stark, R. E., Ansel, B. M., and Bond, J. (1988). Are prelinguistic abilities predictive of learning disability? A follow-up study. In R. L. Masland and M. W. Masland (eds), *Preschool Prevention of Reading Failure*. Parkton, MD: York Press.

Stark, R. E., Bernstein, L. E., and Demorest, M. E. (1993). Vocal communication in the first 18 months of life. *Journal of Speech and Hearing Research*, 36, 548–58.

Stark, R. E. and Nathanson, S. N. (1974). Spontaneous cry in the newborn infant; Sounds and facial gestures. In J. F. Bosma (ed.), *Fourth Symposium on Oral Sensation and Perception: Development in the fetus and infant*. Bethesda, MD: US Government Printing Press.

Stark, R. E., Rose, S. N., and Benson, P. J. (1978). Classification of infant vocalization. *British Journal of Communication Disorders*, 13, 41–7.

Stark, R. E., Rose, S. N., and McLagen, M. (1975). Features of infant sounds: The first eight weeks of life. *Journal of Child Language*, 2, 205–21.

Starkweather, C. W. (1980). Speech fluency and its development in normal children. In N. J. Lass (ed.), *Speech and Language: Advances in Basic Research and Practice*, 4. New York: Academic Press.

Stemberger, J. P. (1988). Between-word processes in child phonology. *Journal of Child Language*, 15, 39–62.

Stemberger, J. P. (1992). A connectionist view of child phonology: Phonological processing without phonological processes. In C. A. Ferguson, L. Menn, and C. Stoel-Gammon (eds), *Phonological Development: Models, research, implications*. Timonium, MD: York Press.

Stemberger, J. P. and Stoel-Gammon, C. (1991). The underspecification of coronals: Evidence from language acquisition and performance errors. In C. Paradis and J.-F. Prunet (eds), *Phonetics and Phonology, 3: The special status of coronals*. New York: Academic Press.

Stern, D. N. (1985). *The Interpersonal World of the Infant: A View from psychoanalysis and developmental psychology*. New York: Basic Books.

Stern, D. N., Hofer, L., Haft, W., and Dore, J. (1985). Affect attunement: The sharing of feeling states between mother and infant by means of inter-modal fluency. In T. Field and N. Fox (eds), *Social Perception in Infants*. Norwood, NJ: Ablex.

Stern, D. N., Spieker, S., Barnett, R. K., and MacKain, K. (1983). The prosody of maternal speech: Infant age and context related changes. *Journal of Child Language*, 10, 1–15.

Stern, D. N., Spieker, S., and MacKain, K. (1982). Intonation contours as signals in maternal speech to prelinguistic infants. *Developmental Psychology*, 18, 727–35.

Stevens, K. N. (1972). The quantal nature of speech: Evidence from articulatory-acoustic data. In E. E. David, Jr. and P. B. Denes (eds), *Human Communication: A unified view*. New York: McGraw-Hill.

Stevens, K. N. (1989). On the quantal nature of speech. *Journal of Phonetics*, 17, 3–45.

Stevens, K. N., Liberman, A. M., Studdert-Kennedy, M., and Öhman, S. E. G. (1969). Cross-language study of vowel perception. *Language and Speech*, 12, 1–23.

Stoel-Gammon, C. (1992). Prelinguistic vocal development: Measurement and predictions. In C. A. Ferguson, L. Menn, and C. Stoel-Gammon (eds), *Phonological Development: Models, research, implications*. Timonium, MD: York Press.

Stoel-Gammon, C. and Cooper, J. A. (1984). Patterns of early lexical and phonological development. *Journal of Child Language*, 11, 247–71.

Stoel-Gammon, C. and Dunn, J. (1985). *Normal and Disordered Phonology in Children*. Baltimore: University Park Press.

Stoel-Gammon, C. and Otomo, K. (1986). Babbling development of hearing-impaired and normally hearing subjects. *Journal of Speech and Hearing Disorders*, 51, 33–41.

Stoel-Gammon, C. and Stemberger, J. P. (1994). Consonant harmony and phonological underspecification in child speech. In M. Yavaş (ed.), *First and Second Language Phonology*. San Diego: Singular Publishing Group.

Straight, H. S. (1980). Auditory versus articulatory phonological processes and their development in children. In G. H. Yeni-komshian, J. F. Kavanagh, and C. A. Ferguson (eds),

Child Phonology, 1: Production. New York: Academic Press.

Strange, W. and Broen, P. A. (1980). Perception and production of approximate consonants by 3-year-olds: A first study. In G. Yeni-komshian, J. Kavanagh, and C. A. Ferguson (eds), *Child Phonology, 2: Perception.* New York: Academic Press.

Streeter, L. A. (1976). Language perception of 2-month-old infants shows effects of both innate mechanisms and experience. *Nature,* 259, 39–41.

Studdert-Kennedy, M. (1975). From continuous signal to discrete message: Syllable to phoneme. In J. F. Kavanagh and J. E. Cutting (eds), *The Role of Speech in Language.* Cambridge, MA: MIT Press.

Studdert-Kennedy, M. (1977). Universals in phonetic structure and their role in linguistic communication. In T. H. Bullock (ed.), *Recognition of Complex Acoustic Signals.* Berlin: Dahlem Konferenzen.

Studdert-Kennedy, M. (1979). Perception. In *Proceedings of the Ninth International Congress of Phonetic Sciences,* 1. Copenhagen.

Studdert-Kennedy, M. (1980). Speech perception. *Language and Speech,* 23, 45–66.

Studdert-Kennedy, M. (1983). Foreword to J. L. Locke, *Phonological Acquisition and Change.* New York: Academic Press.

Studdert-Kennedy, M. (1986). Sources of variability in early speech development. In J. S. Perkell and D. H. Klatt (eds), *Invariance and Variability in Speech Processes.* Hillsdale, NJ: Lawrence Erlbaum.

Studdert-Kennedy, M. (1987). The phoneme as a perceptuomotor structure. In A. Allport, D. MacKay, W. Prinz, and E. Scheerer (eds), *Language Perception and Production.* New York: Academic Press.

Studdert-Kennedy, M. (1989). Feature fitting: A comment on K. N. Stevens' "On the quantal nature of speech". *Journal of Phonetics,* 17, 135–43.

Studdert-Kennedy, M. (1991a). Comment: The emergent gesture. In I. G. Mattingly and M. Studdert-Kennedy (eds), *Modularity and the Motor Theory of Speech Perception: Proceedings of a conference to honor Alvin M. Liberman.* Hillsdale, NJ: Lawrence Erlbaum.

Studdert-Kennedy, M. (1991b). Language development from an evolutionary perspective. In N. A. Krasnegor, D. M. Rumbaugh, R. L. Schiefelbusch, and M. Studdert-Kennedy (eds), *Biological and Behavioral Determinants of Language Development.* Hillsdale, NJ: Lawrence Erlbaum.

Studdert-Kennedy, M. (1993). Discovering phonetic function. *Journal of Phonetics,* 21, 147–55.

Studdert-Kennedy, M. and Goodell, E. W. (1992). Gestures, features and segments in early child speech. *Haskins Laboratories Status Report on Speech Research,* SR-111/112, 1–14.

Studdert-Kennedy, M., Liberman, A. M., Harris, K. S., and Cooper, V. S. (1970). Motor theory of speech perception: A reply to Lane's critical review. *Psychological Review,* 77, 234–49.

Sullivan, J. W. and Horowitz, F. D. (1983). The effects of intonation on infant attention: The role of the rising intonation contour. *Journal of Child Language,* 10, 521–34.

Summerfield, Q. (1991). Visual perception of phonetic gestures. In I. G. Mattingly and M. Studdert-Kennedy (eds), *Modularity and the Motor Theory of Speech Perception: Proceedings of a conference to honor Alvin M. Liberman.* Hillsdale, NJ: Lawrence Erlbaum.

Swoboda, P., Morse, P. A., and Leavitt, L. A. (1976). Continuous vowel discrimination in normal and at-risk infants. *Child Development,* 49, 332–9.

Tees, R. C. and Werker, J. F. (1984). Perceptual flexibility: Maintenance or recovery of the ability to discriminate nonnative speech sounds. *Canadian Journal of Psychology,* 38, 579–90.

Templeton, S. and Scarborough-Franks, L. (1985). The spelling's the thing: Knowledge of derivational morphology in orthography and phonology among older students. *Applied Psycholinguistics*, 6, 371–405.

Templin, M. (1957). *Certain Language Skills in Children*. Minneapolis: University of Minnesota Press.

Thelen, E. (1981). Rhythmical behavior in infancy: An ethological perspective. *Developmental Psychology*, 17, 237–57.

Thelen, E. (1985). Expression as action: A motor perspective of the transition from spontaneous to instrumental behaviors. In G. Zivin (ed.), *The Development of Expressive Behavior*. New York: Academic Press.

Thelen, E. (1989). Self-organization in developmental processes: Can systems approaches work? In M. R. Gunnar and E. Thelen (eds), *Systems and Development*. The Minnesota Symposia on Child Psychology, 22. Hillsdale, NJ: Lawrence Erlbaum.

Thelen, E. (1991). Motor aspects of emergent speech: A dynamic approach. In N. A. Krasnegor, D. M. Rumbaugh, R. L. Schiefelbusch, and M. Studdert-Kennedy (eds), *Biological and Behavioral Determinants of Language Development*. Hillsdale, NJ: Lawrence Erlbaum.

Thomas, D. G., Campos, J. J., Shucard, D. W., Ramsay, D. S., and Shucard, J. (1981). Semantic comprehension in infancy: A signal detection analysis. *Child Development*, 51, 798–803.

Thorpe, L. A. and Trehub, S. E. (1989). Duration illusion and auditory grouping in infancy. *Developmental Psychology*, 25, 122–7.

Tischler, H. (1957). Schreien, Lallen und erstes Sprechen in der Entwicklung des Säuglings. *Zeitschrift für Psychologie*, 160, 209–63.

Trainor, L. J. and Trehub, S. E. (1992). A comparison of infants' and adults' sensitivity to Western tonal structure. *Journal of Experimental Psychology: Human perception and performance*, 18, 394–402.

Trehub, S. E. (1973). Infants' sensitivity to vowel and tonal contrasts. *Developmental Psychology*, 9, 91–6.

Trehub, S. E. (1976a). The discrimination of foreign speech contrasts by infants and adults. *Child Development*, 47, 466–72.

Trehub, S. E. (1976b). Infants' discrimination of multisyllabic stimuli: The role of temporal factors. Paper presented at the annual meeting of the American Speech and Hearing Association, Houston, TX.

Trehub, S. E., Bull, D., and Thorpe, L. A. (1984). Infants' perception of melodies: The role of melodic contour. *Child Development*, 55, 821–30.

Trehub, S. E. and Rabinovitch, M. S. (1972). Auditory-linguistic sensitivity in early infancy. *Developmental Psychology*, 6, 74–7.

Trehub, S. E. and Thorpe, L. A. (1989). Infants' perception of rhythm. Categorization of auditory sequences by temporal structure. *Canadian Journal of Psychology*, 43, 217–29.

Trehub, S. E., Thorpe, L. A., and Morrongiello, B. A. (1987). Organizational processes in infants' perception of auditory patterns. *Child Development*, 58, 741–9.

Trehub, S. E. and Trainor, L. J. (1993). Listening strategies in infancy: The roots of music and language development. In S. McAdams and E. Bigand (eds), *Thinking in Sound: Cognitive aspects of human audition*. Oxford: Oxford University Press.

Treiman, R. (1983). The structure of spoken syllables: Evidence from novel word games. *Cognition*, 15, 49–74.

Treiman, R. (1985). Onsets and rimes as units of spoken syllables: Evidence from children. *Journal of Experimental Child Psychology*, 39, 161–81.

Treiman, R. and Baron, J. (1981). Segmental analysis ability: Development and relation to reading ability. In G. E. MacKinnon and T. G. Waller (eds), *Reading Research: Advances in theory and practice*, 3. New York: Academic Press.

Treiman, R. and Breaux, A. (1982). Common phoneme and overall stimulating relations among spoken syllables. Their use by children and adults. *Journal of Psycholinguistic Research*, 11, 569–97.

Treiman, R. and Danis, C. (1988). Short-term memory errors for spoken syllables are affected by linguistic structure of syllables. *Journal of Experimental Psychology*, 14, 145–52.

Treiman, R. and Zukowski, A. (1991). Levels of phonological awareness. In S. Brady and D. Shankweiler (eds), *Phonological Processes in Literacy*. Hillsdale, NJ: Lawrence Erlbaum.

Trevarthan, C. (1977). Descriptive analysis of infant communicative behavior. In H. R. Schaffer (ed.), *Studies in Mother–Infant Interaction*. London: Academic Press.

Trevarthan, C. (1979). Communication and cooperation in early infancy: A description of primary intersubjectivity. In M. Bullowa (ed.), *Before Speech: The beginning of interpersonal communication*. Cambridge: Cambridge University Press.

Trevarthan, C. and Hubley, P. (1978). Secondary intersubjectivity: Confidence, confiding and acts of meaning in the first year. In A. Lock (ed.), *Action, Gesture and Symbol: The emergence of language*. New York: Academic Press.

Trubetzkoy, N. S. (1949). *Principes de phonologie* (translated by J. Cantineau). Paris: Editions Klincksieck.

Tse, J. K.-P. (1978). Tone acquisition in Cantonese: A longitudinal case study. *Journal of Child Language*, 5, 191–204.

Tyler, L. K. (1984). The structure of the initial cohort: evidence from gating. *Perception and Psychophysics*, 36, 217–22.

Tyler, L. K. and Frauenfelder, U. H. (1987). The process of spoken word recognition: An introduction. In U. H. Frauenfelder and L. K. Tyler (eds), *Spoken Word Recognition*. Amsterdam: Elsevier Science. (Also printed in *Cognition*, 25).

Tyler, L. K. and Marslen-Wilson, W. D. (1981). Children's processing of spoken language. *Journal of Verbal Learning and Verbal Behavior*, 20, 400–16.

Umeda, N. (1975). Vowel duration in American English. *Journal of the Acoustic Society of America*, 58, 434–45.

Užgiris, I. C. (1973). Patterns of vocal and gestural imitation in infants. In L. J. Stone, H. T. Smith, and L. B. Murphy (eds), *The Competent Infant: Research and commentary*. New York: Basic Books.

Užgiris, I. C. (1984). Imitation in infancy: Its interpersonal aspects. In M. Perlmutter (ed.), *Parent–Child Interaction and Parent–Child Relations in Child Development*. Minnesota Symposia on Child Psychology, 17. Hillsdale, NJ: Lawrence Erlbaum.

Velleman, S. L. (1988). The role of linguistic perception in later phonological development. *Applied Psycholinguistics*, 9, 221–36.

Velleman, S. L. (1992). A nonlinear model of early child phonology. Paper presented at the Linguistic Society of America, Philadelphia.

Velleman, S. L. (1994). The interaction of phonetics and phonology in developmental verbal dyspraxia: Two case studies. *Clinics in Communication Disorders*, 4, 66–77.

Velten, H. V. (1943). The growth of phonemic and lexical patterns in infant language. *Language*, 19, 231–92. Reprinted in A. Bar-Adon and W. F. Leopold (eds) (1971), *Child Language: A book of readings*. Englewood Cliffs, NJ: Prentice Hall.

Veneziano, E. (1981). Early language and nonverbal representation: A reassessment. *Journal of Child Language*, 8, 541–63.

Veneziano, E. (1988). Vocal-verbal interaction and the construction of early lexical knowledge. In M. D. Smith and J. L. Locke (eds), *The Emergent Lexicon: The child's development of a linguistic vocabulary*. New York: Academic Press.

Vihman, E. (1974). Estonian quantity re-viewed. *Foundations of Language*, 11, 415–32.

Vihman, M. M. (1971). On the acquisition of Estonian. *Papers and Reports on Child Language Development*, 3, 51–94.

Vihman, M. M. (1976). From prespeech to speech: on early phonology. *Stanford Papers and Reports on Child Language Development*, 12, 230–44.

Vihman, M. M. (1978). Consonant harmony: Its scope and function in child language. In J. H. Greenberg (ed.), *Universals of Human Language*. Stanford, CA: Stanford University Press.

Vihman, M. M. (1980). Sound change and child language. In E. C. Traugott, R. Labrum, and S. Shepard (eds), *Papers from the Fourth International Conference on Historical Linguistics*. Amsterdam: John Benjamins B.V.

Vihman, M. M. (1981). Phonology and the development of the lexicon: Evidence from children's errors. *Journal of Child Language*, 8, 239–64.

Vihman, M. M. (1982). A note on children's lexical representations. *Journal of Child Language*, 9, 249–53.

Vihman, M. M. (1985). Language differentiation by the bilingual infant. *Journal of Child Language*, 12, 297–324.

Vihman, M. M. (1991). Ontogeny of phonetic gestures: Speech production. In I. G. Mattingly and M. Studdert-Kennedy (eds), *Modularity and the Motor Theory of Speech Perception: Proceedings of a conference to honor Alvin M. Liberman*. Hillsdale, NJ: Lawrence Erlbaum.

Vihman, M. M. (1992). Early syllables and the construction of phonology. In C. A. Ferguson, L. Menn, and C. Stoel-Gammon (eds), *Phonological Development: Models, research, implications*. Timonium, MD: York Press.

Vihman, M. M. (1993a). The construction of a phonological system. In B. de Boysson-Bardies, S. de Schonen, P. Jusczyk, P. MacNeilage, and J. Morton (eds), *Developmental Neurocognition: Speech and face processing in the first year of life*. Dordrecht: Kluwer Academic.

Vihman, M. M. (1993b). Early phonological development (ch. 2) and Later phonological development (ch. 3). In J. E. Bernthal and N. W. Bankson (eds), *Articulation and Phonological Disorders* (3rd edn). Englewood Cliffs, NJ: Prentice Hall.

Vihman, M. M. (1993c). Variable paths to early word production. *Journal of Phonetics*, 21, 61–82.

Vihman, M. M. and Boysson-Bardies, B. de (1994). The nature and origins of ambient language influence on infant vocal production and early words. *Phonetica*, 51, 159–69.

Vihman, M. M., Ferguson, C. A., and Elbert, M. (1986). Phonological development from babbling to speech: Common tendencies and individual differences. *Applied Psycholinguistics*, 7, 3–40.

Vihman, M. M. and Greenlee, M. (1987). Individual differences in phonological development: Ages one and three years. *Journal of Speech and Hearing Research*, 30, 503–21.

Vihman, M. M., Kay, E., Boysson-Bardies, B. de, Durand, C., and Sundberg, U. (1994). External sources of individual differences? A cross-linguistic analysis of the phonetics of mothers' speech to one-year-old children. *Developmental Psychology*, 30, 651–62.

Vihman, M. M. and McCune, L. (1994). When is a word a word? *Journal of Child Language*, 21, 517–42.

Vihman, M. M., Macken, M. A., Miller, R., Simmons, H., and Miller, J. (1985). From babbling to speech: A re-assessment of the continuity issue. *Language*, 61, 397–445.

Vihman, M. M. and Miller, R. (1988). Words and babble at the threshold of lexical acquisition. In M. D. Smith and J. L. Locke (eds), *The Emergent Lexicon: The child's develop-ment of a linguistic vocabulary*. New York: Academic Press.

Vihman, M. M. and Roug-Hellichius, L. (1991). The emergence of phonological organiza-tion. In O. Engstrand and C. Kylander (eds), Papers from the symposium, *Current Phonetic Research Paradigms: Implications for speech motor control* (Stockholm, August 13–16, 1991). *PERILUS*, 14, 161–6.

Vihman, M. M. and Velleman, S. L. (1989). Phonological reorganization: A case study. *Language and Speech*, 32, 149–70.

Vihman, M. M., Velleman, S. L., and McCune, L. (1994). How abstract is child phonology? Towards an integration of linguistic and psychological approaches. In M. Yavaş, (ed.), *First and Second Language Phonology*. San Diego: Singular Publishing Group.

Vincent-Smith, L., Bricker, D., and Bricker, W. (1974). Acquisition of receptive vocabulary in the toddler-age child. *Child Development*, 45, 189–93.

Vinter, A. (1986). The role of movement in eliciting early imitations. *Child Development*, 57, 66–71.

Volterra, V. and Erting, C. J, (eds) (1990). *From Gesture to Language in Hearing and Deaf Children*. Berlin: Springer-Verlag.

Volterra, V. and Taeschner, T. (1978). The acquisition and development of language by bilingual children. *Journal of Child Language*, 5, 311–26.

Volterra, V., Bates, E., Benigni, I., Bretherton, I., and Camaioni, L. (1979). First words in language and action: A qualitative look. In E. Bates, I. Benigni, L. Bretherton, L. Camaioni, and V. Volterra (eds) (1979). *The Emergence of Symbols: Cognition and commu-nication in infancy*. New York: Academic Press.

Von Hofsten, C. (1983). Foundations for perceptual development. In L. P. Lipsitt and C. K. Rovee-Collier (eds), *Advances in Infancy Research*, 2. Norwood, NJ: Ablex.

Vygotsky, L. (1962). *Thought and Language* (Edited and translated by E. Hanfmann and G. Vakar). Cambridge, MA: MIT Press.

Wagner, K. R. (1985). How much do children say in a day? *Journal of Child Language*, 12, 475–87.

Wagner, R. K. and Torgesen, J. K. (1987). The nature of phonological processing and its causal role in the acquisition of reading skills. *Psychological Bulletin*, 101, 192–212.

Walley, A. C. (1987). Young children's detections of word-initial and -final mispronuncia-tions in constrained and unconstrained contexts. *Cognitive Development*, 2, 145–67.

Walley, A. C. (1988). Spoken word recognition by young children and adults. *Cognitive Development*, 3, 137–65.

Walley, A. C. (1993a). More developmental research is needed. *Journal of Phonetics*, 21, 171–6.

Walley, A. C. (1993b). The role of vocabulary development in children's spoken word recognition and segmentation ability. *Developmental Review*, 13, 286–350.

Walley, A. C. and Metsala, J. L. (1990). The growth of lexical constraints on spoken word recognition. *Perception and Psychophysics*, 47, 267–80.

Walley, A. C., Smith, L. B., and Jusczyk, P. W. (1986). The role of phonemes and syllables in the perceived similarity of speech sounds for children. *Memory and Cognition*, 14, 220–9.

Warren, R. M. (1970). Phonemic restoration of missing speech sounds. *Science*, 167, 392f.

Waterson, N. (1971). Child phonology: A prosodic view. *Journal of Linguistics*, 7, 179–211. Reprinted in N. Waterson (1987), *Prosodic Phonology: The theory and its application to language acquisition and speech processing*. Newcastle upon Tyne: Grevatt & Grevatt.

Waterson, N. (1978). Growth of complexity in phonological development. In N.

Waterson and C. E. Snow (eds), *The Development of Communication*. Chichester: Wiley & Sons. Reprinted in N. Waterson (1987), *Prosodic Phonology: The theory and its application to language acquisition and speech processing*. Newcastle upon Tyne: Grevatt & Grevatt.

Waterson, N. (1987). *Prosodic Phonology: The theory and its application to language acquisition and speech processing*. Newcastle upon Tyne: Grevatt & Grevatt.

Wayland, S. C., Wingfield, A., and Goodglass, H. (1989). Recognition of isolated words: The dynamics of cohort reduction. *Applied Psycholinguistics*, 10, 475–87.

Webster's Third New International Dictionary of the English Language. (1981). Springfield, MA: G. C. Merriam.

Weinreich, U., Labov, W., and Herzog, M. I. (1968). Empirical foundations for a theory of language change. In W. P. Lehmann and Y. Malkiel (eds), *Directions for Historical Linguistics: A symposium*. Austin: University of Texas Press.

Wellman, B. L., Case, I. M., Mengert, E. G., and Bradbury, D. E. (1931). Speech sounds of young children. *University of Iowa Studies in Child Welfare*, 5.

Wellman, H. M. (1990). *The Child's Theory of Mind*. Cambridge, MA: MIT Press.

Wenk, B. J. and Wioland, F. (1982). Is French really syllable-timed? *Journal of Phonetics*, 10, 193–216.

Wepman, J. M. and Hass, W. (1969). *A Spoken Word Count: Children – ages 5, 6, and 7*. Chicago: Language Research Associates.

Werker, J. F. (1991). The ontogeny of speech perception. In I. G. Mattingly and M. Studdert-Kennedy (eds), *Modularity and the Motor Theory of Speech Perception: Proceedings of a conference to honor Alvin M. Liberman*. Hillsdale, NJ: Lawrence Erlbaum.

Werker, J. F., Gilbert, J. H. V., Humphrey, K., and Tees, R. C. (1981). Developmental aspects of cross-language speech perception. *Child Development*, 52, 349–55.

Werker, J. F. and Lalonde, C. E. (1988). Cross-language speech perception: Initial capabilities and developmental change. *Developmental Psychology*, 24, 672–83.

Werker, J. F. and Logan, J. S. (1985). Cross-language evidence for three factors in speech perception. *Perception and Psychophysics*, 37, 35–44.

Werker, J. F. and McLeod, P. J. (1989). Infant preference for both male and female infant-directed talk: A developmental study of attentional and affective responsiveness. *Canadian Journal of Psychology*, 43, 230–46.

Werker, J. F. and Pegg, J. E. (1992). Infant speech perception and phonological acquisition. In C. A. Ferguson, L. Menn, and C. Stoel-Gammon (eds), *Phonological Development: Models, research, implications*. Timonium, MD: York Press.

Werker, J. F. and Polka, L. (1993). Developmental changes in speech perception: New challenges and new directions. *Journal of Phonetics*, 21, 83–101.

Werker, J. F. and Tees, R. C. (1983). Developmental changes across childhood in the perception of non-native speech sounds. *Canadian Journal of Psychology*, 37, 278–96.

Werker, J. F. and Tees, R. C. (1984). Cross-language speech perception: Evidence for perceptual reorganization during the first year of life. *Infant Behavior and Development*, 7, 49–63.

Werner, H. and Kaplan, D. (1984). *Symbol Formation: An organismic-developmental approach to language and the expression of thought*. Hillsdale, NJ: Erlbaum. (Originally published in 1963, by Wiley, New York).

Whalen, D. H., Levitt, A. G., and Wang, Q. (1991). Intonational differences between the reduplicative babbling of French- and English-learning infants. *Journal of Child Language*, 18, 501–16.

Wijnen, F., Krikhaar, E., and Den Os, E. (1994). The (non)realization of unstressed elements in children's utterances: Evidence for a rhythmic constraint. *Journal of Child Language*, 21, 59–83.

Winitz, H. (1969). *Articulatory Acquisition and Behavior*. New York: Appleton.

Winitz, H. and Irwin, O. C. (1958). Syllabic and phonetic structure of infants' early words. *Journal of Speech and Hearing Research*, 1, 250–6. Reprinted in C. A. Ferguson and D. I. Slobin (eds) (1973), *Studies of Child Language Development*, New York: Holt, Rinehart & Winston.

Wolff, P. H. (1966). *The Causes, Control, and Organization of Behavior in the Neonate*. (Psychological Issues, 5, Monograph 17). New York: Inter-University Press.

Wolff, P. H. (1969). The natural history of crying and other vocalizations in early infancy. In B. M. Foss (ed.), *Determinants of Infant Behaviour*, 4. London: Methuen.

Yeni-komshian, G., Kavanagh, J. F., and Ferguson, C. A. (eds) (1980). *Child Phonology, 1: Production; 2: Perception*. New York: Academic Press.

Zlatin, M. A. (1974). Voicing contrast: Perceptual and productive voice onset time characteristics of adults. *Journal of the Acoustic Society of America*, 56, 981–94.

Zlatin, M. A. (1975). Explorative mapping of the vocal tract and primitive syllabification in infancy: The first six months. *Purdue University Contributed Papers*. Fall: 58–73.

Zlatin, M. A. and Koenigsknecht, R. A. (1975). Development of the voicing contrast: Perception of stop consonants. *Journal of Speech and Hearing Research*, 18, 541–53.

Zlatin, M. A. and Koenigsknecht, R. A. (1976). Development of the voicing contrast: A comparison of voice onset time in stop perception and production. *Journal of Speech and Hearing Research*, 18, 93–111.

Zwicky, A. M. (1982). Classical malapropisms and the creation of a mental lexicon. In L. Obler and L. Menn (eds), *Exceptional Language and Linguistics*. New York: Academic Press.

Index

Children named in text (excepting those included in Appendix C) are cited here, and appear under their first names.